FAMILY TROUBLES?

Exploring changes and challenges in the family lives of children and young people

Edited by Jane Ribbens McCarthy, Carol-Ann Hooper
and Val Gillies

 ͻk is due for return on or before the ⸤

First published in Great Britain in 2014 by

Policy Press
University of Bristol
1-9 Old Park Hill
Clifton
Bristol BS2 8BB
UK
t: +44 (0)117 954 5940
pp-info@bristol.ac.uk
www.policypress.co.uk

North America office:
Policy Press
c/o The University of Chicago Press
1427 East 60th Street
Chicago, IL 60637, USA
t: +1 773 702 7700
f: +1 773 702 9756
www.press.uchicago.edu
sales@press.uchicago.edu

© Policy Press 2014

British Library Cataloguing in Publication Data
A catalogue record for this book is available from the British Library.

Library of Congress Cataloging-in-Publication Data
A catalog record for this book has been requested.

ISBN 978 1 44730 444 9 paperback

Cover design by Policy Press
Front cover: images kindly supplied by Sophie Rae Harding
Printed and bound in Great Britain by www.4edge.co.uk
Policy Press uses environmentally responsible print partners

Contents

Notes on contributors

Janet Boddy is a Reader in Child, Youth and Family Studies, and Co-Director of the Centre for Innovation and Research in Childhood and Youth (CIRCY) at the University of Sussex. Her UK and cross-national research is focused on two interconnected areas: family lives, and mainstream and targeted services for children, young people and families.

Geraldine Brady is a Senior Research Fellow in the Applied Research Centre in Sustainable Regeneration, Coventry University. She has carried out a number of qualitative research projects with children, young people and parents. Her PhD explored children's and parents' experiences of the medically diagnosed condition ADHD, and her research interests include engaging with policy, popular and medicalised discourses that shape ideas about appropriate development and behaviour of children and young people, and discussion of the methodological challenges involved in participatory research.

Elaine Chase is a Research Officer at the Oxford Institute of Social Policy, University of Oxford. Her research interests include the sociological dimensions of poverty, social exclusion, rights, health and well-being with a particular focus on children, young people and families most likely to experience marginalisation and disadvantage.

Harriet Clarke is Lecturer in Social Policy and Social Research in the Institute of Applied Social Studies, School of Social Policy, at the University of Birmingham. She is a member of the School of Social Policy's Families, Policy and Professional Practice research group, and has interests across social care and welfare policy and how they impact on individuals and family relationships. Her research work has often focused on disabled parents' accounts of disability, parenting and family life and their experiences of services.

Karen Clarke was a Senior Lecturer in Social Policy in the School of Social Sciences at the University of Manchester, and is currently an honorary research fellow at the university. Her principal research interest is in family policy in the UK, and the ways in which social policy allocates responsibility for children between mothers and fathers, and between parents and the state.

Hayley Davies is a Lecturer in the Sociology of Childhood at King's College London. Her main research interests are in children's family and personal relationships, family policy and qualitative approaches to researching these areas. Hayley is currently working on a book on children's personal relationships, which encompasses these areas of interest.

Harriet Churchill joined the Department of Sociological Studies at the University of Sheffield in 2008 and is a Lecturer in Social Work. Her research examines everyday experiences of family relations, and policy and practice developments in child welfare, family support and family policies.

Karin Cooper is a Lecturer in Social Work in the Department of Social Sciences at the University of Hull. Her background is in child protection and kinship care and she has worked as a Professional Practice Officer for a Local Safeguarding Children Board (LSCB). She has recently completed her PhD in the area of kinship care. Her research interests now include fostering, child sexual exploitation and multi-agency working. She is a member of a LSCB child sexual exploitation strategic group as well as the Inter-Professionals Services Centre at the University of Hull.

María Claudia Duque-Páramo is Professor at the School of Nursing of the Pontificia Universidad Javeriana, Bogotá (Colombia). She has a PhD in anthropology (University of South Florida) and qualifications in nursing, and community psychology (Pontificia Universidad Javeriana). She is an active member of national and international networks on childhood and migration. She has several publications, among them 'Parental migration in Colombia: Children's voices in national and international perspectives', in the *Journal of Latin American and Caribbean Anthropology* (2012).

Umut Erel, The Open University, UK, has research interests in migration, ethnicity, gender and citizenship. Recent publications include: *Migrant women: Transforming citizenship*, Aldershot: Ashgate (2009); 'Reframing migrant mothers as citizens', *Citizenship Studies* (November 2011); 'Complex belongings: Racialization and migration in a small English city', *Ethnic and Racial Studies* (December 2012); 'Migrating cultural capital: Bourdieu in migration studies', *Sociology* (2010) vol 44, no 4, pp 642-60; 'Engendering transnational space: Migrant mothers as cultural currency speculators', *European Journal of Women's Studies* (November 2012), pp 460-74.

Ruth Evans is a Lecturer in Human Geography at the University of Reading. Her research focuses on socio-spatial dimensions of care and life transitions among children, youth and families. Her research has investigated children's and young people's caring roles in families affected by HIV in the UK, Tanzania and Uganda. Recent work explores bereavement, inheritance and access to land in Senegal and Ghana.

Brid Featherstone is Professor of Social Care at The Open University. She has researched and written extensively in the areas of gender, child protection and child welfare. Her books include *Contemporary fathering: Theory, policy and practice*,

Bristol: The Policy Press (2009). She is joint managing editor (with Tess Ridge) of *Families, Relationships and Societies: an International Journal of Research and Debate.*

Janet Fink is Senior Lecturer in Social Policy at The Open University. Her research interests include the representation of family relationships in British cinema and the value of the 'visual' for exploring the intersections of inequality and family lives. Related publications can be found in *Critical Social Policy, Families Relationships and Societies, Women's History Review,* and *Sociological Research Online.*

Hannele Forsberg is Professor of Social Work at the School of Social Sciences and Humanities, University of Tampere, Finland. She has researched many aspects of family, childhood and child welfare practices, and is currently working on multiple-place housing of children. She is the co-editor (with Teppo Kroger) of *Social work and child welfare politics: Through Nordic lenses,* Bristol: The Policy Press (2010).

Ara Francis has a PhD in sociology from the University of California–Davis and is an Assistant Professor of Sociology at College of the Holy Cross in Worcester, Massachusetts. Interested in the generic processes of disruption in everyday life, she studies how people construct, manage and make sense of troubling circumstances. Her current research examines the experiences of middle-class parents whose children suffer from a wide range of physical, psychological and social problems. Dr Francis teaches courses on the sociological perspective, self and society, deviance, and the sociology of trouble.

Val Gillies is Research Professor in Social and Policy Studies at the Weeks Centre for Social and Policy Research, London South Bank University. Her research interests focus on family, parenting, social class, and marginalised children and young people, and she has published extensively in journals on these topics. Her books include *Making families: Moral tales of parenting and step-parenting* (co-authored with Jane Ribbens McCarthy and Rosalind Edwards), Sociologypress/Routledge (2003), and *Marginalised mothers: Exploring working-class experiences of parenting,* Routledge (2006).

Carol-Ann Hooper is Senior Lecturer in Social Policy at the University of York. She has worked in the overlapping fields of child protection and family support, gender and crime, and violence against women, for over 20 years. Recent books and reports include: *Living with hardship 24/7: The diverse experiences of families in poverty in England* (co-authored with S. Gorin and others), The Frank Buttle Trust (2007) and *Gender and child welfare* (co-edited with Brigid Featherstone and others), Wiley-Blackwell (2007).

Gill Highet was a community worker for many years before establishing a second career in academic research. She is currently employed by NHS Lothian working as a researcher with the Palliative Care Service at the Royal Infirmary of Edinburgh. She retains her links with the University of Edinburgh through her membership of the Primary Palliative Care Research Group.

Lynn Jamieson is Professor, Sociology of Families and Relationships, at the University of Edinburgh. She is a founding co-director of the Centre for Research on Families and Relationships (www.crfr.ac.uk), a consortium across a number of Scottish universities, a hub and network for research and knowledge exchange across academic, policy and practice domains. She is also co-editor of the Palgrave series 'Families and Intimate Life' and associate editor of the journal *Families, Relationships and Societies*.

Anne Kazimirski is Deputy Head of Measurement and Evaluation at NPC (New Philanthropy Capital). Anne has 13 years' experience as a social researcher, including nine years at the National Centre for Social Research (NatCen). Her primary interest is social impact measurement, with particular expertise in the family sector.

Peter Keogh is Senior Lecturer in Sexual Health at the University of Greenwich and Honorary Senior Lecturer at the London School of Hygiene and Tropical Medicine. Prior to this he was at NatCen and Sigma Research. His interests lie in the areas of sexual risk and intimacy as well as clinical and social care issues for people with HIV.

Jill E. Korbin, PhD (1978, UCLA) is Associate Dean, Professor of Anthropology, Director of the Schubert Center for Child Studies, and Co-Director of the Childhood Studies Program at Case Western Reserve University, Ohio. Her research interests include culture and human development; cultural, medical and psychological anthropology; neighbourhood, community and contextual influences on children and families; child maltreatment; and child and adolescent well-being.

Helen Lomax is Senior Lecturer in the Faculty of Health and Social Care at The Open University. She has a longstanding interest in health and wellbeing and in developing visual and discursive methods. Her research interests include working participatively with young people, families and communities to explore well-being and its connection to place. Publications can be found in *Sociological Research Online, International Journal of Research and Method in Education* and the *International Journal of Social Research Methodology*.

Helen Lucey is a Senior Lecturer in Psychology at the University of Bath. She is a psychosocial researcher who draws on psychoanalysis and social theory to look at how internal and external worlds shape one another, rather than being separate spheres. In research with children, young people and adults, she explores individual and group relational identities in the context of the changing nature of social class, the production of gendered identities, educational success and failure, and sibling relationships.

Ruth Maisey is a Research Director at NatCen Social Research. Over the last eight years her research has concentrated on policies affecting families, children and young people. Her work is largely quantitative in focus, and includes secondary analysis as well as a number of large-scale government evaluations.

Dawn Mannay is a Lecturer in Social Sciences (Psychology) at Cardiff University's School of Social Sciences, Wales, and an Associate Lecturer at The Open University; as well as being involved with the Women Making a Difference programme. Her research interests revolve around class, education, gender, geography, inequality, place, violence, and visual research methods.

Jane Ribbens McCarthy is Reader in Family Studies, in the Centre for Citizenship, Identities and Governance (CCIG) at The Open University. Her research interests and publications focus on families and relationships, particularly children and young people's family lives. Recent books include: *Young people's experiences of bereavement and loss: Towards an interdisciplinary approach*, Open University Press (2006); Key concepts in family studies (co-authored with Rosalind Edwards), Sage (2011); and *Understanding family meanings* (co-authored with Megan Doolittle and Shelley Day Sclater), The Policy Press (2012).

Lindsay O'Dell is an academic in the Faculty of Health and Social Care at The Open University. Her research interests focus on 'different' childhoods, including intersections of gender, ethnicity, culture, disability and generation. Specific research projects include work with young carers, language brokers, children with a visible difference and young people with autism. She is interested in constructions of normative childhoods and children who seen to be 'different'. Lindsay is a co-editor of the journal *Children & Society*.

Susan Purdon is a survey statistician. She worked at NatCen Social Research for 13 years, before setting up an independent research partnership in 2009. Her primary research interest is sample design for complex surveys and policy evaluations.

Sir Michael Rutter is Professor of Developmental Psychopathology at the Institute of Psychiatry. He established the MRC Child Psychiatry Research Unit in 1984 and the MRC Social, Genetic and Developmental Psychiatry Centre in 1994. He was elected a Fellow of the Royal Society in 1987; an honorary member of the British Academy in 2002, chairing the working party on Social

Science and Family Policies in 2010; and was a founding Fellow of the Academy of Medical Sciences. He has published over 40 books and 500 scientific papers.

June Statham is Emerita Professor of Education and Family Support at the Institute of Education, University of London. She has over 30 years' experience of conducting and directing UK and cross-national research on issues concerned with the well-being of children and their families, and has a particular interest in services to support vulnerable children and their families, including children in need in the community and children who are cared for away from home.

Arlene Vetere is Professor of Clinical Psychology at Surrey University, UK, and Professor of Family Therapy and Systemic Practice at Diakonhjemmet University College, Oslo, Norway. She is a practising clinical psychologist and systemic psychotherapist and specialises in working with couples and families where violence is of concern.

Sarah Wilson is a Lecturer in Sociology in the School of Applied Social Science at the University of Stirling. She is interested in employing participative methods in research with children and young people and has been involved in several research projects into the effects of parental substance misuse. She is a qualified solicitor with some experience of family, childcare and criminal law.

Foreword

Dorit Braun

This vital new collection provides important research evidence alongside new and fresh concepts about what it means to work with families right across the spectrum – from those we might label 'ordinary' to those labelled 'troubled'. The collection makes a very significant contribution to questioning these labels and the assumptions that underpin the labels, and shows that labelling families and individuals within them might obscure as much as or more than it reveals. The wide variety of issues covered, and the thoughtful nature of all the contributions therefore make this a key text for anyone working with children and families. The authors are expert in their field and have made significant contributions to research about families.

The contributions in this collection examine how best to think about ordinary troubles that affect most families, and about families regarded as being troubled and troubling. All families experience troubles from time to time – illness, sibling rivalry, unemployment, migration, bereavement, and other significant life events can affect all of us. Some families and family members cope pretty well, with help and support from family members and friends. Other families or individuals within them may be less resilient. Seeing families as one unit can obscure the different experiences of different family members, including of course of gender, but also of other family relationships such as grandparenting. Many of the chapters in this book provide insights into the complexities and contradictions of individuals' experiences of their family.

Much research to date has focused on 'troubling and troubled' families, exploring the various interventions that might be required, whether or not these interventions are effective, how effectiveness can be measured, and how best children can be protected and supported. But little research has considered how even the most troubled families have aspects of their lives that are ordinary – yet such research has a great deal to tell us about how individuals in families cope and thrive in what appear to be very unpromising circumstances. And the corollary is also true; there has been little research to date that looks at how 'ordinary' families deal with troubles, and the impact of 'troubles' on individual and family functioning. This all too often means that services are designed to reach families deemed as 'troubled' and are not available to many other individuals and families who are experiencing troubles and would benefit from them. It also means that the experiences of families dealing with troubles who are not getting support from services are largely hidden.

The perspective from social sciences in this important collection provides readers with fresh insights into what might seem familiar territory. The work here helps us to reconsider how we work with individuals and families; to reconsider our assumptions about life events; about troubles; about gender; culture and disability; and about professional roles and responsibilities. It helps us to reflect on the policy directions that we might otherwise follow without much questioning, so that we can consider what these policy ideas might mean for the individuals and the families that we work with.

Family life is much richer and more varied than politicians and policy makers might like. It is also much more complicated. Individuals in families are motivated by a complex set of factors, most of which are rooted in emotion and family history, and few of which are straightforwardly rational. This makes family policy very tricky: good intentions frequently have unintended consequences. The essays in this collection help us all to think more deeply about what it means to live in families; they highlight the complexities, the difficulties and the resources that all families have.

This book makes a significant contribution to what we know and understand about families and should be required reading for anyone developing family policy or working with families.

Dr Dorit Braun, AcSS, OBE. Formerly Chief Executive of Parentline Plus (UK, now Family Lives). Currently Interim Chief Executive of The College of Social Work. Dorit has a background in community and family education, health and social care and has worked mainly in the voluntary and not-for-profit sector to develop and provide services to families, carers and professionals working with them.

Preface

As the everyday family lives of children and young people come to be increasingly defined as matters of public policy and concern, it is important to raise the question of how we can understand the contested terrain between 'normal' family troubles and troubled and troubling families. This edited collection is the outcome of a two-day colloquium held in London, in July 2010,[1] to promote dialogue between researchers addressing mainstream family change and diversity in everyday lives, and those specialising in specific problems that prompt professional interventions, and to consider the implications for policymakers, service users and practitioners.

The Colloquium grew from the editors' friendship and academic conversations over many years, through which we became aware of (and intrigued by) a practical divide that tends to occur – in terms of the conferences we attend, the networks we belong to, the questions that shape research and the literatures that are discussed in these various sites – between those social scientists researching and writing about changes in 'mainstream' family lives, and those researching and writing about family lives that are considered to be 'problematic' and subject to direct policy and professional interventions. Yet, much research on mainstream families incorporates data about how 'troubles' feature in the lives of research participants, although this may not appear in the main outputs of such studies. Similarly, applied research on troublesome family issues may incorporate data on how such family members experience the kinds of change and diversity addressed by 'mainstream' researchers and how they carry on, and 'normalise', their everyday lives in the context of trouble. For the Colloquium, we invited such researchers to take a fresh look at their data to explore how 'troubles' feature in 'normal' families, and how the 'normal' features in 'troubled' families. The response to our call for papers brought forward enthusiastic participants from across the globe, offering to address these questions by drawing on research on a wide range of substantive topics, including infant care, sibling conflict, divorce, parental bereavement, disability, illness, migration and asylum-seeking, substance misuse, violence, kinship care, and forced marriage.

Key questions that we asked participants to consider included:

- If change (whether experienced suddenly or incrementally) is a 'normal' feature of family lives and the life course, at what point does it become experienced, or perceived, as troublesome, and why?
- What similarities and differences are there between different family members' experiences of the same issue, and between different sources of change?
- Can the different events of family change be understood through a common conceptual framework or are some troubling experiences more deeply challenging to those caught up in them and those who seek to support them?
- If so, what is it that makes them different, how can we understand the nature of this difference and how can we best respond?

This edited collection invites you to engage with, and take forward, our debates on these questions.

Note

[1] We are grateful to the Open University's Centre for Citizenship, Identities and Governance for sponsoring the Colloquium, and to London South Bank University for hosting it (http://www8.open.ac.uk/ccig/page/family-troubles-the-ongoing-project).

CHAPTER ONE

Troubling normalities and normal family troubles: diversities, experiences and tensions

Jane Ribbens McCarthy, Carol-Ann Hooper and Val Gillies

Introduction

In setting out to explore changes and challenges in the family lives of children and young people, and whether and how it may be important, useful and productive to consider such experiences as troubling or troublesome, we started from some basic assumptions for framing our thinking across diverse topics and circumstances. The first is that change is an inescapable feature of life, and these changes will often be highly challenging, although in some circumstances, it may be the absence of change that is troubling. The second is that troubles, conflict and painful experiences are common features of children's and young people's lives as these occur in the particular contexts of their families and close relationships, and all families are likely to be troubled at times. Yet, an idealised notion of childhood as a time of protection and innocence in contemporary Western cultures[1] sometimes undermines the ability to acknowledge this and to equip children to deal with such trouble when they encounter it, and this failure may itself exacerbate the impact of trouble. This raises a significant tension between how far to understand troubles as pervasive and, indeed, universal and to build expectations of and for children's lives on this basis, and how far to see troubles as avoidable and unacceptable and requiring clear interventions that will state this unequivocally, and seek to remedy and/or prevent such troubles.

A further tension concerns how to understand and prioritise children's needs in the context of their family relationships. Recent decades in affluent Western societies have seen a dramatic shift in public policy and popular media towards the nature of parenting and the 'skills' needed to perform it satisfactorily, promoting what has been described as 'intensive mothering' (Hays, 1996) and 'concerted cultivation' (Lareau, 2003). The demanding nature of such parenting in terms of parents' (generally mothers') time and devoted attention, and the increased expectations of parenting skills, has occurred amidst a process of increased surveillance and regulation of parents (Burman, 2007) and moral discourses that have led to a 'responsibilisation' of parents (Ribbens McCarthy, 2008). The belief that changes in parenting will rectify many, if not most, societal problems is proffered at the expense of attention to the impacts of poverty and inequality on the challenges of parenting. At the same time, there have been important gains in the raised aspirations for childhood reflected in international frameworks such as the UN Convention on the Rights of the Child (UNCRC) (discussed further by Ribbens McCarthy, Chapter Twenty-Six), and in the growth of attention to children and young people's experience as worthy of attention in its own right, rather than simply for its implications for their futures, brought by the new sociology of childhood (James et al, 1998; Uprichard, 2008; Kassem et al, 2010).

Our further assumptions were:

- that all children and young people will experience family troubles of some shape or form (using 'family' to refer broadly to their personal relationships with those responsible for their care);
- that besides the major significance of material resources in how such troubles are lived and experienced, there may be variable cultural resources available – across the globe as well as within differing groups within societies – to help children, young people and other family members to make sense of troubles in their lives;
- that troubles are not restricted to particular issues, families or situations, but that some troubles in some contexts may, nevertheless, be seen (by family members or others) to raise particular concerns about the potential for harm; and
- that researchers, policymakers and professionals, as well as family members themselves, may struggle to know when to stress the continuities of broad human experiences in response to the changes and challenges of young people's relational lives, and how and when to draw the lines and boundaries around particular family troubles that may invoke interventions.

In this volume, we do not envisage answering such questions in any fixed way, even though policymakers and professionals may want firm answers. Since we began this project, the UK government has established a dedicated 'Troubled Families Unit' to target 120,000 households deemed to be clearly identifiable as having serious problems, with local authorities being tasked to 'turn their lives around'. Behind this initiative lies a troubling attempt to define, measure and map families who are seen to cause society the most problems – although the definition used to locate such families clearly targets the most socially and economically disadvantaged. In the process, the concepts of 'troubled' and 'troublesome' are conflated through an equation of multiple disadvantage with disorder and anti-social behaviour (Levitas, 2012; Portes, 2012).

While we continue to draw on the language of troubles from which our project started, we are very aware of the developing political associations, even as we seek to carve out a particular space for careful reflection and critical engagement. The goal of our project on family troubles is thus very different: not to 'other' the troubled, however defined, but to invite debate and to explore how the normal and the troubling are perceived, experienced and presented by different actors in different contexts, whose definition of trouble prevails in particular contexts, where responsibility is located for particular troubles, with what consequences and so on.

In this opening chapter, we set out some of the debates invoked by these contentious and complex issues, and begin to consider what theoretical and conceptual frameworks are available to help us to think about these questions. Many of the chapters in this volume are based in the UK, where the original Colloquium was held; others are written by authors based in other countries and continents. Some take an explicitly cross-cultural or historical approach, while one section of the book is specifically devoted to family troubles across space and culture, including mobilities across the globe. While some of the issues discussed in relation to social policies and professional interventions are specific to particular national contexts, the breadth of the topics and contexts at stake are highly productive in helping us to unsettle assumptions and be open to the ambiguities of children's relational and family lives, and hence to think creatively on ever-changing territory.

In the first part of this introductory chapter, we consider some of the basic concepts underpinning the debates presented in this book: children and families, and the meanings implicated by individuality and relationality; and change and challenges, and how far they may be understood to constitute troubles and what conceptual frameworks may be pertinent to this question. We then consider some of the gains and losses that may be seen to have occurred in specific debates and research studies that have sought to normalise troubles, or trouble the normal. This then sets the scene for moving onto processes of power in how definitions of normality and trouble emerge and become institutionalised, and how such definitions and boundaries may be perceived by diverse social actors. We conclude the chapter by introducing the main structure and outline of the book as a whole.

Children, families and relationality

Children and families are concepts at the heart of this book, although these terms are often taken for granted in a more or less implicit way (Ribbens McCarthy et al, 2012). They are, however, embedded in, and productive of, particular – and highly charged – sets of meanings, implicating understandings of connections, dependencies and what it means to be an 'individual' or a member of a collectivity (Ribbens McCarthy, 2012). Some such meanings are institutionalised and powerful, while some are very much taken for granted in mundane aspects of daily lives.

In Western societies, the lives of children have been predominantly theorised and researched from the perspective of child development, rooted in a psychological disciplinary framework. This perspective has become almost hegemonic in such societies, while also extending its reach worldwide. It is important here to distinguish between the use of 'development' to indicate, on the one hand, that the early years are important for life in later years and, on the other, a model of progressive movement towards developmental goals with each stage being seen to be of a higher order than the previous stages (Ribbens McCarthy and Edwards, 2011). As a discipline, child development generally builds on the latter idea of development, and it has grown as a field into a highly complex and sophisticated body of work, underpinned by an extensive research basis largely premised on the basis of 'good science' (Rutter, Chapter Four). This field of study has not been without its critics within psychology, however, not least because of the potential for unrecognised cultural myopia (eg Burman, 2007; Woodhead, 2009). Thus, while Woodhead warns of the danger of throwing the developmental baby out with the bathwater, he also points out that 'as a generalization, it is fair to say that knowledge of developmental experiences for the great majority of the world's children has been and still is in very short supply' (2009, p 52) (see also Korbin, Chapter Two).

The cultural critique of developmental models includes theoretical concerns about the nature of 'the child' that is implicated, and the goals to which he or she is seen to be progressing, as well as the significance and meanings of the varying contexts and relationships in which children's lives are embedded. Some forms of developmental psychology have sought to build on different theoretical models to take account of such issues (eg Rogoff [2003], who takes a Vygotskyan approach), while others have sought to 'strip back' the fundamentals that can be said to be universally applicable in terms of children's needs (eg Woodhead, 1990), opening up greater space for considering how far understandings of children's 'needs' are themselves culturally constructed.

One such approach, for example, concerns the importance of 'attachment' in early life for children's future mental health and social adjustment. There is now a significant body of work on the underpinning theoretical model, building on the original work of Bowlby (Oates, 2007) and relevant empirical work in various different cultures around the world (discussed by Burman, 2007; van Ijzendoorn et al, 2007). Some of this work has pointed to surprising cultural variabilities, for example, in terms of how Japanese children react to separation from their mothers compared to children from North America, alongside evidence of the widespread relevance across the globe of this theoretical approach to children's development. Some writers continue to urge caution in assessing the universal relevance of attachment theory, for example, avoiding the presumption that 'only one [attachment] style is truly adaptive and of value to society' (Barrett, 2006, p 196), as well as the need to bear in mind how many questions surrounding attachment theory still need further research. It is noteworthy also that it is families living in poverty and situations of deprivation who are the most likely to be compromised in their ability to provide the care appropriate for secure attachments (Belsky, 2007). Helen Barrett (Chair of the International Attachment Network) comments:

> Specifically, we … make a plea for greater tolerance of diversity and
> for more efforts to be made towards understanding minority group

attachment patterns. It would be a pity if a theory conceived so ambitiously with the aim of improving chances of psychological health and so potentially empowering of parents and children turned out only to make disadvantaged parents feel even more alienated. (2006, p 359)

The needs of very young children for care for their survival, and the extent to which this is linked to the deeply social nature of human beings, are not in doubt, however. Various psychological and sociological theories also point to the significance of some level of security and reliability for human well-being, including Giddens' (1991) concept of ontological security, which posits a need for a degree of continuity in the events, and meanings given to them, in a person's life (see Chase and Statham, Chapter Eighteen). Both psychological and sociological theories – including Schutz's (1954) notion of 'typifications', Kelly's (1955) 'personal construct' theory and Janoff-Bulman's (1992) work on 'assumptive worlds'– also suggest a human endeavour, from the earliest years of life onwards, to develop some sort of workable framework for ordering perceptions, understandings and daily interactions.

Developmental psychology has also been critiqued from other disciplinary viewpoints, including history, anthropology and sociology, and in the growing field of 'childhood studies'. These critiques highlight the historical and cultural specificity of contemporary Western understandings of 'childhood' as a time of innocence to be protected (although within affluent Western societies, this framing of childhood may itself be classed and raced; see Giroux, 2000). And, in other contexts, a very different and perhaps wider range of everyday experience may be accepted for children (Montgomery, 2009). In affluent Western societies, however, the dominant view of childhood, along with processes of industrialisation and the growth of compulsory education (Woodhead, 2009), has been particularly influential in the separation of children's lives from those of adults, and the significance of the home and the school as the appropriate sites of a 'proper childhood', protected from the potential moral corruption of the workplace or the street. The field of child development has been closely tied to the institutionalisation of this understanding of childhood (Ribbens McCarthy and Edwards, 2011), which is also promoted worldwide through the power and reach of the media, and through international legislation and policies.

At the same time, images and understandings of children and young people remain contested, both within and across cultures. Ribbens (1994), for example, found differing typifications of children in the accounts given by English mothers of their lives with their children – as natural innocents, little devils or small people – each implicating a different understanding of the relationship between individual and society. Varying images, partial and often dichotomous, pervade policy and practice, for example, children as victims or villains/threats, a dichotomy that obscures the extensive overlap between victimisation and offending (Hooper, 2010). The changing constitution of 'childhood' in contemporary societies is also debated, for example, between childhood as increasingly democratised or familialised (Ribbens McCarthy and Edwards, 2011), or as the focus for anxieties associated with rapid social, technological and economic change. And throughout these debates about the nature of childhood and of child development, there is the general tension between analysing the child as an individual or as part of a family or other household (Qvortrup et al, 2009) and see Vetere, Chapter Twenty-two.

There are also cultural variabilities with regard to the nature of the relationships through which care is given, and the understanding of 'self' that is being cared for and nurtured. In this regard, families are generally seen as the crucial and appropriate place for the care of children, although understandings of what is meant by 'family' are both widely variable and highly charged with emotion and rhetoric (Ribbens McCarthy et al, 2012). The nature of the linkage between 'the child', 'the self' and 'the family' is thus open to significant debate. While a focus on the family lives of children and young people inevitably highlights themes of interdependence and relationality, with the (developing) self embedded in interpersonal relationships, understandings of the nature of 'adulthood' towards which the child is seen to be moving implicate very differing notions of personhood across the globe. Notions such as 'individuation', 'autonomy' and 'independence' – which are commonly regarded as appropriate goals for child development in the West – may thus be quite marginalised in other cultural contexts, while understandings of 'family' may invoke a range of meanings of 'relationality' both within and across different societies (Ribbens McCarthy, 2012). These are complex issues that underpin the concerns of the work reported in this volume, and it is important not to underestimate the complexity of relationality – its multidimensionality (Ribbens McCarthy and Prokhovnik, under review), variability and paradoxes – and how these are played out in relation to ideas of 'family'.

At the same time, Western discourses of the autonomous self – as the underpinning of liberal democracy and the goal of child development – also construct a rational self stripped by secularisation of any spiritual content. In many cultures around the world, however, it is the child as a spiritual being that is the central concern. In Orissa in India, for example, the individual is understood through the idea of the 'soul' and its dharma, but this idea of the soul or self:

> is more closely connected in Oriya discourse to the role structure of a community than to the themes of this-worldly self-sufficiency and individual freedom of choice … personal identity is more closely associated with its statuses and relationships than with its individuality or distinctness. (Shweder et al, 1997, p 145)

In this context, responsibility for the satisfaction of individual desires is seen to lie not with the individual concerned, but with others, and even when a person is capable of independence, it might not be considered appropriate to be so. Similarly, in East Asian contexts more generally, troubles that would be located in the individual in the West, such as illness, may be framed as residing in interpersonal processes, the family and/or wider networks (Kleinman and Kleinman, 1997). This resonates with some approaches to family troubles in Western societies, such as family therapy (see Vetere, Chapter Twenty-two), or calls to focus on support for the families in which children's lives are embedded in preference to 'interventions' focused on individual children (Featherstone et al, under review).

Cultural and relational contexts may thus frame experiences of individuality, personal lives and relationships in quite different ways, with fundamental consequences for how children and their family troubles may be understood. We turn next, however, to understandings of changes and challenges in children's family lives.

Changes, challenges and troubles

Change is an inevitable part of human experience generally – the only other certainty besides death. For family lives in particular, changes may be seen most fundamentally around the key events of births and deaths, with partnering often an additional feature of the experience of birth and child-rearing. For children and young people, change is generally seen through a dominant developmental lens (Burman, 2007), such that change is very much expected and normal – indeed, its absence would itself be troubling. Concomitantly, some forms of change in family lives are also seen as 'natural' and inevitable, associated with children's development and adults' aging. The idea of 'change' is also the assumed bedrock for the notion of the 'life course' through which much research on personal lives is framed (Ribbens McCarthy and Edwards, 2011). Alongside this central theme, the language of personal change can include turning points, critical moments, biographical disruptions, transitions, development, growth, decline, crisis and trauma.

Some of these terms implicate ideas of personal change that are more or less orderly, part of the natural sequence, the ebb and flow of life, perhaps invoking ideas of development or deterioration. Others suggest unexpected disruption to that ebb and flow and/or events that overwhelm the capacity to cope with or manage them. Personal change may occur at a specific moment in time, occur over a period (sometimes barely discernible except in retrospect) or be a recurring circular, if complex and uneven, pattern, potentially evoking the 'chaotic lifestyle' of some families referred to in social work discourse. And change may also be desired and desirable, such that professionals at times urge families to change, and crucial contestations may occur over whether or not sufficient change has occurred. As a concept, then, 'change' is highly politically charged, both with regard to how we understand change in particular family lives and how we construct general narratives of change and continuity in contemporary family lives more broadly (Ribbens McCarthy and Edwards, 2011).[2]

We chose to use the language of 'change' rather than that of 'loss', appropriate though the latter may be to capture the emotional response to unwelcome change implicated in a range of family troubles. While change arguably always entails loss (Craib, 1994), the former concept provides us with more space to see the benefits that may be associated with change, though it may also risk us avoiding its painfulness (Ribbens McCarthy, 2006). But, if (some) changes are a 'normal' part of the family lives of children and young people, how do people understand these and at what point do they and others start to be deeply troubled by changes – or, indeed, their absence? When and how do some changes become troublesome to those involved, and troubling to others who may have concerns about harm to those involved – perhaps implicating profound levels of human suffering? Such questions lead to further issues about which changes might be seen as inevitable or expectable on the one hand, or as avoidable and contestable, and therefore to be struggled against, on the other. While these questions are important to pose, the chapters in this volume make clear that such categories and boundaries may be complex, and often ambiguous, to apply to the realities of particular children's family lives in particular contexts and circumstances.

So, while the term 'troubles' is itself open to varying nuances (eg as referring to what may be troubled, troubling or troublesome), what conceptual resources are available to help us understand and frame change that has become problematic, to constitute troubles, adversity or suffering? The anthropologist Michael Carrithers uses the term 'vicissitudes' to refer to 'difficulties or hardships erupting into a life, career, a course of action or an ordered scene and usually beyond one's control', involving 'the ruin of expectations' (2009, pp 2–3). He suggests that such experiences are a general feature of the human condition, vicissitudes being addressed at the cutting rhetorical edge of culture as this is created and recreated in daily interactions – a process involving both adults and children with varying degrees of agency and power. Carrithers' discussion draws attention particularly to sudden disruptions, but some vicissitudes might also occur slowly over time, until the original ideas of order (the ordered scene) and normal change (the life, career or course of action) are overturned. These terms in themselves draw attention to the significance of expectations and how these are culturally and personally both shared and variable, and we find the attention to 'expectations' important to hold on to as we develop our discussion here.

Expectations also link to the work of the sociologist and psychoanalyst Ian Craib, discussing 'the importance of disappointment'. Unexpectedly perhaps, Craib's discussion is directed more towards the affluent sections of contemporary Western societies who, he suggests, have come to 'hope for too much' (1994, p 5), including, we might add, sometimes for their children. And, in so doing, Western culture generally may have fostered unrealistic expectations about what is or is not possible in contemporary lives, since 'we are inevitably frustrated by the social world and by our own psychological and physical make-up' (Craib, 1994, p 6). These unrealistic expectations, Craib argues, may be associated with a denial of disappointment and a retreat from reality that may be profoundly unhelpful to all.

A somewhat different, multi-disciplinary, literature focuses on the concept of 'suffering'. These debates consider the ways in which suffering may be framed by different cultures as a more or less avoidable or inevitable feature of human experience: 'The cultural meanings of suffering (eg as punishment or salvation) may be elaborated in different ways … but the intersubjective experience of suffering, we contend, is itself a defining characteristic of human conditions in all societies' (Kleinman and Kleinman, 1991, p 280). Elsewhere, Kleinman argues that acute pain in particular constitutes 'a ubiquitous feature of human experience' (Kleinman et al, 1992, p 1), although chronic pain may not be universal in the same way.

While troubles frequently involve pain and suffering, linked to a range of unwanted states and losses (Kleinman and Kleinman, 1991; Schweder et al, 1997; Kellehear, 2009), the cultural resources available for meeting the existential challenges they pose vary in different contexts, for example, with more or less attention to spiritual dimensions. These issues are explored further by Ribbens McCarthy (Chapter Twenty-six), but Carrithers' (2009) discussion is also useful here, since the non-fulfilment of expectations may constitute a form of loss in itself, potentially entailing deeply held if implicit expectations for oneself, those we care about or for the way we expect life to be. Das (1997) argues that attention to everyday suffering also highlights the ways in which social institutions are involved in the production of suffering and, on the other hand, the creation of 'moral communities' (Das, 1997, p 563) to address suffering. At the same time, Kellehear quotes Bowker (1970) as suggesting that, '"To talk about suffering is to talk not of an academic problem but of the sheer bloody agonies of existence"' (Kellehear, 2009, p 388).

Some chapters in this volume portray forms of suffering – by children and other family members – for which the concept of trauma may be useful (eg see Chapters Twelve, Thirteen, Twenty-three and Twenty-four by Mannay, Wilson, Churchill and Clarke, and Forsberg, respectively). While expectations can again play a key part in trauma – Janoff-Bulman (2004, p 32) describes trauma as 'a case of massive expectancy disconfirmation' – a developmental perspective may also be useful here, particularly if trauma is seen to overwhelm capacity (Herman, 1992; Perry and Szalavitz, 2006). Building on the theoretical framework of trauma, the growing research literature indicates that, while what is experienced as traumatic may differ between individuals, dependent on context and previous experiences and relationships, such experiences may often underlie the behaviour that others define as troubling in children and young people. Where this remains unrecognised, there is the potential for interventions to exacerbate the problem (Perry and Szalavitz, 2006; Hooper, 2010). The framework of trauma has important implications for interventions with children, young people and their families. Perry and Szalavitz (2006) suggest that some form of traumatic experience is widespread but that appropriate responses open up the space, even in the face of severe adversity, to hold the potential for positive change over time. If human nature, as Sayer argues, is one of 'becoming', a 'shared incompleteness' (2011, p 111), change – for the young and the older – can create stimulation towards an enlargement of ourselves.

Personal responses to changes, troubles and suffering may thus include both negative elements (potential trauma and harm, or the spoiling of identities and hopes) and more positive elements. This latter possibility has been recognised particularly in the literature on post-traumatic growth that has developed in recent years – although, as Tedeschi and Calhoun (2004, p 1) point out, while the concept may be new, the idea that 'great good can come from great suffering is ancient'. Janoff-Bulman (2004, p 30) suggests that coping with trauma entails 'the arduous task of reconstructing an assumptive world'. Post-traumatic growth, she suggests, can involve strength gained through suffering, but the positive and negative are inextricably linked: 'The long-term legacy of trauma involves both losses and gains' (Janoff-Bulman, 2004, p 34). In the chapters contained in this volume, such complexities and ambiguities of responses to the changes and challenges in the family lives of children and young people are evocatively and robustly documented.

At the same time, besides such personal responses to family lives, where changes become troubling or troublesome to society more broadly, a variety of institutional responses may be involved, ranging from education, health and welfare systems to punishment and justice. Such institutions may work in complex ways with discourses and practices of support, nurturance, containment or punishment, constructing children as more or less competent in different contexts (Tisdall, 2006), often through dichotomous constructs such as victims versus villains (Seaford, 2001). Each of these institutionalised discourses frame specific family troubles in particular ways, which may take more or less account of, and provide more or less recognition for, the understandings and experiences of those family members whose lives and actions are at stake. Whether or not such institutional and professional responses are helpful or harmful in themselves may also be highly variable – as also evidenced by the research included in this volume (eg see Chapters Eighteen and Nineteen by Chase and Statham, and Evans, respectively). And whether at personal or institutional levels, Carrithers importantly points to the ways in which some rhetorical responses to vicissitudes may be productive, but others may themselves 'deepen the crisis, create more vicissitudes, and require yet further marshalling of ideas and interpretations' (2009, p 3).

It is thus important to recognise that the changes and challenges faced by individual family members may also challenge the world-as-normal for social scientists, social policymakers and professionals. Issues of language, concepts, rhetoric and meaning are key sites over which power struggles may be fought, in more or less explicit fashion, between diverse social actors, using whatever resources – personal, inter-personal, material, institutional or cultural – they can find to hand. It is thus crucial to attend to the complexities of how meanings and contexts are intertwined, as these are drawn upon and reshaped by social interaction in a great variety of circumstances, as well as by institutionalised discourses, interpersonal dynamics and material resources and situations. We turn next to illustrate such complex processes by reference to particular substantive issues.

Troubling normalities and normalising troubles

One way of thinking about the questions raised by a focus on family troubles, and how such questions have been raised and addressed in existing literatures, is to recognise two conflicting directions of argument within feminist and other research on families and its overlapping fields: one direction is to trouble the 'normal'; and the other is to normalise perceived 'trouble'. These different approaches coexist in some areas of debate, but they have also developed in historically specific contexts. While both approaches have been necessary and valuable – the first to name oppressive practices such as violence and abuse as such, and the second to counter the pathologisation of family change and diversity – both are also echoed in other contexts with different purposes, and those echoes suggest some pitfalls or risks too.

Troubling the normal

The highlighting of harm/injustice involved in previously oppressive norms and obscured by both functionalist theory (Morgan, 1975) and idealised images of the family was the purpose of feminist work on the 'dark side' of the family (Sommerville, 2000), the naming of domestic violence along with other forms of violence against women, and the growth of recognition worldwide of child abuse and neglect. Research driven by this agenda was more visible in sociology in the 1970s and 1980s than latterly, though campaigns continue to have these issues taken seriously as harmful troubles and addressed in policy and practice, as does applied research expanding the knowledge base on specific issues and considering its implications for professional practice. So troubling the normal has been an important direction for feminist research and activism, and for those concerned with child poverty.

The normal may be troubled in more negative ways however, in ways inflected by the politics of class, gender, age and 'race'. This can result in certain groups being pathologised, demonised, othered against dominant norms: teenage parents, when they are identified as a problem category to be reduced rather than a group for some of whom the circumstances in which they parent may undermine capacity; young people, when they are represented in the media in predominantly negative terms, associated with drinking, drugs and other forms of socially disapproved behaviour; and black and minority ethnic groups, when debates about issues such as forced marriage and honour crimes are used to stigmatise whole communities (for some of the difficulties in defining and measuring the prevalence of this particular trouble, see Keogh et al, Chapter Twenty).

Pathologising or stigmatising may also be a risk encountered in the naming of harms for example, and hence to the troubling of the 'normal', since naming harm easily slides into the presumption of damage on the one hand, or malice on the other. Alongside the important public recognition of child sexual abuse as a form of harm, there is now a critique of the 'harm story' being emphasised at the expense of recognising resilience, resistance and recovery, and the diversity of experiences and impacts (O'Dell, 2003). There is also a growing critique of the child protection system that has developed in the UK and other Anglophone countries, which gives risk of harm, framed as maltreatment, a more central place as grounds for intervention in families than most other European countries, where grounds for intervention tend to be framed in terms of child welfare (see Boddy, Chapter Twenty-one). There are many aspects to the critique in the UK, but one is the way parents and children often experience their interaction with Children's Services negatively (Lonne et al, 2009; Children's Commissioner, 2010), such that the intervention may at times exacerbate the problem.

Normalising troubles

A research agenda geared to normalising what had been presented as family troubles developed a bit later in the UK and the US, in response to the New Right's concern at what was understood to be undesirable family change involving the 'breakdown of the traditional family' – rising divorce, lone parenthood, cohabitation and so on (reviewed by Abbott and Wallace, 1992). This approach of normalising troubles thus sought to query whether such changes in family patterns should be seen as necessarily harmful, either for children or for society at large. Increasing divorce, for example, may be seen to reflect women's greater independence and freedom to refuse to live in circumstances and relationships that they find unacceptable, including relationships that may be abusive to them and/or their children.

From this perspective, culturally variable family practices may also be seen to have been pathologised and treated as 'dysfunctional', for example, through the inclusion of black and minority ethnic family lives in research as a pathologised presence or a normalised absence (Phoenix and Husain, 2007). In Korbin's terms (Chapter Two), such evaluations involve the mistake of confusing culture with harm. From this direction, then, the aim has been to recognise diversity, change and some element of adversity as 'normal', and to counter the pathologisation of whole groups by placing diverse practices in context, exploring them through the eyes of those involved.

This has also been important and influential, but, again, trouble is also normalised in other contexts in ways that are more problematic. Abusive parents and partners often normalise their own behaviour, presenting themselves in ways that may persuade and confuse other members of their families and professionals, obscuring harmful practices. Researchers sometimes counter a negative picture of a pathologised group with a more positive one, highlighting resilience and showing similarities with, as well as differences from, other groups, which is an important corrective, but parts of the picture that do not fit with that aim may also be lost sight of.

The risk in this direction of argument, then, is that in normalising trouble, the recognition of harm/injustices/particular vulnerabilities may be obscured, as may the variable needs of the different individuals involved, especially in the context of highly political debates. Policymakers in the UK have recently problematised teenage mothers as a group, concerned partly at costs to the public purse. Research, however, shows the complexity and diversity of the circumstances in which young women mother (Duncan et al, 2010), the variability of outcomes for their children, and the common context of teenage pregnancy as poverty and disadvantage, with an absence of alternative routes to independent adulthood for young women with limited education. In debates where broad generalisations are often exchanged, the needs for support of the most vulnerable mothers – those with histories of being looked after in public care or of sexual abuse, for example – and of their children (SmithBattle, 2000) may sometimes be overlooked.

Another example followed an earlier, but similarly highly political, debate between feminists and family systems therapists on the role of mothers whose children had been sexually abused, in which feminists argued that sexual abuse was the responsibility solely of the perpetrator, and family systems therapists at the time regarded both parents as equally responsible. Hooper (1992) conducted qualitative research with women whose children had been sexually abused, and the exploration of their perspectives helped to increase understanding of their experience and the challenges they faced, and to counter blame and pathologisation. However, the ensuing policy and professional developments took up the distinction between abusing and non-abusing parent in a way that offered a cheap solution (to require the non-abusing parent to eject and/or prevent contact with the perpetrator), but which often failed to recognise ongoing difficulties in the mother–child relationship and the vulnerability and need for support of both children and their mothers in this situation (Hooper and Humphreys, 1998).

The divide that we have explored here – between troubling the normal and normalising trouble – is schematic of course, but it may offer a useful reference point. Some of the chapters in this volume bring in more complexity, for example, illustrating how such diverse issues as domestic abuse (Mannay, Chapter Twelve), children caring for sick parents (Clarke and O'Dell, Chapter Six; Evans, Chapter Nineteen) and migration (Chase and Statham, Chapter Eighteen; Duque-Páramo, Chapter Seventeen; Erel, Chapter Sixteen; Evans, Chapter Nineteen; Jamieson and Highet, Chapter Eleven) can be both normalised and problematic, both troubling and ordinary, at the same time, and how ideals of the normal pervade the experience of trouble and influence available narratives and meanings through which to make sense of such experiences (Jamieson and Highet, Chapter Eleven; Wilson, Chapter Thirteen).

However, the most polarised debate at the Colloquium itself, which concerned the issue of smacking, reflected both directions of argument. For some participants, smacking was an oppressive practice to be named, given that the defence of reasonable chastisement persists for parents (in the UK) – albeit to a more limited extent than formerly – in order that children should be granted the same rights as adults to protection from assault; that is, it was a normalised practice in need of troubling. For others, the problematising of smacking was a way of pathologising working-class parents; a perceived trouble in need of normalising. The point here is not to resolve the debate but to clarify what was going on. The shifts and currents stirred up by these different movements of normalising trouble, or troubling the normal, can work in complex ways as discourses, policies, practices and everyday understandings are reshaped by these debates (particularly apparent in Duque-Páramo, Chapter Seventeen).

Expectations, power and contestations

These various debates and examples highlight how the transgression of expectations of what is typically normal, and what is normatively the way things should be, can constitute troubles, while at other times, it may be the expectations themselves that are seen as troubling. This resonates with one of our core questions, which asks to what extent troubles themselves are a 'normal' – expected and expectable – part of life. Are troubles, as unexpected disruptions and/or as disruptive changes, and/ or as a chronic failure of life to live up to expectations, an endemic and perennial feature of human experience in general, and children's family lives in particular, with which better preparation and more realistic expectations would help to cope? At what point do family troubles become defined as 'harmful', 'oppressive', 'abusive' or 'neglectful' of the needs of the less powerful (often meaning children), and hence requiring intervention? And at what point do 'normal troubles' entail (perhaps avoidable and unacceptable) suffering? Are there clear cut-off points or is it more arbitrary than this, and who sets these cut-off points?

Such processes point directly to the issues of contestation, negotiation and power in the determination of such boundary definitions and their evaluations. Just as the normal may be troubled in ways that others might want to question, troubles may also be normalised in other contexts in ways that others may find problematic. Some of this boundary-setting, and drawing of lines, around the normal and the troubling may involve power interpersonally in everyday domestic and relational lives, but, of course, it is also involved in other settings too, from social science debates (including this volume), to institutionalised policy and professional practices, including those involved in voluntary support for families. These issues are thus political with both a large and a small 'p', in parallel terms to the ways in which 20th-century feminists sought to find a way to talk about (gendered) troubles that had no language, and to recognise the personal as political.

In developing this volume, in conversations between ourselves as editors, debates at the Colloquium and elsewhere, we are conscious that there are many forms of tension at stake here, and we are not attempting to bring them to any tidy resolution. Asking differing questions, taking differing theoretical points of view, taking account of historical and cultural changes, understanding the perspectives and interests of different family members, and researching through differing methodologies, each brings differing rewards that bring particular things into view, while also risking leaving other things out, and other questions unanswered. This is the nature of the social science enterprise and its relevance to family troubles in everyday lives and professional practice. Some of the tensions that are particularly apparent have been:

- methodological tensions around differing research methods and the gains and losses of a focus on scientific measurement and understandings of causality on the one hand, or the prioritising of attention to process, context and complexity on the other, each underpinned in different ways by the significance of everyday, professional and academic meanings in which the research is situated;
- disciplinary and professional tensions around the desirability of a (more or less) detached analysis and the asking of difficult questions about how to value and include differing points of view, versus the more engaged perspective required of those concerned with interventions and change, political and policy issues, and/or professional practices;
- associated with this, tensions around how and whether to focus on the desirability of developing universal or abstract principles against the (pervasively recognised) need to attend to concrete practicalities and local specificities, and, linked to this, the risks of voyeurism and violation in focusing on and exposing the difficult concrete realities of particular troubling family relationships (eg as in reality TV shows; see Ray, 2012);
- tensions around the discourses of particular disciplinary perspectives, for example, how far to use a language of health in considering family lives (functional/dysfunctional, healthy/pathological etc), a language of morality (the ethics of care, right and wrong, selfish and unselfish etc), a political language (rights, fairness, oppression etc) or more anthropological language that seeks to stay close to everyday language and understandings;
- tensions around how to understand the needs of individuals as individuals (whatever their age) and to attend properly to individual needs, while also attending fully to the significance of the 'social person' (Ribbens McCarthy, 2012) that underpins widespread cultural understandings of family, as well as some particular therapeutic interventions, without risking 'subsuming' the individual within the group (Smart, 2007);
- tensions around how to take account of the multiplicity of perspectives involved, whether it is the multiplicity of differing family members, other social actors such as professionals or advocates, or institutions such as legal and welfare systems, and when to prioritise one perspective over another; and
- running through many of these tensions, tensions around the ambiguity and ambivalences of complex emotions and different values and priorities, through which we may see both losses and gains – to variable extents – in the risk and challenges children and young people may encounter in their everyday family lives.

While not generally posed in such stark dichotomous terms, these tensions made themselves felt during the Colloquium itself, as exemplified earlier, and have made themselves known in the production of this book (and some are explored further by Ribbens McCarthy, Chapter Twenty-six). The authors of different chapters may thus be at odds with one another at times, and we, as editors, sometimes have our differences with each other and with some of the discussions – although they all offer us important food for thought and significant research conclusions. A variety of disciplines and therapeutic orientations are represented in the chapters in this collection, including psychoanalysis, systemic approaches, anthropology, history, sociology, psychology, social policy analysis and more, and we have drawn on a range of such sources for this chapter here. While a multidisciplinary approach is vital to engaging with the complexity of this territory, tensions are inevitable – although hopefully productive – in bringing together such different approaches.

At a more general level, we discussed earlier how social science has come to see childhood, and children's interests, as socially, historically and institutionally constructed, with children's needs perhaps constituting one of the very few moral imperatives still apparent in contemporary Western cultures (Ribbens McCarthy et al, 2000). But there is a tension for us here, in our own writing in this volume, that we are ourselves working with, and contributing to, this social construction of childhood and youth. This in itself raises particular issues about how far we also want to work around the moral imperative of meeting children's needs. For example, what are the implications of this analysis for how we consider outcomes for children and young people? While sociologists may use the word 'normal' to refer to what is common or typical (statistically average) or normative (what is the dominant set of morally inflected expectations), in the field of social welfare, a consideration of the optimal (understood as health/well-being/development) is generally part of the picture too. In such a context, the growing body of outcome research makes a valuable contribution. But it is also important to avoid using children's best interests in a way that assumes it is simple to know what they are, and that even when we agree what they are, that they necessarily trump all other considerations.

In our introductory discussion here, we have pointed to the problems and issues of categorisation, resources, power and politics, which are, of course, central features of the academic enterprise itself. So we may need, as researchers as well as professionals, to recognise and explicate the political choices and values that may be present in the concepts we use, the questions that we ask and the theoretical models we construct and work with. In considering family troubles, we suggest, there are 'big issues' of morality, existential meanings, human care and kindness at stake, alongside the possibilities – or inevitability – of power, inequalities, conflict and suffering (considered further in Ribbens McCarthy, Chapter Twenty-six). In the case of family troubles, these big issues may not be writ large but may nevertheless be the underlying existential challenge of everyday relational lives, challenges that may sometimes lead to a fresh evaluation of the mundane.

Interwoven with all this, in the present volume, may be the authors' (and readers') 'own' personal experiences of family troubles. Indeed, our involvement as editors and instigators of this project very probably reflects at some level, conscious or unconscious, and in different and changing ways, our own efforts to create meaning around our personal family troubles. While Judith Butler (2005) reminds us that accounts of ourselves are always partial and limited, provisional and susceptible to change – and we do not therefore see it as useful to tell what could only be one version of our own stories here – in our discussions, we have often been reminded of the ways these issues touch us personally, and of the need to consider our personal histories, identifications and investments in varying perspectives and debates. This underscores just how difficult is the work expected of professionals who intervene in family troubles, requiring them: to keep in mind all parties as well as the social, cultural, economic and political context of their troubles; to be an ally for the most vulnerable when required; and to manage their own experience when they too are likely often to be touched personally by these encounters (Ferguson, 2011). Readers will no doubt also engage with these issues in ways influenced by their personal lives as well as their professional and/or academic interests.

Introducing the book as a whole

These, then, are some of the questions raised, and tensions explored, through this volume. We have structured the book into five main parts, and each part is introduced by one of the editors to consider the issues and themes addressed across the chapters included in that section. We begin in Part One by setting the scene overall in terms of the contexts (both cultural and historical) and methodologies (of varying approaches) that may frame academic work on family troubles. Then, in Part Two, authors explore issues at the edges of the definitions and practices of troubles, and ask whose views prevail. Part Three then takes this further, raising questions of when the normal and the troubling may become the harmful, while the focus broadens across the globe in Part Four to consider troubles and transitions as these may occur over space and culture. Part Five then considers more directly how interventions may occur as policies and professional practices seek to work with children and their carers to address family troubles. This part concludes with a discussion of what is at stake in family troubles, and what cultural and philosophical resources may be available to help us to address them, thus reviewing some of the broader and underpinning issues invoked across the collection as a whole.

Across these chapters, many variable substantive issues are considered, enabling a wide-ranging exploration of how troubles may be experienced across a variety of sources of family change. The topics in the first four parts range from child maltreatment to different perspectives on infant feeding in encounters between mothers and midwives, from disability to deviance, from kinship care to parental separation, from conflict between siblings to young asylum-seekers escaping conflict in their countries of origin, from parental death to family migration, from forced marriage to parentless households orphaned through AIDS. And, in Part Five, working with families includes a variety of therapeutic perspectives and policy contexts, particularly across Europe. At the same time, there are many more family troubles and therapeutic approaches that are not included in this volume, and the gaps partly reflect the nature of the papers that were offered at the original Colloquium. But we hope that the issues raised here across the topics that are addressed may be taken further, perhaps, by others.

Notes

[1] We use this term here without explicit discussion of the difficulties and dilemmas in the terms being used, i.e. 'Western', and 'culture'. See Ribbens McCarthy, Chapter Twenty-Six, for further consideration of how to refer to and describe 'cultural differences' without reifying or fixing them in unrealistic and unhelpful ways.

[2] It should be noted that we here consider only the concept of 'change' in terms of its assumptions, evaluations and political usage. Similar analysis could be undertaken for other concepts that appear in this volume, such as 'abuse', 'exploitation', 'harm', 'well-being' or 'flourishing'. Later in this chapter, we consider some alternative – perhaps more neutral – languages that might be useful in considering the issues at stake in our discussion of family troubles. In Chapter Twenty-six, Ribbens McCarthy returns to the question of how to frame and evaluate the family troubles of children and young people.

References

Abbott, P. and Wallace, C. (1992) *The family and the new right*, London: Pluto Press.

Barrett, H. (2006) *Attachment and the perils of parenting*, London: National Parenting and Family Institute.

Belsky, J. (2007) 'Childcare matters', in J. Oates (ed) *Attachment relationships: quality of care for young children*, Milton Keynes: The Open University.

Burman, E. (2007) *Deconstructing developmental psychology* (2nd edn), London: Routledge.

Butler, J. (2005) *Giving an account of oneself*, New York: Fordham University Press.

Carrithers, M. (2009) 'Introduction', in M. Carrithers (ed) *Culture, rhetoric and the vicissitudes of life*, New York, NY: Berghahn Books, pp 1–17.

Children's Commissioner (2010) 'Family perspectives on safeguarding and on relationships with children's services'. Available at: http://www.childrenscommissioner.gov.uk/content/publications/content_405 (accessed 2 June 2012).

Craib, I. (1994) *The importance of disappointment*, London: Routledge.

Das, V. (1997) 'Sufferings, theodicies, disciplinary practices, appropriations', *International Social Sciences Journal*, vol 154, pp 563–72.

Duncan, S., Edwards, R. and Alexander, C. (2010) *Teenage parenthood: what's the problem?*, London: Tufnell Press.

Featherstone, B., Morris, K. and White, S. (under review) 'A marriage made in hell: early intervention meets child protection', *Early Intervention*.

Ferguson, H. (2011) *Child protection practice*, Basingstoke: Palgrave Macmillan.

Giddens, A. (1991) *Modernity and self identity: Self and society in the late modern age*, Cambridge: Polity Press.

Giroux, H.A. (2000) *Stealing innocence: youth, corporate power, and the politics of culture*, New York, NY: St Martin's Press.

Hays, S. (1996) *The cultural contradictions of motherhood*, New Haven, CT: Yale University Press.

Herman, J. (1992) *Trauma and recovery*, London: Pandora.

Hooper, C.-A. (1992) *Mothers surviving child sexual abuse*, London: Routledge.

Hooper, C.-A. (2010) 'Gender, child maltreatment and young people's offending', in B. Featherstone, C.-A. Hooper, J. Scourfield and J. Taylor (eds) *Gender and child welfare in society*, Chichester: Wiley-Blackwell.

Hooper, C.-A. and Humphreys, C. (1998) 'Women whose children have been sexually abused: reflections on a debate', *British Journal of Social Work*, vol 28, pp 565–80.

James, A., Jenks, C. and Prout, A. (eds) (1998) *Theorizing childhood*, Cambridge: Polity Press.

Janoff-Bulman, R. (1992) *Shattered assumptions: towards a psychology of trauma*, New York, NY: The Free Press.

Janoff-Bulman, R. (2004) 'Posttraumatic growth: three explanatory models', *Psychological Inquiry*, vol 15, no 1, pp 30–4.

Kassem, D., Murphy, L. and Taylor, E. (eds) (2010) *Key issues in childhood and youth studies*, London: Routledge.

Kellehear, A. (2009) 'On dying and human suffering', *Palliative Medicine*, vol 23, pp 388–97.

Kelly, G. (1955) *The psychology of personal constructs*, New York, NY: W.W. Norton.

Kleinman, A. and Kleinman, J. (1991) 'Suffering and its professional transformation: towards an ethnography of interpersonal experience', *Culture, Medicine and Psychiatry*, vol 15, no 3, pp 275–301.

Kleinman, A. and Kleinman, J. (1997) 'Moral transformations of health and suffering in Chinese society', in A.M. Brandt and P. Rozin (eds) *Morality and health*, New York, NY: Routledge, pp 101–18.

Kleinman, A., Brodwin, P.E., Byron, J. and DelVecchio Good, M.J. (1992) 'Pain as human experience: an introduction', in M.J. DelVecchio Good, P.E. Brodwin, B.J. Good and A. Kleinman (eds) *Pain as human experience: an anthropological perspective*, Berkeley, CA: University of California Press, pp 1–28.

Lareau, A. (2003) *Unequal childhoods: class, race and family life*, Berkeley, CA: University of California Press.

Levitas, R. (2012) 'There may be trouble ahead: what we know about those 120,000 'troubled' families', Working Paper No 3, Poverty and Social Exclusion UK, Available at: – http://www.poverty.ac.uk/policy-response-working-paper-families-social-justice-life-chances-children-parenting-uk-government (accessed 2 June 2012).

Lonne, B., Parton, N., Thompson, J. and Harries, M. (2009) *Reforming child protection*, London: Routledge.

Montgomery, H. (2009) *An introduction to childhood: anthropological perspectives on children's lives*, Oxford: Blackwell.

Morgan, D.H.J. (1975) *Social theory and the family*, London: Routledge and Kegan Paul.

Oates, J. (ed) (2007) *Attachment relationships: quality of care for young children*, Milton Keynes: The Open University.

O'Dell, L. (2003) 'The "harm" story in childhood sexual abuse: contested understandings, disputed knowledge', in P. Reavey and S. Warner (eds) *New feminist stories of child sexual abuse: sexual scripts and dangerous dialogue*, London: Routledge.

Perry, B. and Szalavitz, M. (2006) *The boy who was raised as a dog, and other stories from a child psychiatrist's notebook: what traumatized children can teach us about loss, love and healing*, New York, NY: Basic Books.

Phoenix, A. and Husain, F. (2007) *Parenting and ethnicity*, York: Joseph Rowntree Foundation/National Children's Bureau.

Portes, J. (2012) '"Neighbours from hell": who is the Prime Minister talking about?'. Available at: http://notthetreasuryview.blogspot.com/2012/02/families-from-hell-who-is-prime.html?m=1 (accessed 1 June 2012).

Qvortrup, J., Corsaro, W.A. and Honig, M.-S. (2009) 'Why social studies of childhood?', in J. Qvortrup, W.A. Corsaro and M.-S. Honig (eds) *The Palgrave handbook of childhood studies*, Basingstoke: Palgrave Macmillan, pp 1–18.

Ray, L. (2012) 'Violence and suffering', paper presented at the Symposium on 'Sociology, Suffering and Humanitarianism', London, British Sociological Association, 3 February.

Ribbens, J. (1994) *Mothers and their children: a feminist sociology of childrearing*, London: Sage.

Ribbens McCarthy, J. (2006) *Young people's experiences of loss and bereavement: towards an inter-disciplinary approach*, Buckingham: Open University Press.

Ribbens McCarthy, J. (2008) 'Security, insecurity and family lives', in A. Cochrane and D. Talbot (eds) *Security: welfare, crime and society*, Maidenhead: Open University Press/McGraw Hill, pp 61–92.

Ribbens McCarthy, J. (2012) 'The powerful relational language of "family": togetherness, belonging, and personhood', *Sociological Review*, vol 60, no 1, pp 68–90.

Ribbens McCarthy, J, Edwards, R. and Gillies, V. (2000) 'Moral tales of the child and the adult: narratives of contemporary family lives under changing circumstances', *Sociology*, vol 3, no 4, pp 785–804.

Ribbens McCarthy, J. and Edwards, R. (2011) *Key concepts in family studies*, London: SAGE.

Ribbens McCarthy, J. and Prokhovnik, R. (under review) 'Embodied relationality and caring after death', *Body and Society*.

Ribbens McCarthy, J., Doolittle, M. and Day Sclater, S. (2012) *Understanding family meanings: a reflective text*, Bristol: The Policy Press.

Rogoff, B. (2003) *The cultural nature of human development*, Oxford: Oxford University Press.

Sayer, A. (2011) *Why things matter to people*, Cambridge: Polity Press.

Schutz, A. (1954) 'Concept and theory formation in the social sciences', *Journal of Philosophy*, vol 51, pp 257–73.

Seaford, H. (2001) 'Children and childhood: perceptions and realities', *The Political Quarterly*, vol 72, no 4, pp 454–65.

Shweder, R.A., Much, N.C., Mahapatra, M. and Park, L. (1997) 'The "big three" of morality (autonomy, community and divinity) and the "big three" explanations of suffering', in A.M. Brandt and P. Rozin (eds) *Morality and health*, London: Routledge, pp 119–69.

Smart, C. (2007) *Personal life*, Cambridge: Polity.

SmithBattle, L. (2000) 'Developing a caregiving tradition in opposition to one's past: lessons from a longitudinal study of teenage mothers', *Public Health Nursing*, vol 17, no 2, pp 85–93.

Sommerville, J. (2000) *Feminism and the family: politics and society in the UK and USA*, Basingstoke: Macmillan.

Tedeschi, R.G. and Calhoun, L.G. (2004) 'Posttraumatic growth: conceptual foundations and empirical evidence', *Psychological Inquiry*, vol 15, no 1, pp 1–18.

Tisdall, E.K.M. (2006) 'Antisocial behaviour legislation meets children's services: challenging perspectives on children, parents and the state', *Critical Social Policy*, vol 26, no 1, pp 101–20.

Uprichard, E. (2008) 'Children as "beings" and "becomings": children, childhood and temporality', *Children and Society*, vol 22, pp 303–13.

Van Ijzendoorn, M.H., Bakermans-Kranenburg, M.J. and Sagi-Schwartz, A. (2007) 'Attachment across diverse socio-cultural contexts: the limits of universality', in K. Rubin and O.B. Chun (eds) *Parenting beliefs, behaviors, and parent–child relations: a cross-cultural perspective*, New York, NY: Psychology Press, pp 108–42.

Woodhead, M. (1990) 'Psychology and the cultural construction of children's needs', in A. James and A. Prout (eds) *Constructing and reconstructing childhood: contemporary issues in the sociological study of childhood*, Brighton: Falmer.

Woodhead, M. (2009) 'Child development and the development of childhood', in J. Qvortrup, W.A. Corsaro and M.-S. Honig (eds) *The Palgrave handbook of childhood studies*, Basingstoke: Palgrave Macmillan, pp 46–61.

PART ONE

APPROACHING FAMILY TROUBLES? CONTEXTS AND METHODOLOGIES

Introduction to Part One

Jane Ribbens McCarthy

In this opening section of the book, we set the scene for some fundamental issues for understanding and researching family troubles in the lives of children and young people, and raise some core questions about how we can consider family troubles in the changeable and changing contexts of varying cultures and historical periods. While each of the four introductory chapters takes a particular focus, the issues they raise are also touched upon through other chapters in this section. Thus, in terms of the methodological issues raised by Michael Rutter and Ara Francis concerning the basis of knowledge around family troubles, questions of context are still as crucial (and troubling) as they are in the more theoretical and substantive chapters by Jill Korbin and Janet Fink. And, as Korbin and Fink consider cultural and historical contexts, respectively, the concerns of their chapters, in turn, suggest significant methodological considerations. And across all of these four chapters, insights are provided into various substantive topics concerning family troubles as these are used to illustrate the arguments made. Korbin particularly focuses on child maltreatment across cultural contexts; Fink considers historically variable concerns regarding 'lost' childhoods and the 'losses' experienced by children and their parents; Rutter's examples of science in action include physical abuse and maltreatment of children, genetic and environmental mediation of mental health outcomes, resilience, and residential care; while Francis particularly considers qualitative research on child abuse, mental health issues, low-income unmarried mothers and middle-class parents whose children are considered to have 'significant problems'.

In the first chapter, Jill Korbin sets out a concise and thoughtful overview of global cultural issues in relation to family troubles – highlighting some major points for consideration. In discussing evidence that culture has been identified as one of 10 major principles affecting human development, Korbin argues that questions of culture have been seriously neglected in traditional child development research, often based on samples from very particular cultural contexts. This, then, points to methodological and ethical issues of complexities and contradictions in researching the everyday settings and practices of child development across cultures as well as between different groups within particular cultures. In Korbin's discussion, culture is crucial in helping to shape the meanings of children's everyday lives and thus in framing what comes to constitute 'trouble', which has to be understood by reference to community expectations of what is considered desirable. At the same time, Korbin warns of the dual dangers of confusing culture with troubles as well as mistaking troubles for culture. In seeking to unravel some of these difficult conundrums, Korbin offers important guidance under the general approach of cultural pluralism while also urging caution in making judgements about what constitutes 'family troubles' in variable cultural contexts.

Fink's chapter also opens with a concise and important overview, regarding the historiography of work on family troubles, before embarking on a meticulous and thoughtful exploration of the specific historical contexts of children's family troubles as represented in popular culture across the 20th century in Britain. Fink pursues this exploration through two films and one particular television series that clearly spoke strongly to concerns of their audiences at the time. By placing these sources firmly in their temporal contexts – including contemporary welfare policies and economic circumstances – Fink is able to show how the meanings of family troubles get worked through, and sometimes reframed at different points in time. In turn, Fink argues that an underpinning emphasis in the defining of family troubles in Britain throughout the 20th century has been the normative persistence of a particular version of family and the stigmatisation of those outside it, along with the prevalence of troubles, even though these may be silenced in some historical circumstances.

The third chapter in this section moves on to the methodological issues raised by Rutter about how to research family troubles through 'good science'. After pointing to pressing reasons for the importance of science in understanding family troubles, and setting out some thoughts on the characteristics of good science, Rutter outlines particular issues requiring a scientific approach. These include: determination of rates of family troubles; patterns of such troubles, including 'normal variations'; their origins and environmental mediation; and variations in the ways in which children experience their upbringing. Eschewing an epistemological discussion of methodologies, Rutter develops certain themes to illustrate the important contributions that good science can make in practice, as seen through both qualitative and quantitative research studies. These themes include: the making of generalisations; responsiveness to the unexpected in research; consideration of the meanings of the measures used; attention to social interactions as well as to the point of view of the individual; and considerations of heterogeneity. Rutter goes on to argue that good science can make key contributions to the field of family troubles through its attention to methodologies and methods, including: systematic sampling and good measurement; well-focused and incisive questions; the use of a range of research strategies; the testing of alternative explanations; and the examination of inter- and intra-group variations.

The section concludes with Francis's chapter on qualitative methodologies for studying family troubles, which she argues include a range of methods sharing a concern with meanings, seeking to stay close to everyday contexts and underpinned by a primarily inductive epistemology. In relation to family troubles, Francis suggests that qualitative methodologies are particularly well-suited to ask two core questions: of how people construct 'family troubles'; and how these constructions are related to social systems of power and inequalities. Using the example of the emergence of child abuse as a significant publicly defined family trouble in 20th-century Western societies, Francis argues that qualitative methodologies can consider the processes through which such troubles are recognised and constructed, including historical considerations of the parts played by particular professional interests and the (classed) resistance to and support for the definitions of child abuse that emerged. Close examination of the social constructions of particular family troubles, Francis proposes, can be important in helping to frame appropriate interventions.

In the title of her chapter, Francis also explicitly draws attention to the tensions and 'divides' concerning methodological approaches to researching family troubles, and some of these tensions are also raised in Rutter's chapter. This is not the place to attempt to settle these questions of the differences and commonalities, the pros and the cons, of qualitative and quantitative methodologies and their relationship to epistemological and ontological positions. Yet, it is important to recognise that, as we see in their respective chapters, different positions and concerns can generate quite different understandings of the arguments. At the same time, there is much common ground, including a concern with producing good science and the need to attend to meanings and contexts (a point that Rutter has also developed at greater length in earlier publications; see Rutter, 1999). Indeed, all four chapters in this section point towards the need to consider cultural and temporal contexts and variations and how these may shape, and respond to, the meanings attached to children's family lives. The question then becomes: which methodologies are best suited to getting closer to 'meanings-in-context' (Ribbens McCarthy et al, 2012) and how far is this a central concern for researching family troubles?

Other key methodological issues that emerge from these discussions, but with differing emphases and understandings, include:

- What is meant by generalisability and how it can be achieved: while Rutter suggests that small or poor samples are a particular weakness of qualitative methods, Francis argues that generalisability of a different sort can be achieved through the use of 'sensitising concepts', and, we might add, the careful compilation and comparison of a range of pertinent qualitative studies bearing on the topic under investigation. At the same time, while qualitative studies do not generally incorporate probability sampling, the nature of the samples obtained do require careful consideration and scrutiny for any systematic processes that have shaped the characteristics of the research participants as a whole. Further, while Rutter argues that differences between and within groups are more carefully considered in quantitative methodologies, there may also be specific techniques used by qualitative researchers – such as the search for negative cases (Hammersley and Atkinson, 2007) – to explore both what is shared and what is variable among the research participants.

- Ability to deal with the unexpected in research: Rutter argues that good science, using a range of methodologies, can be flexible and responsive to unexpected findings, although Francis argues that this is a particular strength of qualitative methodologies with their more open-ended research methods and inductive processes of knowledge production.
- The ability to identify processes and mechanisms underlying family troubles: this is an important issue for a range of methodologies. While quantitative and qualitative methodologies may differ in terms of how they understand and prioritise the search for causality, their various contributions can also be complementary in important ways (as Rutter points out) towards understanding family troubles as these occur over time.
- The importance of the questions being asked and the nature of the questions: while sharing an emphasis on the former, there may be different approaches to the nature of the questions between methodologies. Thus, while Francis argues that qualitative methodologies are concerned with the origins of research questions and the significance of social contexts for their construction, Rutter argues that good science requires well-honed and precise research questions for investigation, along with a close correspondence between concepts and their measurement. At the same time, issues of power and inequality are stressed by Francis as central themes that qualitative methodologies can encompass as a key part of the questions and processes under investigation, as well as within the production of knowledge itself in the social contexts of Western academic hierarchies.

The sensitivity and 'troublesome' nature of some of these methodological issues is clearly apparent in relation to these chapters. As discussed in Chapter One, these are not the only tensions arising in this edited collection, and we are pleased to offer these robust debates and thoughtful conversations within this volume. At the same time, there is a shared view that social science research of all forms requires being open to scrutiny and debate among one's academic peers, and of the need for thoughtful, creative, rigorous and robust work for the production of knowledge. It is only through such work that the development of appropriate interventions can take account of complexity and diversity as these occur in cultural and historical contexts.

References

Hammersley, M. and Atkinson, P. (2007) *Ethnography: principles in practice*, London: Routledge.

Ribbens McCarthy, J., Doolittle, M. and Day Sclater, S. (2012) *Understanding family meanings: a reflective text*, Bristol: The Policy Press.

Rutter, M. (1999) 'Resilience concepts and findings: implications for family therapy', *Journal of Family Therapy*, vol 21, pp 119–44.

CHAPTER TWO

Cultural context, families and troubles

Jill Korbin

The cultural context provides a perspective that is core to understanding families and their troubles. Families around the world vary in the forms that they take, the circumstances in which they live and the troubles that they experience. There is not a single consensus definition of culture, of family or of trouble that offers an opportunity to explore how diversity and variability can contribute to understanding the connections among these phenomena. This chapter will first consider the relationship of the cultural context to understanding families and troubles and will then turn to a consideration of child maltreatment as an illustration of the complexities of these issues.

Families are fundamental building blocks of human societies. We spend most of our lifetimes as family members, from the family or families in which we are reared to the family or families that we form or relate to as adults. The 'right' to a family is prominent in the United Nations' Convention on the Rights of the Child, and when families are disrupted or absent, a substitute arrangement with as many familial features as possible is most often sought (McCall et al, 2011). Yet, despite the centrality of families in social organisation and human development, families are rife with contradictions. Families, by their very nature, are at once both cooperative and conflictual, both stable and changing, and both safe and dangerous. 'Troubles' arise both from within and from outside families, and are variably experienced by different family members by virtue of attributes including age, gender, sibling position or family role.

The cultural context offers an important framework for understanding families and 'troubles'. A major review of child development research identified culture as one of 10 major principles impacting human development, but yet one that was poorly studied and understood:

> Culture influences every aspect of human development and is reflected in childrearing beliefs and practices designed to promote healthy adaptation.... Given the magnitude of its influence on the daily experiences of children, the relative disregard for cultural influences in traditional child development research is striking. (Shonkoff and Phillips, 2000, p 25)

Further, to move towards a fuller understanding of families and 'troubles' in cultural context requires a broader sample of the world's peoples than we generally find in the literature on human development: 'The study of child development has been largely confined to children in North America, Europe, and other Western countries, who comprise less than 10 per cent of all children in the world' (LeVine and New, 2008, p 1). The overwhelming majority of research findings are based on undergraduate students enrolled in basic psychology courses in Western, Educated, Industrialised, Rich and Democratic (WEIRD) societies: 'Overall, these empirical patterns suggests that we need to be less cavalier in addressing questions of human nature on the basis of data drawn from this particularly thin, and rather unusual, slice of humanity' (Henrich et al, 2010, p 61).

Ecological and ecocultural models have been applied to understanding families in their cultural contexts. Bronfenbrenner's (1979, 1995) widely cited ecological model of human development allows a perspective on families both in terms of the individuals composing them and the broader social and cultural context. Individuals are nested in families, shaping and influencing their families through the individual characteristics and developmental stages members bring to the family unit. Families are then nested in communities and the larger sociocultural context, again bringing the characteristics of both the individuals composing families and the family units to the larger context. The transactions or interactions across ecological levels describe and explain how families mediate between the individuals that compose them and the larger context. The family is one ecological level, with the point of an ecological framework being that levels do not exist independently. While the Bronfenbrenner model is not, in and of itself, a causal model, it provides a framework for forming hypotheses that take multiple levels into consideration. The transactions or interactions across the levels are of primary interest (Cicchetti and Lynch, 1993). For example, a child with aggressive behaviours in a family with spousal and other forms of violence living in a community with a higher rate of violent crime would be postulated to fare worse than a similar child in a more nurturing and low-violence community. These are testable hypotheses based in the framework. The Bronfenbrenner model has been expanded and elaborated on by others, for example, including a time component of whether factors at each level are transient or enduring, and a risk component of whether they are protective or risk-enhancing (Cicchetti and Lynch, 1993).

Ecocultural models of human development (eg Weisner, 2002; Worthman, 2010) build on the work of the Whitings (eg Whiting, 1977; Whiting and Edwards, 1988). Harkness and Super (1994) introduced the idea of the 'ecological niche' to link cultural context, particularly parental ethnotheories (ideas about how parenting influences child development as shaped by culture and environment) to parenting practices and childcare patterns around the world. Ecocultural theory, as proposed by Weisner (2002), focuses on the developmental pathways grounded in settings that include daily activities, tasks and routines in their ecological and cultural (ecocultural) context. Worthman (2010) adds important biological components in her and her colleagues' bioecocultural model (for an excellent review of these three models, see Worthman, 2010). These models have provided the basis for a rich empirical tradition of studying children in their contexts, including the family.

Increasing interest is being directed to the scientific study of families that takes into account the complexity of families and the need for rigorous and mixed-methods approaches (Yoshikawa et al, 2008; Institute of Medicine and National Research Council, 2011; Weisner and Fiese, 2012).

The cultural context includes the settings in which behaviours occur and are given meaning. The cultural context, then, provides others with whom to interact, activities in which to engage, expectations and scripts for behaviour, and the attribution of values and meaning to these contextual features. Further, all of these aspects of an ecological or ecocultural framework are dynamic. Individuals change through the process of development in context, families change through the processes of managing the developmental trajectories of their members and changes in the larger sociocultural context, and cultures also are in a constant state of flux due to both internal and external forces. Rogoff (2003) conceptualises these processes of ongoing change, showing how individuals develop as participants in their cultural contexts.

Cultural pluralism, or cultural contextualism, is the orientation that there are multiple pathways afforded by different cultural contexts; that is, there is a multitude of ways that families can accomplish their goals, in this case, child-rearing, all of which are suited to their context and circumstances. Cultural pluralism/contextualism differs from cultural relativism in that relativism asserts that all cultural practices have equal value if only culture is well understood. Cultural pluralism/contextualism, in contrast, argues for understanding the multiple pathways afforded by the cultural context. Both cultural pluralism/contextualism and cultural relativism are in opposition to ethnocentrism, which holds that one's own culture is not only preferable, but superior, to all others. Ethnocentrism, then, takes a *deficit* perspective towards all cultures other than one's own. Cultural relativism takes a *difference* perspective that precludes evaluation or comparison, while cultural pluralism/contextualism takes a *difference* perspective that can be empirically studied. Within this framework, then, family forms and practices that may seem difficult to understand or accept from outside the culture may be quite well suited both to the individuals in the family and the family in its larger context. With cultural pluralism/contextualism, understanding such differences becomes a matter for study rather than a judgement measured against some universal standard.

Even a brief examination of the cross-cultural record yields a multitude of family forms that can be organised and categorised in various ways, for example: by number of spouses (monogamy, polygyny, polyandry); by power relationships (egalitarian, patriarchal, matriarchal); or by descent (matrilineal, patrilineal). Families can also be categorised along lines of religious and cultural traditions and values (Therborn, 2009) or their modes and styles of interacting with one another (Kagitcibasi, 1997). Kinship, too often thought of as an anachronistic exercise of diagrams and terminology, affords the basic principles by which individuals understand and exercise their mutual rights and obligations to one another. Kinship can be reckoned by a combination of genetic relationships, by social relationships such as marriage and by mutual agreement, sometimes spoken of as fictive kin. Family forms are not static, and also emerge in response to changing conditions and social circumstances. Child-headed households have arisen in response to the HIV/AIDS crisis that has left orphans and children without adults who can care for them. Around the world, same-sex partners are increasingly recognised as marriage partners and forming legally recognised families.

Viewed dynamically, families may move in and out of 'troubles' and 'troubles' may be experienced by some, but not all, family members. By their nature, families are in a near-constant state of change, in response to both external and internal forces. Conditions of poverty, warfare, famine and natural disasters create troubles for families. Troubles also arise from changes within the family that occur as a consequence of normal human development. In the course of development from one life stage to the next, as one member changes, so too must the other members adjust their interaction patterns and expectations. The importance of the cultural context is in ascribing meaning to human development and structuring how these individual changes impact the family and whether they are a source of 'trouble' or not. The 'terrible twos', or oppositionality in young children, is often a source of 'troubles' for families in Western countries, with usually only a single, and maternal, caregiver. In much of the world, however, where young children are cared for by multiple caregivers, including other children, there may be no such culturally ascribed stage. Similarly, adolescence is culturally variable in its expression and experience (LeVine, 2011).

Both child well-being and child maltreatment must be seen in cultural context. Child well-being has been conceptualised and measured in a variety of ways (eg Ben-Arieh, 2008; Ben-Arieh and Frones, 2011). In a broader cross-cultural perspective, child well-being can be defined as the 'engaged participation in the daily activities of a cultural community that that community deems desirable' (Weisner, 2010, p 211). If a major cultural project of families is the successful rearing of their young, however culturally defined, child maltreatment is a quintessential 'trouble'. A fundamental challenge is not to confuse culture as child maltreatment or child maltreatment as culture. This is akin to what Ribbens McCarthy and colleagues (Chapter One) refer to as 'troubling the norm' and 'normalising troubles'.

Child abuse and neglect violate some of our most cherished views of human relationships. Parents are expected to nurture and care for their offspring, providing the foundation for families and societies. Nevertheless, child abuse and neglect have occurred throughout history and across cultures. Child maltreatment became a concerted field of inquiry and a matter of public and professional attention in the US in the early 1960s. Many nations had similar experiences of first denying the existence of child maltreatment within their boundaries, only to later 'discover' its existence. This stimulated interest in the broader cross-cultural record.

Child maltreatment is thought to arise from a complex interaction of factors, ranging from individual to cultural (Board on Children, Youth, and Families, 2012; National Research Council, 1993). Cultural pluralism/contextualism requires knowledge not only about culture broadly conceptualised, but also about variability both within and between cultures to assess which aspects of a family's behaviours are 'cultural' and which are 'abusive' or 'neglectful'. Seriously abused and neglected children look sadly similar across cultural contexts. Nevertheless, child maltreatment encompasses many grey areas and what constitutes abuse or neglect is often highly contested across cultures.

The cross-cultural literature offers multiple examples of how child maltreatment is differentially regarded (eg Korbin, 1981, 1997; Fontes, 1995; Korbin and Spilsbury, 1999; Dubowitz and Merrick, 2010). Four cautions are in order. First, childcare practices taken for granted as normative or positive in any one society may be regarded as bad for children, abusive or neglectful by others. Second, for the most part, we have limited empirical evidence on the outcomes, including the harmfulness, of most cultural practices. Third, as noted earlier, what evidence we have is limited by a sample largely restricted to Western cultures (Henrich et al, 2010). And fourth, differences in childcare practices may be highly contested both across and within cultural contexts. Identifying any one cultural group as an example of either 'good' or 'bad' childcare practices risks relying on anecdotal evidence and stereotyping, and also diminishes recognition of intracultural variability.

What, then, are some examples to illustrate these points? In the US, common paediatric advice has been that it is developmentally important for infants and young children to sleep independently. Yet, this has not stifled debate about the advantages and disadvantages of co-sleeping versus letting children cry at night, with both sides of the debate viewing the other as improperly raising their children. Cross-culturally, it is rare for infants and young children to sleep independently, which may be regarded as unkind or even dangerous to child well-being and survival.

Medical and health care practices offer examples of differences in what is defined as maltreatment. One illustrative example is 'coin rubbing' as a medical practice among the Vietnamese. This practice involves using metal coins, often heated, to push out the illness, often resulting in a striking linear pattern of bruises. When first observed in US medical facilities, these families were investigated for abuse. However, 'coin rubbing' is a culturally accepted curing practice administered with good intentions, without anger or rage, and usual medical practice has been not to report these families for abuse. The quandary is that 'coin rubbing' results in bruising, which is generally reportable as abuse. In this example, the context of the bruises makes a difference.

Questions in the international arena, and arising from globalisation, underline the importance of considering context. Child labour, for example, is a matter of some controversy. The anthropological literature has documented the positive effects of children socialised while working alongside their families in agricultural, foraging or other subsistence activities. When children's labour becomes exploitative, however, most often with children labouring away from their families in factories or industries making exports, international advocacy groups may include this as a category of child maltreatment.

Intracultural variability and the ranges of acceptable and unacceptable behaviour within any cultural context delineates how cultural practices can best be differentiated from maltreatment. Within any culture, children are not equally protected from harm. Some categories of children, such as children with diminished social supports (eg orphans) or demographic profiles (eg girls in some cultures), may receive a lesser standard of care and protection than their cultural peers. This may be confounded with the level of harm or deprivation that the larger society allows or is willing to tolerate for some or all children, and is not necessarily a straightforward issue of cultural difference, but may also reflect the structural disadvantage of some children within that society which permit circumstances that would not be considered acceptable for more advantaged children in the same society. Examples include exploitative child labour (ie labour outside of a family or apprenticeship context), high rates of child poverty, disparities in health, child sex trafficking and so on. Culture, then, should not be confused with structural conditions detrimental to children and families. However, some children, not all, from some families, not all, find themselves in these circumstances.

Internationally, these issues can become quite complex. Comparing the UK and Kenya, Lynch and Onyango (2012) point out that Western nations, like the US and the UK, have focused on carer, notably parental, abuse and neglect of children. In contrast, in developing countries, such as Kenya and other African nations, attention has focused on issues such as child labour, sex trafficking and exploitation, children in poverty, and children involved in warfare (notably, as child soldiers). In either case, families are the fulcrum between their individual children and larger social and cultural forces. Lynch and Onyango argue that neither approach has necessarily been in the best interests of children's well-being and protection from abuse and harm. In the first case, concern with parental behaviour has outweighed the societally based harms to which children are subjected, while in the second, parental maltreatment has not been well addressed.

The cultural context surrounds the daily lives of families, shaping both the settings in which troubles occur and the meanings afforded to the experiences of these troubles. Child maltreatment is one such trouble that illustrates the challenges of culturally informed work. Continued progress towards better research, practice and policy concerning family troubles will demand systematic attention to the cultural context.

References

Ben-Arieh, A. (2008) 'The child indicators movement: past, present, and future', *Child Indicators Research*, vol 1, pp 3–16.

Ben-Arieh, A. and Frones, I. (2011) 'Taxonomy for child well-being indicators: a framework for the analysis of the well-being of children', *Childhood*, vol 1, no 94, pp 460–76.

Board on Children, Youth and Families (2012) *Child maltreatment. Research, policy, and practice for the next decade. Workshop summary.* Washington, DC: National Academies Press.

Bronfenbrenner, U. (1979) *The ecology of human development: experiments by nature and design*, Cambridge, MA: Harvard University Press.

Bronfenbrenner, U. (1995) 'Developmental ecology through space and time: a future perspective', in P. Moen, G.H. Elder, K. Luscher and U. Bronfenbrenner (eds) *Examining lives in context: perspectives on the ecology of human development*, Washington, DC: American Psychological Association, pp 619–47.

Cicchetti, D. and Lynch, M. (1993) 'Towards an ecological/transactional model of community violence and child maltreatment: consequences for children's development', *Psychiatry*, vol 56, pp 96–118.

Dubowitz, H. and Merrick, J. (eds) (2010) *International aspects of child abuse and neglect*, New York, NY: Nova Science Publishers.

Fontes, L. (1995) *Sexual abuse in nine North American cultures. Treatment and prevention*, Thousand Oaks, CA: Sage.

Harkness, S. and Super, C.M. (1994) 'The developmental niche: a theoretical framework for analyzing the household production of health', *Social Science and Medicine*, vol 38, pp 218–26.

Henrich, J., Heine, S.J. and Norenzayan, A. (2010) 'The weirdest people in the world?', *Behavioral and Brain Sciences*, vol 33, pp 61–135.

Institute of Medicine and National Research Council (2011) *Toward an integrated science of research on families: workshop report*, Washington, DC: National Academies Press.

Kagitcibasi, C. (1997) *Family and human development across cultures. A view from the other side*, Mahway, NJ: Earlbaum.

Korbin, J.E. (ed) (1981) *Child abuse and neglect: cross-cultural perspectives*, Berkeley and Los Angeles, CA: University of California Press.

Korbin, J.E. (1997) 'Culture and child maltreatment', in M.E. Helfer, R. Kempe and R. Krugman (eds) *The battered child* (5th edn), Chicago, IL: University of Chicago Press, pp 29–48.

Korbin, J.E. and Spilsbury, J. (1999) 'Cultural competence and child neglect', in H. Dubowitz (ed) *Neglected children: research, practice and policy*, Newbury Park, CA: Sage Publications, pp 69–88.

LeVine, R.A. (2011) 'Traditions in transition: adolescents remaking culture', *Ethos*, vol 3, no 94, pp 426–31.

LeVine, R.A. and New, R.S. (2008) 'Introduction', in R.A. LeVine and R.S. New (eds) *Anthropology and child development. A cross-cultural reader*, Malden, MA: Blackwell Publishing, pp 1–7.

Lynch, M.A. and Onyango, P. (2012) 'Understanding child abuse and neglect across cultures: reflections from Kenya and the UK', in R.D. Krugman and J.E. Korbin (eds) *C. Henry Kempe: A 50 year legacy to the field of child abuse and neglect*, Dordrecht: Springer Scientific, pp 247–56.

National Research Council (1993) *Understanding child abuse and neglect*, Washington, D.C., National Academy Press.

McCall, R.B., Van Isendoorn, M.H., Juffer, F., Groark, C.J. and Groza, VK (2011) 'Children without parents: research, practice, and policy', *Monographs of the Society for Research in Child Development*, vol 76, no 4, pp 1–289.

Rogoff, B. (2003) *The cultural nature of human development*, Oxford: Oxford University Press.

Shonkoff, J.P. and Phillips, D.A. (eds) (2000) *Neurons to neighborhoods. The science of early childhood development*, Washington, DC: National Academy Press.

Therborn, G. (2009) 'Family', in R. Shweder (ed) *The child: an encyclopedia companion*, Chicago, IL: University of Chicago Press, pp 333–8.

Weisner, T.S. (2002) 'Ecocultural understanding of children's developmental pathways', *Human Development*, vol 4, no 54, pp 275–81.

Weisner, T.S. (2010) 'Well–being, chaos, and culture: sustaining a meaningful daily routine', in G.W. Evans and T.D. Wachs (eds) *Chaos and its influence on children's development: an ecological perspective*, Washington, DC: American Psychological Association, pp 211–23.

Weisner, T.S. and Fiese, B.H. (2012) 'Introduction to special section of the *Journal of Family Psychology*, advances in mixed methods in family psychology: integrative and applied solutions for family science', *Journal of Family Psychology*, vol 2, no 56, pp795–98.

Whiting, J.W.M. (1977) 'A model for psychocultural research', in P.H. Leiderman, S.R. Tulkin and A. Rosenfeld (eds), *Culture and infancy: Variations in the human experience*, New York: Academic Press, pp. 29–48.

Whiting, B.B. and Edwards, C.P. (1988) *Children of different worlds. The formation of social behavior*, Cambridge, MA: Harvard University Press.

Worthman, C.M. (2010) 'The ecology of human development: evolving models for cultural psychology', *Journal of Cross-Cultural Psychology*, vol 4, no 14, pp 546–62.

Yoshikawa, H., Weisner, T.S., Kalil, A. and Way, N. (2008) 'Mixing qualitative and quantitative research in developmental science: uses and methodological choices', *Developmental Psychology*, vol 4, no 42, pp 344–54.

CHAPTER THREE

Representing family troubles through the 20th century

Janet Fink

Histories of family troubles in Britain through the 20th century have been written from a number of different perspectives and have taken a range of conceptual and analytical approaches. Autobiographical and biographical accounts have thrown much light on personal experience (Sage, 2001; Harding, 2006) and the effects of welfare encounters through which families with perceived troubles were identified, regulated or supported (Steedman, 1986). Social histories of family lives have been equally revealing about the ways in which the constitution of 'normal' family relationships has shifted over time (Gillis, 1997; Davidoff et al, 1999; Davidoff, 2012). Tracing, *inter alia*, demographic, economic, political and cultural change as well as shifts in gender relations, familial ties and patterns of employment, such accounts have illustrated the significance of context not only for understanding how the norms of family lives are always contingent and in flux, but also for mapping their continuities. Other accounts have been generated in legal and policy histories concerned with the more public arenas of political intervention and professional accountability around family troubles, wherein the work of government commissions, legislative reform and public inquiries has been interrogated (Parton, 2004; Cretney, 2005). There are also rich analyses that take as their focus a particular dimension of what have been regarded as family troubles in the past, such as unmarried motherhood (Evans and Thane, 2011), bereavement (Jalland, 2010), unemployment (Burnett, 1994), disability (Atkinson et al, 2003), migration (Webster, 1998), child abuse (Ferguson, 2004) and child poverty (Platt, 2005). These variously illustrate how experiences and discourses of 'troubles' have changed and how, in turn, they have impacted upon and shaped the dynamics of family relationships and practices.

As a whole, this historiography points to the continuing centrality of marriage, motherhood and the male breadwinner in normative constructions of British families across the 20th century and how those whose personal and intimate relationships fell outside such constructions were stigmatised or problematised as a result (Clark, 1991; Oram and Turnbull, 2001; Houlbrook, 2005; Holden, 2007). At the same time, it demonstrates the variety and diversity of family experience and, in some instances, suggests that 'trouble' was a commonly experienced, though frequently silenced, aspect of family lives (Davidoff et al, 1999; Smart, 2007). Indeed, the enormous popularity of genealogical research by family historians

(Kramer, 2011), which is similarly reflected in British TV programmes such as *Who do you think you are?*, has reinforced awareness of the incidence of long-held family secrets, such as illegitimate births, desertion and bigamy, and attested, in turn, to the 'normality' of such troubles in the past.

My approach here has many similar threads to other histories in this field, not least a concern with the importance of context, shifting policy and welfare practices, and the continuity of the nuclear family norm. However, my empirical focus is on the representation of family troubles and 'the practices of meaning making' (Clarke and Fink, 2008, p 226) by which troubles were defined and understood in 20th-century popular culture, and, more especially, how family troubles were frequently portrayed through experiences of loss. With its exploration of loss as represented through issues of child abandonment, bereavement and deprivation and questions about men's personal and familial identities, the chapter unpicks the ways in which particular forms of loss came to the fore at particular moments in 20th-century British popular culture. In turn, it examines how these different forms of loss might also be interpreted as reflecting wider anxieties about the effects of socio-economic and political change upon family lives. For this reason, my analysis draws upon Raymond Williams' thesis that culture is dynamic and constituted not just from dominant ways of seeing and knowing, but also from residual elements that have their origins in the past, and emergent meanings, values, relationships and practices (Williams, 1977, pp 121–3, *passim*). My aim, therefore, is to illustrate how the representation of family troubles in popular culture can be effectively interrogated through the wider social contexts in which they are generated and embedded, and how changes and continuities in the meanings of those representations might be productively teased out.

Contexts and sources

My analysis is organised around three periods in the 20th century that are connected by concerns about children's well-being and perceived crises in masculinity and men's familial relationships. The first is the beginning of the 1920s, when the high mortality rates of young men in the First World War, a declining birth rate and concerns about the mortality rates of illegitimate children resulted in 'changes in the ideology of childhood and the social value of children' (Ferguson, 2004, p 87). These years were also marked by the return of a generation of men from the war, often shell-shocked and disabled, who expected to be restored to their homes, families and employment, and by a profound economic recession that resulted in high levels of unemployment (Fink and Holden, 2010). The second period is the beginning of the 1950s, when the effects of the Second World War upon family lives continued to haunt post-war Britain. The rise of divorce rates from 5,750 in 1937 to 48,501 in 1947, with 71% of divorce petitions being granted during 1947 on the grounds of adultery (Fink, 2000), suggested that the norm of monogamous marriage had been at particular risk. Thus, the potential impact of disrupted family lives for children's well-being was increasingly recognised in 1950s' policy and legislation, which sought to acknowledge their rights to physical and emotional security (Hendrick, 2003a). The third period of my discussion is the beginning of the 1980s, when Thatcherite policies were committed to 'cutting public spending, reducing inflation at the cost of high unemployment, privatizing nationalized industries ... and reducing the power of the unions' (Monaghan, 2001, p 3). As a result, poverty and unemployment became endemic 'troubles' in some working-class communities and families, with the identity of the working-class man and his breadwinner role often fundamentally undermined and children increasingly impoverished.

My sources for this 'drilling-down' approach have been selected because they represent a particularly popular cultural production from each period and, thereby, reflect something of the different 'structures of feeling' (Williams, 1977) around family troubles through the 20th century. These sources are: *The Kid*, a silent film released in 1921 and recognised as one of Charlie Chaplin's greatest films; *The Kidnappers*, a well-received British film from 1953 when film-going was just beginning to decline as a leisure activity but when British cinema arguably 'connected with its home audience more successfully than at any time in its history' (MacKillop and Sinyard, 2003, p 2); and *Boys from the Blackstuff*, a TV series, which has been described as 'a landmark of British television' (Auty, 1984, p 93). *Boys from the Blackstuff* attracted total viewing figures of 20 million for the first broadcast on BBC2 and 30 million when reshown on BBC1 just three months later (Monaghan, 2001).

These sources draw upon the conventions of different genres. *The Kid* includes elements that could be defined as comedy and melodrama. Notably, the opening title declares: 'a picture with a smile, and perhaps, a tear ...'. *The Kidnappers* is a family film about the lives of two young brothers and a historical romance, featuring a 'forbidden love' between the boys' aunt and a local doctor. The characters and plots of *Boys from the Blackstuff* are part of a tradition of Northern realism, but the series also engages 'in parody of a number of different genres (including the police thriller, the escape film and the science fiction series)' (Millington, 1993, p 124). Such hybridity is significant because, as Lisa Cartwright (2002, p 58) has argued, a juxtaposition of different genres opens up a transitional space for 'the acting out and working through' of social issues, which can often be left unspoken because of stigma and shame. It is by paying attention to this 'working through' of residual, dominant and emergent meanings around family troubles that changes and continuities in their portrayal over the years can be productively traced.

The Kid (1921): working through loss and abandonment

Although *The Kid* is an American production, it was enormously popular with British audiences. It spoke to British concerns about the 'choices' available to unmarried mothers in this period and drew upon Chaplin's own 'lost and miserable' childhood experiences of the Poor Law system in Victorian Britain (Chaplin, 1966, p 27). Through the 19th century, unmarried mothers without material or familial resources had few opportunities to keep their children, frequently 'losing' them to institutional care because of child welfare reformers' determination to separate poor children from their parents in order to fashion them into future citizens of the nation and Empire (Murdoch, 2006). However, one of the significant changes brought about by the First World War was the improvement of statutory provision for all mothers and children, which arose out of a concern to 'save the babies'. Moves were also made in the voluntary sector to improve the health and welfare of unmarried mothers through the founding of the National Council for the Unmarried Mother and Her Child in 1918. Nevertheless, perceptions of unmarried motherhood continued to be contested in this period, with, for example, national conferences of the Church of England in 1920 and 1924 condemning the punitive treatment of unmarried mothers and their children and, at the same time, suggesting that 19th-century ideas of repression were one solution (Middleton, 1971) to such family troubles.

This, then, was the social, moral and welfare context through which *The Kid*, an archetypal abandoned–child–found–in–the–wilderness story (Weissman, 1987), was viewed in Britain. As a baby, the kid is first abandoned by his unmarried mother and then found by the character of a tramp, played by Chaplin. The tramp is not immediately affected by the baby's plight; indeed, much of the comedy in their first encounter lies in the tramp's consideration of whether and how he can 'lose' the baby again. Yet, there is also a serious undercurrent to the film and its portrayal of impoverished characters who, as Sinyard (1992) has pointed out, inhabit the barren landscapes of the industrialised city and whose only protection against a hostile society is a fragile sense of family. Thus, over the years together, the tramp and the kid patch together (practically and symbolically) a close and loving family for themselves, albeit one outside the boundaries of blood relations and one in which conventional familial roles are frequently reversed.

The discovery that the tramp is not the child's father threatens this family unit, with officials from the child orphan asylum and the police taking the boy away to the distress of both characters. It is their separation and reunion, following the tramp's dogged determination to resist the state's claim upon the child, which form the emotional climax of the film. This claim also throws into question what is meant by 'saving the child' when so little compassion or understanding is shown towards those perceived as living outside the family norm. This small episode presents a damning portrayal of the punitive and officious nature of interactions between child welfare officials and poor families and it reflects the long history of fear and resentment that individuals and their families, experiencing such troubles as unemployment, homelessness, poverty and the birth of an illegitimate child, felt towards the Poor Law (Doolittle, forthcoming, 2013). As such, the scene draws much of its emotive strength from residual elements of 19th-century memories and understandings of working-class powerlessness that continued to shadow experiences of welfare provision in the early decades of the 20th century.

Yet, changes in the meanings of the 'normal' family emerge in the concluding scenes of the film. Although still unmarried, the child's mother is able to reclaim her 'lost' son because she has redeemed herself through charitable works and because she is also financially independent. The powerful ideal of the mother–child dyad is thus extended in the film to include the unmarried mother and her illegitimate child, albeit that, at the same time, this results in the tramp's loss of 'his' kid. Nevertheless, the boundaries of this newly constituted family are shown to be inclusive and the tramp is welcomed into the domestic space of the mother's affluent home. Ultimately, then, this resolution affirms the rights of unmarried mothers to raise their children and suggests how the meanings of family troubles, associated with the figure of the child 'lost' to mothers and society because of illegitimacy, might begin to shift and be reworked in the second half of the 20th century.

The Kidnappers (1953): working through loss and bereavement

Experiences of loss and the changing meanings of family relations are similar features in the next film of my discussion, *The Kidnappers*, and the context in which it was produced and released. The early 1950s was a period of tremendous social, cultural and economic change that, with full employment, rising living standards and increased levels of welfare provision, brought significant financial and material improvements to the lives of many families. At the same time, ensuring the well-being of children became a key element in the post-war Labour government's development of social and welfare reforms, particularly through the Children Act (1948), which sought to improve the services provided to children and their families. Through such policy shifts, the home and family life were constituted as sites wherein children were provided with the nurture, stability and protection needed for their successful development (Riley, 1983; Hendrick, 2003b), while also being inflected with anxieties about potential family troubles, which might damage not only a child's emotional and psychological health, but also, by extension, Britain's future.

The relationship between wartime experiences and family troubles is an implicit theme throughout *The Kidnappers*. The film is set in Nova Scotia, Canada at the beginning of the 20th century and features two brothers, Harry and Davy, who are shown moving to their grandparents' home following the death of their mother. She had had sole care of them after their father was killed in the Boer War. The brothers are portrayed adjusting to the bleakness of their education in the local school and the emotional and material austerity of family life, in which their grandmother and aunt are kindly presences but frequently overruled by their authoritarian grandfather. It is the bond between the brothers that is shown to sustain them emotionally and psychologically from their family troubles, especially the younger boy. This bond does not, however, preclude their intense longing for a dog; a pet that will allow them to love and be loved unconditionally but that their grandfather refuses to countenance. So, when Harry 'finds' a baby while out playing, she becomes the secret object of their unstinting care and affection as they feed, change and tend to her needs in their hideaway in the woods. Following the search for and discovery of this 'lost' child, Harry is charged with her kidnapping but ultimately released by the local magistrate after the intervention of the baby's father, a Dutch settler. The grandfather's apology to the settler and thanks for speaking up for Harry is a pivotal moment in the film because the settler, and the Dutch community more generally, had been a constant focus of the grandfather's anger following the death of his son in the war.

In such ways, the figure of the grandfather is used to critique residual ideas about masculinity and the ways in which men's emotional detachment might generate trouble not only for other family members, but also for themselves. The grandfather's inability to grieve the loss of his son, seeking refuge instead in blame and revenge, is portrayed as corroding not only his relationships with the wider community, but also those within his own family. However, his recognition of the effects of these ways of being upon his young grandchildren is demonstrated in the concluding scene of the film in which the boys are allowed to have their much-desired dog. In order to buy the dog, the grandfather sells his boots, a gift from his deceased son, and, as a result, returns to the farm with bare, dirty feet. This act of symbolic humbling represents his recognition that the emotional needs of his bereaved grandchildren have to be acknowledged and addressed. It also illustrates how emergent ideas about masculinity and childcare are deployed in the film to constitute a challenge to the uses and abuses of patriarchal authority in the home and its potential damage to children whose interests are not placed over those of their parents and carers (Geraghty, 2000). Ultimately, the film suggests, a child's successful emotional development will ensure that family troubles such as delinquency, reflected by Harry's appearance in court, can be avoided, while new ideas about the meanings and practices of loving care between men and children will have equally positive benefits for men's emotional well-being and 'normal' family life more generally.

Boys from the Blackstuff (1982): working through loss and deprivation

Moving forward 30 years to the early 1980s takes my discussion into another period of intense social, political and economic change, which is played out through different emphases on experiences of loss. The Conservative government, elected in 1979, was transforming the post-war political consensus through 'a rhetoric of "rolling back the state", "cutting the costs of welfare" and reinstituting personal enterprise and self-reliance' (Lewis, 1998, p 58). Working people were encouraged to participate in the new enterprise culture but, at the same time, unemployment soared in those working-class communities where job opportunities were limited to rapidly declining industrial and manufacturing sectors (Monaghan, 2001). In some parts of the country, a generation of children was being 'lost' to poverty while the 'loss' of the male breadwinner role was a significant feature of domestic relations, putting pressure on women to find (often additional) paid employment outside the home and exacerbating other family troubles such as the breakdown of couple relationships, financial insecurity and poor physical and psychological health.

The TV series *Boys from the Blackstuff* is set in one such area, Liverpool, and is recognised as an 'exceptional intervention' (Millington, 1993, p 119) in these wide-reaching political and economic shifts. The series is made up of five episodes, but my focus is upon the character of Yosser, whose story of unemployment, fatherhood and breakdown forms one episode and whose desperate catchphrase, 'Gizza [give me a] job. I can do that', not only made him a folk hero, but was also appropriated and reworked in popular culture through the 1980s (Millington, 1993). Yosser has been the focus of other analyses (Millington, 1993; Paterson, 1997; Kirk, 1999; Monaghan, 2001) in which the losses of male identity and working-class masculinity as a result of the New Right's political agenda have been carefully explored. However, there are other issues raised by Yosser's story about the losses being experienced by his children and these throw light equally on the portrayal of family troubles in this period.

Yosser has three children, two boys and a girl, who form a largely silent but always visible screen presence. Like bodyguards, they consistently huddle around their father, seeking to protect him and themselves from the 'hostile society' that was such a feature of *The Kid*. In this context, however, home and family life are portrayed as offering them little safety. Their troubles encompass a mother who has abandoned them and a father who is portrayed as unable to cope with even the most basic of domestic tasks because of his rapidly deteriorating psychological health. The children are dirty and dishevelled with few playthings and little to eat other than what can be bought at the local takeaway. Their protective role means that they go everywhere with Yosser, including the working-men's club, a consultation with his doctor and the benefits office. When the children are depicted in a place more commonly associated with childhood – the local park – they sit listlessly with their father watching 'normal' families playing together on the swings and slides.

The consequences of unemployment are portrayed as fundamental to Yosser's children's experiences of troubled family life. Equally, interventions by the state are shown to be inadequate, lacking in care and unnecessarily punitive. As such, they illustrate both residual views about encounters between welfare professionals and poor families, exemplified so powerfully in *The Kid*, while also signifying emergent understandings of the far-reaching effects of the Conservative government's determination to restructure the economy and reform welfare services. Thus, as Millington (1993, p 119) has argued, the series' haunting tragic-comic images of unemployment and life on the dole 'engaged the collective anxiety of the nation and fuelled the debate in the real world'. The climax of Yosser's story reinforces this anxiety still further by portraying his violent and prolonged beating by the police and the removal of his children by social workers. Unlike earlier periods, then, the representation of family troubles in the 1980s offered no opportunities for their resolution but rather a bleak despondency about the future. Like Chaplin's character of the tramp, Yosser is a 'lost' man, but there are no possibilities that he might be 'healed' by his children or restored by family life. His troubles, like those of his children, are long-term and permanent and, as this TV series suggests, can only be accepted because of the powerful New Right ideological interventions that generated them.

Conclusion

Although these examples from popular culture span the 20th century, they illustrate many commonalities. The child 'lost' to its family and wider society, as a result of illegitimacy, abduction and deprivation, and the child's loss of a parent, because of abandonment, bereavement and psychological ill-health, point to a long-standing concern with the suffering child in the depiction of family troubles. Similarly, questions of loss feature with regard to men's identity, breadwinner role and self-esteem and suggest, in turn, their significance for understanding the meanings of family troubles through the lens of masculinity. Yet, as the chapter has demonstrated, these examples can also be viewed as reflecting broader questions about the consequences of social change for family lives and family relationships. Sometimes, the portrayal of these consequences suggests positive outcomes for families troubled, for example, by the birth of an illegitimate child or the wielding of patriarchal authority over vulnerable family members. However, family troubles that have their origins in structural problems, such as child poverty and unemployment, are represented as ultimately intractable. Other temporal contexts and other sources would, undoubtedly, point to different concerns about family troubles and the ways in which these have changed or retained their significance through the 20th century. What is not in doubt is the extent of such troubles in the past and the ever-shifting ways in which they were understood, experienced and given meaning.

References

Atkinson, D., Jackson, M. and Walmsley, J (2003) *Forgotten lives: exploring the history of learning disability*, BILD: British Institute of Learning Disabilities.

Auty, M. (1984) 'Boys from the blackstuff', *Monthly Film Bulletin*, vol 51, nos 600/611, pp 92–4.

Boys from the Blackstuff (1982) BFI; script by Alan Bleasdale; directed by Philip Saville (available on DVD).

Burnett, J. (1994) *Idle hands: experience of unemployment, 1790–1990*, London: Routledge.

Cartwright, L. (2008) *Moral spectatorship. Technologies of voice and Affect in postwar representations of the child*, Durham, NC, and London: Duke University Press.

Chaplin, C. (1966) *My autobiography*, London: Penguin.

Clark, D. (ed) (1991) *Marriage, domestic life and social change*, London: Routledge.

Clarke, J. and Fink, J. (2008) 'Unsettled attachments: national identity, citizenship and migration', in W. Oorschot, M. Opielka and B. Pfau-Effinger (eds) *Culture and welfare state: values and social policy in comparative perspective*, Cheltenham: Edward Elgar.

Cretney, S. (2005) *Family law in the twentieth century: a history*, Oxford: Oxford University Press.

Davidoff, L. (2012) *Thicker than water: siblings and their relations, 1780–1920*, Oxford: Oxford University Press.

Davidoff, L., Doolittle, M., Fink, J. and Holden, K. (1999) *The family story: blood, contract and intimacy, 1830–1960*, London: Longman.

Doolittle, M. (forthcoming, 2013) 'Providing and the poor: fathers, families and the workhouse in England 1880–1914', in B. Althammer, A. Gestrich and J. Gründler (eds) *At the margins of the welfare state: changing patterns of including and excluding the 'deviant' poor in Europe 1870–1933*, Basingstoke: Palgrave Macmillan.

Evans, T. and Thane, P. (2011) 'Special Issue: Lone Mothers', *Women's History Review*, vol 20, no 1, pp 1–160.

Ferguson, H. (2004) *Protecting children in time: child abuse, child protection and the consequences of modernity*, Basingstoke: Palgrave Macmillan.

Fink, J. (2000) 'Natural mothers, putative fathers and innocent children: the definition and regulation of parental relationships outside marriage in England, 1945–1959', *Journal of Family History*, vol 25, no 2, pp 178–95.

Fink, J. and Holden, K. (2010) 'Paradoxes of gender and marital status in mid-20th century British welfare', in J. Fink and A. Lundqvist (eds) *Changing relations of welfare: family, gender and migration in Britain and Scandinavia*, Aldershot: Ashgate, pp 87–109.

Geraghty, C. (2000) *British cinema in the fifties: gender, genre and the 'New Look'*, London: Routledge.

Gillis, J. (1997) *A world of their own making: myth, ritual and the quest for family values*, Harvard: Harvard University Press.

Harding, J. (2006) *Mother country: a memoir*, London: Faber & Faber.

Hendrick, H. (2003a) 'Children's emotional well-being and mental health in post-war Britain', in M. Gijswijt-Hofstra and H. Marland (eds) *Cultures of child health in Britain and the Netherlands in the twentieth century*, Amsterdam: Rodopi.

Hendrick, H. (2003b) *Child welfare: historical dimensions, contemporary debate*, Bristol: The Policy Press.

Holden, K. (2007) *The shadow of marriage: singleness in England 1914–1960*, Manchester: Manchester University Press.

Houlbrook, M. (2005) *Queer London: space, identities and male practices, 1918–1957*, Chicago, IL: Chicago University Press.

Jalland, P. (2010) *Death in war and peace: a history of loss and grief in England, 1914–1970*, Oxford: Oxford University Press.

Kirk, J. (1999) 'Class, community and "structures of feeling" in working-class writing from the 1980s', *Literature and History*, vol 8, no 2, pp 44–63.

Kramer, A.-M. (2011) 'Kinship, affinity and connectedness: exploring the role of genealogy in personal lives', *Sociology*, vol 45, no 3, pp 379–95.

Lewis, G. (1998) '"Coming apart at the seams": the crises of the welfare state', in G. Hughes and G. Lewis (eds) *Unsettling welfare: the reconstruction of social policy*, London: Routledge.

MacKillop, I. and Sinyard, N. (2003) 'Celebrating British cinema of the 1950s', in I. Mackillop and N. Sinyard (eds) *British cinema of the 1950s: a celebration*, Manchester: Manchester University Press, pp 1–10.

Middleton, N. (1971) *When family failed: the treatment of the child in the care of the community in the first half of the century*, London: Gollancz.

Millington, B. (1993) '*Boys from the Black Stuff* (Alan Bleasdale)', in G.W. Brandt (ed) *British television drama in the 1980s*, Cambridge: Cambridge University Press.

Monaghan, D. (2001) 'Margaret Thatcher and the struggle for working-class identity', *Journal of Popular Film and Television*, vol 29, no 1, pp 2–13.

Murdoch, L. (2006) *Imagined orphans: poor families, child welfare and contested citizenship in London*, New Jersey, NJ: Rutgers University Press.

Oram, A. and Turnbull, A. (2001) *The lesbian history sourcebook: love and sex between women from 1780 to 1970*, London: Routledge.

Parton, N. (2004) 'From Maria Colwell to Victoria Climbié: reflections on public inquiries into child abuse a generation apart', *Child Abuse Review*, vol 13, no 2, pp 80–94.

Paterson, R. (1997) 'Restyling masculinity: the impact of *Boys from the Blackstuff*', in J. Curran, A. Smith and P. Wingate (eds) *Impacts and influences: essays on media power in the twentieth century*, London: Methuen.

Platt, L. (2005) *Discovering child poverty: the creation of a policy agenda from 1800 to the present*, Bristol: The Policy Press.

Riley, D. (1983) *War in the nursery*, London: Virago Press.

Sage, L. (2000) *Bad blood*, London: Fourth Estate.

Sinyard, N. (1992) *Children in the movies*, London: Batsford.

Smart, C. (2007) *Personal life: new directions in sociological thinking*, Cambridge: Polity Press.

Steedman, C. (1986) *Landscape for a good woman*, London: Virago.

The Kid (1921) Warner Brothers; written and directed by Charles Chaplin (available on DVD).

The Kidnappers (1953) Group Film Productions; screenplay by Neil Paterson; directed by Philip Leacock (not available on DVD).

Webster, W. (1998) *Imagining home: gender, 'race' and national identity, 1945–64*, London: Routledge.

Weissmann, S.M. (1987) 'Chaplin's, *The Kid*', in J.H. Smith and W. Kerrigan (eds) *Images in our souls: Cavell, psychoanalysis and cinema*, Baltimore/London: Johns Hopkins University Press.

Williams, R. (1977) *Marxism and literature*, Oxford: Oxford University Press.

CHAPTER FOUR

The role of science in understanding family troubles

Michael Rutter

The need to give science a central role in understanding family troubles arises from three different, but somewhat related, considerations. First, both the media and political statements, as well as all too many supposedly scientific papers, make all manner of claims about the family that are based on anecdotal reports by unrepresentative samples of volunteers, together with the use of weak, and often biased, measures. It is, therefore, crucial to check these claims through the appropriate application of high-quality science (British Academy Working Group Report, 2010). Second, even when evidence of associations is based on proper sampling and appropriate measurement, there is all too often a sliding from the demonstration of an association to an assumption that it must reflect a causal effect. There is an abundance of evidence that that is not justified but, equally, that there are good scientific approaches that can do much to test the causal inference (Academy of Medical Sciences, 2007; Rutter, 2007; Jaffee et al, 2012). Third, when moving from evidence, of whatever kind, to policy implications, there is a tendency for people to assume that because they are in some way part of a family, they are thereby an expert on families. Accordingly, it is essential to examine carefully the paths leading from evidence, through causal inference to policy implications (British Academy Working Group Report, 2010).

What constitutes good science?

Before turning to the different questions on which science may have something to offer, it is necessary to begin by considering what constitutes good science. How do we differentiate between good and poor science? In 1973, Merton (1973) proposed that there were three main features that characterised good-quality science. First, the research must involve a search for principles that can be generalised beyond the sample studied. Second, the approach should involve organisation – meaning conceptualising the meaning or the mechanism underlying any set of findings or observations. Third, there must be an attitude of scepticism; that is, there must be a norm of questioning, challenging and always looking for alternative counter-explanations to the proposition being put forward.

Nearly three decades later, the US National Research Council (2002), when considering scientific research in education, put forward six criteria. Although these differed from those suggested by Merton in the way they were framed, the overall message was basically the same. Thus, they argued that: research should pose significant questions that could be investigated empirically; there should be a linking of research to relevant theory; methods should be used that permitted direct investigation of the question and employed a range of complementary research strategies; the research ought to provide a coherent and explicit chain of reasoning and particularly consider and test plausible counter-explanations; there was also a need to replicate and generalise across studies; and it was essential to disclose research details to encourage professional scrutiny and critique. It is against that backcloth of criteria for high-quality science that we can turn to the questions needing scientific input.

Questions needing scientific input

Rates

The first question has to be the rate of the family 'trouble' being considered. As recently as the time when I started my scientific career, physical child abuse was viewed as rare and not something that needed to be routinely considered in clinical referrals. Good epidemiological studies have made clear that the rate of physical abuse is probably in the order of 5–10% but there is a large overlap between physical abuse and emotional neglect (with a paucity of good evidence on the frequency of neglect). Accordingly, all responsible clinicians would now see it as mandatory to consider the possibility of abuse with any clinical referral (Glaser, 2008). The rate of sexual abuse was viewed as equally rare but it is now evident that its frequency is at least as high as that of physical abuse. Moreover, most of it occurs within the family or by other people known to the child and not by strangers. In addition, although girls are at greater risk, it is evident that boys are sexually abused as well.

The characteristic of the science is that the research must use: systematic sampling with adequate numbers in the samples being investigated; sound methods of measurement; and confidence intervals to show the degree of heterogeneity within the sample.

Patterns

A related issue, but a somewhat different one, concerns the pattern of the 'trouble' and whether it shows continuity with normal variations. The issue is well illustrated by considering an important study by Jaffee et al (2004), which compared the genetic and environmental mediation of the effects of corporal punishment and physical abuse, using a twin design. The findings were striking in showing that the pattern was quite different for corporal punishment and physical abuse, with genetic factors playing a negligible role in physical abuse but a substantial role in corporal punishment. The implication was that corporal punishment was often a response by the parent to genetically influenced behaviours of the child. This was not the pattern with abuse. On the other hand, the findings also showed that frequent use of corporal punishment was associated with a predisposition to a slide into the use of abuse. Other research has shown that abuse usually occurs in the context of more widespread domestic violence and conflict (British Academy Working Group Report, 2010). It is apparent that a particular characteristic of science here lay in the use of research designs that could compare and contrast alternatives and could ask penetrating questions about likely mechanisms.

Origins

The third question needing scientific input concerns the experiential, as well as the genetic, 'origins' of the trouble. That is, we need to determine the origins of a risk factor as well as the effects of that risk factor on children's development. For example, there is evidence that children's behaviour influences parental negativity. O'Connor et al (1998) showed this using a longitudinal adoption design. The negativity shown by the adoptive parents (who, of course, had no genetic connection with the child) was increased when the child came from a genetically high-risk group. Further analyses showed that the effect was mediated by the child's disruptive behaviour. There is also evidence of modest intergenerational continuity in physical abuse (Dixon et al, 2005a, 2005b).

In relation to this question, the characteristic of the science was the use of quantitative adoptee data to test the effect of biological mother characteristics on adoptive mother parenting. It also involved testing whether the evocative effect was specific to a genetic risk group, with the finding that the evocative effect was almost as strong in those not at genetic risk.

Environmental mediation

The fourth question asks whether the experience of family adversity has a truly environmentally mediated causal effect on later mental disorder in the offspring. This question has been tackled in several different ways, but they may be illustrated by focusing on discordant twin analyses. For example, Kendler and Prescott (2006) examined the possible causal effects of the experience of sexual abuse on the liability to mental disorder in adult life. The focus was on twins, one of whom had experienced sexual abuse whereas the other had not. The findings showed that the odds ratio in the twin comparison for the risk of mental disorder was just about as great as in the general population. The implication is that the introduction of a genetic control confirmed the likely causal effect of the sexual abuse – moreover, a causal effect that extended into adult life.

The number of twins in that particular study did not allow direct comparison of effects of discordant monozygotic, as compared with discordant dizygotic, twins. However, a study undertaken by Caspi et al (2004) did have that comparison. They focused only on discordant monozygotic pairs for the risk experience of maternal negative expressed emotion as determined at age five in relation to the outcome of disruptive behaviour as reported by teachers two years later. In other words, the mother was negative to one twin and not to the other. It is clear that the design involved a high degree of methodological rigour in using different measures and different informants for the risk factor, as compared to the outcome variable. It also involved looking at effects across a time span of two years – a time period that involved a change of context from home to school. The findings showed a significant effect of maternal negative expressed emotion, with the strong implication that this was indeed an environmentally mediated effect. The overall characteristic of this sort of science is that it has used a variety of 'natural experiments' (involving longitudinal data) that served to pull apart variables that ordinarily went together. In this way, they have been able: to differentiate between genetic and environmental mediation; to test for the direction of effects; and to rule in or out social selection (Rutter, 2007, 2012).

Child-rearing experiences

The fifth question needing scientific input concerns whether adverse child-rearing experiences affect all children to a similar degree. The relevant evidence comes from two rather different sorts of studies. First, there is evidence from a general population longitudinal study that the effects of non-maternal care (which includes care in someone else's home, care at home by a relative or non-relative, and care in a day care centre) differ according to whether the family have high-risk characteristics (Geoffroy et al, 2007; Côté et al, 2008). The Canadian study showed that there were strong selection effects involved in whether or not children had maternal care or some form of non-maternal care and that maternal care had a protective effect in those from a high-risk background but no such effect in those from a low-risk background

The second sort of evidence is derived from the gene–environment interaction studies undertaken by Caspi et al (2002, 2003). Substantial, and statistically significant, gene–environment interactions (GxE) were found for both the onset of a major depressive disorder and the liability to antisocial behaviour. However, what is crucially important in these findings is that the genetic liability with respect to these two rather different outcomes was not the same. The particular form of GxE found for antisocial behaviour was not the same as that for depression. In both cases, maltreatment constituted the environmental risk factor but the interplay with genes differed, although both involved GxE.

Quantitative and qualitative research

Many words have been written about the supposed differences between these two styles of research, but without much understanding of the issues. Unfortunately, all too often the style of debate involves ideological evangelism rather than reason and logic. Part of the problem lies in the insistence by qualitative researchers that epistemology provides the guidance (see Becker, 1996). This is a branch of philosophy (not science) that deals with the varieties of grounds of knowledge in order to draw conclusions on their supposed validity. The problem is that some researchers act as if this means an ideologically influenced 'quasi-philosophy'. As a scientist, my firm preference is for using epistemics – that is, the science of knowledge and understanding – using empirical investigations to settle the issues.

Howard Becker (1996), while claiming that he believes that the two styles of research actually share the same epistemology, emphasises the supposed differences between the two. Most turn out to be largely fiction. Thus, he contrasts the qualitative focus on observing behaviour in situ with the quantitative focus on using questionnaires as proxies for observation. That is especially wrong in the field of family studies in which a high proportion of quantitative research is based on observations – as exemplified by parenting (Patterson, 1981), attachment (Cassidy and Shaver, 2008), marriage (Gottman, 1995) and family interactions (Brown and Harris, 1978). Moreover, the use of questionnaires is recognised by quantitative researchers as having many weaknesses (see later). What is different is that quantitative researchers make more use of experimental, as well as naturalistic, research strategies.

Becker also claims a second difference with respect to qualitative researchers; concern with the accuracy, precision and breadth of their observations and interviews, as distinct from the quantitative researchers' preoccupation with procedural issues of reliability and validity. While I agree that neither of these can 'trump' the other (and all too often both sides think that their focus does trump that of the other), it is clear that *both* sets of criteria need attention by both types of researchers (see Lieberson, 1992).

A further difference put forward by Becker is that whereas qualitative research provides many opportunities for unexpected findings, surveys involving fully structured interviews or questionnaires determine in advance all the information that can be acquired. That is correct, but it entirely ignores the wide range of methods used by quantitative researchers, many of which place a premium on the importance of the unexpected and non-predicted. Rather than continue with further fruitless epistemology, let me take an epistemic approach to what researchers actually do and what they achieve.

Generalisations

All studies, whether qualitative or quantitative, regardless of whether the sample size is 20, 200 or 2,000, necessarily raise queries over the extent to which the findings can be generalised to other populations. There are qualitative researchers who claim that that is not a question that concerns them because they are interested only in the accuracy of the findings as they apply to the sample studied. That may be research, but it is not science. Presumably, the justification is that any case example illustrates some general principle. However, that can never be assumed because there are numerous examples in which findings have a different meaning in different groups. That is, context may be critical, whereby variables and their effects can acquire their meaning because of their social effect. For example, Christensen's (1960) comparison of three communities suggested that the consequences of a premarital pregnancy differed markedly according to the prevailing sexual mores. Where there were strong taboos against premarital sex, premarital conception appeared more likely to lead to early marriage and to marital breakdown later. Goody (1970) described how in certain groups in Africa, having one's children fostered lent prestige to the family, whereas in the UK, it had the reverse effect. The style of research was quite different in the two cases – Christensen was a quantitative sociologist whereas Goody was a qualitative social anthropologist – but both were similar in using cross-cultural comparisons to derive meaning from findings. Social context matters (Rutter, 1999) and it is a mistake to assume that it does not. Moreover, it is quite wrong to argue that qualitative researchers do not accept the need to test for generalisation. Becker (1996) gave several telling examples of well-known, highly respected qualitative studies that deliberately brought together a range of methods in order to do just that. For example, Mercer (1973) used unstructured interviews combined with community surveys and official records to draw her conclusions about the social character of mental retardation – a mixture of qualitative and quantitative methods that provided different sorts of evidence for the same overall purpose.

Spotting the unexpected

There is general agreement among both qualitative and quantitative researchers that if new knowledge is to be obtained, it is highly desirable to use methods that facilitate spotting the unexpected in findings. Cox and his colleagues (Cox et al, 1981) were one of the very few groups to investigate (using both naturalistic and experimental strategies) which clinical interviewing techniques were most effective in eliciting both factual information, including self-disclosures, and also emotions and feelings. Systematic probing for detailed descriptions of actual occurrences aided the eliciting of factual information but an 'open' interviewing style was preferable to a 'closed' one relying on yes/no answers to closed or leading questions. Experienced interviewers proved to be considerably better than trainees, both because they chose probes in a more effective fashion and because they were more responsive to cues in what was said. All four experimental styles picked up a large number of clinically significant but individually idiosyncratic factual information. Perhaps surprisingly, the four interviewing styles did not differ in this respect.

A rather different type of example is provided by Robins' (1993) follow-up study of Vietnam soldiers with respect to their use of heroin both in Vietnam and on return to the US. Completely contrary to nearly everyone's expectations, a majority of the heroin users in Vietnam spontaneously gave up taking heroin after leaving Vietnam. It might be supposed that the stress of combat was the key factor but this proved not to be the case. Robins went on in a creative, imaginative fashion to explore the implications of her findings. As with other research, it turns out that the key requirement is not the particular method used but the skill in spotting the unexpected and knowing how to investigate it (Lieberson, 1992).

The UK study of English and Romanian Adoptees (ERAs) produced a host of unexpected findings (Rutter and Sonuga-Barke, 2010), but here I focus on just a few that illustrate the value of both qualitative and quantitative approaches. First, there were significant sequelae of institutional deprivation that persisted after the children reached six months of age, but the rate of persisting deficits went up to nearly half the sample when the deprivation extended up to one year of age. Only quantitative research could have shown this. The follow-up to the age of 15 years involved both the use of standardised interviews and questionnaires and open 'qualitative-style' interviews. The initial findings based on structured measures suggested that the early problems often diminished with time, but the 'open' interviews indicated that this impression derived from the fact that some problems ceased to meet the usual diagnostic criteria. The more 'open' interviews showed, nevertheless, that the problems persisted, albeit in somewhat different ways. Quantitative analyses confirmed the reality of the persistence and its strong association with institutional deprivation. The last example is provided by the evidence that the persistence of problems was often associated with changes for the better and with notable successes. If the outcome had been assessed only through the use of some quantitative composite summary, that would have been missed. The research did not have explicitly quantitative and qualitative parts; rather, it was guided by the need to use both approaches in an integrated fashion.

It needs to be added, however, that unexpected findings, whether based on quantitative or qualitative research, are notoriously likely to be accompanied by unwarranted claims or misinterpretations of their meaning (see medical examples in Goldacre, 2010). Good science, of all varieties, requires the careful consideration of alternative explanations, the use of multiple research methods and replication by independent scientists.

Meaning of measures

All comparative research, whether qualitative or quantitative, requires careful attention to the comparability of measures across the groups being studied. This has been especially an issue in cross-cultural research (see Rutter and Tienda, 2005; Nikapota and Rutter, 2008). Both quantitative and qualitative methodologies have been used to identify differences and their meaning. Thus, using qualitative approaches, Kleinman (1977) noted that in some societies, emotional disturbances were particularly likely to be reported in terms of somatic symptoms rather than altered mood. Deater-Deckard et al (2005), using quantitative methods, showed that whereas corporal punishment tended to be associated with *more* disruptive behaviour in white Americans, it tended to have the reverse effect in African-Americans. Weisz et al (1997) used a mixture of methods to compare psychopathology in Thailand and the US, finding that differences in perception and expectation had quite marked effects on rates of *reported* disorder but little effect on overall prevalence. In the cognitive arena, a range of studies have shown marked differences in problem-solving according to whether the problem is expressed in abstract terms or, rather, in practical terms, such as those familiar to unschooled street vendors (see, eg, Schliemann and Carraher, 1994).

Creative quantitative researchers have long been alert to the need to respond to differences in the meaning of measures. For example, Ainsworth et al's (1978) development of the 'Strange situation' procedure as a means of assessment of attachment security/insecurity was found to work well in most circumstances, but it sometimes led to apparently anomalous findings in young children experiencing a grossly abnormal upbringing. This led to the development of new attachment categories, such as 'disorganised attachment' (Main and Solomon, 1986, 1990). Brown and Harris (1978) were alert to the fact that life events differed in their meaning according to their personal social context, and devised new measures to reflect that effect.

The meaning of measures has to be a key issue for both quantitative and qualitative researchers. Of course, that does not mean that appropriate steps have always been taken to respond to that need. Meta-analyses pooling rather disparate questionnaire and interview measures well illustrate the problems (Uher and McGuffin, 2010; also, in relation to studies of adoption, see Rutter et al, 2009a, 2009b; in relation to studies of gene–environment interaction, see Karg et al, 2011).

The point of view of the individual

As Howard Becker (1996) pointed out, most qualitative researchers undertaking ethnographic research place their major emphasis on the essential need to grasp the point of view of the individual (something that is lacking in the use of questionnaires and structured interviews). That is a valid point, but, as Becker points out, all of us always attribute meaning to both our own experiences and those we observe. This is part of the universal human tendency to process experiences. With respect to family studies (the focus of this volume), it is crucial to appreciate that there never is, or could be, just one individual. Moreover, different family members frequently differ in their interpretations. This has been brought out most clearly in quantitative studies. Thus, in a meta-analysis of 119 published studies (Achenbach et al, 1987), the average correlations on child behaviour between pairs of adult informants was only .28. This is likely to have been a consequence of both situation specificity and differences in perception. However, there has been regrettably little research into the meaning of these differences among informants. An exception is provided by early research undertaken by Wesley Becker (1960, 1962), who found that mothers who reported themselves as anxious were reported by their husbands as having become hostile. In a very real sense, both were correct because people who become anxious or depressed often also become negative in their interactions with others. However, any attempt to assess 'meaning' by interviewing just one of the family members will necessarily provide a misleading impression of the whole.

The key feature is that all of us perceive what we expect to find, and there are numerous examples of distinguished researchers being led astray by that. It is not just what we observe or report but the inferences we make about their meaning. However, it is also that humans both evoke and respond to others in their interactions. Thus, numerous studies of parent–toddler attachment security have shown that father–child and mother–child attachment show only modest agreement (Cassidy and Shaver, 2008). Because the interactions are observed and scored in the same way, this is unlikely to reflect perceptual differences. Rather, it reflects two-way social interactions.

Heterogeneity

The final issue to note concerns heterogeneity. Zigler and Styfco (2006) noted that most quantitative studies comparing groups reported their findings in terms of the between-group differences in the mean score of some variable of interest, ignoring their own finding that the within-group differences usually exceeded the between-group differences. They criticised what they termed the 'tyranny of the mean'. This heterogeneity has been shown to be an almost universal feature irrespective of whether the measures concern biological features, psychological functioning or social interactions. Any account that implies homogeneity is almost certainly wrong. Although highlighted by quantitative research, the problem is particularly acute in qualitative research, if only because of the typically small sample sizes. Either homogeneity is implied or meaningful heterogeneity is claimed on the basis of numbers far too small to delineate valid within-group differences.

The problem and possible solutions may be illustrated by several examples of social experiences and social institutions. Goffman's (1961) study of asylums, which he classified as 'total institutions', is rightly regarded as a classic because he successfully highlighted their characteristics and what this meant for the life of staff and patients. However, the implication that all institutions are the same turned out to be wrong (Tizard et al, 1975; Richardson, 1984). Wing and Brown (1970) showed this in their comparative study of mental hospitals, with findings indicating the association between institutional characteristics and patient outcomes. More recently, Rutter et al's (1979) study of secondary schools in London showed the same with respect to school effects on pupil outcomes. Their use of a longitudinal strategy to examine outcomes after taking into account intake differences was explicitly quantitative in concept. However, it made extensive use of observations and it was not framed by any theory (it could not be, because the data that could form the basis for such a theory did not exist at the time). It is most appropriately viewed as a quantitative study making use of qualitative approaches. The St Petersburg Group–USA Orphanage Research Team (2008) comparative study of Russian residential institutions for children had similar features, except that, in addition, it made use of interventions designed to test for causal effects.

Studies of resilience (meaning relative resistance to stress/adversity) go further in their explicit focus on the meaning of within-group heterogeneity (Rutter, 2003). The best of such studies have started with rigorous quantitative analyses but have then moved to detailed qualitative studies in order to gain a better understanding of the possible mechanisms involved. Laub and Sampson (2003) did this in their follow-up study to age 70 years of individuals with severe delinquency in adolescence. Purposive sampling was undertaken to provide Laub with 52 individuals who varied greatly in their outcomes. Among other things, the findings showed the multiple routes by which marriage could exert a protective effect. Hauser et al (2006) similarly started with a quantitative study of outcomes in a group of young people hospitalised in adolescence for a mental disorder. Qualitative interviews were undertaken to compare those who had shown resilience in having an unusually good outcome and those who had turned out as average. The findings highlighted self-reflection, a commitment to relationships and personal agency, and a concern to overcome adversity – variables that would not necessarily have been expected from the quantitative findings. Again, what makes these studies so informative is their thoughtful, creative use of an integrated combination of quantitative and qualitative approaches. The qualitative findings cannot prove or disprove a mediating mechanism; quantitative methods will be needed to do that. On the other hand, the qualitative findings enabled the research to go well beyond the initial quantitative results.

Overall conclusions on the role of science

It may be concluded that science has a key role in the understanding of family troubles because of: its use of systematic samples and good measurement; the asking of well-focused incisive questions; the use of a range of different research strategies (especially those involving 'natural experiments'); the testing of alternative explanations for findings; and the examination of both between-group differences and within-group heterogeneity. The examples given illustrate the power of both quantitative and qualitative research at its best. Nevertheless, it has to be admitted that much social research does not live up to those standards and some of it is mediocre. However, the future does not lie either in focusing on the limitations of past research or on a continuation of a fruitless battle between those espousing qualitative or quantitative research and denigrating the other. Both have much to offer and many of the successes have involved an integration of the principles of both.

References

Academy of Medical Sciences (2007) *Identifying the environmental causes of disease: how should we decide what to believe and when to take action?*, London: Academy of Medical Sciences.

Achenbach, T.M., McConaughy, S.H. and Howell, C.T. (1987) 'Child–adolescent behavioural and emotional problems: implications of cross-informant correlations for situation specificity', *Psychological Bulletin*, vol 101, pp 213–32.

Ainsworth, M.D.S., Blehar, M.C., Waters, E. and Wall, S. (1978) *Patterns of attachment: a psychological study of the strange situation*, Hillsdale, NJ: Erlbaum Associates.

Becker, H.S. (1996) 'The epistemology of qualitative research', in R. Jessor, A. Colby and R.A. Shweder (eds) *Ethnography and human development: context and meaning in social inquiry*, Chicago, IL: University of Chicago Press, pp 53–71.

Becker, W.C. (1960) 'The relationship of factors in parental ratings of self and each other to the behaviour of kindergarten children as rated by mothers, fathers and teachers', *Journal of Consulting Psychology*, vol 6, pp 507–27.

Becker, W.C. (1962) 'Developmental psychology', *Annual Review of Psychology*, vol 13, pp 1–32.

British Academy Working Group Report (2010) *Social science and family policies*, British Academy Policy Centre, UK.

Brown, G.W. and Harris, T.O. (1978) *The social origins of depression: a study of psychiatric disorder in women*, London: Tavistock.

Caspi, A., McClay, J., Moffitt, T.E. et al (2002) 'Role of genotype in the cycle of violence in maltreated children', *Science*, vol 297, pp 851–4.

Caspi, A., Sugden, K., Moffitt, T.E. et al (2003) 'Influence of life stress on depression: moderation by a polymorphism in the 5-HTT gene', *Science*, vol 301, pp 386–9.

Caspi, A., Moffitt, T.E., Morgan, J., Rutter, M. et al (2004) 'Maternal expressed emotion predicts children's antisocial behavior problems: using monozygotic-twin differences to identify environmental effects on behavioral development', *Developmental Psychology*, vol 40, no 2, pp 149–61.

Cassidy, J. and Shaver, P.R. (eds) (2008) *Handbook of attachment: theory, research and clinical applications* (2nd edn), New York, NY: Guilford Press.

Christensen, H.T. (1960) 'Cultural relativism and premarital sex norms', *American Sociological Review*, vol 25, pp 31–9.

Côté, S.M., Borge, A.I., Geoffroy, M.-C., Rutter, M. and Tremblay, R.E. (2008) 'Non-maternal care in infancy and emotional/behavioral difficulties at 4 years old: moderation by family risk characteristics', *Developmental Psychology*, vol 44, pp 155–68.

Cox, A., Rutter, M. and Holbrook, D. (1981) 'Psychiatric interviewing techniques. V. Experimental study: eliciting factual information', *British Journal of Psychiatry*, vol 139, pp 29–37.

Deater-Deckard, K., Dodge, K.A. and Sorbring, E. (2005) 'Cultural differences in the effects of physical punishment', in M. Rutter and M. Tienda (eds) *Ethnicity and causal mechanisms*, New York, NY: Cambridge University Press, pp 204–26.

Dixon, L., Browne, K.D. and Hamilton-Giachritsis, C. (2005a) 'Risk factors of parents abused as children: a mediational analysis of the intergenerational continuity of child maltreatment (Part I)', *Journal of Child Psychology and Psychiatry*, vol 46, no 1, pp 47–57.

Dixon, L., Hamilton-Giachritsis, C. and Browne, K.D. (2005b) 'Attributions and behaviours of parents abused as children: a mediational analysis of the intergenerational continuity of child maltreatment (Part II)', *Journal of Child Psychology and Psychiatry*, vol 46, no 1, pp 58–68.

Geoffroy, M.-C., Côté, S.M., Borge, A.I., Séguin, J.R. and Rutter, M. (2007) 'Association between non-maternal care in the first year of life and children's receptive language skills prior to school entry: the moderating role of socioeconomic status', *Journal of Child Psychology and Psychiatry*, vol 48, pp 490–7.

Glaser, D. (2008) 'Child sexual abuse', in M. Rutter, D. Bishop, D. Pine, S. Scott, J.S. Stevenson, E. Taylor and A. Thapar (eds) *Rutter's child and adolescent psychiatry* (5th edn), Oxford: Wiley-Blackwell Publishing, pp 440–58.

Goffman, E. (1961) *Asylums: essays on the social situation of mental patients and other inmates*, New York, NY: Doubleday.

Goldacre, B. (2010) *Bad science*, London: Fourth Estate.

Goody, E. (1970) 'Kinship fostering in Gonja', in P. Meyer (ed) *Socialisation: the approach from social anthropology*, London: Tavistock.

Gottman, J.M. (1995) What predicts divorce? The measures, Hillsdale, NJ: Lawrence Erlbaum.

Hauser, S., Allen, J. and Golden, E. (2006) *Out of the woods: tales of resilient teens*, Cambridge, MA: Harvard University Press.

Jaffee, S.R., Caspi, A., Moffitt, T.E. et al (2004) 'The limits of child effects: evidence for genetically mediated child effects on corporal punishment but not on physical maltreatment', *Developmental Psychopathology*, vol 40, pp 1047–58.

Jaffee, S.R., Strait, L.B. and Odgers, C.L. (2012) 'From correlates to causes: can quasi-experimental studies and statistical innovations bring us closer to identifying the causes of antisocial behaviour?', *Psychological Bulletin*, vol 138, pp 279–95.

Karg, K., Burmeister, M., Shedden, K. and Sen, S. (2011) 'The Serotonin Transporter Promoter Variant (5-HTTLPR), stress, and depression meta-analysis revisited: evidence of genetic moderation', *Archives of General Psychiatry* vol 68, pp 444-54.

Kendler, K.S. and Prescott, C.A. (2006) *Genes, environment, and psychopathology: Understanding the causes of psychiatric and substance use disorders*, New York, NY: Guilford Press.

Kleinman, A.M. (1977) 'Depression, somatization and the "new cross-cultural psychiatry"', *Social Science and Medicine*, vol 11, pp 3–10.

Laub, J.H. and Sampson, R.J. (2003) *Shared beginnings, divergent lives: delinquent boys to age 70*, Harvard, MA: Harvard University Press.

Lieberson, S. (1992) 'Einstein, Renoir, and Greely: some thoughts about evidence in sociology: 1991 presidential address', *American Sociological Review*, vol 57, pp 1–15.

Main, M. and Solomon, J. (1986) 'Discovery of an insecure-disoriented attachment pattern', in T.B. Brazelton and M.W. Yogman (eds) *Affective development in infancy*, Norwood, NJ: Ablex, pp 95–124.

Main, M. and Solomon, J. (1990) 'Procedures for identifying infants as disorganized/ disoriented during the Ainsworth Strange Situation', in M. Greenberg, D. Cicchetti and E.M. Cummings (eds) At*tachment during the preschool years: theory, research and intervention*, Chicago, IL: University of Chicago Press, pp 121–60.

Mercer, J. (1973) *Labeling the mentally retarded*, Berkeley, CA: University of California Press.

Merton, R.K. (1973) *The sociology of science. Theoretical and empirical investigations*, Chicago, IL: University of Chicago Press.

National Research Council (2002) *Scientific research in education*, Washington: National Academy Press.

Nikapota, A. and Rutter, M. (2008) 'Sociocultural/ethnic groups and psychopathology', in M. Rutter, D. Bishop, D. Pine, S. Scott, J.S. Stevenson, E. Taylor and A. Thapar (eds) *Rutter's child and adolescent psychiatry* (5th edn), Oxford: Blackwell, pp 199–211.

O'Connor, T.G., Deater-Deckard, K., Fulker, D. et al (1998) 'Genotype–environment correlations in late childhood and early adolescence: antisocial behavioral problems and coercive parenting', *Developmental Psychology*, vol 34, pp 970–81.

Patterson, G.R. (1981) *Coercive family process*, Eugene, OR: Castalia Publishing.

Richardson, S.A. (1984) 'Institutionalization and deinstitutionalization of children with mental retardation', in H.W. Stevenson and A.E. Siegel (eds) *Child development research and social policy*, Chicago, IL: University of Chicago Press, pp 318–66.

Robins, L.N. (1993) 'Vietnam veterans' rapid recovery from heroin addiction: a fluke or normal expectation?', *Addiction*, vol 88, pp 1041–54.

Rutter, M. (1999) 'Social context: meanings, measures and mechanisms', *European Review*, vol 7, pp 139–49.

Rutter, M. (2003) 'Categories, dimensions, and the mental health of children and adolescents', *Annals of the New York Academy of Sciences*, vol 1008, pp 11–21.

Rutter, M. (2007) 'Proceeding from observed correlation to causal inference: the use of natural experiments', *Perspectives on Psychological Science*, vol 2, pp 377–95.

Rutter, M. (2012) 'Natural experiments as a means of testing causal inferences', in C. Barzini, P. Dawid and L. Bernardinelli (eds) *Statistical methods in causal inference*, Chichester: Wiley, pp 253–72.

Rutter, M. and Sonuga-Barke, E.J. (eds) (2010) 'Deprivation-specific psychological patterns: effects of institutional deprivation', *Monographs of the Society for Research in Child Development*, vol 75, p 1.

Rutter, M. and Tienda, M. (eds) (2005) *Ethnicity and causal mechanisms*, New York, NY: Cambridge University Press.

Rutter, M., Maughan, B., Mortimore, P., Ouston, J. and Smith, A. (1979) *Fifteen thousand hours: secondary schools and their effects on children*, Cambridge, MA: Harvard University Press.

Rutter, M., Kreppner, J. and Sonuga-Barke, E. (2009a) 'Emanuel Miller lecture: attachment insecurity, disinhibited attachment, and attachment disorders: where do research findings leave the concepts?', *Journal of Child Psychology and Psychiatry*, vol 50, pp 529–43.

Rutter, M., Thapar, A. and Pickles, A. (2009b) 'From JAMA: commentary on paper by Risch et al (2009) – Gene–environment interactions: biologically valid pathway or artefact?', *Archives of General Psychiatry*, vol 66, pp 1287–9.

Schliemann, A.D. and Carraher, D.W. (1994) 'Proportional reasoning in and out of school', in P. Light and G. Butterworth (eds) *Context and cognition: ways of learning and knowing*, Hillsdale, NJ: Lawrence Erlbaum Associates, pp 47–73.

St. Petersburg–USA Orphanage Research Team (2008) 'The effects of early social-emotional and relationship experience on the development of young orphanage children', *Monographs of the Society for Research in Child Development*, vol 73, pp 1–262.

Tizard, J., Sinclair, I. and Clarke, R.V.G. (1975) *Varieties of residential experience*, London: Routledge & Kegan Paul.

Uher, R. and McGuffin, P. (2010) 'The moderation by the serotonin transporter gene of environmental adversity in the etiology of depression: 2009 update', *Molecular Psychiatry*, vol 15, pp 18–22.

Weisz, J.R., McCarty, C.A., Eastman, K.L., Chaiyasit, W. and Suwanlert, S. (1997) 'Developmental psychopathology and culture: ten lessons from Thailand', in S.S. Luthar, J.A. Burack, D. Cicchetti and J.R. Weisz (eds) *Developmental psychopathology: perspectives on adjustment, risk, and disorder*, Cambridge: Cambridge University Press, pp 568–92.

Wing, J.K. and Brown, G.W. (1970) *Institutionalism and schizophrenia*, Cambridge: Cambridge University Press.

Zigler, E. and Styfco, S.J. (2006) 'Epilogue', in N.F. Watt, C. Ayoub, R.H. Bradley, J.E. Puma, and W.A. LeBoeuf (eds) *The crisis in youth mental health: critical issues and effective programs. Volume 4: early intervention programs and policies*, Westport, CT: Praeger, pp 347–71.

CHAPTER FIVE

Family troubles, methods trouble: qualitative research and the methodological divide

Ara Francis

Research in the social sciences is characterised by a healthy fragmentation; scholars operate within multiple paradigms of inquiry that are premised upon different assumptions about the nature of reality and the purposes of scholarship. Guba and Lincoln (1994) identify five orientations to social research and delineate the ontological premises of each. As their work suggests, most traditions can be seen as falling somewhere on an ontological continuum of realism and relativism.[1] On the side of realism, positivism views the social world as operating much like the natural world, according to laws that have predictable, measurable effects and are consistent across time and space. From this perspective, social and psychological forces animate individuals in much the same way that gravity animates physical objects. At the other end of this continuum, constructivism holds that the social world is different from the natural world because humans use symbols, are highly reflexive and make meaningful choices about their conduct. From this perspective, social life is patterned but not predictable, and all human conduct is culturally and situationally contingent.

Although the relationship is imperfect, different paradigms of inquiry tend to align with particular methodological traditions. Positivism often partners with quantitative methods, most often in the form of surveys and experiments, and these methods follow the same logic of inquiry that is used in the natural sciences. Because the primary goal is to identify the causes of human conduct, quantitative researchers' chief concerns include objectivity, the isolation of variables and control over the conditions of research. Constructivism, on the other hand, often couples with qualitative methods, such as in-depth interviews and participant observation. These methods are designed to capture and convey meaning. Because the primary goal is to understand how people make sense of the world and their own conduct, most qualitative researchers view empathy as an asset and social context as a prerequisite for understanding.

As Michael Rutter (Chapter Four) notes, it is important not to overstate the differences between such contrasting methodological approaches. Insofar as these traditions are empirical and systematic, they adhere to the scientific ethos that characterises all research in the social sciences. They have explicit criteria for assessing robustness and generate knowledge that is generalisable (although the manner by which they move from the specific to the general is different, as I later discuss). Finally, there are scholars of family trouble who employ both qualitative and quantitative methods with great success (eg Green, 2003; Umberson, 2003; Cherlin et al, 2004). Why, then, should we pay heed to the seemingly abstract differences outlined here?

There are at least two justifications for doing so. First, a rich and productive examination of family troubles requires scholars to think across methodological boundaries, and it is difficult to appreciate the contribution of one research tradition without understanding fully what distinguishes it from its counterpart. Second, an acknowledgement of the differences between these approaches may help us to bridge what I see as a methodological divide. In order to overcome what amounts to a language barrier between scholars trained in different traditions, we must examine the syntax that governs each approach. This chapter focuses on the contribution of qualitative methods to studies of family trouble, but the subject of difference and division is a central theme. At the discussion's close, I offer suggestions for how scholars of family trouble might ameliorate methods trouble and reach across the qualitative–quantitative divide.

The logic of qualitative inquiry

Scholars who employ qualitative methods are a diverse bunch with varied philosophical, theoretical and methodological orientations (see Denzin and Lincoln, 2008). Nonetheless, it is fair to characterise most qualitative research as operating according to a logic of inquiry rooted in Max Weber's (2001) notion of *verstehen*. As noted earlier, the foremost goal of most qualitative scholarship is to *understand* the meanings of human conduct, not to identify its causes.

Research on the family members of people with clinical depression, schizophrenia, bipolar disorder and other forms of mental illness illuminates this distinction as it pertains to family trouble. One line of quantitative scholarship in this area uses survey data to identify the factors, such as race or age, that increase or mediate the financial, physical and psychological costs of caring for mentally ill spouses, children, parents or siblings (see Rungreangkulkij and Gilliss, 2000). The question of what *causes* 'caregiver burden' is a driving premise of this scholarship. In contrast, David Karp's (2001) ethnographic research sets out to examine what it *feels like* to be the spouse, child, parent or sibling of someone who is mentally ill. Drawing from observations of a support group and 60 in-depth interviews, his book, *The burden of sympathy*, highlights the deep ambivalence that people experience as they try to determine the boundaries of their obligation to mentally ill family members.

Karp's research reveals that trying to help sick loved ones without becoming consumed by their misery is an agonising, near-impossible undertaking. This micro-social struggle, Karp argues, reflects cultural contradictions about what people in the US owe to themselves and to one another. 'Taught to believe simultaneously in the sanctity of the self and of attachment to others' (Karp,

2001, p 242), caregivers are torn apart – physically and psychologically – as they attempt to care for mentally ill family members and themselves. As Karp's research demonstrates, qualitative scholarship focuses not on the causes of family trouble, but on capturing 'the more emotionally nuanced, subjective, and cognitively complex features' of people's experiences (Karp and Watts-Roy, 1999, p 471).

A second defining characteristic of qualitative inquiry is that it prioritises direct observation in everyday contexts (Lofland and Lofland, 1995). Even interviews are structured loosely in order to approximate mundane interaction. This reflects the constructivist position that human conduct cannot be understood when separated from the larger systems of meaning in which it is embedded. To use the example popularised by Clifford Geertz (1973), the contraction of an eyelid may be a twitch, a wink or a parody of a wink. Recognising the difference requires the observer to know something about the intention of the actor, the established social code and the situation at hand. Qualitative methods such as participant observation and in-depth interviews are designed to maximise researchers' ability to grasp these subjective and contextual aspects of human conduct.

Somewhat paradoxically, this means that qualitative studies are often in a good position to consider *why* people do what they do (Maxwell, 2004). Consider research on low-income, unmarried mothers, a group that the public often deems to be 'troublesome' or 'in trouble'. While non-marital childbearing, cohabitation and divorce have increased among most demographic groups in the US, quantitative research demonstrates that rates of non-marital births are particularly high among women who are economically disadvantaged (eg Ellwood and Jencks, 2004). Why this group of women so often puts motherhood before marriage is a question with important political implications; although data suggest that having a child does not significantly impact the life chances of young, unmarried mothers, it may diminish the life chances of their children (eg Haveman et al, 2001).

Kathryn Edin and Maria Kefalas (2005) spent two and a half years doing fieldwork in eight Philadelphia neighbourhoods and conducted 162 interviews with low-income, single mothers. Their rich data suggest that the negative relationship between socio-economic status and non-marital childbearing is due, in part, to what marriage and motherhood *mean* to women growing up in impoverished communities. Edin and Kefalas's participants believed that the best time to marry is after both members of a couple have achieved some modicum of independence and economic security. With few opportunities to achieve this kind of stability in the inner cities of Philadelphia, women delayed marriage. However, these participants did not view higher education or steady employment as prerequisites for having children. Unlike affluent women, for whom early motherhood means relinquishing other opportunities, this group of women had little to lose. In fact, motherhood was one of the few accessible roles that they could take pride in performing. With few avenues for crafting valuable identities, Edin and Kefalas's participants saw childlessness as a much greater tragedy than having children too early.

As demonstrated by Edin and Kefalas's work, qualitative researchers' deep immersion in participants' everyday lives allows them to see how conduct is embedded in particular social contexts. This is not easily achieved with survey or experimental methods, which tend to decontextualise people's experiences in an effort to control the research environment and make broad generalisations. Although studies like Edin and Kefalas's cannot make definitive assertions about the causes of family trouble, they offer important windows into the black boxes of so much quantitative research. As Edin et al (2004, p 1013) explain, 'the meanings ascribed to cohabitation and marriage are vitally important to explaining family-formation behaviors'.

Consistent with a commitment to honouring the emergent and complex features of human life, most qualitative work takes an inductive approach. Of course, no study is *purely* deductive or inductive; to claim otherwise is a misrepresentation of how research actually gets done (Medawar, 1969). Nonetheless, there are different points of departure in research. While quantitative studies usually begin with theoretical propositions that tightly frame what kinds of data are gathered and analysed, most qualitative studies begin with broadly stated interests and questions. Qualitative researchers set out to collect the richest data possible, and most sharpen their foci only after data collection is well under way. Their rationale for doing so is to privilege the empirical world, unclouded as much as possible by preconceptions, theoretical or otherwise. This does not mean that qualitative researchers begin their work free from assumptions. Rather, they endeavour to bracket those assumptions and give primacy to participants' words and actions (see Blumer, 1969; Becker, 1996).

One advantage of this inductive orientation is that it offers a degree of flexibility that is not available in survey or experimental research. For example, when I set out to study middle-class men and women who identify their children as having 'significant problems', I was interested in the parents' role in the problematisation and medicalisation of childhood. Although my questions for parents reflected these topics, I structured my interview guide loosely so that participants could discuss what they viewed as the most important aspects of their experiences. When I began talking with parents, I was struck by how children's problems had disrupted their lives, not just in terms of parenthood, but in terms of their relationships with family members and friends, career trajectories, notions of self as 'normal' middle-class people, and plans and hopes for the future. Upon witnessing the wide-ranging ramifications of children's problems, I expanded my focus to examine parents' experiences of stigma, loneliness, responsibility, guilt, loss and grief (Francis, 2012a). In sum, the flexibility of qualitative methods makes a great deal of room for unexpected observations and unanticipated conclusions (Becker, 1996).

Finally, the logic of generalisation in qualitative scholarship is distinct. While quantitative scholars favour large, random samples so that their findings will be generalisable to larger populations of people, most qualitative scholars aim to generate, refine and extend what Herbert Blumer (1969) referred to as 'sensitising concepts'. These flexible constructs call attention to certain empirical possibilities without offering strict definitions or propositions. Developed from the 'ground up' in one research context and then used by scholars in multiple settings, sensitising concepts are one means by which qualitative research is made 'generalisable' (Hanson, 2008).

Goffman's (1963) notion of courtesy stigma, or the stigma that stems from close association with stigmatised others, offers a relevant example. In his classic text *Stigma*, Goffman (1963, p 30) spends just a few pages discussing the 'tendency of stigma to spread from the stigmatized individual to his close connections'. Since Goffman's introduction of the concept, scholars have used courtesy stigma to analyse cases ranging from the family members of people with Alzheimer's disease to the parents of children with Attention Deficit Disorder (MacRae, 1999; Koro-Ljungberg and Bussing, 2009). Researchers have critiqued, retooled and adapted the concept in ways that reflect diverse and ever-changing empirical worlds (Craig and Scambler, 2006; Farrugia, 2009; Francis, 2012b).

So far, this discussion has focused on the logic of qualitative inquiry, using studies of family trouble as cases in point. Now I consider more directly the contribution of qualitative scholarship to family troubles research. I argue that because of its special focus on meaning in social life, qualitative scholarship makes important substantive contributions by commonly addressing two questions: how do people construct 'family trouble', and how are those constructions related to social systems of power and inequality?

Qualitative contributions to the study of family trouble

It is not as though quantitative research cannot or does not address these questions. In fact, large sample surveys are excellent tools for capturing how people's perceptions of family trouble change over time, and this is one means by which scholars demonstrate the culturally and historically contingent nature of family trouble (see Best, 1990, pp 151–75). However, qualitative methods are particularly well suited for exploring the *processes* of trouble construction. As illustrated by Stephen Pfohl's (1977) piece 'The "discovery" of child abuse', the content analysis of historical documents works well in this regard. It is well known that, prior to the 1960s, people did not widely view as deviant many of the actions now categorised as 'child abuse' in the late-modern West (eg Best, 1990, pp 66–71). A number of historical shifts – such as the emergence of childhood as a discrete and special stage of life – paved the way for rising concerns about children's health and welfare (DeMause, 1974). Drawing from legal records and medical publications, Pfohl demonstrates how the fragmented and hierarchical nature of the medical profession positioned radiologists to further categorise child abuse as deviant behaviour and help construct it as a pressing social problem. At the time, radiology was a marginal specialty that involved little risk-taking and no patient contact, and child abuse provided paediatric radiologists with an opportunity to improve their standing. 'By linking themselves to the problem of abuse', Pfohl explains, 'radiologists became indirectly tied into the crucial clinical task of patient diagnosis. In addition, they became the direct source of input concerning the risky "life or death" consequences of child beating' (Pfohl, 1977, p 319).

While the content analysis of historical documents, medical texts and popular media allows scholars to examine the processes by which particular definitions of family trouble become culturally dominant, in-depth interviews are a good method for capturing how people support, resist and make sense of these definitions in everyday life. Maxine Jacobson's (2002) study of a child protection team in rural Montana illustrates how culturally dominant understandings of family trouble sometimes conflict with local realities. The urban service model of child protection is predicated on the notion that childhood is a period of innocence and play. However, people in post-industrial farm settings view children as a valuable part of the labour force. This understanding of childhood, together with a frontier ethos of bearing up under difficult circumstances and a reluctance to acknowledge problems, posed challenges to team members' implementation of contemporary child welfare philosophies. Instead of using the psychological and medical treatments that characterise interventions in urban settings, the team that Jacobson studied developed creative solutions focusing on the community rather than individuals.

In the course of examining how people construct family troubles, qualitative studies often explore the intersection of trouble, power and inequality. Who defines trouble – and who gets defined as 'troubled' or 'troublesome' – is inextricably bound to a society's distribution of symbolic and material resources. In our late-modern, highly medicalised society, medical science itself is an object of critical inquiry. For example, social histories of child abuse, Fetal Alcohol Syndrome and learning disabilities illustrate how medical categories reflect middle-class interests and sensibilities (Pfohl, 1977; Coles, 1989; Golden, 2005). Ethnographic scholarship often contributes to these substantive concerns by examining how dynamics of power unfold in interactions between service providers and 'troubled' individuals and by examining how people internalise, manage and resist biomedical labels (Beard and Fox, 2008; Nack, 2008; Stacey et al, 2009).

In sum, qualitative methods are well-suited to capturing and conveying particular aspects of the empirical world. However, social-scientific research does more than document reality; it also *generates* reality through the production of knowledge (Law, 2009). Methods are central to this process, and different methods can be said to generate different kinds of reality. This is one source of what I see as a methodological divide in studies of family trouble.

The methodological divide

The conference that inspired this volume offers evidence that there exists an uneasy relationship between quantitative and qualitative approaches to studying family troubles. The conference programme was comprised almost entirely of qualitative work, even though topics like divorce, unemployment, illness, migration, domestic abuse and addiction are commonly studied using quantitative methods. That a general call for papers on the broad topic of 'family trouble' yielded such a disproportionate number of qualitative studies illustrates how scholars are often situated within niches of research divided along methodological lines. The existence of different intellectual 'tribes' reflects the fragmented organisation of social science more generally (Becker, 1996).

When the conference's qualitative and quantitative scholars did encounter one another, they sometimes talked at cross-purposes. Quantitative researchers spoke the language of hypothesis-testing and expressed dismay at qualitative researchers' small sample sizes and inability to generalise to larger populations. Qualitative researchers discussed emergent patterns and sensitising concepts and complained about the failure of quantitative scholars to recognise the constructed nature of variables. Nowhere were these tensions more evident than during a large group discussion of child abuse; when one scholar commented on the high rates of child abuse, another pointed out that such claims were culturally and historically relative. The discussion quickly reached an impasse, each group surprised and disconcerted by the other's orientation towards family trouble.

These tensions reflected the different goals of family scholars and family practitioners as much as they reflected different methodological orientations. Indeed, the trouble stemmed not from methods themselves, but from the different types of knowledge generated by different traditions of research. Quantitative research is more apt to conceive of child abuse as an obdurate social fact; scholars define it, measure it and attempt to discern its causes. Quantitative studies of maltreatment in the US are, by and large, premised on objective definitions and pay less attention to the subjective or relative aspects of abuse (see the review by Manly, 2005). In fact, some studies of maltreatment prevalence cite respondent subjectivity as a limitation that hinders accurate measurement (eg Hussey et al, 2006, p 940). Although some large sample surveys in the UK recognise and account for cultural variability and respondents' own perspectives (eg May-Chahal and Cawson, 2005), survey methods themselves impose reification; measurement requires clear definition, and settling upon any meaning – or even multiple meanings – requires researchers to bracket the fluid, ongoing processes that generate and maintain those definitions. Qualitative scholarship tends to produce a different image of reality, conceiving of child abuse as an ongoing construction. As noted earlier, scholars employ qualitative methods to observe how the meanings people ascribe to abusive actions change over time and across contexts. Although they may seem incompatible, neither of these portrayals of reality is 'incorrect'. Definitions of child abuse are all at once flexible and durable, created by humans even as they bear down upon us as separate and obdurate phenomena. Different orientations to research reflect the paradoxical nature of social life itself, but scholars too often dismiss one vantage point or the other as misguided.

The hierarchy of academic life also fuels methods trouble. Although social science is well populated with constructivist, qualitative scholarship, many scholars view positivism and quantitative methods (especially the experimental method) as the gold standard of scientific research. As Howard Becker (1996) argues, this status differential usually means that quantitative scholars can call upon qualitative scholars to account for their work using the language of positivism, but qualitative scholars cannot, in turn, demand that quantitative scholars answer to the standards of constructivism. Some scholars use the standards of positivism to challenge the legitimacy of qualitative research. However, answers to the question 'What constitutes good science?' have as much to do with the social organisation of academic life as they do with the acquisition of truth. To the extent that quantitative research is ostensibly superior to qualitative research, divisions and tensions are sure to persist.

Given what I have outlined here, how might scholars reach across the methodological divide in order to further our understanding of family troubles? Any attempt to bridge these differences must begin with the respectful recognition that differences exist. Following Howard Becker (1996), I have used the analogy of a language barrier to describe the relationship between qualitative- and quantitative-minded scholars. This comparison suggests that one way to mitigate tension is to do as anthropologists do: avoid using the precepts of one's own group to evaluate the actions of the other. It is unwise for qualitative researchers to demand that quantitative scholarship richly illustrate how taken-for-granted categories such as gender, race, mental illness or child abuse are socially constructed. Similarly, quantitative researchers cannot reasonably expect qualitative studies to be generalisable to larger populations of people. What each can request, however, is that the other understands and appreciates the general tenets under which they conduct research.

Much like the conference that inspired this volume, collaborative projects that acknowledge and critically examine paradigmatic tensions hold more promise than research that is, simply, 'multi-methodological'. The integration of qualitative and quantitative methods has the potential to generate new knowledge and novel ways of thinking, but separating methods from their ontological assumptions diminishes this potential. Indeed, if our representations of family troubles are to be accurately textured, the field must contain the unique vantage points offered by qualitative and quantitative methods. Our challenge, it seems, is to understand what each has to offer and to integrate our substantive knowledge without relinquishing the distinct logics that inform our varied traditions.

Note

[1] This ontological continuum is not one-dimensional but may be cross-cut by other perspectives. For example, critical realism may have an objectivist ontological position but reflect a constructivist epistemological position.

References

Beard, R.L. and Fox, P.J. (2008) 'Resisting social disenfranchisement: negotiating collective identities and everyday life with memory loss', *Social Science and Medicine*, vol 66, no 7, pp 1509–20.

Becker, H.S. (1996) 'The epistemology of qualitative research', in R. Jessor, A. Colby and R.A. Shweder (eds) *Ethnography and human development: context and meaning in social inquiry*, Chicago, IL: University of Chicago Press, pp 53–71.

Best, J. (1990) *Threatened children: rhetoric and concern about child victims*, Chicago, IL: University of Chicago Press.

Blumer, H. (1969) *Symbolic interaction: perspective and method*, Berkeley, CA: University of California Press.

Cherlin, A.J, Burton, L.M., Hurt, T.R. and Purvin, D.M. (2004) 'The influence of physical and sexual abuse on marriage and cohabitation', *American Sociological Review*, vol 69, no 6, pp 768–89.

Coles, G. (1989) *The learning mystique: a critical look at learning disabilities*, New York, NY: Pantheon.

Craig, G.M. and Scambler, G. (2006) 'Negotiating mothering against the odds: gastrostomy tube feeding, stigma, governmentality and disabled children', *Social Science & Medicine*, vol 62, no 5, pp 1115–25.

DeMause, L. (1974) *The history of childhood*, New York, NY: Psychohistory Press.

Denzin, N.K. and Lincoln, Y.S. (eds) (2008) *The SAGE handbook of qualitative research* (3rd edn), Thousand Oaks, CA: Sage Publications.

Edin, K. and Kefalas, M. (2005) *Promises I can keep*, Berkeley, CA: University of California Press.

Edin, K., Kefalas, M.J. and Reed, J.M. (2004) 'A peek inside the black box: what marriage means for poor unmarried parents', *Journal of Marriage and Family*, vol 66, no 4, pp 1007–14.

Ellwood, D.T. and Jencks, C. (2004) 'The uneven spread of single-parent families: what do we know? Where do we look for answers?', in K.M. Neckerman (ed) *Social inequality*, New York, NY: Russell Sage, pp 3 77.

Farrugia, D. (2009) 'Exploring stigma: medical knowledge and the stigmatisation of parents of children diagnosed with Autism Spectrum Disorder', *Sociology of Health & Illness*, vol 31, no 7, pp 1011–27.

Francis, A. (2012a) 'The dynamics of family trouble: middle-class parents whose children have problems', *Journal of Contemporary Ethnography*, vol 41, no 4, pp 371–401.

Francis, A. (2012b) 'Stigma in an era of medicalization and anxious parenting: how proximity and culpability shape middle-class parents' experiences of disgrace', *Sociology of Health and Illness*, vol 34, no 6, pp 927–42.

Geertz, C. (1973) *The interpretation of cultures*, New York, NY: Basic Books.

Goffman, E. (1963) *Stigma: Notes on the management of spoiled identity*, New York, NY: Aronson.

Golden, J. (2005) *Message in a bottle: the making of fetal alcohol syndrome*, Cambridge, MA: Cambridge University Press.

Green, S.E. (2003) 'What do you mean "What's wrong with her?"': stigma and the lives of families of children with disabilities', *Social Science & Medicine*, vol 57, no 8, pp 1361–74.

Guba, E.G. and Lincoln, Y.S. (1994) 'Competing paradigms in qualitative research', in N.K. Denzin and Y.S. Lincoln (eds) *Handbook of qualitative research*, Thousand Oaks, CA: Sage, pp 105–17.

Hanson, B. (2008) 'Wither qualitative/quantitative? Grounds for methodological convergence', *Quality and Quantity*, vol 42, no 1, pp 97–111.

Haveman, R., Wolfe, B. and Pence, K. (2001) 'Intergenerational effects of non-marital and early childbearing', in B. Wolfe and L.L. Wu (eds) *Out of wedlock*, New York, NY: Russell Sage, pp 287–316.

Hussey, J.M., Chang, J.J. and Kotch, J.B. (2006) 'Child maltreatment in the United States: prevalence, risk factors, and adolescent health consequences', *Pediatrics*, vol 118, no 3, pp 933–42.

Jacobson, M. (2002) 'Local realities: a frontier perspective on child protection team practice', *Child Welfare*, vol LXXXI, no 5, pp 737–55.

Karp, D. (2001) *The burden of sympathy: how families cope with mental illness*, New York, NY: Oxford University Press.

Karp, D.A. and Watts-Roy, D. (1999) 'Bearing responsibility: how caregivers to the mentally ill assess their obligations', *Health*, vol 3, no 4, pp 469–91.

Koro-Ljungberg, M. and Bussing, R. (2009) 'The management of courtesy stigma in the lives of families with teenagers with ADHD', *Journal of Family Issues*, vol 30, no 9, pp 1175–200.

Law, J. (2009) 'Seeing like a survey', *Cultural Sociology*, vol 3, no 2, pp 239–56.

Lofland, J. and Lofland, L.H. (1995) *Analyzing social settings*, Belmont, CA: Wadsworth/Thomson Learning.

MacRae, H. (1999) 'Managing courtesy stigma: the case of Alzheimer's disease', *Sociology of Health and Illness*, vol 21, no 1, pp 54–70.

Manly, J.T. (2005) 'Advances in research definitions of child maltreatment', *Child Abuse & Neglect*, vol 29, pp 425–39.

Maxwell, J.A. (2004) 'Using qualitative methods for causal explanation', *Field Methods*, vol 16, no 3, pp 243–64.

May-Chahal, C. and Cawson, P. (2005) 'Measuring child maltreatment in the United Kingdom: a study of the prevalence of child abuse and neglect', *Child Abuse and Neglect*, vol 29, pp 969–84.

Medawar, P.B. (1969) *Induction and intuition in scientific thought*, Philadelphia, PA: American Philosophical Society.

Nack, A. (2008) *Damaged goods: women living with incurable sexually transmitted disease*, Philadelphia, PA: Temple University Press.

Pfohl, S.J. (1977) 'The "discovery" of child abuse', *Social Problems*, vol 24, no 3, pp 310–23.

Rungreangkulkij, S. and Gilliss, C.L. (2000) 'Conceptual approaches to studying family caregiving for persons with severe mental illness', *Journal of Family Nursing*, vol 6, no 4, pp 341–66.

Stacey, C.L., Henderson, S., MacArthur, K.R. and Dohan, D. (2009) 'Demanding patient or demanding encounter? A case study of a cancer clinic', *Social Science & Medicine*, vol 69, no 5, pp 729–37.

Umberson, D. (2003) *Death of a parent: transition to a new adult identity*, Cambridge, MA: Cambridge University Press.

Weber, M. (2001) *The protestant ethic and the spirit of capitalism* (3rd edn), trans S. Kalberg, Los Angeles, CA: Roxbury.

WHOSE TROUBLE? CONTESTED DEFINITIONS AND PRACTICES

Introduction to Part Two

Val Gillies

In this part, themes around difference and conformity are brought into focus, highlighting the personal and public struggles framing the construction of family troubles. All five chapters engage to some extent or another with the politics of definition, revealing how understandings are shaped by prevailing normativities as well as private meanings and relationships. In some instances, this involves family members managing the public problematisation of behaviour that might be experienced as commonplace or more or less ordinary. As many of the chapters in this part illustrate, such dissonance can be a core source of trouble for families, provoking feelings of guilt and anxiety and demanding extensive discursive work to explain and justify perspectives or choices.

For example, Helen Lomax's chapter explores how everyday infant feeding practices are moralised and troubled in professional and policy arenas through the presentation of breastfeeding as 'natural' and best for baby in a context where a majority of mothers bottle-feed. In a meticulous analysis of mothers' discussions with midwives during the early days of motherhood, Lomax draws out the often-defensive rhetorical labour engaged in by mothers in response to the subtle pressures exerted by midwives. This troubling of the ordinary is also addressed in Harriet Clarke and Lindsay O'Dell's chapter on disabled parents and child carers, showing how policy and practice can overlook the everyday concerns of family life for a risk-focused lens. As a consequence, the need to access services can be viewed as a potential threat rather than a support to maintain everyday normality. Similarly, both Geraldine Brady's and Ara Francis's chapters show how the public gaze is instrumental in shaping parents' interpretations of conduct in children, leading in some cases to a medicalisation of behaviour that might alternatively be viewed in terms of difference and nonconformity. Francis presents a detailed examination of how a group of middle-class parents in the US come to construct their children as having significant problems in relation to their behaviour and or mental health, highlighting the formative role of wider family members, friends, school officials and medical professionals in reinforcing perceived maternal responsibilities to monitor and cultivate development. In a

British context, Brady focuses, in particular, on families where a child has been diagnosed with attention deficit hyperactivity disorder (ADHD) to show how troublesome differences in behaviour become formally problematised through interaction with dominant biomedical models of health and illness.

But while troubling the normal, public discourses can also normalise the troubled, as Karin Cooper's chapter on the children of kinship carers so effectively shows. A 'pro-family' rhetoric employed by social workers positions the placement of children in the care of friends and family as a more 'natural' option, thereby obscuring and delegitimising the difficulties experienced by carers' own children. The promotion of ideals through professional, administrative and medical orthodoxies and the extent to which this papers over real-life conflicts and difficulties is a thread running through many of the chapters. Helen Lomax demonstrates how the concerns and discomforts associated with breastfeeding were 'glossed and silenced' in midwives' interactions with new mothers, while Harriet Clarke and Lindsay O'Dell highlight how differing policy and research agendas can prioritise particular perspectives as the expense of others' troubles. In this same vein, parents in Ara Francis's research fought hard to gain public recognition that their children's problems were legitimately medical as opposed to the more 'ordinary' consequences of bad parenting. In the specific context of an ADHD diagnosis, the parents discussed in Geraldine Brady's chapter expressed similar experiences and concerns, albeit with greater ambivalence.

All of the chapters here provide a fascinating insight into the social mechanisms through which understandings of family troubles are constructed, contested and reconstructed to varying ends. They also draw attention to the power dynamics mediating and containing such representations and experiences. Questions as to 'Whose problem?' illuminate contrasting perspectives within families as well as wider public–private disjunctures, feeding in to broader debates about cause, effect and, perhaps inevitably, blame. Experiences of family troubles are morally charged, especially where the welfare of children is at stake. While parents are accorded responsibility for the protection and well-being of children and young people, this accountability is situated within social, material and economic contexts that limit agency and capacity. Individual struggles to manage practical and interpersonal demands within these constraints are well documented here. In particular, gender and generation feature as key axes. The role that mothers, in particular, assumed in striving to ensure that their interpretation of a family problem is recognised and addressed is to the fore in several of the chapters. For example, in Ara Francis's work, mothers sought to convince fathers, wider family members and presumably the children themselves that challenging behaviour was attributable to a medical disorder. In relation to generation, Karin Cooper's chapter highlights the distinctly less powerful position that children may occupy in defining and dealing with family troubles, while also drawing attention to the role that they assume as active moral agents in negotiating the difficulties they encountered.

As the chapters here also demonstrate, presumptions around gender and generation are strong features of family interactions with institutions and professionals. With respect to gender, this extends from the mother–centric focus on post–natal feeding choices, exemplified in Helen Lomax's research, to more general accounts from mothers of feeling judged and under scrutiny (as explored in Francis's, Brady's and Clarke and O'Dell's chapters). Contemporary discourses tightly tying the well–being of children and society at large to the precise child–rearing practices pursued, have compounded this gendered focus on mothering as a source of trouble. The new significance accorded to parenting has also routinely set children's needs apart from their parents, in some cases obscuring more complex and interlinked experiences. This is particularly evident in Harriet Clarke and Lindsey O'Dell's consideration of how disabled parents' support needs are sometimes overshadowed by a policy and practice concern to protect young carers from the damaging consequences of their responsibilities. Their nuanced and fluid account foregrounds a more normalised experience of care in the context of the family, while underlining how access to resources plays a central role in mediating all family troubles.

The mismatch between policy and practice agendas and everyday experience is one of the strongest themes running across this part of the book. While many of the research participants featured in the chapters actively sought help and support, it was rarely accessed on their own terms.

In encounters with professionals, new mothers were forced to justify feeding choices for their babies in a context where breastfeeding was presented as a moral commitment (see Lomax's chapter). Young carers had to fit themselves into the problematised policy framework of 'young carer' in order to access resources and support (see Clarke and O'Dell's chapter), while the children of kinship carers struggled to voice their difficulties in a situation constructed by social workers as 'normal' and 'natural' (see Cooper's chapter). For parents raising children with challenging behaviour, a medical frame of reference became at once the source of the problem and the solution (see Francis's and also Brady's chapters). In teasing out the interrelationships and ruptures between real–life experiences and normative systems of support and intervention, the chapters here offer a sophisticated insight into the way the material and the discursive shape and contain the everyday management of family troubles.

CHAPTER SIX

Disabled parents and normative family life: the obscuring of lived experiences of parents and children within policy and research accounts

Harriet Clarke and Lindsay O'Dell

Introduction

This chapter examines understandings of family life where a parent has an impairment or experiences chronic health difficulties. Over the past two decades, the experiences of families that include a disabled parent have become increasingly visible through research, wider awareness-raising activity and policy debate and development. The strands of research and conceptual work in this area (including our separate work, on which we draw here) often centre around *either* young people with caring responsibilities for a family member, *or* disabled adults with dependent children. This is reflective of divisions in academic enquiry (such as 'childhood studies' and 'disability studies') and in policy and practice (such as 'children and families' and 'adult social care').

Prior to the 1990s, work in relation to disabled people as parents was often impairment-specific and concerned with 'risks' as regards child development (Olsen and Clarke, 2003). A developing policy focus on carers in the 1980s was built upon in the 1990s to identify experiences of care-giving that had previously been under-recognised. One of the most influential strands of work was that developed by Becker and his colleagues in relation to 'young carers' (Aldridge and Becker, 1993a, 1993b). Early work in this field was focused on the experience of young carers, who were considered to have missed out on the choices and opportunities of a 'normal' childhood: the policy and practice response was to develop services focused on redressing children's losses. This was critiqued as marginalising and problematising disabled adults and as producing a welfare category that insufficiently examined how young people (carers and non-carers) might experience disadvantage and loss of opportunity resulting from lack of support for their parents (eg Morris, 1997; Olsen and Parker, 1997). Further important contributors to debate and understanding in the 1990s and 2000s include disability and parenting organisations (eg the Disabled Parents Network and the Disability, Pregnancy and Parenting International), young carers organisations (eg Princess Royal Trust for Carers) and practice-focused research and development work (eg Morris and Wates, 2006, 2007; Commission for Social Care Inspection, 2009).

As social researchers, we have worked separately on research focused primarily on the experiences of disabled parents (Clarke) and of young carers (O'Dell), but share an interest in conducting research that engages with people's lived experience and seeks to contribute to service and policy development, but avoids a service-led approach. We are aware of the potential positive and negative power of administrative categories (such as 'young carer', 'mental health service user' or 'parent with learning disabilities') and are concerned that these are not imposed on the participants we engage with or in the knowledge and debates we seek to contribute to. We have both tended towards looking at family experience of disability and care in a normative way and here bring together our work to offer insights into disability and family life.

Children and young people's experience of parental disability: the 'young carer' approach

In the 1990s, children who care for a family member became subject to the public gaze and their lives became part of the national agenda for policy and research in social care. This resulted in the funding of support for young people categorised as 'young carers' and so is a strong example of research that has mobilised resources in response to an identified 'family trouble'. Arguably, this has been predicated on an understanding of care experience as problematic (although not problematic enough to remove the need for excessive young caring through resourcing support for parents), and has been based on a notion that many difficulties faced by young carers are qualitatively different to those faced by peers who may not have a specific caring experience.

The early work publicising the 'plight' of young carers involved a negative portrayal, whereby young caring was articulated as a 'curse on children' (Siddall, 1994, p 15). Aldridge and Becker (1993c) titled an early article 'The lost children', where they described children who had lost out on their childhood because of the caring duties enforced upon them. Much of the debate and concern about children as carers stems from the assumption that, in some way, they are transgressing expected roles within the family (Cass, 2007), whereby children are assumed to be dependants and should be cared for rather than caring for others. Activities of young carers are seen to be unusual and problematic because they are assumed to be outside of the usual expectations of children's activities in families (Earley et al, 2007).

It is evident that very difficult family situations and relationships are part of some young carers' family experience; sometimes this is extreme and has been directly related to involvement in inappropriate levels of care and not accessing support. In April 2007, the inquest of 13-year-old Deanne Asamoah, who had overdosed on morphine, highlighted her role over four years as a carer, reporting that she had 'struggled to care' for her terminally ill mother (Seneviratna, 2007, p 21). This tragic example was used to illustrate the need for the visibility of (and funding for) young carers, but also identified that young people providing excessive support for parents were usually doing so because of a lack of adult social care support.

Discourse about 'young carers' has often focused on loss as a consequence of care-giving itself: loss of childhood, friendships and loss of opportunities to engage fully in school and in friendship groups (O'Dell et al, 2010). Research has suggested that young carers have reduced education and employment prospects in addition to reduced social networks (Newman, 2002; Cass, 2007). Young carers often report feeling different to other children, feeling 'a freak' (Roche and Tucker, 2003, p 444), which can affect their ability to make friends and talk about their situation. This was noted by young carers in O'Dell's work:

> because of things with my mum being disabled I didn't fit in well with other people because when it came down to it the way I saw it was 'well I will try but they don't understand where I'm coming from so its very hard to relate to them because I don't go through typical issues that they do'. I mean, they would come on to the school going 'oh my mum's a bitch, she won't let me do this, she won't let me do that' and I'm sitting there thinking 'oh my God, how superficial are you, you don't even know what the hell you're talking about'. (Helena, quoted in O'Dell et al, 2010, p 648)

Young carers were positioned within these debates as 'adults before their time' (Eley, 2004, p 66), often suggesting a role reversal: 'They are in effect becoming their own parent's parents' (Aldridge and Becker, 1993c, p 378). It is this *parentification* of a child that has been presented as a significant risk, as potentially damaging for young carers. The notion that temporary or ongoing responsibility taken by children for *aspects* of their parents' well-being is a risk has been critiqued as being predicated on fixed constructions of 'adult' and 'child' roles (Keith and Morris, 1995) and for not enabling an exploration of how much involvement in care might be 'too much' (Earley and Cushway, 2002).

In order to explore why some young carers find the process of caring a more positive experience, it is useful to consider the ways in which the practices that they are engaged in are considered appropriate to their age and understanding (Aldridge, 2006; Earley et al, 2007). Activities that are within a typical range for a child of a similar age, for example, such as washing up, will be more achievable and understandable to the child. Activities that involve a high degree of skill or invasion of personal boundaries, such as giving medication or toileting an adult, are not within the realm of typical childhood experiences and thus may make more cognitive and psychological demands. The 'age appropriateness' of child involvement in supporting a parent or other family members might form part of a dialogue between social care workers and parents. It is questionable, however, how much assessments and, where received, care provision ensures 'appropriate' involvement (eg as assessed by parents and young people):

> The care manager said my 9 and 15 year olds could do housework like making beds and washing up. But in practice my daughter ended up doing my care to put me to bed with the hoist, to empty my catheter. My daughter was doing her GCSEs and I was absolutely devastated and that situation hasn't been addressed. (Disabled mother, Commission for Social Care Inspection [CSCI] Workshop Participant, quoted in CSCI, 2009, p 25)

If there is a disconnect between expressed or felt acceptable levels of care activity and the level of support a child actually has to give to a parent, this could be an isolating experience for family members. It is not surprising that young people may themselves value the recognition of their needs through a 'carer' lens, even if the predominant difficulties they face by their own assessment are not related to engaging in care itself. This may be about having one's own experiences and concerns acknowledged, or having the opportunity to connect with others who share a family experience of disability.

O'Dell et al's work elicited normative accounts of young carers that contrasted with the view of caring as negative and damaging, instead offering a more complex and fluid picture of family life in which all members contribute. The assumption that families (including children) should and do support and care for each other was a strong theme in interviews with a diverse range of 15- to 18-year-olds who took part in the study (O'Dell et al, 2006). In contrast, the 'young carer' lens in social research, policy and practice has increased awareness that some children are meeting the support requirements of their disabled parents through drawing on a discourse of family trouble and pathologising caring by children and young people. As has been discussed, while there are contexts within which care is problematic and difficult, there are also times in which care is a normative and expected aspect of family life. In addition, the dominant discourse of young carers arguably marginalised disabled parents by positioning them as the 'objects' of care rather than the active carers of their children (O'Dell et al, 2010).

Disabled parents' perspectives

Over the past two decades, both disabled parents' organisations and research with parents have challenged the invisibility and othering that has occurred in policy and research, which can be experienced in concrete ways on a regular basis. Recent work by the CSCI (2009)[1] found that insufficient visibility and excessive othering of disabled people as parents (or, indeed, as potential parents) remain significant concerns:

A lot of the problems we face are because there is a perceived contradiction between being a parent and being disabled, as if you can't actually be both. Parks can be inaccessible – many are to me and I'm a wheelchair user. Physical access to playgrounds and schools is variable. It's the perceived contradiction between being a disabled person and being a parent. It's even shown up by how disabled loos don't have condom machines – as though disabled people won't have sex! (Disabled mother, CSCI Workshop Participant, quoted in CSCI, 2009, p 21)

Researchers (including those who are themselves disabled mothers, such as Lois Keith, Jenny Morris, Ora Prilleltensky and Michele Wates) have challenged the often-present, if implicit, notion that 'being disabled' (ie having an impairment or experiencing chronic ill health) prevents people from being good parents. These writers (eg Keith and Morris, 1995; Morris, 2001; Wates, 2002; Olsen and Wates, 2003; Prilleltensky, 2004), among others (such as Newman, 2002), argue that the way in which the young carers debate has been framed (around parental dependency on children, rather than barriers to social participation, including parenting) implies that parents are failing in their duties: 'the continuing emphasis on the needs of young carers remains an accusation to disabled parents that they are failing in their duty towards their children' (Newman, 2002, p 619).

Such messages can be associated with a risk lens, whereby services are viewed as a potential threat to, rather than a support for, family life. Managing others' perceptions of children's involvement in domestic activity and 'care' might be said to be part of the 'work' of managing family life: this can be particularly acute where parents are concerned about a professional gaze on their parenting, but may also relate to concerns about day-to-day perceptions of one's mothering or fathering. One mother told Olsen and Clarke (2003, p 87) that while she was upset that her garden did not look well kept, she 'would rather have grass six foot in the air, than have people think I am getting my kids to do too much'. When parents find it difficult to access or afford appropriate external assistance, managing dilemmas and instigating strategies to mitigate any potential negative impacts of the child(ren)'s involvement in providing support can be a source of trouble for them as well as for their children.

Olsen and Clarke (2003) reported that families were concerned that services could be difficult to access, and that when services were accessed as a result of a family crisis, parental capacity rather than previous lack of appropriate support could be the central issue for professionals. The risk-focused lens on disabled people's parenting, supported by the dominant carer-focused approach, contrasts starkly with current personalisation agendas in adult social care, where support for an individual to maintain choice and control in their own lives to overcome barriers is a central part of the discourse:

> We have been a pilot on Individual Budgets ... we are mainstreaming, and self-directed support is more around barriers than function.... I would say we are moving from being impairment focused to barriers focused, as the disability equality duty and DDA [Disability Discrimination Act] kick in. (CSCI interview with Assistant Director, Adults' Social Care Services, quoted in CSCI, 2009, p 34)

While personalisation has some potential to challenge risk-focused analyses, a continued focus on risk in family focused policy can support an understanding of disability that problematises impairment and focuses on 'care' (Clarke 2010). If a pathologised visibility for disabled parents remains, bolstered by a dominant young carer lens alongside restrictive eligibility criteria for adults' services, this could make it difficult for individual disabled parents to approach, access or accept formal support ('personalised' or not). A pathologised visibility also risks masking much of the parenting work conducted by disabled parents to protect children from the negative impacts of caring (sometimes alone, sometimes alongside other family members, eg, the other biological parent or step-/social parents). Retaining the risk lens, this could mean that some children and young people are excessively protected from, rather than supported to engage in, domestic and care activity.

While a young carer lens may be problematic, research does suggest that parents can use 'young carer' to describe their child without it centring on the young person's engagement in caring activity – indeed, 'young carer' could be seen as an appropriate term by parents for some children *not* significantly involved in supporting their mother or father (Olsen and Clarke, 2003). This might be: because of the administrative access a carer label can provide to some services; because for some parents, support requirements are not routine and predictable but intermittent and varied; because the young person is seen to support others (eg the non-disabled parent or siblings) or have a general caring disposition; or because it signifies that other young people and other families share similar experiences and concerns.

The normative thread was present in Olsen and Clarke's research, with accounts of disabled parents, partners and children often more focused on what was shared with other families than what was different. This study, which engaged with families whether or not social care services were accessed (ie a 'community' sample), found that factors that support disabled people in parenting are the same as other (non-disabled) parents' requirements for caring for their children (such as adequate income, appropriate housing, the opportunity to support children to deal with problems etc) (Olsen and Clarke, 2003, p 149). For mothers and fathers, experiencing social and interpersonal (eg attitudinal) barriers or medical concerns might be experienced as distinctive, but the fact of parenthood and raising children was not. Specific personal experiences of impairment (eg pain, fatigue, self-care) could be experienced as private trouble (personally distressing), and interpersonal family experiences related to impairment (eg 'protecting' a child by deciding what information to provide or decisions concerning involving a child in care/domestic activity) could be experienced as privately troubling, in that decisions about 'what is right' in complex circumstances can be difficult. The management of private troubles and engaging in moral decision-making are likely to be familiar issues to other individuals and families where disability and impairment are not a significant part of lived experience.

Conclusion

Research can support policy and personal recognition of 'hidden' troubles (and so bring them into the public frame), yet such recognition is often dependent on accentuation of the unusual rather than the normative features of individual and family experience. In order to impact on narrow understandings of disability and family life in policy, research, practice and public discourse, we require research that presents accounts of disability from both disabled and non-disabled people, in relational contexts, outside of a service-led – or policy-led – frame. Research that operates almost exclusively within the terms of narrow policy fields (eg young carers' support and adult social care) can risk obscuring both individual and family experiences. There is evidence that administrative categories, and perhaps particularly 'carer', have become a culturally available shorthand for other facets of a personal and family life affected by disability. Research with disabled parents and family members, including young carers, demonstrates that it is valuable to focus on the ways in which adults and young people experience, understand, change and maintain their family contexts, and to explore explicitly how personal troubles (understandings and experiences) are partly shaped by service structures and policy frames.

Notes
[1] Harriet Clarke led the fieldwork and analysis for a CSCI project on support for disabled parents and their families, which involved interviews with lead informants in 50 councils and workshops with family members and professionals in four council areas.

References

Aldridge, J. (2006) 'The experiences of children living with and caring for parents with mental illness', *Child Abuse Review*, vol 15, pp 79–88.

Aldridge, J and Becker, S. (1993a) *Children who care: inside the world of young carers*, Loughborough: Loughborough University.

Aldridge, J. and Becker, S. (1993b) 'Punishing children for caring: the hidden cost of young carers', *Children & Society*, vol 7, no 4, pp 376–87.

Aldridge, J. and Becker, S. (1993c) 'The lost children', *Community Care*, 18–24 March, p 23.

Cass, B. (2007) 'Exploring social care: applying a new construct to young carers and grandparent carers', *Australian Journal of Social Issues*, vol 42, no 2, pp 241–54.

Clarke, H. (2010) 'Supporting parents to support family life: a central challenge for family minded policy', *Social Policy & Society*, vol 9, no 4, pp 567–77.

CSCI (Commission for Social Care Inspection) (2009) *Supporting disabled parents: a family or a fragmented approach?*, London: CSCI.

Earley, L. and Cushway, D. (2002) 'The parentified child', *Clinical Child Psychology and Psychiatry*, vol 7, no 2, pp 163–78.

Earley, L., Cushway, D. and Cassidy, T. (2007) 'Children's perceptions and experiences of care giving: a focus group study', *Counselling Psychology Quarterly*, vol 20, no 1, pp 69–80.

Eley (2004) '"If they don't recognise it, you've got to deal with it yourself": gender, young caring and educational support', *Gender and Education*, vol 16, no 1, pp 65–75.

Keith, L. and Morris, J. (1995) 'Easy targets: a disability perspective on the "children as carers" debate', *Critical Social Policy*, vol 15, nos 44/5, pp 36–57.

Morris, J. (1997) 'A response to Aldridge and Becker "Disability rights arguments and the denial of young carers: the dangers of zero-sum arguments"', *Critical Social Policy*, vol 17, no 51, pp 133–5.

Morris, J. (2001) 'Impairment and disability: constructing an ethics of care that promotes human rights', *Hypatia*, vol 16, no 4, pp 1–16.

Morris, J. and Wates, M. (2006) *Supporting disabled parents and parents with additional support needs*, SCIE Knowledge Review 11, London: Social Care Institute for Excellence.

Morris, J. and Wates, M. (2007) *Working together to support disabled parents*, SCIE Resource Guide 9, London: Social Care Institute for Excellence.

Newman, T. (2002) 'Young carers and disabled parents: time for a change of direction', *Disability & Society*, vol 17, no 6, pp 613–25.

O'Dell, L., Abreu, G., Cline, T. and Crafter, S. (2006) 'Young people's representations of conflicting roles in child development', final project report to the Economic and Social Research Council.

O'Dell, L., Crafter, S., Abreu, G. and Cline, T. (2010) 'Constructing "normal childhoods": young people talk about young carers', *Disability & Society*, vol 25, no 6, pp 643–55.

Olsen, R. and Clarke, H. (2003) *Parenting and disability: disabled parents' experiences of raising children*, Bristol: The Policy Press.

Olsen, R. and Parker, G. (1997) 'A response to Aldridge and Becker "Disability rights arguments and the denial of young carers: the dangers of zero-sum arguments"', *Critical Social Policy*, vol 17, no 50, pp 125–33.

Olsen, R. and Wates, M. (2003) *Disabled parents: examining research assumptions*, Dartington: Research in Practice.

Prilleltensky, O. (2004) 'My child is not my carer: mothers with physical disabilities and the well-being of children', *Disability & Society*, vol 19, no 3, pp 209–23.

Roche, J. and Tucker, S. (2003) 'Extending the social exclusion debate: an exploration of the family lives of young carers and young people with ME', *Childhood*, vol 10, no 4, pp 439–56.

Seneviratna, C. (2007) 'They are not asking a lot', *Community Care*, 21–27 June, pp 20–1.

Siddall, R. (1994) 'Lost childhood', *Community Care*, 9–15 June, pp 14–15.

Wates, M. (2002) *Supporting disabled adults in their parenting role*, York: Joseph Rowntree Foundation.

CHAPTER SEVEN

Normal problems or problem children? Parents and the micro-politics of deviance and disability

Ara Francis

Introduction

The research presented here is part of a more comprehensive study of middle-class parents who identify their children as having significant problems, such as learning and developmental disabilities, mental illnesses, and substance addictions. The data are drawn from in-depth interviews with 34 mothers and 21 fathers who are predominantly white and middle-class. Focusing on the processes of problem construction, this chapter examines how parents came to view their children as having significant problems of a particular kind.

The author's analysis is informed by a social constructionist perspective that views all problems as emerging in social interaction. This does not imply that problems are 'mere' social inventions. On the contrary, the constructionist perspective holds that problems are *real* precisely because people identify and respond to them as such. All maladies, regardless of aetiology, require social acknowledgement in order to have meaningful consequences. In the words of Charles Rosenberg and Janet Golden (1992, p xxiv), an unknown disease is like a 'tree falling in the forest with no ear to hear'.

As Robert Emerson and Sheldon Messinger (1977) argue in their seminal work on trouble, problems also are the outcomes of micro-political processes. Since every condition or behaviour contains multiple interpretive possibilities, the construction process can be fraught with uncertainty and conflict. Given the indeterminate nature of trouble, the micro-politics framework asks: who are the relevant social actors? What are their sources of power? What are their vested interests? Whose definitions of trouble prevail, in which contexts and why? This chapter draws from parents' accounts to address these questions as they relate to the construction of children's problems.

There are a number of factors important to the construction process that are not fully addressed in this discussion. Central among these is what parents perceived to be the signs and symptoms of children's troubles. Children's conditions and behaviours provided a baseline for what interpretive trajectories were possible.

In the contemporary West, for example, people view frequent seizures as medical problems, not products of wilful deviance. Although the meanings of children's problems were not inherent in their conditions and behaviours, dominant cultural understandings of those conditions and behaviours set the parameters for parents' interpretations. Children's ages, the proliferation of information about particular problems (such as autism), and parents' personal biographies also shaped definitions of the situation.

From mothers' and fathers' perspectives, mothers played a greater role than other actors (fathers, non-professionals, school personnel and medical experts) in constructing children's problems. Although women's power stemmed from their role as children's primary carers, interviews reveal that women's agency was constrained by an ever-present threat of mother-blame. Women worked to define problematic conditions and behaviours in ways that offered potential solutions and ameliorated their own ostensible culpability.

Method and participants

This research project was designed to explore how children's problems impact middle-class parents' lives. The decision to focus on middle-class parents to the exclusion of low-income or elite groups was intentional and stemmed from the sociological literature on an anxious, child-centred parenting culture, which has gained prominence in the contemporary US. Scholars of motherhood argue that this culture is characterised by an 'ideology of intensive mothering' that constructs child-rearing as an altruistic, emotionally consuming and labour-intensive project (Thurer, 1994; Hays, 1996; Douglas and Michaels, 2004). Although this model of parenting is highly feminised, research suggests that fatherhood is becoming more intensive as well (Pleck, 1987; Coltrane, 1997). In fact, data show that both mothers and fathers devote more time to childcare than their counterparts did 40 years ago (Gauthier et al, 2004; Bianchi, 2006). While the ideology of intensive parenting is widely shared, its successful performance requires symbolic and material resources. Not only do middle-class parents have more time, money and education, but their desire to maximise children's opportunities for success leads them to orchestrate children's activities, further bolstering this orientation to child-rearing (Lareau, 2003). This study was designed with this cultural landscape in mind and considers, specifically, what it is like to be the *middle-class* parent of a 'problem child' in this era of intensive, child-centred parenting.

The recruitment parameters were broad: any middle-class parent who identified his or her child as having a 'significant problem' was eligible to participate, as long as he or she could meet for a face-to-face interview in the Northern California area.[1] The author sought participants through support and advocacy groups, non-profit organisations, and schools for children with additional needs. Friends, colleagues and previous participants also referred potential participants.

Parents' annual household incomes ranged from US$30,000 to US$250,000, and the median for household incomes was US$90,000 per year. All participants had completed high school and most were college-educated. All but five participants owned their own homes, and all but three identified as Caucasian.[2]

Children's problem types varied widely. Table 7.1 summarises the problems that participants described. Children often suffered from more than one condition, and Table 7.1 reflects only primary labels and diagnoses.

Table 7.1: Summary of children's problems

Types of problem	N
Learning disabilities (attention deficit hyperactivity disorder, dyslexia and auditory processing disorder)	7
Developmental disabilities (pervasive developmental disorder, autism, Asperger's syndrome, Down's syndrome, cerebral palsy and fetal alcohol syndrome)	16
Mental health problems (depression, anxiety, attachment disorder, obsessive compulsive disorder, trichotillomania, bipolar disorder, oppositional defiance disorder)	8
Drug or alcohol addiction	8
Medical problems without developmental disabilities	1
Total	40

Interviews were structured informally to reflect an inductive, grounded approach to conducting qualitative research (see Lofland et al, 2006). Twelve participants preferred to be interviewed with their spouses, but the remaining mothers and fathers were interviewed separately. During these guided conversations, the author encouraged parents to emphasise what had been the most salient aspects of their experiences while also prompting them to discuss matters relevant to the stated purposes of the research. Each interview was documented with a handheld audio-recorder and the conversations were later converted into verbatim transcripts. This allowed data to be sorted into analytically relevant categories, a process referred to as 'coding' (Lofland et al, 2006, p 200).

The micro-politics of children's problems

As indicated by children's eventual labels and diagnoses, parents deemed a wide range of conditions and behaviours to be troublesome. Initial 'signs' and 'symptoms' that something was amiss included: underachievement in school or sports; disobedience; inability to participate in commonplace interactions; emotional outbursts; not acting one's age; and physical ailments. In most cases, trouble was fully realised only after prolonged periods of ambiguity and uneasiness, as this quote illustrates:

> Around a year old, we began to notice that he was very hypersensitive to sound, like [the] vacuum cleaner. He was a very intense baby....

> [We] put him in a toddler class when he was about two. [He] didn't want anything to do with the other kids, absolutely nothing. Cried, fussed, tended to be a very picky eater. Terrified of water splashing on him … and I began to start thinking, 'This is not normal. This is not right.' (Carol, whose son was diagnosed with Asperger's syndrome when he was four years old)

Even in cases when the first signs or symptoms of trouble seemed unambiguous, the process of naming the problem was protracted:

> The doctors never used the word 'epilepsy' with us. They always said, 'A seizure disorder, a seizure disorder' … and it's like, 'Just say it! Tell me something so I can hang on, just don't give me some general fluff term!' (Bill, whose son started having seizures when he was five months old and is now developmentally delayed)

Trouble took shape over the course of weeks, months and sometimes even years as parents interacted with their children, one another, family members and friends, school officials, and medical professionals. People commonly disagreed about the nature of children's conditions or behaviours, and out of these disagreements emerged provisional consensus about the existence and nature of children's problems.

Mothers

Although each child's problem had a unique definitional history, parents' interviews repeatedly indicated that, more than other actors, mothers marshalled the construction of children's conditions and behaviours as seriously troublesome:

> [My daughter] was starting to act … moderately depressed. And she was doing some weird stuff. She was complaining about the kids at school staring at her. 'Nobody liked her' and 'they were staring at her' and she started wearing dark glasses a lot.… I knew something was going on. And dad was denying it. (Megan, whose teenaged daughter attempted suicide and was prescribed medication for depression)

Men's interviews substantiated women's accounts; in most cases, it was mothers who initiated formal labelling processes by seeking professional help, and it was women's definitions of children's conditions and behaviours that won out in the end.

Women's power stemmed, in part, from their role as primary cares. Approximately half were stay-at-home mothers, and, in all but three cases, women who worked outside of the home still performed a majority of routine childcare. Because mothers spent more time with their children, they believed that they were in the best position to make decisions about their care:

> I'm more engaged with the kids, I'm not home more often. [My husband and I] both work full-time but [my husband] is much more of a loner and tends to spend a lot of time in his office ... we have very different approaches to [our son], and I feel like over the years I've been able to find things that will work some of the time. (Sandra, whose 13-year-old son takes a series of medication for temper tantrums, aggressive behaviour and learning problems)

At first glance, women seemed to exercise a great deal of power in the construction of children's problems. However, further examination of these data suggests that women's agency was tremendously constrained. Mothers were acutely sensitive to their ostensible responsibility for children's conditions and behaviours, and they feared that others would hold them culpable if children did not develop into 'normal' middle-class adults. In this way, their definitions of the situation emerged in response to the actions and perceived opinions of other actors.

Fathers

Compared to other relevant actors, fathers played a peripheral role in the definitional process. By their own accounts, they were initially reluctant to view their children as having significant problems. They were more apt to view children's conditions or behaviours as normal, as personality quirks or as temporary stages that they would likely grow out of (see also Singh, 2003):

> [At first I had] that mentality of, 'Oh, he'll grow out of it. He's just having a bad day, just snap out of it.' You know, and [my wife would say], 'You don't know what you're talking about'. I was in denial. (Sergio, whose 15-year-old son has mental health problems suggestive of schizophrenia)

As this quote suggests, fathers did assert their definitions of the situation, at least initially. However, their spouses persuaded them in nearly every case to see their children as having significant problems.

Mothers achieved definitional victories by tenaciously researching what they believed were significant problems and presenting themselves to their spouses as experts. Some women said that they used the information they garnered from books, articles, internet discussions and support groups as leverage: "I would come in with my new book, my new self-help, kid-has-a-problem book, and say, 'Well, check out this paragraph. Doesn't this sound like her? ... read this part'" (Martha, whose 13-year-old daughter has had learning problems since kindergarten).

What were women's vested interests in convincing fathers that their children had significant problems? First and foremost, women had a genuine desire to help their children, and they assumed that the successful identification of children's problems – particularly in biomedical terms – would lead to effective solutions. At the same time, some women were responding to the blame that they perceived as emanating from extended family members, friends, acquaintances and strangers. These non-professional actors encouraged women in a number of ways to seek professional help for their children's conditions and behaviours.

Non-professional actors

Although they did not have the power to officially label children as having particular types of problem, and although they were without formal leverage of any kind, extended family members, friends, acquaintances and even strangers played a key role in constructing children's conditions and behaviours as problematic, particularly when children were young. Women used others as sounding boards for their own concerns and looked to them for confirmation of their definitions of the situation:

> When [my daughter] was two-and-a-half, a neighbour mentioned [that] maybe I should get her hearing tested. And I thought, 'Oooh, maybe other people are noticing it now too.' And I thought, 'It's not just me.' Because I began to notice it when she was two. (Anna, whose adult daughter is developmentally delayed)

Children's condition and behaviours also disrupted parents' interactions with family members, friends, acquaintances and strangers. This served as a signal to parents that something was wrong:

> I think deep down I knew something was off about him ... it's been a slow process.... [In preschool], he'd always be the epicentre of problems. [Other parents] would give me the looks, or they would avoid me and not talk to me because they figured I was a bad parent ... I thought, 'Maybe they're right!' (Paula, whose son was diagnosed with attention deficit hyperactivity disorder [ADHD] when he was four years old)

The mothers of young children were particularly vulnerable to interactions like these, in part because they spent more time accompanying children in public venues and had formed relationships that revolved around children's activities.

As Paula's comment suggests, the power of family members, friends, acquaintances and strangers to define children's conditions and behaviours stemmed from their ability to informally sanction women for their maternal practices. Consistent with a legacy of mother-blame in the modern and late-modern West (eg Thurer,

1994; Ladd–Taylor and Umansky, 1998; Garey and Arendell, 2001), mothers often anticipated and interpreted others' responses to children's conditions and behaviours as poor estimations of their own parenting:

> Actually my own family, one of my sisters, didn't get it at all ... I imagine they think that my parenting is poor, I'm not setting enough limits, the kid is getting away with things he shouldn't, he's spoiled. (Jessica, whose six-year-old son has ill-defined mental health problems)

Uncomfortable interactions that intimated blame encouraged women's efforts to identify and, more importantly, fix whatever was wrong. This may seem like a contradictory response. If others assumed that they were culpable, why did mothers not insist that their children were problem-free? There may have been two reasons that they did not do so. First, faced with the suggestion that something was seriously wrong, a refusal to concur might be construed as 'denial'. This could further mark women as bad parents. As noted earlier, several parents, most often fathers, described themselves as having been 'in denial' about the onset of children's problems. Mothers' comments indicate that this was an undesirable state of mind, something that they had to work through or overcome:

> For many parents, there's a real denial at first ... they try to explain it away. And I think I did that, certainly [laughs]. Like, 'He'll grow out of it.' [But] I wouldn't be afraid to get evaluated ... [don't be] afraid to get support sooner rather than later, for everybody's sake. (Jessica, giving advice to other parents whose children may have mental health problems)

As discussed later in more detail, psychological and biomedical definitions of the situation ameliorated women's ostensible culpability for having caused children's problems. This also might explain women's eagerness to seek professional help. Indeed, given the ever-present threat of mother-blame, many women worked hard to secure labels that both indicated solutions and situated problems firmly within the child, rather than between child and parent.

Schoolteachers and administrators

Parents' accounts suggest that school officials played a key role in the construction of teenaged children's deviance, as well as young children's learning disabilities and behavioural problems. Unlike family members, friends, acquaintances and strangers, school personnel could formally sanction children. They suspended and expelled teenagers for drug use, truancy and fighting. They gave children poor grades. They called meetings to discuss students' deficiencies, and sometimes told parents, in no uncertain terms, that their children had problems requiring professional intervention. In many cases, parents who had been ambivalent about their children's conditions or behaviours felt compelled in these circumstances to define them as seriously troublesome:

> We were always, I think, a little concerned. [But] again, I put it off more to – as I told you earlier – boy being boy.... It wasn't until really his freshman year ... we really started to get some inkling I think, of 'There's some real deep issues here...'. He got in some trouble and missed the first day [of school], [and] I think we were nervous from that point forward ... and then, of course, he had the fights [when he was a sophomore] and was expelled right around Thanksgiving of that year. (Phil, who sent his teenaged son to a therapeutic boarding school when he was found using and selling drugs)

Occasionally, schoolteachers and administrators encouraged parents to view their children's problems in medical terms and to administer pharmaceutical treatments, even when parents were reluctant to do so:

> [Our son's] behaviour or wiring was becoming more and more of a problem for [his] teachers within the dynamics of the classroom. And so we said, 'Ok, well, we need to try something.' We had talked with the teachers and [were] a little reticent to medicate him ... [but] we finally did it and that day, the first day that [he was] medicated, both teachers said 'Oh my God, what a huge difference.' (Mike, whose son was diagnosed with ADHD when he was four years old)

At the same time, schoolteachers and administrators were key sources of mother-blame, often implying quite strongly that women had caused children's problems:

> [The teachers] were just saying ... 'What's the situation at home? What's going on at home?' I'd say, 'Excuse me? We're talking about a first-grader, and you're thinking I'm doing something wrong at home or our home life is in disarray? I mean, where are you going with this?' And they'd back off a little, but they'd say, 'Well, you know, you just never know with these things, and children are very sensitive to things going on at home.' (Martha, whose 13-year-old daughter has had learning problems since kindergarten)

Beyond a desire to help children, it is likely that teachers and administrators had their own reasons for taking action. When children's conditions or behaviours upset the dynamics of the classroom and made their jobs more difficult, or when a particular label gave them the bureaucratic means to secure educational funding from the state, it was in their own interests, and the interests of their schools, to advocate for particular constructions of children's problems:

> Even the school psychologists, they'll say 'autistic type tendencies'.
> So they really haven't labelled him … autistic. [But] they need to put
> something on him. So the school's special education just basically
> slapped autism [on him] because they get a bigger pot of money, or a
> better source of money … if they put that label on him. (Bill, whose
> son has developmental disabilities and an ill-defined seizure disorder)

As this quote suggests, educational placement and funding are often contingent
upon specific biomedical labels. By suggesting that parents (most often mothers) are
to blame for children's problems, while, at the same time, suggesting that children's
conditions and behaviours are medically diagnosable, teachers and administrators
catalysed mothers' efforts to seek professional intervention.

Medical professionals

At the level of popular discourse, the widespread medicalisation of childhood
is an important context for understanding mothers' role in the construction of
children's problems. While medical and biological accounts did not necessarily
protect parents from blame, self-doubt or guilt, they did have the potential to
diminish their culpability for having caused children's problems:

> Then it came time for the findings, and [the doctor] says, 'Well the
> good news is it's not your parenting style. You're doing as well and
> more as can be expected … based on 10 traits that are indicators of
> ADD/ADHD [Attention Deficit Hyperactivity Disorder], [your son]
> has eight of 'em real strongly.' And he says, 'So considering he has eight
> of 'em real strongly, you guys are doing amazingly well.' (Mike, whose
> son was diagnosed with ADHD when he was four years old)

Some women used biomedical accounts of their children's problems to avoid or
manage stigma and blame (see also Farrugia, 2009):

> [My sister] thought I wasn't limit-setting enough … I think she gets
> it now … it's not just me telling her that there's some neurological,
> biological thing going on. It's like, you know, this is finally somebody
> [else], an expert, said [it]. (Jessica, whose six-year-old son has ill-defined
> mental health problems)

While medical discourse strongly shaped parents' understandings of children's
problems, interviews suggest that mothers – rather than individual doctors –
were the chief purveyors of medicalisation. Doctors played a key role in the
construction of *traditional disabilities*, such as cerebral palsy, fragile X syndrome and
hyperinsulinism. However, when it came to invisible disabilities, such as learning
problems, mild developmental delays and mental health problems, doctors more

commonly served to verify or refute mothers' pre-existing definitions of the situation. As mentioned earlier, the mothers in this study often framed themselves as experts and did extensive research on their children's conditions and behaviours. By the time they sought professional intervention, they often had particular diagnoses in mind:

> Actually, I found [attachment disorders] on the internet, is what happened. I, like, typed in [our daughter's] symptoms. 'Cause it was so frustrating not to know what was going on! And it was clear that that's what it was. (Jen, whose 13-year-old daughter later received a formal diagnosis from an attachment specialist)

When doctors or psychologists did not confirm mothers' definitions of the situation, women sought second and third evaluations. One mother was convinced her son was suffering from mental health problems because her own brother had committed suicide. She visited multiple doctors until she found one who shared her opinion. Sergio, her spouse, explained:

> We just kept going to doctors. And [our son] has had so many different diagnoses … we got to the point where we were going to doctors on a weekly basis, just to find the best [care] for our son. [One doctor kept] going back to ADHD, whatever, and we knew it wasn't that.

Sociologists argue that the health care system in the US increasingly positions doctors as go-betweens who manage the interests of insurance and pharmaceutical companies on the one hand, and the interests of health care consumers on the other. This limits doctors' power and makes patients themselves key players in the processes of medicalisation (Conrad, 2005). Parents' accounts lend support to this thesis. With an increasing number of medical and psychological ailments that have no sensitive or specific markers, educated and affluent health care consumers, like the mothers in this study, shop for diagnoses and treatments that align with their definitions of the situation.

Conclusion

This chapter has examined parents' construction of children's problems, focusing in particular on the role of mother-blame in encouraging women to define children's conditions and behaviours as indicative of serious, underlying problems. Much of the scholarship on children's problems focuses on aetiology, without considering how problems are socially constructed. The analysis offered here raises important questions about whose interests are served by the widespread problematisation and medicalisation of children's conditions and behaviours. Whose interests are served by learning disability diagnoses and pharmaceutical interventions? Whose interests are served when teenaged children are sent to therapeutic boarding schools in order to treat their drug problems? This research highlights how children's problems are constructed in ways that reflect the interests of the adults that surround them. The extent to which children benefit from this process is an empirical question that deserves further attention.

When considering the relevance of these findings to other studies, it is important to keep two things in mind. First, these data are drawn from parents' own accounts, and it is quite possible that mothers and fathers portray themselves as having had more or less power than they actually did. Second, this study's conclusions pertain to a largely white, affluent and highly educated group of parents. We cannot assume that the power relationships described here would hold true for less privileged mothers and fathers. Future research on the micro-politics of children's problems would do well to examine whether or not parents' experiences vary across social class and to explore the accounts of other relevant actors, such as doctors, teachers and children. Finally, this study accords children a passive role in the problem construction process, but we know that children can actively pursue or resist problem labels (eg Gillies, 2011, pp 196–7). A more comprehensive understanding of this topic would consider not just the role of adults in interpreting and naming children's conduct, but also the role of children themselves.

Notes

[1] 'Middle class' is defined by reference to annual household income, level of education and home-ownership status.

[2] The remaining three participants identified as Filipino, Asian and Mexican.

References

Bianchi, S., J. P. Robinson and Milkie, M. (2006) *Changing rhythms of American family life*, New York, NY: Russell Sage Foundation.

Coltrane, S. (1997) *Family man*, New York, NY: Oxford University Press.

Conrad, P. (2005) 'The shifting engines of medicalization', *The Journal of Health and Social Behavior*, vol 46, no 1, pp 3–14.

Douglas, S. and Michaels, M. (2004) *The mommy myth: The idealization of motherhood and how it has undermined women*, New York, NY: Free Press.

Emerson, R.M. and Messinger, S.L. (1977) 'The micro-politics of trouble', *Social Problems*, vol 25, no 2, pp 121–35.

Farrugia, D. (2009) 'Exploring stigma: medical knowledge and the stigmatisation of parents of children diagnosed with autism spectrum disorder', *Sociology of Health & Illness*, vol 31, no 7, pp 1011–27.

Garey, A. and Arendell, T. (2001) 'Children, work, and family: some thoughts on "mother-blame"', in R. Hertz and N. Marshall (eds) *Working families: the transformation of the American home*, Berkeley, CA: University of California Press, pp 293–303.

Gauthier, A.H., Smeedeng, T.M. and Furstenberg, F.F. (2004) 'Are parents investing less time in children? Trends in selected industrialized countries', *Population and Development Review*, vol 30 , pp 647–71.

Gillies, V. (2011) 'Social and emotional pedagogies: critiquing the new orthodoxy of emotion in classroom behaviour management', *British Journal of Sociology of Education*, vol 32, no 2, pp 185–202.

Hays, S. (1996) *Cultural contradictions of motherhood*, New Haven, CT: Yale University Press.

Ladd–Taylor, M. and Umansky, L. (eds) (1998) *'Bad' mothers*, New York, NY: New York University Press.

Lareau, A. (2003) *Unequal childhoods: class, race and family life*, Berkeley, CA: University of California Press.

Lofland, J., Snow D., Anderson, L. and Lofland, L.H. (2006) *Analyzing social settings*, Belmont, CA: Wadsworth/Thomson Learning.

Pleck, J. (1987) 'American fathering in historical perspective', in M.S. Kimmell (ed) *Changing men: new directions in research on men and masculinity*, Thousand Oaks, CA: Sage Publications, pp 83–97.

Rosenberg, C. and Golden, J. (1992) *Framing disease*, New Brunswick, NJ: Rutgers University Press.

Singh, I. (2003) 'Boys will be boys: fathers' perspectives on ADHD symptoms, diagnosis and drug treatment', *Harvard Review of Psychiatry*, vol 11, no 6, pp 308–16.

Thurer, S.L. (1994) *The myths of motherhood*, Boston, MA: Houghton Mifflin Company.

CHAPTER EIGHT

Troubled talk and talk about troubles: moral cultures of infant feeding in professional, policy and parenting discourses

Helen Lomax

Introduction

This chapter examines the ways in which policy agendas and contemporary notions of the 'good mother' frame infant feeding practices, rendering them a site of moral and interactional trouble. Drawing on analysis of mothers' talk with midwives during the first days of motherhood, the chapter explores the ways in which breastfeeding confers a positive maternal identity, while choosing not to do so is associated with a deficit identity against which mothers struggle to present themselves as good parents. The chapter suggests that mothers' interactions with professionals are important places for exploring the ways in which 'ordinary' family practices may be troubled by professional and policy agendas that may conflict with women's embodied experiences and cultural beliefs about what constitutes a healthy, well-fed baby. A focus on these encounters makes visible the rich texture of maternal labour and its complex and troubling relationship with policy.

Infant feeding: a troubled policy terrain?

Despite widely reported health benefits and a national and international policy agenda to increase the uptake and duration of breastfeeding, the UK has one of the lowest breastfeeding rates in the developed world (WHO, 2003; Bolling et al, 2007; DH, 2007; ONS, 2007). While both the Department of Health and the World Health Organization recommend that mothers breastfeed exclusively for the first six months, most do not, and by six months of age, only 2% of infants are wholly breastfed and 75% receive no breast milk at all (Bolling et al, 2007; ONS, 2007; Hoddinott et al, 2008). However, while formula-feeding might be considered 'normal' in statistical terms, survey and interview-based research suggests that, for many, it is experienced as 'non-normative' and troubling. While the majority of mothers report their intentions to breastfeed, a significant number express regret at stopping breastfeeding earlier than they had anticipated and feel stigmatised for their decisions not to breastfeed or to stop breastfeeding (Dykes, 2005; Hoddinott et al, 2008), indicating a troubling gap between mothers' expectations and experiences.

A useful perspective on this issue is offered by Lee's suggestion that mothers' breastfeeding troubles are symptomatic of a wider political agenda and the intensification of parenting, such that matters that were once the private concerns of families are increasingly contested and problematised (Knaak, 2005; Lee and Bristow, 2009; Lee et al, 2010). As Lee and others argue, the construction of breastfeeding in UK policy as the only reasonable maternal choice reflects the currency of the idea that parents themselves present a significant risk to their children's health and a means by which mothers are increasingly measured and measure themselves (Blum, 2000; Murphy, 1999; Marshall et al, 2007; Kukla, 2008; Knaak, 2010; Lee et al, 2010). However, while this analysis offers an important critique of UK public policy, in empirical terms, its restriction to an examination of policy documents and survey and interview data is such that it offers limited insight into mothers' lived experiences at this time.

Of further relevance are the tensions suggested by policy and guidance, which tasks midwives, the primary providers of care during this period, with both working to a woman-centred agenda and also promoting and supporting breastfeeding (Page and McCandlish, 2006; Leap, 2009). This may be illustrated with reference to the Royal College of Midwives' (2004, p 1) breastfeeding position statement, which affirms midwives' requirement to 'promote informed choice and support women in their chosen method of infant feeding', and in the National Institute for Clinical Excellence (NICE, 2006) guidance in which the importance of information, advice and support for breastfeeding is prioritised alongside an emphasis on woman- and baby-centred care that recognises 'the views, beliefs and values of the woman, her partner and her family'. However, despite wider feminist interest in mothers' 'complicated relationship with medical institutions and spaces' (Kukla, 2008, p 69), the ways in which these policy priorities are mobilised in practice has been little researched.

Methods and analysis

This chapter addresses this deficit in the literature in order to examine the ways in which mothers and midwives talk about and practically manage infant feeding at the level of service delivery. Drawing on researcher-generated videotapes of midwives' routine visits to mothers (Lomax, 2005, 2011), the analysis considers the ways in which policy priorities are 'talked into being' (Heritage, 1984) and the implications for women's moral identities. For brevity, the analysis focuses on three visits to three mothers: 'Megan', who is successfully breastfeeding her first baby; 'Emily', who is experiencing difficulties breastfeeding her second baby; and 'Chloe', a first-time mother who is formula-feeding her daughter. Data, which was transcribed and analysed using a modified form of conversation analysis (c.a.) and discursive analysis (d.a.) (Reynolds and Taylor, 2005; Wooffitt, 2005; Heath et al,

2010), is presented in the form of transcribed sequences in order to make visible the ways in which dominant and residual narratives (eg about what constitutes appropriate mothering) are deployed and resisted.

A focus on the 'architecture of talk' (Heritage, 1984), which encompasses the ways in which turns at talk are allocated – whether they proceed smoothly or dysfluently, or display agreement or resistance – enables an exploration of the ways in which particular maternal identities are discursively constructed. Drawing on these examples, the analysis explores the ways in which mothers' infant feeding choices are discursively sanctioned and how this is made visible through the absence or presence of 'trouble'. This includes the ways in which breastfeeding is acknowledged to present both practical and corporeal challenges for mothers (talk is *about* troubles), but, more particularly, the ways in which midwives' questions and mothers' responses generate accounts that are universally positioned vis-a-vis a discourse of 'breast is best' (through which talk *is* troubled). Accordingly, mothers who do not breastfeed or who are contemplating stopping can be seen do a great deal of rhetorical work to present their decisions as legitimate in order to defend against the implicit allegation of a less than ideal 'choice'. As the chapter explores, the degree to which mothers acknowledge or rebuke this charge is apparent in the ways in which talk is visibly dysfluent or 'troubled'.

Breast is best? A morally sanctioned maternal identity

The idea that breastfeeding confers a particular identity as a 'good mother' is immediately evident in the midwife's opening remarks in Megan's consultation (reproduced in Figure 8.1[1]).

Analysis of this sequence suggests unequivocal support for the mother's decision to breastfeed. The midwife's repeated use of positive and enthusiastic descriptions of the baby as 'look[ing] so happy' (line 5) and the mother herself as 'a <u>wonderful</u> breastfeeder' (line 11) convey the appropriateness of Megan's choice and its association with a positive maternal identity. However, the midwife's construction of the mother as 'doing so brilliantly' is not entirely unproblematic, Megan's question 'how do you know if he's actually taking anything in?' (lines 3–4) articulates a familiar concern that it is not possible to measure the amount a breastfed baby consumes. The midwife's response, which includes the assessment that Megan is 'doing brilliantly', implies that she is succeeding at something that is potentially quite difficult in a way that also sidesteps Megan's concerns. As a strategy, its limitations may be deduced by the re-emergence of Megan's unease moments later (line 17: 'is it normally – are there normally problems?'). Of significance, too, are the ways in which Megan phrases her unease, foregrounding it as connected to her own inexperience in ways that moderate its threat to the midwife's construction of untroubled breastfeeding. In this way, Megan's talk acknowledges the dominance of a rhetoric in which breastfeeding is constructed as natural and uncomplicated, while also making visible the midwife's rights within the asymmetrical order of interaction to define it as such.

Figure 8.1: Megan: a sanctioned identity

1	M	I don't like to (.) ur: interrupt you when you are
2		feeding so beautifully
		(2.3)
3	C	I was just-I don't-how do you know if he's actually
4		taking anything (in) (.)
5	M	well he certainly looks as if he is he looks so happy
		(0.9)
6		u↑m (.) he's getting collostrum of course at the
		[
7	C	um:
8	M	moment (.) you haven't got gallons
9		there of course but I mean you know
10	C	it does look like it ahahah
11	M	you're going to be a <u>wonderful</u> breastfeeder
12		I mean you're you're doing so brilliantly
13		is this ↑really your first baby
14	C	um::
15	M	I can't believe it ahaha (0.8) how
16		did you get to be so good! ahah
17	C	((smiling)) is it normally-are there
18		normally problems?

Breastfeeding as troubling: a deficit maternal identity?

The theme of glossed and silenced troubles is continued in Emily's encounter with her midwife (see Figure 8.2), which begins with Emily's vivid description of leaking breasts (lines 71–77), a fractious and unhappy baby (lines 3–5) and her efforts to manage these difficulties, including her decision to supplement with formula milk (line 5).

Emily's talk presents her experiences as practically difficult but herself as a morally active mother. Analysis of the ways in which her talk is organised reveals the ways in which she robustly constructs her decision to formula-feed as predicated not on 'choice' – which might engender a charge of self-interest – but as the desperate last resort for a baby that 'wouldn't settle' and 'was gettin' in a state'. Moreover, her explanation that formula was only offered *after* she had breastfed positions her action as a supplement offered by a mother who is ordinarily committed to breastfeeding, in ways that defend against the 'moral danger' associated with formula-feeding (Murphy, 1999). The midwife's response 'That's a shame' (quietly delivered and accompanied with mild laughter) displays and makes visible that this is indeed a less than ideal practice.

The imperative for Emily to justify her decision is evident in the embodied and practical context in which she elaborates her explanation. As the video and transcript reveal, Emily, who has experienced an extended hospital stay following her baby's admission to special care, is struggling to catch up with

Figure 8.2: Emily: a troubled maternal identity

1	M	Are you-you're putting her on and she's
2	M	going on alright is she?
3	C	Yeah she's going on alright (.) Last night she
4		wouldn't settle um and I tried to feed and she
5		was gettin' in a state so I did make up a bottle
		of SMA
6	M	Oh right
7	C	Um and I gave her that
8	M	*That's a shame when you have got all that ahaha*
9	C	That's right yeah ((laughter))
10		But um she was getting frustrated and um
		((Mother gets up to let dog in))
11	M	yeah
12	C	she had fed a lot off me but then um
66	M	And you know she might feed every two
67		hours one day and then she'll gradually sort
68		herself out ((inaudible – dog barking))
69	C	Because last night I mean – Whistler ((dog))
70		GO AND LIE DOWN– I
71		um I mean last night I put towels under
72		the sheet because I was actually saturated
73	M	((inaudible – dog barking))
74	C	Um and I thought well it ain't getting on the
75		mattress and I thought well if it is going to
76		be like this I was going to give up you know
77		like breastfeeding because I can't you know
78	M	Oh no don't do that!

housework (there are piles of laundry waiting to be sorted, her attention to which constitutes an ongoing disruption to proceedings), she also has a toddler and two large dogs, whose noisy presence continually threatens to disrupt the flow of the visit. Physically, she is in considerable discomfort. Her breasts leak, she has perineal trauma, untreated cystitis and severe bruising to her thigh caused by the administration of pain relief during labour. However, within the context of breastfeeding 'advice', these difficulties appear themselves insufficient to justify her decision. They are barely acknowledged by the midwife, who deploys minimal response tokens (Heritage, 1984) (lines 6: 'Oh right'; and line 11: 'yeh'), which avoid engagement with the emotional content of Emily's speech. Moreover, the suggestion that breastfeeding may necessitate feeding every two hours (line 66) ignores the very evident practical difficulties this will entail in this context. What it does illustrate, however, is the ways in which the imperative to improve breastfeeding rates may conflict with a policy agenda that seeks to prioritise woman–centred care.

Formula-feeding: troubling the normal?

This final sequence considers the ways in which Chloe's decision to formula-feed is troubled in her encounter with her midwife (see Figure 8.3). The ensuing talk indicates a wider moral and policy framework within which mothers are called to account for their decisions in ways that can be seen to trouble 'normal' decisions to formula-feed.

Figure 8.3: Chloe: a stigmatised maternal identity

51	M	Are you feedin' her?(.2) yourself breastfeeding?
		[ ]
52	C	no
53	M	bottle-feeding yes?
		[ ]
54	C	bottle-feeding yes
55	M	right
		(1.2)
56	M	that's what you planned to do was it?
57	C	yes
		[
58	M	yeah^
59	C	It's never really appealed to me
60	M	^Fair enough^ she'll survive alright love
61	C	/That's it/ She's doin' fine
62	M	and what you given' her SMA? Cow and Gate?
		[ ]
63	C	oyster *is it oyster?*
64	M	Oster-
65	C	-Oster?
66	M	yeah
		(1.5) ((smiling at baby))
67	M	She's lovely
		(.)
68	M	I'll leave he asleep for a bit ...

This is immediately evident in the midwife's opening question, which assumes (incorrectly) that Chloe is breastfeeding (line 51:'Are you feedin' her?'), generating an uncomfortable pause and necessitating a clarification (the tag 'yourself breastfeeding?'). Further difficulty is generated by Chloe's negative response, which, as the c.a. literature elaborates, is 'dis-preferred' in the normative order of conversation. While speakers usually organise questions in ways that solicit agreement and social cohesion (Hutchby and Wooffitt, 1998), talk in this sequence becomes rapidly dysfluent, characterised by non-normative pauses in which the mother negates to speak, signalling her increased disengagement and discomfort with this topic (lines 55–56, 66–67 and 67–68). Chloe's refusals necessitate the midwife's additional turns (eg at line 56 'that's what you planned to do was it?').

However, rather than repairing the interaction, this generates further trouble, obliging Chloe to reveal that breastfeeding 'never really appealed'. In terms of a policy and popular discourse in which good mothers are positioned as acting in the best interests of their children, Chloe's explanation is fragile at best. It also generates some difficulty for the midwife, who, in policy terms, is unlikely to sanction such a 'choice' but is also obliged to support the mother's decision-making. The midwife's discomfort is evident in the way in which she articulates her response; as a higher pitch utterance that acknowledges the mother's right to make this choice (line 60: 'fair enough') and the (less than ideal) consequences for Emily's daughter (that she will 'survive'). The mother's response (line 61: '/ That's it/ She's doin' fine') upgrades the midwife's appraisal, while it's production (rapidly uttered, with an emphasis on 'fine') indicates disagreement with the midwife's assessment (Pomerantz, 1984).

Discussion and concluding remarks

Analysis of these sequences makes visible the ways in which breastfeeding provides a morally sanctioned identity for mothers in ways that can be seen to trouble mothers' 'normal' infant feeding practices. As the data reveal, mothers experience breastfeeding as practically and physically difficult, troubles that are exacerbated by the alignment of breastfeeding with a policy and professional agenda in which it is positioned as the embodiment of good mothering. Midwives' construction of breastfeeding as a positive expression of maternal identity appears to gloss over mothers' embodied experiences, such that mothers who are experiencing problems breastfeeding have difficulty giving voice to their experiences. In contrast, mothers who choose not to breastfeed struggle to construct a positive maternal identity and, moreover, are subject to a particular form of surveillance as they are called to account for their decisions. This analysis suggest that professional–mother interactions are important places to explore the ways in which 'ordinary' family practices are framed and troubled by policy agendas and their mobilisation. Analysis of the ways in which mothers are discursively positioned and position themselves in relation to a political and professional hegemony of 'breast is best' reveals the ways in which, irrespective of infant feeding 'choice', mothers are acutely attentive to and troubled by a rhetoric of ideal mothering that negates the complexities of maternal labour.

Note
[1] A summary of transcription notation is contained in the Appendix at the end of this chapter.

References

Blum, L. (2000) *At the breast: ideologies of breastfeeding and motherhood in the contemporary United States*, Boston, MA: Beacon Press.

Bolling, K., Grant, K., Hamlyn, B. and Thornton, A. (2007) *Infant feeding survey*, United Kingdom: Information Centre, Government Statistical Service.

DH (Department of Health) (2007) *Standard 1: promoting health and well-being, identifying needs and intervening early, national service framework for children young people and maternity services*, London: Crown.

Dykes, F. (2005) '"Supply" and "demand": breastfeeding as labour', *Social Science and Medicine*, vol 60, no 10, pp 2283–93.

Heath, C., Hindmarsh, P. and Luff, P. (2010) *Video in qualitative research: analysing social interaction in everyday life*, London: Sage.

Heritage, J. (1984) *Garfinkel and ethnomethodology*, Cambridge: Polity Press.

Hoddinott, D., Tappin, D. and Wright, C.(2008) 'Breastfeeding', *British Medical Journal*, vol 336, p 881.

Hutchby, I. and Wooffitt, R. (1998) *Conversation analysis: principles, practices and applications*, Cambridge: Polity Press.

Knaak, S. (2005) 'Breastfeeding, bottle feeding and Dr Spock: the shifting context of choice', *Canadian Review of Sociology and Anthropology*, vol 42, pp 197–216.

Knaak, S. (2010) 'Contextualising risk, constructing choice: breasting and good mothering in risk society', *Health, Risk and Society*, vol 12, no 4, pp 345–55.

Kukla, R. (2008) 'Measuring mothering', *The International Journal of Feminist Approaches to Bio-ethics*, vol 1, no 1, pp 67–90.

Leap, N. (2009) 'Woman–centred or women–centred care: does it really matter?', *British Journal of Midwifery*, vol 17, no 1, pp 12–16.

Lee, E. and Bristow, J. (2009) 'Rules for feeding babies', in S.D. Sclater, F. Ebtehaj, E. Jackson, E. and M. Richards (eds) *Regulating autonomy: sex, reproduction and family*, Oxford: Hart, pp 73–91.

Lee, E., Macvarish, J. and Bristow, J. (2010) 'Risk, health and parenting culture', *Health, Risk & Society*, vol 12, no 4, pp 293–300.

Lomax, H. (2005) 'Mothers, midwives and the interactional accomplishment of the birth story during routine postnatal care', unpublished PhD thesis, Department of Sociological Studies, University of Sheffield.

Lomax, H. (2011) 'Visual identities: choreographies of gaze, body movement and speech in mother–midwife interaction', in P. Reavey (ed) *Visual methods in psychology: using and interpreting images in qualitative research*, Abingdon: Routledge.

Marshall, J., Godfrey, M. and Renfrew, M. (2007) 'Being a "good mother": managing breastfeeding and merging identities', *Social Science and Medicine*, vol 65, no 10, pp 2147–59.

Murphy, E. (1999) '"Breast is best": infant feeding decisions and maternal deviance', *Sociology of Health & Illness*, vol 21 no 2, pp 187–208.

NICE (National Intitute for Clinical Excellence) (2006) 'Postnatal care: routine postnatal care of women and their babies', Clinical Guidelines CG37, July.

ONS (Office for National Statistics) (2007) *Infant feeding survey 2005*, London: ONS.

Page, L. and McCandlish, R. (2006) *The new midwifery: science and sensitivity in practice*, London: Churchill Livingstone.

Pomerantz, A. (1984) 'Agreeing and disagreeing with assessments: some features of preferred/dispreferred turn shapes', in J.M. Atkinson and J. Heritage (eds) *Structures of social action: studies in conversation analysis*, Cambridge: Cambridge University Press.

Reynolds, J. and Taylor, S. (2005) 'Narrating singleness: life stories and deficit identities', *Narrative Enquiry*, vol 15, no 2, pp197–215.

Royal College of Midwives (2004) 'Position statement on infant feeding, no. 5', RCN.

WHO (World Health Organization) (2003) *Global strategy for infant and young child feeding*, Geneva: WHO.

Wooffitt, R. (2005) *Conversation analysis and discourse analysis: a comparative and critical introduction*, London: Sage.

Appendix

Table A8.1: Transcription notation

Symbol	Explanation
M	Midwife
C	Mother
[ ]	Overlap in speakers' talk
(0.5)	Pause in speech, in this case, of 0.5 seconds
(.)	Pause of less than one tenth of a second
<u>word</u>	Speaker's <u>stress</u> on a word or phrase
SHOUT	Word or phrase spoken much louder than surrounding text
/That's it/	Word or phrase spoken more rapidly than surrounding text
^Fair enough^	Word or phrase spoken at higher pitch than surrounding text
word	Word or phrase spoken more quietly than surrounding text
(word)	Transcriber's uncertainty about what was said
wo::rd	Extension of the sound preceding the colon (the more colons the longer the sound)
word↑	A rise in intonation occurring in the sound preceding the symbol
((raises head))	Contains transcriber's description

CHAPTER NINE

Children's non-conforming behaviour: personal trouble or public issue?

Geraldine Brady

Introduction

In the UK, government policy increasingly seeks to define the meaning of 'good' parenting and to link responsible parenting with successful outcomes for children. This is just one of a number of powerful discourses which influence family life. Parents' perceptions of their child when development or behaviour does not appear to conform to societal norms are influenced by the pervasive discourses of health, normality, childhood and, indeed, parenting. In this chapter, I explore how a subsection of parents makes sense of 'difference' in their child in comparison to other children, providing insight into how family troubles, such as children's challenging and non-conforming behaviour, become in some cases normalised and in others a matter for wider concern, often requiring intervention. Drawing on data from qualitative research into the experience of attention deficit hyperactivity disorder (ADHD) diagnosis, I illustrate how the behaviour of some children becomes differentiated from the norm and problematised through a process that is underpinned by the dominant biomedical model of health. There are, in turn, unforeseen implications when troubles within the family become troubles outside of the family. Reflection on the following tension is encouraged: biomedical diagnosis of emotional and behavioural difficulties (including ADHD) leads to children's behaviour being framed as a specific medical condition, which prompts specialist intervention, thereby rendering a somewhat private, family trouble as a more public issue (Mills, 1959). Simultaneously, a medical diagnosis can work to depoliticise troublesome behaviour so that it is regarded not as intrinsically related to the structure of the social system, but as an individualised problem (Zola, 1972; Conrad, 1976).

'Medicalisation' of non-conforming behaviour

The ways in which 'problems' become defined in medical terms, as an illness or a disorder requiring a medical intervention, have long concerned critics of medicine (Freidson, 1970; Zola, 1972; Conrad, 1975, 1976, 1992; for discussion, see also Ballard and Elston, 2005). The process by which children's behaviour becomes medicalised is greatly influenced by discourses of 'health', 'normality', 'childhood' and, indeed, parenting, with the construction of new medical categories often being heavily promoted by pharmaceutical companies and growing consumer power (Conrad, 1976). One of the consequences of the growth of medical knowledge in the 20th century was the proliferation of different types of 'child', differentiated into categories of perceptual difference from some notional model of the 'normal' child (Armstrong, 1983) and linked to an overriding concern with the health of the nation (Armstrong, 1995). ADHD could be said to be one of these categories. As yet, there is no definitive test, it is diagnosed with reference to the *American Psychiatric Association's diagnostic and statistical manual* (*DSMIV* APA, 1994, Version V is currently under review), and the three main dimensions are inattention, impulsivity and overactivity. Assessment is made by obtaining a full case history, conducting a physical examination (including measures of height, weight and blood pressure, and the testing of fine and gross motor skills), observing behaviour, gathering information from parents and schools and by considering other explanations for concerning behaviour. Representations of ADHD within the media fall into two categories: the biological or the psychosocial. At first sight, these explanations appear to compete, but what both have in common is their implication that 'something must be done to regulate young people, parenting and society in general' (Horton-Salway, 2011, p 546).

ADHD can be said to be partly based on observations of unacceptable, inappropriate, deviant behaviour that flouts social norms. Over time, what may previously have been thought of as a social problem becomes a medical issue; the various social, psychological and environmental factors that influence behaviour become downplayed, leading to the problem being located within the individual. Effectively, the issue (or problem) is depoliticised so that the focus is then on seeking to change the individual, rather than looking for causes and solutions to complex social problems within the social system (Zola, 1972). Alternatively, it can be argued that the behaviour of children is a *private* matter for families and should be managed by families, but by conceptualising aspects of children's behaviour as a medical condition, namely ADHD, the matter becomes one of *public* concern, to use C. Wright Mills' term, the 'personal trouble' becomes a 'public issue' (Mills, 1959). In a somewhat contradictory manner, the illness label of ADHD tends to *homogenise difference*, while *reinforcing* the focus *on individual deficit*. My aim here is not to question the validity of the diagnosis of ADHD, but to situate the process of assessment, diagnosis and treatment within a socio-cultural context, arguing that the problematisation of behaviours is strongly related to the social construction of both childhood and deviance.

Research design/methodology

The data drawn upon here form part of a larger sociological study that explored the experience of living with ADHD from the perspectives of both children who had the medical diagnosis of ADHD and their parents (Brady, 2004). The research sample was recruited through a Child and Adolescent Mental Health Service (CAMHS). Eleven parents (seven mothers, two fathers, two step-fathers) and seven children (six boys and one girl, aged between 6 and 15 years of age) took part in in-depth interviews on one to three occasions over a 12-month period. Within the sample, three families were owner-occupiers, three were in social housing and one was privately renting their home. All but one family lived in the same city and within two to six miles of the CAMHS. Parents had a range of occupations, including nurse, care assistant, childminder, social worker, security guard, lorry-driver, full-time mother, sales representative and civil engineer. Interviews took place within the family home, with few constraints on time and allowing for rapport to develop; a combination of oral, written and artistic tools gave children the opportunity to participate and contribute their views. Mothers were the principal carers and provided rich descriptions of their lives with their children. The focus of this chapter is on one predominant theme that emerged, namely, the way in which parents made sense of their child's perceived difference in comparison to normative understandings of children. This, in turn, sheds light on the process by which ADHD becomes constructed.

Early concerns with children's behaviour

The stories shared by parents were underpinned by theories of developmentalism and socialisation, demonstrating a tacit understanding of normal health and development. For mothers, in particular, the idea of normal growth and development is not confined to physical or mental health but incorporates their child's level of social acceptability (Buswell, 1980; Pelchat et al, 2009). As Mayall states: 'Normal children are the goal, judged according to physical, developmental and social criteria' (Mayall, 1996, p 51). In this study, parental expectations were that 'normal' children are healthy, unproblematic, relatively compliant, reach developmental milestones when expected to and are not a source of constant challenge or frustration. Parents recounted how they 'just knew' from an early stage that their child was not like others as they did not behave like a 'normal' baby or child, a situation that caused various degrees of distress within different family and social contexts:

> I knew she was different, right from 10 months, because she put her foot on the bar of the buggy, she didn't have the shoulder straps on, just the waist ones, and did a backwards somersault and hung out of the buggy ... she didn't walk, she ran, she took two walking steps and that was it, she just ran. Same as talking, she didn't babble, just straight into talking. (Mother of 10-year-old Emma)

Various comparisons were made: to other children of the same age; to siblings when they were the age of the child in question; to what parents had been told about themselves as children; and to parenting ideals explicated by popular child development experts. Most sought to confirm the 'difference' by conferring with mothers in their lay, informal networks, before approaching health care professionals. It was often much later, sometimes years, before their intuition was legitimated by medical professionals. Other research supports this finding, parents are often the first to suspect that there is something concerning about their child's development, but issues raised are not always taken seriously (Read, 2000; McLaughlin and Goodley, 2008). As one mother described:

> At first you put it down to 'Oh well, he's only three', then only four, or only five, but you get to six and you can't keep putting it down to age. They act very immature, I mean, it sounds silly to call an eight year old immature because they are but it's too young – you'd expect that kind of behaviour at about four, and that would be acceptable, but of course as they get older, it gets more and more worrying. (Mother of eight-year-old Danny)

Parents had expectations of children as they reached a particular age or developmental milestone, and if children did not fulfil expectations, they may be deemed to be 'immature' or 'behind', not to be trusted with responsibility or unable to assess risks appropriately. Such accounts drew heavily on dominant understandings of a linear model of child development and although such immaturity could be tolerated within the family environment, it became more apparent and difficult to handle within a public space.

Public disapproval of children's behaviour

Children who appear to behave inappropriately, or not respond to discipline, can lead to parents' competence being called into question. The traditional division of labour and prevailing ideologies of motherhood left mothers responsible for the welfare of children. Mothers felt judged and frustrated when people showed little understanding of the difficulties faced, as one mother said:

> When he was five, you could tuck him under your arm, but when he got to that age, you couldn't take him on the bus anywhere, he'd be running up and down the aisles, up the stairs, ringing the bell, climbing under them and over them. What do you do when everyone's looking at you thinking – and saying – 'Can't you control that child?' and the answer to that was, short of putting him in a straitjacket and hanging him on a hook, 'No!' (Mother of 12-year-old Sean)

Such encounters played a crucial role in shaping parents' resolve to seek support and an explanation for their child's inappropriate behaviour. Accounts contained evidence of 'internalised concern' relating to what others may think of them (Ryan, 2010) when children behaved in unacceptable ways in public, so parents routinely engaged in emotion management to ameliorate relationships between their children and wider society. However, a unique worldview, a desire to question and discover, a dissatisfaction with routine and monotony, and a need for continual stimulation were sometimes regarded by parents as positive qualities and they accepted that children were individuals with varied temperaments. In some instances, the ways that differences were explained drew on notions of individual characteristics, with comments such as "No two children are the same" or "It was his personality" revealing resistance to see the differences as a problem. As 'normal' and 'different' are relational concepts, what is regarded as not normal must be different, but difference need not necessarily be viewed negatively.

Seeking external support for children's behaviour

Scientific understandings and medicalised conceptualisations of child health conditions pervasively influence public policy, leading to an increasing focus on the elimination of 'risks' – including a preoccupation with children's development and behaviour – and thus implicit messages about normality (Olin Lauritzen and Sachs, 2001). Parents (primarily mothers) are responsible for promoting health, identifying signs of illness as well as treatment and medication (Olin Lauritzen, 2004). This amounts to negotiations between their own lay perspective and biomedical classifications. Parenting, however, can also be a relatively private endeavour, with many families expected to cope with a range of difficult issues without formal support unless or until a point of crisis is reached. McLaughlin and Goodley (2008, p 323) argue that parents seek certainty about what might be wrong with their child in the 'privileged grand narrative of medicine', yet the naming of a condition can be an illusory certainty and, moreover, may shape the nature of the developing parent–child relationship.

All of the children in this study were assessed, diagnosed with ADHD and prescribed psychostimulant medication, usually methylphenidate (Ritalin) by the CAMHS. Following diagnosis, medical vocabulary began to be used by parents, other adults and the children themselves to define behaviour. The uncertainty that prevailed in the period prior to diagnosis had led parents to be anxious as to the cause of the behaviour of their child. Some mothers expressed a sense of guilt or self-blame if they felt that their child's difficulties could have been caused or made worse by their own actions. In common with mothers of disabled children (James, 1993; Read, 2000), mothers asked themselves what they had done wrong or differently during the pregnancy, birth and formative years. Many struggled to hold onto a belief in their ability to be a 'good' parent (sometimes, despite parenting their other children successfully) if they felt lacking in the competence and skill required to deal with their child. Parents' moral character had also been called into question, so the meaning of diagnosis was highly significant, reducing blame and providing a frame of reference. Some parents may have felt more open to public scrutiny than others as the particular model of parenting currently promoted is a middle–class ideal (Gillies, 2005). Socially disadvantaged parents are generally less protected and more likely to be in closer contact with the state, leading them to be more visible and subject to professional monitoring.

A complex interplay of factors influenced parents' health beliefs, their accounts demonstrated a shift in terms of their understanding of where the source of the trouble might be located following diagnosis. In common with other research that has sought to examine the meaning of diagnosis to lay people (Anderson and Bury, 1988; Scambler and Hopkins, 1990; Weinbren and Gill, 1998), parental responses were a mixture of relief, vindication, sorrow and concern. The diagnosis of ADHD had both practical and social consequences, but also a deeper, 'symbolic' significance (Bury, 1997). At a symbolic level, if their child's behaviour had been perceived as 'different' to other children of a similar chronological age, regarded as being of concern and assigned to a medical category, parents felt that they had been vindicated, and that their child's difficulties were legitimated by medical professionals:

> When he was first diagnosed it was such a weight off my shoulders, both mine and my husband's shoulders, cos you just blame yourself, your parenting skills, everything…. I felt I needed to talk to somebody about it, those who knew about this behaviour, and for me to say 'Well, he's not the naughty child that you always thought he was, he's got a diagnosis.' (Mother of 10-year-old Marcus)

It can be argued that the medical frame of reference was productive in the absence of other alternatives (Brady, 2004). 'Every culture generates frames of reference to understand why people behave the way they do' (Halldén, 1991, p 334), and a further parental perceived advantage to diagnosis was that families were brought into contact with potential systems of support. Such agencies, however, were also systems of monitoring and surveillance. Children who may previously have been regarded as regular children began to be scrutinised by the 'psy complex' (Donzelot, 1980). Mayall (1996) argues that care and control are inextricably linked across the public–private divide, where public institutions intervene in the private decisions of families. For example, in the case of Chris, a Year 11 student, his school had offered very limited educational and social support since his diagnosis of ADHD yet would not permit Chris to come onto school premises to take his GCSE examinations unless he had taken his medication. This normalisation of practice relating to 'the trouble' (ie taking psychostimulant medication to aid concentration and ability to focus) had taken place over a very short period of time, namely, during the course of the data collection period of 12 months.

This new frame of reference, however, did influence the views of the children themselves. Children who gave an explanation of what ADHD meant to them tended to give biologically determinist accounts, referring to ADHD as an illness: "It's something not working in your brain that makes you want attention and that" (Sean, aged 12). Moreover, their accounts illustrated the ways in which they were affected by the general stereotyping of the ADHD child. For example, when Emma's peers found out that she had a diagnosis of ADHD and took medication, they called her a psycho and spread rumours about her. She said: "I would like to be normal and popular" (Emma, aged 12). In a further example, Ross had internalised the notion that being talkative was problematic and could be controlled with medication: "I think when my tablet's worn off I talk too much" (Ross, aged 12).

There are implications for children's sense of agency in the examples given; if children feel that their destiny is biologically determined, that they are part of a group who 'have' ADHD, they may experience little sense of control or even a fatalistic attitude towards the future. It can be argued that such views are more likely when the psychosocial and environmental context are excluded from the explanations given by professionals and parents (for discussion of the impact of diagnosis and medication on children's identity, see Brady, 2005) and the explanatory framework emphasises individual deficit. This is not to say that some children who are diagnosed with ADHD have not always felt that they were different to other children (Gallichan and Curle, 2008; Shattell et al, 2008) or that children do not sometimes strategically engage with the diagnosis when it is to their advantage. There is, therefore, a place for non-biological accounts of the behaviours referred to as ADHD (Rostill and Myatt, 2005) and, in turn, for non-pharmacological interventions.

The process of change through diagnosis and the intervention of medication was also not unproblematic for parents. Some experienced it as emotional loss. This loss most pertinently related to changes in behaviour that were closely related to personality, identity and, ultimately, selfhood:

> Getting back to the personality thing, it does change his personality, that is one of the things that makes me very sad about having to medicate him. It mellows him, he loses his appetite, he is not quite as sociable as when he doesn't take it. (Mother of 12-year-old Ross)

This indicates the complexity of this issue. Parents had strived to obtain an explanation for their child's 'difference' and wanted a route out of their family difficulties; biomedical diagnosis provides an explanation. However, the changes to behaviour associated with stimulant medication, which were previously perceived by parents to be desirable, provided only part of the solution, as this change was then experienced as troubling when it led to fundamental modifications to the embodied young person. Perhaps more importantly, experience of bodily difference impacted on children's development of social identity, as cultural stereotypes of what constitutes a normal child are important to children as well as parents (James, 1993).

Benefits of medical diagnosis

Reliance on the theory of child development, with the development of children perceived to unfold along predetermined lines, has meant that children who do not 'measure up' have been regarded as problematic; in short, such a concept of childhood has facilitated the expansion of the diagnosis of ADHD, as a growing emphasis on early assessment and identification of any developmental issues has led to the early intervention of support services, including medical professionals, in the intimate lives of families. Parents are not passive in their encounters; they may be active in inviting professional scrutiny of their problematic child.

The diagnosis of ADHD provides parents with a legitimated framework from which to understand their child's behaviour and the opportunity to access practical help. As well as offering an explanation for their child's 'difference', it also, arguably, provides absolution from blame for both parents and children, and encourages all to see that they are not the only family with this experience, providing a commonality of experience. Treichler (1990) argues that benefits can be gained from placing problems within the medical remit; gaining legitimation from the medical profession can also be of help in a variety of social relationships (Kohler–Reissman, 1989; Broom and Woodward, 1996). This aspect of relief at medical validation is also captured in Rafalovich's (2004) study, which is a critical examination of the framing of ADHD children. Drawing on the work of Emerson and Messinger (1977), he describes how the process by which a trouble becomes normalised and forgotten or progressively interpreted as a specific form of deviance is directly related to the social organisation of the persons associated with the trouble.

Following on from this, it has been claimed that advocates and proponents of the concept of ADHD (such as Barkley, 1990; Goldstein and Goldstein, 1990) possess an essentially functionalist view of society, regarding society as given and individuals as being required to fit in (Ideus, 1995). Therefore, identifying and treating ADHD is regarded as protecting individual rights and promoting equality of opportunity; untreated individuals are at risk of long-term social failure (Anderton, 2007). Yet, although children who are medically diagnosed and treated with medication may be less troublesome to society, what constitutes troublesome behaviour is nevertheless related to 'implicitly held cultural assumptions' (Ideus, 1995, p 86) that help to define categories of mental illness.

Limitations of medical diagnosis

Through the adoption of a biomedical frame of reference, children's non-conforming or problematic behaviour (the problem) is constructed as a mental health issue and medication is accepted as the primary source of intervention. Yet, the location of the cause of behavioural and emotional difficulties within individual children seems to suggest that children need to be helped to change in order to better fit with societal expectations. Conrad (1976, p 250) argues that medicalisation 'diverts our attention from the family or school and from seriously entertaining the idea that the "problem" could be in the structure of the social system'. Furthermore, linked to this is the question of the source of the trouble: are troubles generally located within individual children or perhaps, more convincingly, in the interaction between individuals, families and wider discourses and understandings of appropriate parenting and childhood? Singh (2004) argues that while mothers may have previously been blamed for their child's behaviour, blame tends to shift to the child's brain following diagnosis of ADHD. Recognition that their child 'has it' exacerbates or refocuses parental concerns, particularly as children diagnosed with ADHD can be demonised in public discourse – associated with anti-social behaviour, educational failure, crime and poor mental health. Yet, even with a focus on children's brains and individual deficit, mothers are once again implicated. An increasing reliance on neuroscience to underpin claims for early intervention draws on 'evidence' which suggests that pregnancy and the gestational period are crucial in terms of children's development. Literature aimed at informing parents-to-be claims that 'raised levels of stress in pregnancy can increase the risk of later emotional and behavioural problems in children aged five years' (Puckering, 2011).

Reflections: personal trouble or public issue?

Taking as a starting point C. Wright Mills' (1959, p 187) concept of personal troubles/public issues, at the point of medical assessment and diagnosis, the parental and child respondents' 'personal trouble' became a public issue. Children's problematic behaviour, originally thought to be a matter of individual personality – a private trouble to be contained within the family – gradually became a public issue when the behaviour came within the remit of a medical frame of reference and a diagnosis of ADHD was made. This framework, coupled with ideals of 'good parenting' and 'normal' childhood behaviour, facilitated the involvement of mental health care, and the child became regarded as part of a cohort of children so diagnosed.

What an individual:

> feels to be personal troubles are very often also problems shared by others, and more importantly, not capable of solution by any one individual but only by modifications of the structure of the groups in which he lives and sometimes the structure of the entire society. (Mills, 1959, p 207)

This leads to the following tension: according to Zola (1972) and Conrad (1992), medicalisation tends to point to the behaviour of children being regarded as a 'private', individualised matter, which leads to the issue becoming depoliticised. Yet, at the same time, the private matter of a child behaving inappropriately becomes a public issue, as the child becomes part of the system of medical surveillance.

Simultaneously both a private trouble and a public issue, a psycho-medical frame of reference has become more dominant, and parents turn in this direction for answers to children's non-conformist and challenging behaviour. An increasing UK policy focus on the behaviour of individuals and on the advancement of expert interventions, rather than on support for families, is likely to facilitate this process.

References

Anderson, R. and Bury, M. (eds) (1988) *Living with chronic illness: the experience of patients and their families*, London: Unwin Hyman.

Anderton, P. (2007) *The tipping points: what professionals should recognise as the social impact of ADHD*, Middlesex: ADDISS.

Armstrong, D. (1983) *The political anatomy of the body: medical knowledge in Britain in the twentieth century*, Cambridge: Cambridge University Press.

Armstrong, D. (1995) 'The rise of surveillance medicine', *Sociology of Health and Illness*, vol 17, no 3, pp 393–404.

Ballard, K. and Elston, M.A. (2005) 'Medicalisation: a multi-dimensional concept', *Social Theory and Health*, vol 3, no 3, pp 228–41.

Barkley, R.A. (1990) *Attention deficit disorder: a handbook for diagnosis and treatment*, New York, NY, and London: Guildford Press.

Brady, G. (2004) 'Children and ADHD: a sociological exploration', unpublished PhD thesis, University of Warwick.

Brady, G. (2005) 'ADHD, diagnosis and identity', in C. Newnes and N. Radcliffe (eds) *Making and breaking children's lives*, Ross-on-Wye: PCCS Books.

Broom, D.H. and Woodward, R.V. (1996) 'Medicalisation reconsidered: towards a collaborative approach to care', *Sociology of Health and Illness*, vol 18, no 3, pp 357–78.

Bury, M. (1997) *Health and illness in a changing society*, London: Routledge.

Buswell, C. (1980) 'Mothers' perceptions of professionals in child health care', Paediatric Community Research Club paper, Rugby.

Conrad, P. (1975) 'The discovery of hyperkinesis: notes on the medicalisation of deviant behaviour', *Social Problems*, vol 23, pp 12–21.

Conrad, P. (1976) *Identifying hyperactive children: the medicalization of deviant behavior*, Lexington, MA: Lexington Books.

Conrad, P. (1992) 'Medicalisation and social control', *Annual Review of Sociology*, vol 18, pp 209–32.

Conrad, P. and Schneider, J. (1980) *Deviance and medicalisation: from badness to sickness*, Philadelphia, PA: Temple University Press.

Diagnostic and Statistical Manual of Mental Disorders IV (1994) American Psychiatric Association

Donzelot, J. (1980) *The policing of families: welfare versus the state*, London.

Emerson, R.M. and Messinger, S.L. (1977) 'The micro-politics of trouble', *Social Problems*, vol 25, pp 121–34, cited in Rafalovich, A. (2004) *Framing ADHD children: a critical examination of the history, discourse, and everyday experience of attention deficit/hyperactivity disorder*, Maryland, MA: Lexington Books.

Freidson, E. (1970) *Professional dominance: the social structure of medical care*, Chicago, IL: Aldine.

Gallichan, D.J. and Curle, C. (2008) 'Fitting square pegs into round holes: the challenge of coping with attention deficit hyperactivity disorder', *Clinical Child Psychology and Psychiatry*, vol 13, pp 343–63.

Gillies, V. (2005) 'Meeting parents' needs? Discourses of "support" and "inclusion" in family policy', *Critical Social Policy*, vol 25, no 1, pp 70–90.

Goldstein, S. and Goldstein, M. (1990) *Managing attention disorders in children*, New York, NY: John Wiley.

Halldén, G. (1991) 'The child as project and the child as being: parents' ideas as frames of reference', *Children and Society*, vol 5, no 4, pp 334–46.

Horton-Salway, M. (2011) 'Repertoires of ADHD in UK newspaper media', *Health*, vol 15, no 5, pp 533–49.

Ideus, K. (1995) 'Cultural foundations of ADHD: a sociological analysis', in P. Cooper and K. Ideus (eds) *Attention deficit/hyperactivity disorder: educational, medical and cultural issues*, Kent: The Association of Workers for Children with Emotional and Behavioural Difficulties.

James, A. (1993) *Childhood identities: self and social relationships in the experience of the child*, Edinburgh: Edinburgh University Press.

Kohler-Reissman, C. (1989) 'Women's medicalisation: a new perspective', in P. Brown (ed) *Perspectives in medical sociology*, California, CA: Wadsworth.

Mayall, B. (1996) *Children, health and the social order*, Buckingham: Open University Press.

McLaughlin, J. and Goodley, D. (2008) 'Seeking and rejecting certainty: exposing the sophisticated lifeworlds of parents of disabled babies', *Sociology*, vol 42, pp 317–35.

Mills, C.W. (1959) *The sociological imagination*, New York, NY: Oxford University Press.

Olin Lauritzen, S. (2004) 'Lay voices on allergic conditions in children: bodily signs and the negotiation of a diagnosis', *Social Science and Medicine*, vol 58, no 7, pp 1299–308.

Olin Lauritzen, S. and Sachs, L. (2001) 'Normality, risk and the future: implicit communication of threat in health surveillance', *Sociology of Health and Illness*, vol 4, pp 497–516.

Pelchat, D., Levert, M. and Bourgeois-Guérin, V. (2009) 'How do mothers and fathers who have a child with a disability describe their adaptation/transformation process?', *Journal of Child Health Care*, vol 13, no 3, pp 239–59.

Puckering, C. (2011) 'Getting in early: a good start in life doesn't just begin at birth'. Available at: www.mellowparenting.org (accessed 8 August 2012).

Rafalovich, A. (2004) *Framing ADHD children: a critical examination of the history, discourse, and everyday experience of attention deficit/hyperactivity disorder*, Maryland, MA: Lexington Books.

Read, J. (2000) *Disability, the family and society: listening to mothers*, Buckingham: Open University Press.

Rostill, H. and Myatt, H. (2005) 'Constructing meaning in the lives of looked after children', in C. Newnes and N. Radcliffe (eds) *Making and breaking children's lives*, Ross-on-Wye: PCCS Books.

Ryan, S. (2010) '"Meltdowns", surveillance and managing emotions: going out with children with autism', *Health and Place*, vol 16, pp 868–75.

Scambler, G. and Hopkins, A. (1990) 'Generating a model of epileptic stigma: the role of qualitative analysis', *Social Science and Medicine*, vol 30, pp 1187–94.

Shattell, M.M., Bartlett, R. and Rowe, T. (2008) '"I have always felt different": the experience of ADHD in childhood', *Journal of Pediatric Nursing*, vol 23, no 1, pp 49–57.

Singh, I. (2004) 'Doing their jobs: mothering with Ritalin in a culture of mother-blame', *Social Science and Medicine*, vol 59, pp 1193–205.

Treichler, P.A. (1990) 'Feminism, medicine and the meaning of childbirth', in M. Jacobus, E.F. Keller and S. Shuttleworth (eds) *Body/politics: women and the discourses of science*, New York, NY: Routledge.

Weinbren, H. and Gill, P. (1998) 'Narratives of childhood epilepsy: have I got epilepsy or has it got me?', in T. Greenhalgh and B. Hurwitz (eds) *Narrative based medicine: dialogue and discourse in clinical practice*, London: BMJ Books.

Zola, I.K. (1972) 'Medicine as in institute of social control', *Social Review*, vol 20, pp 487–503.

CHAPTER TEN

Revealing the lived reality of kinship care through children and young people's narratives: "It's not all nice, it's not all easy-going, it's a difficult journey to go on"

Karin Cooper

Introduction

This chapter examines kinship carers' own children's experiences of the kinship care arrangement (also known as family and friends care). The research emanated from the author's professional role as a kinship social worker and the identified invisibility of kinship carers' own children within research and social work policy and practice. The research was underpinned by the sociology of childhood and informed by a children's rights framework, which viewed children as social actors and active participants within the research. The aim of the study was to illuminate the positions and perspectives of kinship carers' own children through multiple narratives. Illustrative data are drawn from a qualitative doctoral study. The research consisted of seven kinship care families, involving semi-structured interviews with eight kinship carers, ten kinship carers' own children and seven placed children aged between three and 21 years old. Data were gathered using art, photo elicitation and audio research techniques and involved individual, dyad and family group interviews. Data also consisted of four focus groups and individual semi-structured interviews with a total of 35 social workers.

Social workers' narratives were set against a pro-family legislative backdrop and child welfare policy context that seeks permanency for children who can no longer reside with their birth parents. The use of kinship care is reflected in the duty to place children with a relative or family friend contained within the Children Act 1989, a requirement strengthened through changes under the Adoption and Children Act 2002, Public Law Outline 2008 and the replacement of section 23 of the Children Act 1989 by the insertion of section 22(C) of the Children and Young Persons Act 2008. Herein, preference must be given to placing a child with a relative, friend or other connected person who can safeguard and promote their welfare. However, as explored later, this pro-family rhetoric was, at times, contested by the voices of kinship carers' own children as a perspective that did not always reflect their lived experiences.

Kinship care: 'normal' and 'natural'

The discursive construction of kinship care as 'normal' and 'natural' emerged in social workers' narratives as a powerful rationale for placing children within their familial and social network and legitimised this caring experience above others:

> we're keeping that child with the family, you know research shows that family is best for the children ... that it's more normal for the child, it's more of a normal family situation, it's not as upheaving. (Senior Social Worker [1])

Indeed, it has been argued that kinship care can serve to promote the child's sense of identity and cultural heritage and increase their sense of belonging and security (McFadden, 1998; Broad et al, 2001; Doolan et al, 2004; Farmer and Moyers, 2008). It also has the potential to facilitate family relationships, to promote contact with, and reduce the trauma of being separated from, birth parents (Broad et al, 2001; Doolan et al, 2004; Farmer and Moyers, 2008). Importantly, children are often placed with people that they know and experience a way of life that may be not only familiar to them, but consistent with their previous life experiences, and this, in turn, might make placed children feel more secure and reduce their anxiety (Greeff, 2001; Hunt, 2009).

Social workers' narratives were shaped and framed not only by the pro-family legislation, but also by assumptions regarding the pre-existing connections between the children in kinship care arrangements. For example, when comparing the experiences of kinship carers' own children with those of stranger foster carers, one social worker stated that it was "more normal to have a family member in". Indeed, a significant difference between kinship carers' own children and those of stranger foster carers lies in the relationship and/or biological connection the former may have with a child prior to placement. However, research and literature highlights the significant impact that fostered children can have upon the daily lives of stranger foster carers' own children (Watson and Jones, 2002; Spears and Cross, 2003; Höjer, 2007; Twigg and Swan, 2007). Moreover, as Greeff (2001, p 54) notes:

> One of the key concepts in systems thinking is that one change within a system will have 'knock-on' effects on all other members of the system. Thus the adjustments will involve not only the carers, the parent and the child, but the birth children of the carers.

The following section, drawing upon data from formally approved kinship care arrangements, considers the relationship differences experienced between co-resident siblings and the placed child.

Co-resident siblings, placed children and relationships: revealing dynamics

Social workers the author spoke with commented that the relationships between placed and kinship carers' own children would be more intimate than those of stranger foster carers' own children. This was closely associated with and demarcated by the placement being perceived as 'natural' and reflected in family practices such as physical displays of affection towards children by kinship family members:

> KSW3(FG):   Whereas I think them boundaries never exist in a family placement.

> KSW4(FG):   Things like hugs and kisses, it's quite natural for a cousin to hug their cousin and kiss their cousin, whereas if it was a stranger child, it's difficult …

> KSW3(FG):   They wouldn't.

> KSW4(FG):   … the adults and the birth children and the kids alike all those things are different when it's a stranger child in a stranger placement.

Clearly, kinship social workers' co-constructed accounts considered the quality of the relationship experienced by placed children to be literally bounded by the placement type, and defined and shaped by familial relationships.

The depth of the bond between resident children and placed relatives was, at times, borne out by children's narratives, as exemplified by Sofia (eight years old) who stated in relation to her niece: "I loved, I loved, I loved Emilia really, really lots. And I was just really excited for her to come to live with us". The intimacy shared between kinship carers' own children and placed family friends was also articulated by Alfie (17 years old) who described his relationship with the friend they fostered as "like a brother". However, it is interesting to note that it was not unusual for placed and resident children to actively renegotiate and redefine 'family' in the context of kinship care by altering their actual relationship in public and private. For example, Noah (12 years old) and Jonah (10 years old) verbally conveyed to others that their relationship with their cousin Sasha (seven years old) was that of brother and sister, this not only prevented unwanted intrusion into their private family life as to why she lived with them, but also actively displayed their emotional commitment to their cousin Sasha (Finch, 2007). In doing so, the children actively posed a challenge to social workers' construction of kinship care as 'normal' and 'natural'. For example, Noah and Jonah clearly demonstrate that they are behaving in intimate ways, as illuminated by social workers' narratives. However, what they challenge are social workers' perceptions that welcoming their cousin, a member of their wider family, into the kinship family is unproblematic. They seek to construct a 'normalised' family that they present outside the realms of the immediate family, wherein their cousin becomes their sister and this makes sense to the outside world.

In spite of the positive relationship kinship carers' own children experienced prior to placement, some had to renegotiate the kin relationship following transition from overnight stays to permanence and this was fraught with difficulties:

Beatrice (six years old):	But when Flora moved in she was a pain in the bum.
Karin:	Oh tell me about that.
Beatrice (six years old):	'Cos she always bites us and smacks us and hits us and er she kicks us, punches us sometimes and she pushes us.

The difference in the dynamics between co-resident siblings and their relationship with placed children was evident in the interviews with Miranda and her sister Beatrice. However, in comparison to Beatrice, Miranda's adverse feelings towards Flora (three-and-a-half years old) at the time she participated in the research were more strongly expressed:

Beatrice (six years old):	We like her living here, but she's naughty.
Karin:	So what do you like best about Flora?
Miranda (eight years old):	Nothing.
Beatrice (six years old):	That we can look after her.
Miranda (eight years old):	But I don't like nothing.
Beatrice (six years old):	Miranda that's horrible.
Miranda (eight years old):	I've got nothing to say. I hate her.

Although impossible to know how this unfolded over the longer term, the intensity of Miranda's feelings were reinforced later when I asked the question: "If you could change one thing about your family what would it be?":

Miranda (eight years old):	My cousin.
Karin:	Flora?
Miranda (eight years old):	Yeah.
Karin:	What would you change?
Miranda (eight years old):	That she was never naughty and never, ever, ever, my cousin and never lived with me.

As this example demonstrates, Miranda's narrative was permeated by highly emotive terminology and reflected her oppositional relationship with Flora as she struggled to cope with the situation. Triseliotis and colleagues (2000), writing about stranger foster carers' own children, and Farmer and Moyers (2008), regarding kinship carers' own children, refer to the rivalry and jealousy exhibited by these children towards placed children. Miranda's view contrasted heavily with Beatrice's response, as she referred to Flora's negative behaviour towards them rather than the child herself, stating: "I would change about Flora being naughty and smacking and biting me". Interestingly, Miranda's resentment around Flora's presence also spilled over into the research arena, as she thwarted Flora's attempts to enter the kitchen at the start of their first interview with me. However, during the interview, Beatrice also did the same. For these children, then, the research interview may well have created a space over which they could exercise autonomy and that they were reluctant to concede.

A further reflection of the difficult relationship with Flora was evident in, and reinforced through, the advice Miranda would give to those considering fostering a relative, as she stated that she would tell them: "[i]t's hard fostering people, so don't try it yourself". To this extent, it is possible to identify the differentiated sibling relationships experienced by co-resident siblings with the placed child. Unlike her sister Beatrice, at no point did Miranda speak warmly of the relationship or interactions between herself and Flora. Interestingly, Nicole (mother) tried to ensure that she created an opportunity for her children to have space and time away from Flora:

> they was just used to having each other, but now it's changed again to where they're back to the same old selves, where they will go and play in one room, and we'll entertain Flora in another. (Nicole/parent)

Clearly, Nicole's own children had to negotiate not only the changed physical relationship with their parent as she spent more time with their cousin, but also the transition in terms of the altered emotional relationship with Flora, which became more intense and difficult for them all once she moved in. Hunt et al, (2008) and Farmer and Moyers (2008) argue that difficult behaviour of the placed child is one of the underlying factors in placement disruption. For example, in the former's research regarding placement stability, it was found that while 29% of disruptions related to the placed child's behaviour, in a further 23% of cases, 'relationship difficulties between the child and either the carer or other children in the household' was the cause of placement disruption (Hunt et al, 2008, p 76). These findings have practice implications in terms of the pre- and post-placement assessment of relationships between placed and kinship carers' own children.

The differences between siblings' experiences of kinship care were also apparent within Helena's (17 years old) family, who fostered her brother's friend:

> it was less difficult for Thomas because … it was his mate … from school and he was looking after his mate and that was fine. For Helena, it was an awful, awful experience and it wasn't until she was a little bit older that we realised he was bullying her. (Julianne/parent)

The difference in the relationship with Liam (fostered family friend) was combined with feeling unsafe and insecure, as Helena said: "I was scared stiff of him 'cos he just used to look over me and just push me about". Helena's narrative illuminated not only the strong relationship between Thomas and Liam, but also the emotional distance this created between herself and her brother Thomas: "it felt like Thomas was closer to Liam than he was with me. So I felt like the outcast in the family, because Thomas was always with Liam", which effectively reinforced her feelings of insecurity.

Helena, aged eight years old when the placement commenced, hid the difficulties she experienced from her parents despite the negative consequences for herself, which, in turn, served to sustain the kinship arrangement. However, throughout my interview with her, the many and varied ways in which she attempted to distance herself from Liam became increasingly apparent. Helena elected not to discuss fostering within her family network, although her 'nana' acknowledged Liam as family, thus blurring the boundaries between what is essentially social with what is considered biological, and, in so doing, validated Liam's place within their family (Almack, 2008):

Karin: What did your other family members think about you fostering?

Helena (17 years old):	I'm not actually sure. I don't really; I haven't really spoken to them about it 'cos I didn't want to speak about fostering anyway. But ... I think my nana loved it because she got called nana by another person. It weren't just Thomas being her grandson it was Liam.

This distancing was mirrored in the public sphere with Helena's school peers; she refused to discuss fostering with her friends, and although Liam attended the same school, she had very little contact with him: "I didn't really talk about it [fostering] much. I just used to say right that's my foster brother 'Hi' and 'Bye'". Helena distanced herself verbally in terms of her connection with Liam, as she referred to Thomas as her "real brother" while, more often than not, she referred to Liam as her "foster brother". This was particularly significant as other sons and daughters I spoke with defined the personal tie to the placed child either in terms of their actual genealogical relationship, their friendship or as a 'brother' or 'sister'. By referring to Thomas as "real" and Liam as "fostered", Helena was able to 'demarcate the "we" [family] from the "other" [Liam]' (Hill, 2005, p 88). This not only enabled her to deal (albeit unsuccessfully) with the rocky terrain of kinship family life, but also define and display to the outside world who constituted her family (Finch, 2007).

Helena's selflessness went some way to explain why she chose not to disclose the bullying experienced from Liam, as she stated: "'cos he was a foster brother and 'cos I thought we was helping him out I didn't want to say anything". This was also closely tied up with her concerns around the security of her place both within the family and in the affections of her parents and sibling, coupled with her lack of visibility in the family:

Helena (17 years old):	And ... I don't know, I think at the time I felt like he was taking my mum and dad away as well.
Karin:	Did you?
Helena (17 years old):	Because ... like I say, I was always locked in my room and there was my brother and Liam and it felt like I was invisible in my own home.

Helena was constrained by the view that she fostered on the premise that she wanted to help someone. This was further compounded by the fact that she had been able to exercise choice and influence the initial decision to foster. To state that the placement was not working was made all the more difficult by the pre-existing relationship the family had with her brother's friend. This resulted in Helena exercising agency in a way that had a profound effect upon her engagement in kinship family life, as she resorted to locking herself away. Previous research has highlighted children's use of distancing techniques in managing change within the family. For example, Heidbuurt's (1995) research on boundary maintenance suggests that stranger foster carers' own children engaged in 'partial seclusion' as a means of coping with the fostering situation (cited in Twigg and Swan, 2007, p 55). Similarly, Nuske (2004, p 8) talks about this in terms of caregivers' own children 'removing themselves'.

Essentially, the idea of being 'locked' in her room was not only a physical response, as she sought to distance herself from Liam, but also an emotional locking away from her parents and sibling, which had serious implications for Helena. This self-enforced disengagement from her immediate family resulted in the deterioration in her emotional well-being, as explained by her mother, Julianne, who stated: "in the end fostering ... made her life miserable ... and she cut herself, she cut her wrists twice ... and it was all to do with the fostering". The inability to explore her concerns with her parents for fear of the repercussions for Liam resulted in Helena choosing more ethereal means of addressing her situation:

Helena (17 years old):	erm I decided to write notes ... because we used to write notes in school to each other and close them up into like this square and then send them on to our mates. So I thought 'Oh well if we can pass them on to our mates' then I had this tin box that my nana left me when she died ...
Karin:	Yeah.
Helena (17 years old):	and erm I put these letters in that, said my thoughts about my foster brother....And I'd write that I hate him, I don't want to be with him anymore, he's done this and he's done that. I'd put it in the tin and think 'Right my nana's going to hear all this because it's in her box and she'll sort it out for me without me telling anyone.'

In essence, Helena created a safe place in the liminal space occupied by her 'nana' within which she felt emotionally able to cope with the adversity she faced in her daily life. In doing so, she actively avoided confrontation with her family, and, as such, restricted the consequences of her actions to herself.

Helena's experience led her to advise other sons and daughters to "spend more time with them [foster child] then we did with the foster person ... because anything can happen". This is a view echoed by Mitchell and colleagues' (2010) research regarding fostered children. The children in their study desired more information prior to placement in foster care, which, the authors argued, could assist in 'minimising ambiguity' (Mitchell et al, 2010). Recent developments in government guidance and regulations may go some way to redress the balance regarding these issues for placed and resident children (Department for Education, 2011a, 2011b, 2011c). However, the urgency and level of crisis apparent in the need to place a child within a kinship care arrangement were powerful forces within the author's research that prevented consultation with resident children pre-placement. Heidbuurt (2004, p 8), in relation to stranger foster carers' own children, states that 'participation in family decision-making was critical to feeling a valued part of the family'. However, the author suggests that in the context of kinship care, taking on the care of a family member was perceived, particularly by the adults spoken with, as something inevitable and what families do at a time of crisis.

Conclusion

This chapter has presented data that illustrate the complexity of kinship family life for kinship carers' own children. Social workers' normalisation of kinship care through the use of pro-family rhetoric was contested by the voices and experiences of some kinship carers' own children. Familiarity and/or an emotional bond prior to placement were a positive experience for some kinship carers' own children. In contrast, as indicated by Helena's and Miranda's accounts, the pre-existing relationship did not always reflect the type of relationship experienced post-placement. The data demonstrate the different ways in which co-resident siblings responded to the emotional and behavioural difficulties displayed by placed children. This resulted in the need for the former to make adjustments, which, in turn, altered the dynamics of their family life and impacted upon their emotional well-being. In comparison to her brother, fostering for Helena was not an easy experience as she aptly summed up: "It's not all nice, it's not all easy-going, it's a difficult journey to go on".

This chapter has illustrated that the placement of children in kinship care, an option assumed by social workers to be 'normal' and 'natural', disrupted some kinship carers' own children's everyday lived experiences in nuanced ways not discussed in social work discourses. The data, therefore, raise questions regarding the entrance of known or related children into an established family, and whether their (agreed or imposed) placement, in turn, creates a troubled family. Such findings further validate Hunt's assertion that '[t]here is perhaps, still an assumption that because kinship care is "natural" it is also unproblematic' (2009, p 112).

References

Almack, K. (2008) 'Display work: lesbian parent couples and their families of origin negotiating new kin relationships', *Sociology*, vol 42, no 6, pp 1183–99.

Broad, B., Hayes, R. and Rushforth, C. (2001) *Kith and kin: kinship care for vulnerable young people*, London: National Children's Bureau.

Department for Education (2011a) *Family and friends care: statutory guidance for local authorities*, London: Department for Education.

Department for Education (2011b) *The Children Act 1989 guidance and regulations volume 4: fostering services*, London: Department for Education.

Department for Education (2011c) *Fostering services: national minimum standards*, London: Department for Education.

Doolan, M., Nixon, P. and Lawrence, P. (2004) *Growing up in the care of relatives or friends: delivering best practice for children in family and friends care*, London: Family Rights Group.

Farmer, E. and Moyers, S. (2008) *Kinship care: fostering effective family and friends placements*, London: Jessica Kingsley Publishers.

Finch, J. (2007) 'Displaying families', *Sociology*, vol 41, no 1, pp 65–81.

Greeff, R. (2001) 'Family dynamics in kinship foster care', in B. Broad (ed) *Kinship care: the placement choice for children and young people*, Lyme Regis: Russell House Publishing.

Heidbuurt, J. (2004) All in the Family Home: The Biological Children of Parents who Foster. Foster Family–Based Treatment Association's 18th Annual Conference on Treatment Foster Care, on-line research abstract at http://www.ffta.org/research_outcomes/abstracts18_heidbuurt.pdf (accessed 10 April 2011).

Hill, M. (2005) 'Children's boundaries: within and beyond families', in L. McKie and S. Cunningham-Burley (eds) *Families in society: boundaries and relationships*, Bristol: The Policy Press.

Höjer, I. (2007) 'Sons and daughters of foster carers and the impact of fostering on their everyday life', *Child and Family Social Work*, vol 12, no 1, pp 73–83.

Hunt, J. (2009) 'Family and friends care', in G. Schofield and J. Simmonds (eds) *The child placement handbook: research, policy and practice*, London: BAAF.

Hunt, J., Waterhouse, S. and Lutman, E. (2008) *Keeping them in the family: outcomes for children placed in kinship care though care proceedings*, London: BAAF.

McFadden, E.J. (1998) 'Kinship care in the United States', *Adoption and Fostering*, vol 22, no 3, pp 7–15.

Mitchell, M.B., Kuczynski, L., Tubbs, C.Y. and Ross, C. (2010) 'We care about care: advice by children in care for children in care, foster parents and child welfare workers about the transition into foster care', *Child and Family Social Work*, vol 15, no 2, pp 176–85.

Nuske, E.M. (2004) 'Beyond the double edged sword: the contradictory experiences of biological children in foster families'. Available at: http://pandora.nla.gov.au/pan/56368/20060224-000www.croccs.org.au/downloads/2004_conf_papers/040709PaperElaineNuskePUBLISH.pdf (accessed 10 April 2011).

Spears, W. and Cross, M. (2003) 'How do "children who foster" perceive fostering?', *Adoption and Fostering*, vol 27, no 4, pp 38–45.

Triseliotis, J., Borland, M. and Hill, M. (2000) *Delivering foster care*, London: BAAF.

Twigg, R. and Swan, T. (2007) 'Inside the foster family: what research tells us about the experience of foster carers' children', *Adoption and Fostering*, vol 31, no 4, pp 49–61.

Watson, A. and Jones, D. (2002) 'The impact of fostering on foster carers' own children', *Adoption and Fostering*, vol 26, no 1, pp 49–55.

THE NORMAL, THE TROUBLING AND THE HARMFUL?

Introduction to Part Three

Carol-Ann Hooper

While the potential for harm to children and young people, sometimes along with other family members, in a range of family troubles is a theme throughout this book, Part Three illuminates some of the complexities of identifying those who are particularly vulnerable. To a large extent, families construct their own version of the normal, and children and young people may be unable to detach sufficiently from the power and significance of the relationships on which they depend to perceive alternatives and name their own experience as harmful (see the chapters by Mannay and Wilson). Whether particular troubling events or experiences create lasting harm is also influenced by many aspects of their context: relational, social, material and cultural (see the chapter by Jamieson and Highet and the chapter by Davies). Furthermore, emotions within family relationships are complex – involving love and hate in all families, as well as the intensified anger, shame and guilt associated with abuse or neglect – and the expression of aggression may be creative as well as destructive (see the chapter by Luccy). Different figures are cited to draw a boundary around the troubled – the UK government's Troubled Families Unit identified 120,000 'troubled families' in 2011, while a year later, after the discovery that young people involved in riots in the summer of 2011 did not predominantly come from those families, a further 500,000 'forgotten families' were named. Both groups have focused largely on the poor and marginalised, but harmful troubles are potentially much more widespread and not confined to families who 'bump along the bottom of society' (Riots, Communities and Victims Panel, 2012, p 7).

Exposure to domestic violence (the subject of Dawn Mannay's chapter) is associated with an increased risk of all forms of child maltreatment and is now recognised as a form of emotional abuse of children itself in the UK (HM Government, 2010) – a recent survey found that over a quarter of 18- to 24-year-olds reported experiencing this at some point in their childhoods (Radford et al, 2011). The number of children living with parents misusing drugs (the subject of Wilson's chapter) was estimated by the Advisory Council on the Misuse of Drugs in 2003 as between 200,000 and 300,000 children in England and Wales

(2–3% of all children under 16) and may well have increased since. The disruption to family relationships or loss of a parent, through divorce, separation or death (covered in the chapter by Jamieson and Highet and the chapter by Davies) are even more widespread – it has been estimated that between a third and a half of children experience the breakdown of their parents' relationships (Bradshaw, 2011). All these situations appear, directly or indirectly, on lists of risk factors for child maltreatment and youth offending (an increased risk of the latter itself being associated with the former), but such lists, derived from quantitative research, conceal as much as they reveal, and may distort professional perceptions of the families they work with. The influence of poverty and the role of public policy remain invisible, while certain categories of household adversely affected by both are problematised, and the messy, dynamic, complex, changing, embedded nature of family life is also obscured. The qualitative approach taken by each of the studies in this part show how the range of circumstances in which particular troubles occur, the influence of context on their impact and children's active engagement in attributing meaning to them make each family story, and each family member's story within it, unique.

Lynn Jamieson and Gill Highet draw on interview data with children and young people aged between 10 and 14 years who have lived through contrasting forms of family household change to explore what influences their ability to sustain and refashion their sense of self in the context or aftermath of loss. While children who experience the death of a parent, or parental separation or divorce, must cope with disruption to, or loss of, a primary relationship central to their development and identity, and children whose families relocate across countries to seek asylum more often lose everything but these primary relationships – extended family, community and place of origin – the influence of relational, social, cultural and material contexts on the experience is a common thread. Mannay takes a case study approach, using one woman's narrative journey from childhood to motherhood to explore the ongoing permeating presence of her childhood experience of domestic and family violence. While the influence of childhood experience on parenting is well recognised, she also highlights the wider context of the normalisation of male violence and the centrality of care in the construction of femininity, and their influence on the everyday life and aspirations of girls and women in work as well as family contexts.

Sarah Wilson draws on interviews with young people affected by parental substance misuse (among other family troubles), arguing for greater attention to difficult family relationships in contemporary sociological thinking on personal and family lives. Her analysis highlights the challenges such young people face in constructing a morally acceptable self in the absence of expected parenting practices and the family narrative they support in a cultural context where the primacy of family relationships to children and young people is so taken for granted as to obscure and devalue alternative sources of self-worth and identity. Hayley Davies uses interview data from children aged 8–10 years who had experienced parental separation and/or divorce (and sometimes multiple family transitions) to discuss their accounts of contact with non–resident parents and the negotiations involved in maintaining both the practice and the meaning of connection. While contact may have mixed implications for children (as Forsberg's chapter in Part Five also indicates), loss or lack of contact was often a source of distress that children were active in attempting to change, although their ability to negotiate this successfully was highly dependent on the adults in their lives and the relationships between them.

Helen Lucey offers a psychoanalytically informed psychosocial perspective on aggression between sisters, illustrated by case studies from a qualitative study of children and young people's sibling relationships. While aggression is commonly associated with harm (and, indeed, often defined as involving the intent to harm), and also with masculinity, she highlights the centrality of ordinary aggression to relationships with self and others, as much for girls as for boys, and its creative uses in family relationships for the development of identity and individuality. Sibling relationships may, of course, be a source of harm, where bullying or other forms of abuse occur (Hooper, 2011), but her analysis further complicates the picture of the relationship between the normal and the troubling.

All these chapters make readily apparent the profound significance of children's family relationships for their everyday lives, development and well-being, as quantitative research also confirms – the quality of children's family and peer relationships are among the strongest influences on their well-being (ESRC, 2010; Hobcraft and Kiernan, 2010; Rees et al, 2010). While the fundamentals of child development, such as attachment, play a key part in that picture, the more sociological approach taken here also brings into focus the influence of material resources, public policy and cultural discourse. While poverty makes all family troubles harder to manage and its impacts on child well-being can be argued to make child poverty a form of 'societal neglect' (Hooper et al, 2007), its impact is also specific to different troubles – managing post-separation relationships is easier, for example, for families with space to spare in their housing (see the chapter by Jamieson and Highet and the chapter by Davies). The precariousness of life for some families, especially those who have sought asylum but have not yet been granted leave to remain in the UK, is a direct result of public policy (see the chapter by Jamieson and Highet; see also the chapter by Evans and the chapter by Chase and Statham in Part Four). Cultural discourses that idealise family life, pathologise certain families ('broken' or asylum-seeking) or children (eg the 'wounded by tragic loss', bereaved of a parent), normalise aggression in men and disallow it in women, and support the making of decisions with a profound effect on children's lives without their participation must all be negotiated as family members attempt to maintain both a positive (or at least liveable with) identity and the relationships that sustain them. Discourses change over time – it is significantly easier to name domestic violence as a wrong now (see the chapter by Mannay) than it was 50 years ago, at least in some parts of the world, although not universally – but the discursive space for those with difficult and damaging family relationships to define positively their achievement in 'breaking the chains' of their legacy remains very limited (see the chapter by Wilson).

The potential impacts of troubles on children's well-being in childhood, the risks of long-term negative outcomes into adulthood and their ripple effects, and the associated costs to the public purse – domestic violence alone was estimated to cost £23 billion per annum in 2001 – form the case for intervention in response to, or to prevent, harm. Debates on the form that intervention takes are addressed in Part Five. The chapters in this part all indicate the limitations of locating trouble within an easily defined minority of the population however – such an attempt might arguably be seen as a projection of the collective shadow (or 'dark side' of family life), a disowning of much more widespread and ordinary trouble by locating it in an 'othered' minority group.

References

Bradshaw, J. (2011) 'Demography of childhood', in J. Bradshaw (ed) *The well-being of children in the UK* (3rd edn), Bristol: The Policy Press, pp 13–25.

ESRC (Economic and Social Research Council) (2010) *Britain in 2011: the state of the nation*, Swindon: ESRC.

Hobcraft, J.N. and Kiernan, K.E. (2010) 'Predictive factors from age 3 and infancy for poor child outcomes at age 5 relating to children's development, behaviour and health: evidence from the Millenium Cohort Study', *Social Science and Medicine*, vol 69, no 10, pp 1476–83.

Hooper, C.A. (2011), 'Child maltreatment', in J. Bradshaw (ed) *The well-being of children in the UK* (3rd edn), Bristol: The Policy Press, pp 191–211.

Hooper, C.A., Gorin, S., Cabral, C. and Dyson, C. (2007) *Living with hardship 24/7: the diverse experiences of families in poverty in England*, London: The Frank Buttle Trust.

Radford, L., Corral, S., Bradley, C., Fisher, H., Bassett, C., Howatt, N. and Collishaw, S. (2011) *Child abuse and neglect in the UK today*, London: NSPCC.

Rees, G., Bradshaw, J., Goswami, H. and Keung, A. (2010) *Understanding children's well-being: a national survey of young people's well-being*, London: The Children's Society.

Riots, Communities and Victims Panel (2012) *After the riots: the final report of the Riots, Communities and Victims Panel*, London: Riots, Communities and Victims Panel.

CHAPTER ELEVEN

Troubling loss? Children's experiences of major disruptions in family life

Lynn Jamieson and Gill Highet

Introduction

This article draws on young people's perspectives on extraordinary changes – the disruption of biographies, families and households – that may be experienced as loss. We take it for granted that young people's own insights into the constraints and possibilities of adjusting to, recovering from or repairing such disruptions are of intrinsic value and interest. The focus is not on the psychological mechanism involved in mourning (Bagnoli, 2003) or on how the absent are dealt with in memory (Cait, 2008), but, rather, on the interpersonal, systemic and discursive processes involved in deflecting, minimising or amplifying the trouble loss brings. The theoretical starting point draws from insights shared by a range of sociological understanding of the development of selves (Mead, 1934; Goffman, 1959; Berger and Luckman, 1967; Giddens, 1984; Bourdieu, 1986; Smith, 1987; Holdsworth and Morgan, 2007; Holmes, 2010). This approach places the biographical origins of the self-reflexive self, 'me' and 'I', in emotionally charged relationships with primary carers during infancy. In childhood, the influences shaping and sustaining the self rapidly open out to a larger constellation of close relationships and other social systems bestowing a sense of belonging, competence and worth, including the education system and other institutions rewarding performance. Scholars of personal life have used various terms to describe the constellation of close relationships that are influential to a sense of self as well as a source of practical and emotional support and 'capital' (Bourdieu, 1986): 'significant others' (Berger and Luckman, 1967; Ketokivi, 2008), 'network of care' (Hansen, 2005), 'personal communities' (Wellman et al, 1988; Spencer and Pahl, 2006), 'connected lives' (Smart, 2007) and 'family configurations' (Widmer and Sapin, 2008). Such personal relationships and wider social systems bestowing belonging and competence are often intertwined. Micro worlds of personal interaction are always framed by institutionalised social and discursive cultural systems, which structure access to resources and ideas, shaping the possibilities for working on and imagining the self. This theoretical approach regards the self and subjectivity as always open to at least partial refashioning. Working with the limits of inner resources and the affordances of wider social and cultural systems, people, children and adults, refresh and remake something of themselves in social interaction with significant others and through their performances.

The primary data are children and young people reflecting on one or more of: the death of a parent; their parents separating or divorcing; or the dramatic dislocation from place of origin involved in seeking asylum. These different types of change are brought together for theoretical reasons. Two of the types deal with circumstances involving a parent: disruption due to parental death or divorce/separation. Objectively, the former is a much more profound loss. The latter may be an unresolved and 'ambiguous loss' (Boss, 1999) or, in some circumstances, experienced as rearrangement rather than loss. Nevertheless, both biographical occurrences theoretically have the potential to unsettle a child's sense of self and of their place in the world (Bagnoli, 2003). Both involve disruption of parenting relationships, which typically play a key role in the early formation of an inner sense of self and might also impact on the constellation of relationships sustaining the self. Each form of disruption could also change the child's access to resources, simultaneously modifying the materials the child has to work with when seeking to rebuild their selves and lives. Both events are associated with public discourses about children without two resident parents, framing the child as victims of loss: 'tragic loss' or the somewhat stigmatising discourse of 'broken families', 'absent fathers' and difficulties with stepfamilies. Examples of children experiencing death or divorce/separation are brought together with children from asylum-seeking families as a contrasting case. They are with their parents but have experienced losing or coming close to losing almost everything else – access to most of their social network of friends and wider kin, along with their homeland, language, culture and material resources. The public discourse that potentially frames the child and his or her asylum-seeking family is stigmatising and unsympathetic. This provides another line of insight into the relative importance of parents as key significant others versus the wider social, material and cultural context in children's experiences of recovery from biographical disruption.

There are also empirical reasons for bringing these three examples of biographical disruption together: they were found together in children's classrooms, albeit in very different proportions. Parents separating was the most statistically common experience shared by over a quarter of the 10- to 14-year-old children who took part in a screening survey in a small number of participating UK schools.[1] Of the children, 4% had lost a parent through death, close to estimates of the figure for the UK (Harrison and Harrington, 2001; Ribbens McCarthy and Jessop, 2005; Ribbens McCarthy, 2006), and 4% were children of families seeking leave to remain in the country as refugees. Any practitioner working with groups of children in Europe or North America, particularly those from less privileged backgrounds, is likely to encounter a similar mix, albeit not in these specific proportions. More than one form of disruption can also be found together in some children's lives. Among our interviewees, Catherine, for example, had experienced the death of her father and then an episode of her mother re-partnering, her mother's boyfriend moving in, followed by the breakdown of this relationship and his exit. This, in turn, precipitated a period of mental illness and hospitalisation for her mother, during which time she and her brother lived with an uncle. Some asylum-seeking children will also experience the death of a parent or the dissolution of their parents' relationship. Multiple changes in parenting and household arrangements are not the statistical norm among children in Britain, but they are not an uncommon domino effect of extraordinary family change.

The Scottish-based research[2] was initiated in dialogue with practitioner audiences and was intended to inform their services for children. One-to-one interviews about experiences of change were conducted with 55 children and young people aged 10–14 years who had lived through family household change identified through a questionnaire administered in selected primary and secondary schools teaching pupils from a range of socio-economic circumstances and ethnic backgrounds in a Scottish city. The sample was diverse and children living in fairly disadvantaged circumstances were well represented. The majority of the children interviewed had experienced change in their household and parenting arrangements precipitated by the separation of their parents, but eight had experienced the death of a parent, two had a father in prison and four were children of asylum-seeking families. A third of the children were interviewed a second time to provide more detailed cases across this range of circumstances and to gain deeper insight into children's views of change over time. A small number of children's accounts are described here, providing at least one detailed account of each type of change and highlighting features that were typical of children in similar circumstances.

Age and 'stage'

Psychoanalytic theoretical traditions give significant weight to unremembered events of early childhood, but the sociological traditions drawn on here restrict their focus to those unconscious processes that are potentially accessible to self-reflection in inner dialogue or interaction with others. Some of the interviewees who had experienced their parents' divorce or death were under five years old at the time. For them, these events, as part of early childhood that was not remembered in any detail, by definition, carried little conscious sense of drama or trauma. They typically responded to enquiries or polite sympathy by explaining that they were 'too young' to remember.

In his interview, Danny used age at the time of his parents' separation to explain why he was less upset than his older siblings:

> Well, I remember the night they told us because, em, we were, eh, they called us into our lounge, me and my big brother and my big sister. And I remember my big brother being really, really, really upset about it, and my sister being a little bit less upset about it. But I wasn't really that upset because I was too young to really understand. I was just five, I think, so I didn't really think it was anything. (Danny, age 11)

At the same time, reference to age and length-of-time-ago provides an acceptable vocabulary for explaining a reduced sense of being troubled by loss that may not always tell the whole story. So, for example, while two of our interviewees, Rebecca and Catherine, experienced the death of their father at age seven, only Rebecca minimised the troubling nature of the loss by reference to her young age; Catherine stressed the magnitude of the loss. The extent of being troubled was obviously not about age as such. An important factor is found in differences between their 'personal communities': for example, Rebecca's immediate family had a rich support network and sense of everyone rallying round, while Catherine's immediate family had been cut off from most of her kin by a recent acrimonious dispute around her grandfather's will and Catherine lamented that they did not even attend her father's funeral.

The significance of age is often conceptualised as contingent on the interaction between age and 'stage', either referring to a theory of levels of competence and development (eg Erikson, 1950) or used more loosely to refer to passing socially defined milestones such as completing the various years or stages of education. From the sociological perspective adopted here, what matters theoretically is the current state of play in terms of quality, extensiveness and resilience of sources of support for the self beyond the person or persons who are 'lost' that can continue to sustain a sense of self, help rebuild a damaged self or provide alternative narratives to the dominant discourse of troubling loss. In this sense, a child who is engaged by her or his schooling and derives pleasure and worth from schoolwork as well as having a range of positive personal relationships is relatively well placed to withstand the loss of a parent. They are at a multiply better 'stage' than the child who feels disengaged at school and has a very small constellation of personal relationships that are orchestrated by the parent and likely to be damaged without him or her.

Death and being more or less troubled

The death of a parent is typically experienced by children unequivocally in terms of loss (Ribbens McCarthy and Jessop, 2005; Ribbens McCarthy, 2006), but it is also possible for children to speak about no longer being troubled. Rebecca's account of her father's death at age seven is an example. She identified factors reducing troubling aspects of loss – in addition to being "too young to understand" at the time – and distancing herself at age 13: "if people talk to me they're like 'Oh I'm really sorry for talking about it.' I'm like, 'It's fine, I'm over it. It's not a big deal'" (Rebecca, age 13).

The range of factors she itemised as helping to contain her sense of loss mostly referred to the practical and emotional work her mother undertook on behalf of the family. But she also raised doubts about whether the quality of the relationship she had with her father was sufficient for his absence to create a durable sense of loss: "it didn't really make a difference about how the way I feel about my family because I didn't really feel that I got to know him that well" (Rebecca, age 13).

Her father had a long illness that was known to have no cure. Her mother's response included: researching his illness and providing information pre-warning of death; ensuring opportunities for good memories by organising a long overseas family holiday when her father was well enough to travel; and, ultimately, providing an orchestrated occasion to say goodbye, creating a shared sense of a 'good death':

> I got to say goodbye to him so it was easier that way instead of not knowing.... We had like, on the day, we had a lot of family and close friends round, just for everyone to say goodbye and he himself, he was, he'd been ill for ages and he kinda wanted all the pain to be over but we were all, it sounds sad but we were all happy for him. (Rebecca, age 13)

Rebecca also talked of her mother setting the emotional scene of their family life by not dwelling on sadness:

> She has been like really good about it and not being all down and wasn't depressed or anything. She just tried to keep, keep going. I think that helped us.... We didn't think 'God, it's the end of the world.' (Rebecca, age 13)

Rebecca's family is relatively affluent and socially rich. Throughout the story, the figure of an aunt, her mother's sister, who is 'like a second mum', and her cousin, who is her best friend, play key supportive roles.

The story of getting through the death together and then moving on with a positive life was not available to all. Some children experienced life since their parent's death as significantly more difficult and spoke of factors that amplify the troubling nature of loss. Susie wrote on her questionnaire about her mother's death: "I have been lonely at home. She [mum] was my best friend". The sociology of the family literature has long documented that mothers are typically key orchestrators of practical arrangements for children, including maintaining contact with kin, as well as providing a first line of emotional support. Susie's father did not step into any of these roles; she saw less of her grandparents following her mother's death than before, despite needing their support more. Susie had anticipated her father drawing closer after her mother's death, but, instead, he had effectively absented himself: "he's always at work. He goes, after he drops us off at school and then he comes in like half nine at night, so. And then he goes on the internet, so you never get to see him" (Susie, age 13).

In Susie's case, the discourse of 'tragic loss' continued to fit and frame her experience. The loss of her mother had the effect of impairing the practices of intimacy of her father and was associated with an overall contraction in her 'personal community' and sources of support. At the same time, no other system of self-affirmation was stepping in to provide compensation.[3]

Keeping or losing your post-separation dad

Research continues to show that, even if commonplace, living through parental separation or separation and re-partnering does not typically feel ordinary for children (Batchelor et al, 1994; Maclean and Eekelaar, 1997; Brannen and Hepinstall, 2000; Douglas et al, 2000; Dunn and Deater-Decker, 2001; Smart et al, 2001; Wade and Smart, 2002; Ribbens McCarthy et al, 2003; Smart, 2003, 2004). Some children lamented a sense of stepping outside of the normative family of popular discourse in which their idealised parents loved and cherished each other (see also Bagnoli, 2003). Many complained about the radical reduction of times and occasions in which those making up their 'family' all got together. Many also reported that the absence of their father from their family home had an impact on their relationship with their mother. Some experienced a diminished relationship with their father or lost contact with him. The sense of disjuncture was sometimes compounded by other associated changes, such as moving home and school. All of these changes have the potential for some impact on a sense of self. In extreme cases, children lost all contact with their father, their paternal grandparents and his other kin and friends without the 'closure' of death (Boss, 1999). While not all children characterise their experience of parental separation in terms of loss and some, ultimately, have a sense of gain (Smart et al, 2001), unease, an unsettled sense of self, must frequently precede or accompany disavowal of the negative discourses about broken families.

Our interviews with children indicate that the circumstances of some enabled them to confidently repeat their parents' reassurance that separation would not damage their child–parent relationships. As Karen put it: "They still love you and they still try to do the best that they can for you, so it doesn't really make a difference" (Karen, age 12). On the other hand, once their father had left their family home, many children became more aware of and watchful of the practices that underpin intimacy and care in the child–father relationship, such as spending time together, talking and updating their knowledge of each other, and being financially supported. Rather than taking it for granted that their father would actively "always try to do the best that [he] can for you", the relationship was sometimes experienced as fragile and accomplished by effort. The presence of new partners and new children, step-siblings or 'half-siblings', often heightened awareness of the possibility of losing significance in their father's life. Cultural discourse negatively stereotyping 'broken families', absent fathers and stepmothers sometimes seemed to play a part in children's views. Socio–economic circumstances also had an impact by easing or compounding the difficulties of keeping in touch and having space and time together. While some children felt that they were able to maintain a 'good relationship' as a result of mutual effort, others concluded that their father was not willing to do this and was effectively lost to them. These contrasting scenarios are briefly illustrated by Danny's and Julie's accounts.

Danny's account describes the maintenance of a relationship with his father rather than its loss. Nevertheless, the discourse of broken family and uncertainty about his place in his father's life and his father's place in his were an aspect of his account. His first interview painted a rather negative picture of his weekend visits to his father's home. He talked about coping with a stepmother he didn't like and frustration at missing out on being with his friends in order to have a poor-quality experience in his father's home without any real possibility of one-to-one time with his father:

> It's good when I just spend time with my Dad, just me and him, but sometimes that doesn't happen, 'cause, like, we all work together when it's, like, my two stepsisters, my stepmum, and my sister, and me and my Dad. (Danny, age 11, 1st interview)

At a second interview, Danny talked about how things had changed. He had tried suspending visits to his father but his mother and a school friend counselled him that this was a mistake:

> My mum would always say … 'When you're older and you say you've not got a relationship with your dad any more, you'll feel guilty and you'll wish you had gone and even though sometimes you don't like your step mum, she's a nice person most of the time to you.' (Danny, age 11, 2nd interview)

One reason why he was happier with his visits to his father's house was because he had been allowed to bring two friends with him for a sleepover. His father's socio-economic situation permitted this by affording the space and resources to accommodate six children. The sleepover dissipated the tension Danny felt between time with his friends and time with his father's family. It was a symbolically important demonstration to Danny of his father's attention to his needs and willingness to include more of Danny in the new situation. The direct contact of Danny's friends with the characters in his father's family also shrank the possibilities for spinning tales of his hard life as a victim of a broken family and difficult stepmother and instead created further support for the continuing relationship with his father:

> I'll be honest about it, I think most of the time I started to like my stepmum a lot earlier than I wanted to admit but just because I thought it'd make me look good and it'll make me look as if I've got a really hard life. (Danny, age 11, 2nd interview)

In contrast, Julia experienced her father leaving her mother unequivocally in terms of loss. In her second interview, she described how watching a TV portrayal of the normative happy family triggered intense feelings of longing for such a family, of missing her father and becoming "upset for quite a while".

In Julia's assessment of the behaviour of her father, his practices of spending time, giving and caring failed to add up to intimacy. Her observations led her to conclude that her father had chosen not to keep time or space in his life for her: "He seems to have enough time for her [dad's girlfriend] but not enough for his own flesh and blood" (Julia, age 14, 2nd interview).

But another important element of her account was resistance to continuing her relationship with her father, in the context of a general thinning of her 'personal community' and weakening of sources of support, with consequences for her sense of self. Julia had been very close to her paternal grandparents as her only surviving grandparents. However, her paternal grandfather died in the 12 months before her parents' separation and the acrimony around the end of her parents' relationship precipitated the effective loss of her grandmother: "I've only got a Gran left and that's ma Dad's Mum and she was [pause] she doesn't talk to ma Mum, so I don't really like talking to her" (Julia, age 14, 1st interview).

Her mother's attitude was the antithesis of Danny's mother's and exuded hostility to her contact with her father. In the first interview, a few months after her father had left, Julia described a reversal of caring roles as she tried to look after her mother: "'cause my Dad's like recently left us, she kinda gets upset easily so I spend a lot of time with her" (Julia, age 14, 1st interview).

By the time of the second interview, she was not enjoying school and seemed isolated from friends, whom she described as bored with her being upset and sad:

> I suppose I wasn't as happy and up for doing as much things as I used to be, and they all just kind of got bored with that and just stopped hanging about with me, still haven't talked to me. I don't really talk to anyone in school. (Julia, age 14, 2nd interview)

Rather than reporting advice and supportive commentary on her situation from friends, she described school-based incidents involving victimisation by peers.

From the theoretical perspective sketched at the beginning, the separation of parents is less likely to inflict damage on a sense of self at a life-stage when other self-affirming relationships or systems of affirmation are playing major roles. Julia experienced the discourse of broken families as apposite. As in the case of Susie, family disruption coincided with and precipitated shrinkage in her support network. Julia also reported negative experiences at school, which turned a potential source of self-affirmation outside her family into another source of difficulty, undermining her sense of self-worth.

Losses for children in asylum-seeking families

Although asylum-seeking children were living with their parents and siblings, the extraordinary change of asylum modified family relationships. Extended family was lost as a local resource, radically reducing the supportive capacity of kin even when they were still in communication. The possibilities of immediate family life were also reshaped. Family practices and practices of intimacy, including their parents' capacity to care and provide, were constrained by the national policies and discourses framing asylum, the conditions of their immediate environment, and their lack of family-household resources. There was no possibility of parents playing a conventional role of provider since asylum-seekers are prohibited from taking employment while they remain in limbo waiting to hear if they have leave to remain in the country. Asylum-seeking families receive a lower level of subsistence than unemployment benefit, delivered in ways that are stigmatising and constrain consumption practices. Payments are delivered on a card that can only be used in certain shops on certain items. Credits cannot be carried over from week to week, making saving up for items impossible and the purchase of treats and gifts for children very difficult. Asylum-seeker children are aware of these constraints. For example, when attempting to ask Sanjay about his own experience of formal sources of support, he blurted out: "They don't give you, your own nationality, like, staying here [citizenship, a British passport, the right to remain]. We don't have that, so my Dad can't work" (Sanjay, 12).

The asylum-seeking children interviewed were all separated from their previous 'personal community' without any warning or opportunity for anticipatory preparation. Means of keeping in touch across distance were not necessarily effective in mitigating this loss:

> So, well actually I, I was kind of sad because I didn't. If I had thought. If I knew I was coming, I would have [said goodbye to] my grandparents and stuff and like I didn't really take photos or things but. We didn't, like, have that. We didn't bring much stuff, just clothes. (Serila, age 13)

Serila was seven or eight five years ago, when her parents brought her from rural Turkey where she had lived with them in her paternal grandparents' house. They arrived seeking asylum in London and came to Scotland under the Home Office dispersal programme. The experiences described here are typical of the small group of interviewees from asylum-seeking families but her family were advantaged in two respects. By her second interview, they had been given leave to remain in the UK, ending the years of uncertainty. Deportation is a more likely ending; shortly after interviews were completed, another interviewee was transferred to a detention centre before she could sit the exams for which, she told us, she had been studying hard. Serila's family were also fortunate because they had relatives in the UK, while most asylum-seekers have little prospects of ever seeing kin, since overseas travel is impossible and the circumstances of kin rarely enable visits to the UK. On arrival in Scotland, her initial problem was the complete absence of friends combined with her inability to communicate:

> The most difficult thing [in my life] was coming from Turkey to here and settling in here … there was no Turkish people where we lived, the area where we lived. And we didn't know anybody. So it was hard settling in at first and to the new school when I didn't know any English at all and couldn't understand what people were saying. (Serila, age 13)

Her account of loss also focused on her paternal grandparents, whom she placed alongside her parents as the 'most important people' in her life. She had regular telephone contact with them and they "sent videos so we can see what they look like". However, it is not clear whether this close contact moderated or accentuated a sense of loss: "and when I phoned them, they kind of cry, so it makes me so sad, but I know that's only [because] they love me. I really love them as well, so" (Serila, age 13).

Like all asylum-seeking children, she had to overcome significant obstacles in building a local 'personal community' to replace the one wholly or partially left behind on migration. Asylum-seeking parents lack the social, economic and cultural capital that can be used to ease their own or their children's entry into social worlds, beyond making links with other asylum-seekers from the same national, ethnic and religious backgrounds. Not all asylum-seeking children interviewed succeeded in building their own personal relationships. Sanjay, a young Afghani man, for example, never made friends; he had none after two years in primary school and one year in secondary school. Serila was able to name a group of children she was friendly with at school, but after five years, she had no close school friends. Across two interviews, her close friends were two daughters of other Turkish asylum-seekers living nearby and known to her parents. Even these friendships felt insecure because they relied on proximity and dispersal was a constant risk, since the housing of asylum-seekers included the short-term use of condemned property creating churn, and all without leave to remain in the country lived under the threat of deportation. Serila's parents placed restrictions on her that limited her opportunities to develop the friendly relationships she had in school beyond the school gates. She was not allowed to go out alone or to the houses of children whose parents were unknown to them: "I've not gone into sleepovers to my, any like friends, because my dad and my mum they feel like they don't know all my other friends. So they don't feel that it's safe for me to go" (Serila, age 13).

The social world of her immediate environment also worked against the recovery of a more extensive local 'personal community'. While restrictions sometimes rankled, Serila accepted that her parents needed to protect her from the moral and physical dangers of their neighbourhood. Like all asylum-seekers, her family was housed in an area of multiple deprivation, where evidence of drug and alcohol abuse was visible on the streets and regular reports of experiences of racism circulated among asylum-seeking families (Macaskill and Fisher, 2002; Avan and Bakshi, 2004; Heck, 2006; Hopkins and Hill, 2006). She saw her parents as passing on high moral standards that set her family apart from the children who were contributing to graffiti and trouble. Serila talked about "Scottish people" in her neighbourhood swearing and making offensive remarks to asylum-seekers "about their colour, their hair and stuff" and went on to narrate her own experience:

> When I first came here it was my age, like three girls my age, they kind of made me a bit sad.... I told my dad and he's like, 'Well, it's what they think, so you shouldn't get sad for what people say to you' and stuff. So I don't, even if they say it, I don't really get offended much. It doesn't really make me angry any more. (Serila, age 13)

She referred directly to the negative tabloid discourse deployed by "some Scottish and English people" about asylum-seekers "stealing their government's money by coming here".

For Serila, none of the losses of asylum-seeking were experienced as irrecoverable or creating a wounded self (Ketokivi, 2008). School as an institution and her experience of education played an important part in her positive sense of self and place in the world. Her focus at school was learning rather than making friends, getting on with the 'good education' she knew her parents wanted for her; her ambition was to become a lawyer. Nevertheless, the fact that she derived considerable satisfaction from her sense of learning was not unrelated to her experience of school as a friendly and safe place. School gave her some sense of belonging as well as access to the possibility of educational achievement with the promise of enhanced status within her family and the wider social world. When explaining what helped her get through the most difficult time, she talked of her mother and father as always trying to make her happy and two teachers who taught her English. Her mother, then father, loomed largest as her key significant others in her account of important people, but her 'personal community' also included her two Turkish close friends, an older cousin, other visiting UK-based kin and school-based friends/acquaintances. At the time of the second interview, she was anticipating her family getting passports and being able to see her grandparents again in about 12 months. If the ending of the asylum story had been deportation rather than leave to remain, the consequential loss would have been radically modified.

Concluding discussion

The forms of childhood change discussed – the death of a parent, the separation or divorce of parents, and the sudden unexpected migration with parents as an asylum seeker are not equally uncommon, but all are experienced as extraordinary biographical events involving more or less troubling loss. Public discourse attributes different forms of harm, victimhood and sometimes stigma to these events. A sociological framework and children's accounts point to an analysis of how to manage the troubles of loss. This indicates that minimising being troubled includes setting aside negative discourses framing loss as continuing trouble. This can only be confidently achieved with the help of effective interpersonal support and/or systems reaffirming belonging and self-worth by other means. The interpersonal 'network of care' or 'personal community' of 10- to 14-year-old children is typically their co-resident family, local kin and friends. Much depends on the capacity of this network to offer support before and after loss. Schooling is a formal system that most children inhabit with the potential to bestow identity, social recognition and belonging through progress in education as well as interpersonal relationships. For some experiencing troubling loss, school acted to provide self affirmation. A comparison of different types of loss demonstrates both the possibilities of school compensating for or amplifying deficits in the caring capacities of interpersonal networks and the particular significance of a caring parent playing a major role.

Children's accounts indicate that the opposite interpersonal circumstances – loss or threatened loss of a key significant other, a parent (through death or divorce) or the loss of all other interpersonal relationships except the parents (through asylum) – could have elements of similarity in experience softening this contrast. For example, continuities in the impact of these different types of family change can also be found at the level of 'personal communities'. Death and divorce as well as asylum-seeking could sometimes disrupt children's engagement with friends and kin because of emotional withdrawal, geographical mobility or shifting alliances, and asylum-seeking children can sometimes retain some attenuated links with the personal community they have left behind. But also, the continuity of asylum-seeking children's parents was not absolute, since children experienced very different parenting from that of their previous life. As already noted, the conditions of asylum mean new parental restrictions and parents' practices of caring and providing were necessarily different. All three situations of family change could potentially compromise parents' capacities to support their children, and illustrations of this emerged in some interviews. Just as children who lost a parent through divorce or death were vulnerable to being more troubled if their remaining co-resident parent was withdrawn or needy rather than a source of support, so asylum-seeking children are likely to be more vulnerable if the asylum process renders their parents depressed and despairing.

Children provided narratives both drawing on and repudiating or neutralising, and something in between, the negative discourses that frame the death or divorce of parents – victim of tragic loss or victim of broken families, absent fathers, difficult stepmothers. Friends were identified as an important audience for children's accounts of themselves in this respect. A striking example of the 'in between' concerned a self-presentation drawing on stereotypes of victimhood of divorce, while knowing the story to be more negative than the experienced reality. Continued contact with two loving parents does not fit the stereotype but still involves loss of a normative ideal family and ongoing effort that can feel difficult; the unsettling of previous parenting arrangements reveals that keeping a good relationship with a parent who is no longer co-resident cannot be taken for granted and more effortful persistence seems to be involved with the presence of a new partner. Even when the discourse does not fit the facts, it may, nevertheless, resonate with a sense of some loss, additional effort in maintaining interpersonal relationships and a less taken-for-granted sense of the future of personal relationships. In the case of asylum-seeking children, the negative discourse cannot resonate in this way and is not a resource that children can draw on to think about their own lives but rather a resource that tells them about how other people think. There are no possible gains for children in adopting the discourse that their family has come to the UK to 'steal the government's money'; self-respect requires its utter repudiation. At the same time, experiences of racism help create a sense that this is what many people think and reinforce barriers to making the move from being friendly with to being friends with children at school.

The contrast between the three types of family change helps focus attention on the different parts played by interpersonal, systemic and discursive processes in deflecting, minimising or amplifying the trouble loss brings. Interpersonal, particularly parent–child, relationships play a pivotal role in children's accounts of managing troubling loss. In some cases, the loss of a parent, whether by death or following separation, had a domino effect, weakening the supportive capacity of the remaining parent and knocking down other members of their 'personal community'. Children's personal support systems could be radically weakened without triggering any compensatory support mechanism within the school system,[4] where damage was sometimes amplified rather than counteracted. For other children, loss of a parent did not become a rupture in a 'network of care', largely because of the compensatory actions of someone, usually the other parent, substituting or standing in for the absence, sometimes deploying social and economic capital to heighten support from the wider 'personal community'. In the case of asylum-seeking children, parents and siblings were the only local support system on arrival and, not surprisingly, asylum-seeking children affirmed their overwhelming importance as key significant others, but the significance of more formal systems also comes more sharply into focus. Serila's story of survival in the months of not understanding English highlighted her parents' practices of comforting and encouraging, but her salvation was local authority provision of tuition delivered by sympathetic teachers. Asylum-seeking families' lack of social, economic and cultural capital, the other barriers they face against building local 'personal communities', and parental encouragement of engagement with education all heighten the significance of the education system for asylum-seeking children as potentially providing a site of belonging and self-worth.

Notes

[1] The *Cool with change* project (Highet and Jamieson, 2007) investigated the experiences and views of 10- to 14-year-olds of family change. Surveys were conducted in five schools in Glasgow selected as having pupils from diverse ethnic backgrounds and varied socio-economic circumstances. Muslim children with links to the Indian subcontinent were known to be the main ethnic group. The survey identified pupils who had experienced family change. In-depth interviews then explored young people's views. In total, 361

pupils were surveyed. Of these, 22% identified themselves as Muslim. Reflecting national trends, the less economically advantaged children were more likely to experience parental separation (31% of the most disadvantaged group of pupils compared to 18% of the most affluent group), but this was complicated by ethnicity. Muslims from the Indian subcontinent are one of a number of ethnic groups with consistently low rates of dissolution (Hylton, 1995; Berthoud, 2000; Pankaj, 2000): 9% of pupils classifying themselves as Muslim had experienced the separation of their parents compared to 32% classifying themselves as Christian and 29% of those with no religion.

2. *Cool with change* was a collaboration with Scotland's Families (the name then given to a consortium of voluntary organisations that included Couple Counselling Scotland, Family Mediation Scotland, One Parent Families Scotland, Scottish Marriage Care and Stepfamily Scotland) funded by the Community Fund, a form of lottery funding. Of the 361 10–14 year olds surveyed, 26% had experienced their co-resident parents separating, 12% had experienced their father having a new partner and 13% their mother having a new partner. In addition, 43% said that someone close to them had died recently, 4% had lost a parent and 4% had arrived in Britain seeking asylum. The final report of the project can be found on the Centre for Research on Families and Relationships website at: http://www.crfr.ac.uk/researchprojects/rp_cwc.html

3. While gendered divisions of labour may tend to make this outcome more common following the death of a mother rather than a father, the bereavement literature suggests that bereavement can impair women's capacities for intimacy as well as men's.

4. For Scottish secondary school children, the service that is most available and visible to them are 'guidance teachers', teachers within the school who have pastoral responsibilities and are flagged up to pupils as somebody they can go to. Confidentiality was always quickly raised when talking about talk, whether with friends or professionals. Some children strongly expressed the view that the teaching and counselling role could not be combined and confidentiality was not guaranteed. Some accounts expressed fear of stigma attached to seeking help and many endorsed stigmatising stereotypes of formal sources of help outside the school, including the idea that needing a counsellor is a sad indictment on your friends and your own competence (Brownlie, 2009). Many children have heard of Childline but see it as for dire emergencies. The most frequently mentioned attribute of social workers was their power to take children from their families and place them into care. Most interviewees were unaware of websites offering support to young people. When talking around hypothetical possibilities, children liked the idea of somebody who could be trusted who was in the school but not of the school, and this was seen as likely to be less problematic in terms of confidentiality than a peer- or teacher-led system. However, a lot of groundwork would have to be done to normalise use of a professional school-based service if it were not to further stigmatise its users. Not all children took the view that talking about feeling unhappy or worried by family change is helpful, whether with friends or family or anyone else. What some children wanted was diversion not a further focus on such troubles.

References

Avan, G. and Bakshi, N. (2004) 'My mum is now my best friend ... : asylum–seeker and refugee families in Glasgow', Glasgow: Save the Children.

Bagnoli, A. (2003) 'Imagining the lost other: the experience of loss and the process of identity construction in young people', *Journal of Youth Studies*, vol 6, pp 2003–217.

Batchelor, J., Dimmock, B. and Smith, D. (1994) *Understanding stepfamilies: what can be learned from callers to the STEPFAMILY Telephone Counselling Service*, London: Stepfamily Publications, NSA.

Berger, P.L. and Luckmann, T. (1967) *The social construction of reality: a treatise in the sociology of knowledge*, London: Allen Lane, The Penguin Press.

Berthoud, R. (2000) 'Family formation in multi-cultural Britain: three patterns of diversity', Institute for Social Research Working Paper 2000-34.

Boss, P. (1999) *Ambiguous loss: learning to live with unresolved grief*, Boston, MA: Harvard University Press.

Bourdieu, P. (1986) 'The forms of capital', in J.E. Richards (ed) *Handbook of the theory of research for the sociology of education*, New York, NY: Greenwood, pp 241–58.

Brannen, J. and Hepinstall, E.B.K (2000) *Connecting children: care and family life in later childhood*, London: Falmer.

Brownlie, J. (2009) 'Age of grief in a time of talk', *Sociological Research Online*, vol 14, no 5, 22.

Cait, C.-A. (2008) 'Identity development and grieving: the evolving processes for parentally bereaved women', *British Journal of Social Work*, vol 38, pp 322–39.

Douglas, G., Butler, I., Catherine, A., Fincham, F. and Murch, M. (2000) 'Children's perspectives and experiences of divorce', *Children*, vol 21, pp 5–16.

Dunn, J. and Deater-Deckard, K. (2001) *Children's views of their changing families*, York: Joseph Rowntree Foundation.

Erkison, E. (1950) *Childhood and society*, New York, NY: Norton.

Giddens, A. (1984) *The constitution of society: outline of the theory of structuration*, Cambridge: Polity Press.

Goffman, E. (1959) *The presentation of self in everyday life*, New York, NY: Doubleday.

Hansen, K. (2005) *Not so nuclear families: class, gender and networks of care*, London: Rutgers University.

Harrison, L. and Harrington, R. (2001) 'Adolescents; bereavement experiences: prevalence, association with depressive symptoms and use of services', *Journal of Adolescence*, vol 24, pp 159–69.

Heck, R. (2006) *The experiences and needs of refugee and asylum seeking children in the UK: A literature review*, Birmingham: National Evaluation of the Children's Fund, University of Birmingham.

Highet, G. and Jamieson, L. (2007) *Cool with change*, Edinburgh: Scotland's Families and CRFR. Available at: http://www.crfr.ac.uk/researchprojects/rp_cwc.html

Holdsworth, C. and Morgan, D. (2007) 'Revisiting the generalized other: an exploration', *Sociology*, vol 41, pp 401–17.

Holmes, M. (2010) 'The emotionalization of reflexivity', *Sociology*, vol 44, pp 139–54.

Hopkins, P. and Hill, M. (2006) '"*This is a good place to live and think about the future" … the needs and experiences of unaccompanied asylum- seeking children in Scotland*', Glasgow: Scottish Refugee Council.

Hylton, C. (1995) *Coping with change: family transitions in multi-cultural communities*, London: Stepfamily Publications, National Stepfamilies Association.

Ketokivi, K. (2008) 'Biographical disruption, the wounded self, and the reconfiguration of significant others', in E.D. Widmer and R. Jallinoja (eds) *Beyond the nuclear family: families in a configurational perspective*, Bern: Peter Lang.

Macaskill, S. and Fisher, S. (2002) *Starting again: Young asylum seekers views on life in Glasgow*, Glasgow: Education Services, Glasgow City Council.

McLean, M. and Eekalaar, J. (1997) *The parental obligation: a study of parenthood across households*, Oxford: Hart Publishing.

Mead, G.H. (1934) *Mind, self and society*, Chicago, IL: University of Chicago Press.

Pankaj, V. (2000) *Family mediation services for minority ethnic families in Scotland*, Legal Studies Research Findings 36, Edinburgh: Scottish Executive Central Research Unit.

Ribbens McCarthy, J. (2006) *Young people's experiences of loss and bereavement: towards an inter-disciplinary approach*, Buckingham: Open University Press.

Ribbens McCarthy, J. and Jessop, J. (2005) *Young people, bereavement and loss: disrupted transitions*, London: National Children's Bureau/JRF.

Ribbens McCarthy, J., Edwards, R. and Gillies, V. (2003) *Making families: Moral tales of parenting and stepparenting*, York: Sociology Press.

Smart, C. (2003) 'New perspectives on childhood and divorce', *Childhood*, vol 10, pp 123–9.

Smart, C. (2004) 'Equal shares: rights for fathers or recognition for children?', *Critical Social Policy*, vol 24, p 484.

Smart, C. (2007) *Personal life*, Cambridge: Polity.

Smart, C., Neale, B. and Wade, A. (2001) *The changing experience of childhood*, Cambridge: Polity.

Smith, D. (1987) *The everyday world as problematic: a feminist sociology*, Milton Keynes: Open University Press.

Spencer, L. and Pahl, R. (2006) *Rethinking friendship: hidden solidarities today*, Princeton, NJ: Princeton University Press.

Wade, A. and Smart, C. (2002) *Facing family change: children's circumstances, strategies and resources*, York: Joseph Rowntree Foundation.

Wellman, B., Carrington, P. and Hall, A. (1988) 'Networks as personal communities', in B. Wellman and S. Berkowitz (eds) *Social structures: a network approach*, Cambridge: Cambridge University Press, pp 130–84.

Widmer, E.D. and Sapin, M. (2008) 'Families on the move: insights on family configurations of individuals undergoing psychotherapy', in E.D. Widmer and R. Jallinoja (eds) *Beyond the nuclear family: families in a configurational perspective*, Bern: Peter Lang.

CHAPTER TWELVE

The permeating presence of past domestic and familial violence: "So, like, I'd never let anyone hit me but I've hit them, and I shouldn't have done"

Dawn Mannay

Introduction

As de Beauvoir (1949) argues, for women, the future is often haunted by phantoms of the past, which impact upon the present. This chapter draws on one woman's narrative journey from childhood to motherhood, examining how 'troubles' feature in her life in the form of domestic and familial abuse. Specifically, the permeating nature of 'trouble' is demonstrated in her ideas of what she might become and what she is afraid of becoming; and while she recognises abuse as a harm to be avoided if possible, and/or repaired, it is also routinely normalised in her account.

In the Introduction to Part Three, Hooper established the ways in which domestic abuse remains an insidious presence in the darker side of family life. Domestic abuse has a substantial financial cost to the economy (Walby, 2004) and such violence can also disrupt typical developmental trajectories through psycho-biological effects, post-traumatic stress disorder and cognitive consequences (Margolin and Gordis, 2000; Jarvinen at al, 2008).

Violence was not my initial research focus; nonetheless, as Rock (2007, p 30) contends, there is a 'need to remain open to the features that cannot be listed in advance of the study', and this family trouble was an invasive element in the construction of femininity (see Mannay, 2011). The normalisation of male violence was central in the participants' accounts, where masculinity was tied to aggression and male violence was naturalised.

Adult recollections of violence in childhood supported Henriques et al's (1998) contention that the question of who we are is tied to the memory of who we have been and the imagination of what we might become. In this way, male violence had a pervasive hold over the participants, permeating their everyday lives and aspirations, becoming normalised, and engendering intergenerational journeys that threaten to impinge on their daughters' trajectories.

The study

The data were drawn from a wider research project that employed visual and narrative methods of data production to explore the experiences of mothers and daughters residing on a marginalised housing estate. The research focused on the ways in which the boundaries of the immediate culture and memories of the past mediate their educational and employment histories and futures.

Research was conducted in Hystryd,[1] a predominantly white urban area, which ranks as one of the most deprived communities in Wales (Welsh Assembly Government, 2008). Nine mothers and their daughters participated in the project. I previously lived in Hystryd and this shared sense of geography positioned me as 'experience near' (Anderson, 2002, p 23). Consequently, it was important to address my position as an indigenous researcher and make a deliberate cognitive effort to question my taken-for-granted assumptions of that which I had thought familiar (Delamont and Atkinson, 1995).

Participant-directed visual data production techniques of photo-elicitation, mapping and collage were selected to limit the propensity for participants' accounts to be overshadowed by the enclosed, self-contained world of common understanding (see Mannay, 2010). Participants took photographs, drew maps, and made collages depicting meaningful places, spaces and activities, and then discussed them with me in tape-recorded interviews to ensure that I understood what they intended to communicate (Rose, 2001).

'Possible selves' narratives were also elicited – participants were asked to produce narratives from the retrospective perspective of their childhood self, describing who they wanted to become (positive possible self) and who they feared becoming (negative possible self), and this activity was repeated from the perspective of the present. For this chapter, I have selected data produced with one mother, Zoe,[2] drawing from interviews around her 'possible selves' narratives, to explore the centrality of 'trouble' in family life and the ways in which family troubles are both normalised and pathologised.

"When I was just a little girl"

This section draws on the retrospective accounts of Zoe, thinking back to her childhood possible selves and analyses the connections between individual biography and the future self. The following extract is taken from Zoe's retrospective past 'possible selves' narratives written from the perspective of being a dependent young daughter: "I wanted to be a nurse when I was younger. I've always had a very caring side that wanted to help other people and feel that my daughters are the same."

This narrative fits with wider discourses of appropriate work for women and the naturalisation of women's capacity to care. However, when we examine the accompanying interview, we see how the career aspiration is related to the prevalence of domestic violence:

> I didn't think I would be able to, I didn't think I was intelligent enough
> to become a nurse, so I never bothered, but I think I only wanted to
> be a nurse because of what my Mother went through and everything,
> 'cause I wanted to stop people getting hurt.... Well, to help people
> that got hurt. (Zoe)

The ambition of nursing was not only a vocation embedded in discourses of
women's work, but a reaction to an individual biography where violence in the
home was prevalent and sustained, and one where her mother frequently *'got
hurt'*, a discourse we see in Zoe's retrospective negative 'possible selves' narrative:

> My Dad was quite abusive to my Mum when I was growing up and
> I didn't want to end up with someone like him. Although I love my
> Dad because he's my Dad, I hate him sometimes because of what he
> put my Mum through.... Another negative self would have been that
> I wasn't able to protect my Mum and felt quite helpless when she
> suffered at my father's hands. (Zoe)

The extract illustrates the difficulty of 'loving *and* hating the same person' (Lucey,
Chapter Fourteen, this volume); and throughout the account, there is sadness
about the child's inability to intervene ("I wasn't able to protect my Mum") and
an associated guilt, which although dismissed by adult rationality, still lingers
unforgiving and pervasively regulates Zoe's adult life. An insight into the weight of
this perceived culpability is evident in a memory Zoe shares about the aftermath
of an episode of domestic violence.

Zoe explains how her father broke her mother's arm and after this incident,
her mother wanted him to leave the family home. Zoe's father sat Zoe down and
told her that her mother wanted him to leave but that the decision was in her
hands. Zoe was to decide whether her father should stay or leave. In a violently
charged and highly coercive atmosphere, Zoe said that her father should stay.
The self-reproach of Zoe's narrative is palpable, and although an adult rationality
of the situation is presented in part and echoed by my own interactions with
Zoe, confirming that her father would have remained whatever her reply, these
unanswerable possibilities continue to haunt the present.

The physical violence in Zoe's parental home had, according to Zoe, abated
some years prior to the interview. The catalyst for the change after three decades of
physical abuse was an incident when a grandchild was unintentionally embroiled
in a physical conflict. The near injury of the grandchild resulted in the expulsion
of Zoe's father from the family home, as discussed in the following extract:

> He haven't, he haven't hit her since, I think because of what he done
> to [grandchild], he sort of thought '*Oh my God*, like I just hurt my
> [grandchild] now as well so its got to stop'.... Yeah she kicked him

out ages didn't she, for about a year, and then she had him back, silly cow [laughs] [both laugh], but he haven't hit her since. (Zoe)

Zoe found her mother's decision to take her father back disappointing. Zoe uses the phrase "silly cow" in a humorous tone, illustrated by the responding laughter, but there is an underlying frustration in her voice. In an earlier study, Walkerdine (1997) describes a family in which domestic violence is prevalent. Walkerdine suggests that the daughter holds deep pre-Oedipal feelings about her mother that can be turned into dislike for a woman who it seems must deserve the beatings she is getting.

The pre-Oedipal case may be relevant, but here, for Zoe, this resentment appears to be more connected with the ongoing sense of responsibility carried from childhood and built up through the life of the maternal relationship. Therefore, although actual bodily harm no longer characterises the relationship, the legacy of domestic abuse remains a powerful and pervasive presence, which elicits a new narrative of protection: "Yeah that's what I mean about her, like she likes a full house, she don't like to be on her own with my Dad".

This extract is taken from Zoe's second interview where we discuss her retrospective narrative account of domestic violence. Zoe explains that she endeavours to visit her mother daily and that there is an unspoken rule of protection among her and her siblings. As Page and Jha (2009, p 106) maintain, girls are still often taught to be 'housebound, caring and self-sacrificing' and, in conversations about education and employment, Zoe describes how she has sacrificed her own opportunities to provide a protective presence in her childhood home.

Zoe's own ambitions and her plans to better herself and improve her own family's prospects disrupted this perceived duty of care and caused an unliveable tension, resulting in the abandonment of training and employment opportunities and confinement to low-paid, unqualified care work. Bates (1994) explored male violence in conjunction with working-class girls' involvement with and training for low-level employment in the care sector. In homes where male violence forms part of the everyday, Bates (1994) proposes that family background mediates a set of social attributes that prepare young women to deal with the emotional and physical violence against employees endemic in the caring sector.

Therefore, as well as conforming to a prevailing ideology of 'sacrificial femininity' (Holloway, 2006), the disciplinary socialisation acts as a vehicle for learning 'to take' physical abuse. Importantly, Bates's (1994) focus on violent practices regulated in the culture of the home reinforces the salience of the normalisation of male violence. I expand on this 'normalisation' in the following section.

"But that was just a slap"

Phillips (2003) argues that although it is rare for girls to use physical violence on a regular basis, studies focusing on the meaning of violence in girls' lives show how violence is perceived by many young girls and women as 'normal' and routine. Although Zoe recognises her childhood experiences as abusive, there is a tacit expectance and acceptance of what she interprets as lower-level physical violence, and a distinction between acceptable and expected violence as opposed to the unacceptable, as illustrated in the following extract presented as everyday family life:

Zoe:	Yeah [laughs] [both laugh] I'd beat one [brother] up and then they'd all tie me down and batter me [laughs] all of 'em booting me in the head and all that.
Interviewer:	Oh no.
Zoe:	Yeah [laughs] it's funny thinking about it.
Interviewer:	Was it, did you used to get frightened at the time or didn't you used to care?
Zoe:	No, I mean you just used to rage and didn't care if they used to hit you then, I can remember one time my brother chucked a snooker ball at my head.
Interviewer:	Ah no.
Zoe:	So I picked up the snooker cue and snapped it across his head.

This memoire of sibling fighting is presented as 'normal' family life and the laughter and commentary ("its funny thinking about it") belies the embodiment of violence.

However, Zoe introduces this childhood reflection after discussing her own children and saying "I didn't want to have kids that fought all the time", implying that her upbringing was not as painless as the laughter and colloquialisms suggest. When I ask about her parents' response to this sibling 'play', Zoe's answer reinforces the admissibility of aggressive physicality:

Zoe:	Mum and Dad used to just let us fight, they used to say "Just fight it out".
Interviewer:	Did they?

| Zoe: | Yeah [laughs] they used to just sit back until one of us got hurt and they'd be "Right that's enough now, you deserved that" [laughs] [both laugh], yeah. |

This 'hands–off' parenting process ("just sit back until one of us got hurt") suggests a continuum of aggression that moves from harmless sibling rivalry to something that must be curtailed in response to injury (see Lucey, Chapter Fourteen). The extent of the physical damage acts as a signifier between the harmless and the harmful. The permissive attitude to violence within the home was not reflected in Zoe's use of outdoor space, where her mother's parenting took a more proactive stance:

| Zoe: | I was always taught that I had to fight to defend myself like. |

| Interviewer: | Mmm. |

| Zoe: | So if I ever got into an argument, my Mum used to say "Right get out that street now and batter her now or I'll batter you." |

| Interviewer: | Did she? |

| Zoe: | Yeah [laughs] [both laugh] I'd rather give someone else a hiding than have one off my mother [laughs] … she wanted me to be a stronger person and she was just thinking like "She won't be going through this when she's got boyfriends." |

| Interviewer: | Yeah. |

| Zoe: | "Just make her tough and then she'll never take any of it" … and in a way it's worked 'cause I wouldn't there's no way I would take anyone hitting me. |

Zoe was taught to fight back and non-compliance was met with the threat of physical punishment from her mother, an imagined "hiding" that would make the street fight pale in comparison. Cawson (2002) argues that there is a strong overlap between the physical abuse of children and domestic violence, and from a child protection perspective, Zoe's childhood account could be read as abusive.

However, Zoe reflects on sibling and peer violence within and outside the home pragmatically, explaining that her mother wanted her to be a "stronger person", one who would not become a victim of domestic abuse. This parental protection strategy of 'fighting fire with fire' has had some success according to Zoe, who justifies her mother's actions with the phrase "in a way it's worked". However, tactics to impart the tools of self-defence through the medium of violence can have unintended consequences, in that defence becomes attack:

Zoe: I think that's what frightened me, the once and once he [Zoe's partner] did threaten me when I was sat on the toilet and that and that's when my Dad really battered my Mum when she was sat on the toilet once ... so that brought back memories and I was like "No you're gone", and like that was the second time I kicked him out, but he learnt 'cause he never did it since ... I have punched him in the face and all that.

Interviewer: Oh, have you?

Zoe: Yeah [pause] and I think that's affected me from what my Dad was doing.

Interviewer: Yeah.

Zoe: So, like, I'd never let anyone hit me but I've hit them, and I shouldn't have done.

Interviewer: D'you feel bad then?

Zoe: Yeah I was really violent before, you know I didn't batter him or nothing, but it's just like I punched him in the face, hit him with a sweeping brush, I been nasty and all that.

Interestingly, this conversation evolves from Zoe's retrospective positive possible self narrative, where there is an idealised representation of a future husband "one day I would have a prince charming to marry". However, Towns and Adams' (2000) conception of the Beast Prince is evoked a few minutes after this introduction of 'perfect love', when Zoe talks about how her partner frightened her in an incident that corresponds with a specific childhood memory of domestic violence. Here, the pedagogical training in self-defence and the adage "there's no way I would take anyone hitting me" is tested.

Zoe draws on these resources to challenge and resist domestic abuse, but the recurrence of domestic abuse elicits a violent reaction and engenders a set of new difficulties in which Zoe employs violence to guard against victimisation ("So, like, I'd never let anyone hit me but I've hit them [her partner], and I shouldn't have done"). Zoe acknowledges that this behaviour is wrong and although she does not want to be in the same position as her mother, neither does she want to act like her father, citing him as the source of her aggression ("I think that's affected me from what my Dad was doing"). Identification with either parent has damaging connotations and Zoe needs to establish ground from which she can split the 'bad' mother and the 'bad' father away from her identity as an acceptable self, partner and mother (Klein, 1975).

Again, we see techniques of justification embodied in the type of physical violence. Feminine violence is often viewed as 'doubly deviant' (Phillips, 2003), and Zoe differentiates her actions from perceived 'real' violence ("I didn't batter him or nothing"). Zoe may have "punched him in the face, hit him with a sweeping brush" and she admits "I been nasty and all that". However, the domestic violence endured by her mother went beyond surface physicality, there were injuries sustained and the embodied legacy of bruises, cuts and broken bones affiliated with '*battering*'.

Being '*nasty*' allows for a retention of femininity, the composite 'mean girl' (Ringrose, 2006), in a way that 'battering' cannot allow. '*Battering*' is more than '*just a slap*'; it represents a troubling masculinity embodied in the both loved and hated father figure. Violence, then, cannot sit easily with femininity, but there seems to be something about being feminine that also engenders abuse. This was the impasse that confronted Zoe's mother and now it has become a consideration for the next generation:

> She [her daughter] don't see no violence in my house so I don't understand it [pause] she's always fighting in the street, I've had to stop her going out and all that.... Yeah she's not scared of no one, maybe she got that from me, I don't know but she's never seen me fight or be aggressive like. (Zoe)

Zoe is not sure how to address her daughter's fighting. It is causing difficulties with the neighbours, but learning not to be "scared of no one" has served Zoe well because she is not a victim of domestic violence. The grading of violence has rendered many forms of aggression invisible and Zoe is convinced that her daughter has "never seen me fight or be aggressive". The subjective identification of aggression discounts many words and actions that do not fall within '*battering*' and the following extract is typical of an exchange that describes an argument between her and her brother when they are visiting their mother and father's home:

Zoe:	And if I shouts at him and that, he just gets abusive towards me then call me a stupid C. U. N. T. or …
Interviewer:	Yeah.
Zoe:	… fat bitch or something, or "Shut your fucking mouth or I'll punch you in the face."

This conversation is tied to the rivalry between cousins on visits to Zoe's mother's and the way in which the children's arguments become a bone of contention between siblings. Phrases like "Shut your fucking mouth or I'll punch you in the face" are commonplace in arguments between Zoe's siblings, Zoe's parents and within her intimate relationship.

In this way, violence can be dangerously both an expected and accepted 'family trouble' that although recognised as '*aggression*', is normalised in ways dependent on both the form of abuse and its context. As Page and Jha (2009, p 194) maintain, 'children will continue to absorb the biases of existing understandings of society and reproduce these ways of thinking in the future', and in this familial milieu, Zoe's daughter will negotiate her femininity and face decisions about how abuse should be categorised, avoided, challenged, accepted, expected or rejected.

Concluding remarks

There may well be new opportunities for generations of girls that exceed what was available to their mothers (Nielsen, 2004); nevertheless, this chapter demonstrates how violence actively contributes to the real and symbolic subordination of girls, and often clouds these new horizons across the life course.

A particularly problematic aspect of the data has been the distinction between acceptable low-level violence, which is attached to 'normal' masculinity, as opposed to 'battering'. The prefix '*it was only*' before the description of the attack of a '*slap*' or a '*punch*' indicates that many women and their daughters live with a normalised, yet pathological, presence of danger that they may consider only requires action when they define it as '*battering*'. It is important to lift this delicately veiled guise of the common and the commonplace, and maintain that everyday cultural practices and traditions can no longer be employed to sustain domestic abuse.

Individual biographies can be useful to examine the ways in which women negotiate the darker side of family life. This chapter sought to trouble the 'normal', to restate and make central the salience of embodied violence in the construction and maintenance of lived femininity and masculinity, and to ask why, in a supposedly enlightened and forward-thinking society, brute strength and dominant physicality remain implicit in retaining, enforcing and regulating femininity across generations.

Acknowledgements

I would like to acknowledge Zoe, who made this chapter possible, and also Professor John Fitz, Dr Emma Renold and Dr Bella Dicks, for supervising this research project. The doctoral research project from which this chapter is drawn was titled 'Mothers and daughters on the margins: gender, generation and education' and was funded by the Economic and Social Research Council.

Notes

[1] Hystryd is a pseudonym chosen to maintain the anonymity of the area.

[2.] Zoe is a pseudonym chosen to maintain the participant's anonymity.

References

Anderson, G.L. (2002) 'Reflecting on research for doctoral students in education', *Education Researcher*, vol 31, no 7, pp 22–5.

Bates, I. (1994) '"A job which is right for me?" Social class, gender and individualization', in I. Bates and G. Riseborough (eds) *Youth and inequality*, Buckingham: Open University Press.

Cawson, P. (2002) *Child maltreatment in the family*, London: NSPCC.

De Beauvoir, S. (1949) *The second sex*, London: Penguin.

Delamont, S. and Atkinson, P. (1995) *Fighting familiarity: essays on education and ethnography*, Cresskill, NJ: Hampton Press.

Henriques, J., Holloway, W., Urwin, C., Venn, C. and Walkerdine, V. (1998) *Changing the subject*, London: Routledge.

Holloway, W. (2006) *The capacity to care: gender and ethical subjectivity*, London: Routledge.

Jarvinen, J., Kail, A. and Miller, I. (2008) *Violence against women: hard knock life*, London: New Philanthropy Capital.

Klein, M. (1975) *Love, guilt and reparation, and other works, 1921–1945*, London: Hogarth Press.

Mannay, D. (2010) 'Making the familiar strange: can visual research methods render the familiar setting more perceptible?', *Qualitative Research*, vol 10, no 1, pp 91–111.

Mannay, D. (2011) 'Taking refuge in the branches of a guava tree: the difficulty of retaining consenting and non-consenting participants' confidentiality as an indigenous researcher', *Qualitative Inquiry*, vol 17, no 10, pp 962–4.

Margolin, G. and Gordis, E.B. (2000) 'The effect of family and community violence on children', *Annual Review of Psychology*, vol 51, pp 445–79.

Nielsen, H.B. (2004) 'Noisy girls: new subjectivities and old gender discourses', *Nordic Journal of Youth Research*, vol 12, no 1, pp 9–30.

Page, E. and Jha, J. (eds) (2009) *Exploring the bias: gender and stereotyping in secondary schools*, London: Commonwealth Secretariat.

Phillips, C. (2003) 'Who's who in the pecking order? Aggression and "normal violence" in the lives of girls and boys', *British Journal of Criminology*, vol 47, pp 710–28.

Ringrose, J. (2006) 'A new universal mean girl: examining the discursive construction and social regulation of a new feminine pathology', *Feminism and Psychology*, vol 16, no 4, pp 405–24.

Rock, P. (2007) 'Symbolic interactionism and ethnography', in P. Atkinson, A. Coffey, S. Delamont, J. Lofland and L. Lofland (eds) *Handbook of ethnography*, London: Sage, pp 26–38.

Rose, G. (2001) *Visual methodologies*, London: Sage.

Towns, A. and Adams, P. (2000) 'If I really loved him enough he would be okay: women's accounts of male partner violence', *Violence Against Women*, vol 6, no 6, pp 558–85.

Walby, S. (2004) *The cost of domestic violence*, London: Department of Trade and Industry, Women and Equality Unit.

Walkerdine, V. (1997) *Daddy's girl: young girls and popular culture*, London: Macmillan.

Welsh Assembly Government (2008) *Welsh index of multiple deprivation 2008: summary report*, Cardiff: Welsh Assembly Government.

CHAPTER THIRTEEN

Thinking about sociological work on personal and family life in the light of research on young people's experience of parental substance misuse

Sarah Wilson

Parental substance misuse (PSM) has been the focus of much applied social policy work in recent years (ACMD, 2003, 2007). It has been estimated that two million young people in the UK are affected by PSM (Manning et al, 2009), with significant implications for social work caseloads. Such circumstances are relatively absent, however, from recent mainstream sociological discussion of personal and family life. Here, partly in response to the pathologisation of family diversity and change in some literature (Beck–Gernsheim, 1998; Bauman, 2003) and in the New Right family policy it has influenced, much work has focused on continuities in 'ordinary' family practices (Strathern, 1992; Gross, 2005; Charles et al, 2008) and on 'normalising' to some degree certain family troubles, notably parental separation (Duncan and Edwards, 1999; Ribbens McCarthy et al, 2000). This interest in parental separation has had the result of focusing somewhat greater attention on adult, chosen relationships rather than on those of children and young people. Further, while there is a growing body of work on children's constructions of relationships, this has also focused on more 'ordinary' rather than more 'troubled' families (O'Brien et al, 1996; Mason and Tipper, 2008). Another strand of this recent sociological work has explored the high degree of contemporary anxiety around family life (Illouz, 2007; Mason, 2008) and the importance accorded to 'displaying' family, especially in less conventional circumstances (Finch, 2007). Some of this work has identified the current influence of a 'psychoanalytic imagination' (Illouz, 2007, p 7), according to which the experience of childhood within a nuclear family is viewed as the pre-eminent source of the construction of self, thus reinforcing perceptions of those with difficult early experiences as 'damaged'.

This chapter draws on the author's experience of analysing data from two applied projects exploring young people's experiences of PSM (Bancroft et al, 2004; Houmøller et al, 2011) in the light of this recent sociological work on personal and family life. Presenting the results of this analysis has led to an uneasy 'odd one out' feeling at sociological conferences, where, in recent years (and in contrast to earlier feminist work on domestic violence), family diversity has been explored more in relation to differences of structure and formation than poverty, emotional neglect or physical abuse. This chapter argues for a greater incorporation of such difficult experiences of relationships, including those of children and young people, into current sociological thinking around personal life. The relative absence of such experiences runs the risk of constructing 'an anodyne, cuddly version' of personal and family lives (Smart, 2007, p 54) – a sociology unusually focused on the relatively fortunate perhaps. On the one hand, the data presented in this chapter highlight the continuing discursive power of the family (Charles et al, 2008) or the 'family we live by' (Gillis, 1996). However, these data also point to the importance of exploring what might be seen as the 'flip side' of influential contemporary sociological concepts, and particularly the absence or loss of expected 'family practices' (Morgan, 1996) and the difficulty of 'displaying' a family life recognised as such by others (Finch, 2007) in certain circumstances. It is argued that such analysis also suggests the need to develop a conceptual language that can capture, rather than flatten, the complex and often ambivalent emotional significance of such experience (Smart, 2007).

The chapter will first present data from an empirical study of the effects of PSM on young people before returning to a more theoretical discussion of these findings.

Empirical background

This chapter will draw on a qualitative study with 38 young people (20 women, 18 men) affected by PSM (both drugs and alcohol) (Bancroft et al, 2004).[1] In addition to examining the impact of their parents' substance misuse, this research explored themes of resilience and transitions from the young people's perspectives.

Interviews were carried out in urban and semi-rural locations across mainland Scotland between 2002 and 2004 with young people recruited through a variety of organisations, including universities, young people's health projects, young carers' organisations, youth cafes and community drugs and young offenders' projects. Most respondents were aged 16–21 (with a mean age of 19). Several respondents had experienced one or more family 'reconstructions', nine had grown up primarily with a sole parent, while 15 were from 'intact' families with both birth parents. Some still lived with their substance-misusing parent; all except two had done so within the previous two years and most within the past year. Many of the young people were from deprived urban or post-industrial communities. However, a few (six) were middle-class and varying levels of educational attainment and service use were represented. Some respondents had experienced substance misuse problems themselves, although their number was inflated by a period of recruitment through a substance prescription facility. At the time of their interviews, some had casual jobs or were on benefits, while others were in education, including at university, or in skilled employment.

The 'ordinary complexity of kinship' (Mason and Tipper, 2008, p 443) renders any clear distinction between 'ordinary' and 'troubled' family circumstances difficult to maintain, and 'ordinary' samples will often reveal more difficult situations (Gillies et al, 2001). The respondents in this sample, however, had all experienced circumstances that they had found very difficult, the normalisation of which, as Ribbens McCarthy et al point out in Chapter One, might risk overlooking harm. Such circumstances were often intertwined with their parents' substance misuse problems and included violence and emotional abuse by a parent (experienced by 25 respondents overall) and domestic violence (witnessed by 14 respondents overall), as well as neglect, parental mental ill-health, caring for a parent or siblings, parental imprisonment, and lack of contact with a parent. A small number had experienced longer or more intermittent periods in care.

Since supportive relationships have been identified as critical to the development of young people's resilience in difficult circumstances (Newman and Blackburn, 2002; Gilligan, 2003), the respondents were made aware that the interview would touch on such relationships beforehand. At the beginning of the interview, a life grid exercise facilitated discussion of diverse aspects of the respondents' lives, allowing them to disclose both positive and more sensitive experiences and relationships at their own pace, rather than in response to direct interviewer questioning. The few subsequent questions on 'important relationships' were contextualised by this life grid discussion and seemed to flow relatively easily.

These questions did elicit many accounts of supportive relationships both within and beyond respondents' immediate families as conventionally defined. As such, they allowed respondents to 'display' a coherent family narrative (Finch, 2007). However, some respondents reflected on the absence of such support from expected family sources in response to these questions. That such reflections were often also made at other points in the interview, seemingly unprompted by specific questions, suggests that this was a significant subject that respondents wanted to discuss. While a small minority of respondents were upset by such reflections, all wanted to continue the interview, and the interviewer took care not to return to issues and relationships that the life grid conversation had suggested were particularly sensitive to an individual respondent. Ethical advice and clearance was received from individual agencies, a large statutory social work department and a local NHS Research Ethics Committee. Further details of the conduct of the study are presented elsewhere (Wilson et al, 2007, 2012).[2]

The following section will present data from the project that suggests the importance to the respondents of certain expectations around parenting practices, the difficulties posed to them by the absence or loss of such practices, as well as the difficulties of displaying families in such circumstances.

The significance of the absence and loss of expected parenting practices

Perhaps some of the clearest illustrations of the effects of the absence of expected parental practices are contained in the accounts of a significant minority of respondents (15 overall) who recounted that they had rejected, or were considering rejecting, their biological parents. The following examples indicate that these parents were considered to have breached embedded expectations of parenting practices. Here, Kyle reflects on the absence of his biological father, who he had met only twice:

> Bairns [children] deserve to have two parents eh?... I was always a football player.... And there wasn't any dad there to watch me play, there wasn't any dad to take me to training, there wasn't any dad to go to parents' evenings at school ... to give me a birthday card ... take me places, doing all the normal things what a dad should be doing. (Kyle, age 19, mother drug use)

Others also considered that a parent had abandoned them:

> I went into care and ... he didnae even bother to fucking phone me or fuck all. So I just tell him to fuck off. (Gerry, age 19, father alcohol use)

Sarah Wilson (SW):	So how do you get on with your mother?
Kelly (age 21, mother alcohol use):	[laughs] I don't. Never spoke to her since she threw me out.... You might think this is sad but I wouldnae even bother if she died tomorrow because of the things that were said and done.

At first sight, such angry accounts might suggest a relatively easy breach in relationship, where expectations of certain practices were disappointed. However, closer analysis revealed the continuing dilemmas posed to the young people, Kelly included, when trying to explain such circumstances:

> If I'd just left on my own will ... maybe stuff that's happened might have been my fault.... I think that's maybe why ... I stayed so long. I don't know why I stayed so long.... It was my mum!... But I wasnae the one that chose to leave. (Kelly, age 21, mother alcohol use)

This excerpt suggests the emotional significance of not being easily able to draw on or to display a coherent or conventional family narrative. Kelly's loss seemed to be compounded by a sense of (her own) guilt at breaching embedded moral obligations to parents ("It was my mum!"). In response, she emphasises her mother's, rather than her own, role in severing their relationship ("I wasnae the one that chose to leave"). In spite of her mother's violence and neglect, and the anxiety Kelly had experienced in looking after her, this passage illustrates the difficulty of relating non-contact with a vulnerable parent in the interview encounter while also maintaining a moral self-narrative.

Several other respondents' accounts also suggested how difficulties in constructing or displaying a close-knit family of origin were experienced as a source of shame. For Lucy, the contrast between her own family life and her experience, however idealised, of those of her friends was painful:

> If I was at my chum's house, which I always was because I was never at home ... and just to see how well they got on with their mum and their dad and all their brothers and sisters. They were so happy sitting having meals together. Going out and doing stuff. And I found it pretty hard just to think why could I nae have a family like that? (Lucy, age 17, mother alcohol use)

Carine stated strongly that she had "no family", but also felt embarrassed by this situation and reported finding everyday circumstances that highlighted this absence as difficult:

> The first time I registered [at the doctor's], they asked for an emergency contact ... I put like my support worker ... [upset]. They asked me why I didn't want to put my parents in and I went, I went 'You don't need to know why I don't want to put my parents in you [angry] ... I just don't want to. (Carine, age 19, father alcohol use)

Not only, therefore, did respondents find it difficult or embarrassing to explain their family circumstances, but it also seemed that others were unwilling to allow them to define themselves other than in relation to their families of origin or to choose who to include in their definition of family. In this context, the following exchange with Rachel is interesting:

Rachel (age 17, mother alcohol use):	It's hard but ... I've got to break away, I've got to break the chains.
SW:	That's the way you see it? Like chains? ... Feeling that you should be looking after your mother?
Rachel:	I should be looking after her, but I can't. 'Cos I want to get on with my own life now.

This metaphor of 'breaking the chains', developed alongside friends, provided a more positive narrative for her non-contact with the mother she had previously cared for, a circumstance that she feared others might characterise as 'selfish'.

In the light of such difficult experiences, it is perhaps unsurprising that many respondents drew on narratives in their interviews that allowed them to present themselves as members of a coherent family. For example, some respondents who were not in contact with one biological parent emphasised an excellent relationship with the other. Notably, Kelly highlighted her excellent relationship with her father, in contrast to her mother with whom, as discussed, she had no contact. On one level, this is surprising since, in her view, her father's imprisonment when she was 14 had led to her mother's drinking and an abrupt deterioration in her home environment: "that's when like my dad got the jail and then my mum kind of went off the rails. But everything was fine till I was about 14.... We had a brilliant life ... really happy" (Kelly, age 21, mother alcohol use).

Kelly's determination to praise her father's post-release and continuing commitment to his children, rather than blaming him for the effects of his long imprisonment on the family, may in part reflect a desire to display a strong relationship with at least one biological parent.

Similarly, several respondents emphasised their efforts to maintain, nurture and rebuild relationships with parents, in spite of current or past difficulties. This concern is illustrated by Anna's reflections on her father's attempts to make up for years of heavy drinking:

> I think whatever problems mum and dad both had ... they still loved us and ... want us to be a family and it was a strong sense of like ... they were good people at heart. It's just whatever things got in the way. (Anna, age 19, father alcohol use)

Further several respondents spoke about a substance-misusing parent in a way that shielded this parent from potential criticism:

> She's never, ever believed in hitting any of us kids.... She's always made sure we're bathed, fed, clean bed.... Even though she done [amphetamines] ... she was a good, she is a good mum. (Mia, age 19, mother polydrug use)

> The drink never affected my ... wellbeing.... My mum, she always done her best in me ... made sure that I was at school and that I had nice clothes. (Leanne, age 17, mother alcohol use)

Such accounts suggest expectations of parenting practices influenced, perhaps, by long experience of parents' problems, and potentially also of caring for these parents. At the same time, they reflect a strong sense of the importance to the respondents of having a parent, often a sole parent, as in Leanne's case, who cared *about* them, even if the same parent had not been able to care for them effectively at all times (Backett-Milburn et al, 2008).

In the absence of strong relationships with biological parents, and sometimes in addition to these, a few respondents highlighted strong relationships with adult friends of their parents or with friends' parents or service workers, sometimes identifying them as 'parents', at least for certain periods. As discussed, Carine emphasised that she had no relationship with her biological family. However, in her interview, she highlighted her relationships with two alternative mothers, who, at different times, had acted towards her in the 'motherly' way her own mother had not. One was the supported accommodation keyworker she mentioned in relation to her GP registration, while a friend's mother had played this role when she was still at school:

> We went to our prom night and she was like 'Wait, wait I need to take your picture' [laughs] and 'You need to make sure you get home on time!' acting like my mum.... I would go there [friend's house] so often and her mum would say ... 'You are like a daughter to me.' (Carine, age 19, father alcohol use)

In each case, Carine emphasised the 'mother' figure's, rather than her own, role in creating the relationship. Again, the importance of displaying some sort of family, and one that included parental figures in spite of the difficulties experienced, is clear.

Discussion

Illouz (2007, p 7) highlights the pervasive contemporary influence of the 'psychoanalytic imagination', according to which 'the nuclear family is the very point of origin of the self – the site from which the story and the history of the self could begin'. Charles et al (2008, p 6) argue that 'normal family' practices are embodied in individuals and their identities and desires through habitus. Similarly, Finch (2007) has identified the importance of displaying, and therefore of being able to display, a normative family life. All of this work is helpful in thinking about the data discussed in this chapter, which further suggest the difficulties posed to young people in troubled family circumstances by the absences of expected family practices and by material and discursive barriers to displays of family life and, through them, of moral and 'undamaged' selves.

As younger people, for example, the resources on which the respondents could draw to counter a lack of a happy family of origin and display a coherent family were more limited than those of a middle-aged adult with a well-established 'family of procreation' (Charles et al, 2008) or 'family of choice' (Weeks et al, 1999). Further, for these young people, the display of a coherent family seemed to require a sufficient relationship with at least one parental, as opposed to any other, family figure. As such, Kelly emphasised her relationship with her father, in spite of the negative effects on her family life of his imprisonment. Several respondents defended parents who they felt had fulfilled basic expectations of parenthood, perhaps, in part, because they would otherwise not have been able to speak of a strong relationship with a parent. In the absence of a biological parent to fulfil this role, some respondents, like Carine, had looked for a specifically parental relationship elsewhere. At the same time, her accounts illustrated the difficulty of displaying such relationships as family, and particularly the risk that such narratives of (chosen) family may not be accepted by others and one's claim to belonging to a family structure thereby refused. The non-acceptance of Carine's keyworker as a family member by adult GP staff still upset her in an interview several months later. This may explain why Carine emphasised the role of her friend's mother in creating a parental-type relationship with her, and that it had been her friend's mother who had chosen to call her 'daughter'. It seemed that for Carine and others, the notion of a young person choosing the adult members of their immediate families conflicted with their idea of a 'proper' family. She therefore carefully asserted that this relationship was not exclusively her own construction and, as such, that despite her non-relationship with her family of origin, she was accepted by a parental figure as a daughter.

Kelly, Rachel, Carine and others were therefore deeply aware of the threat to their self-presentation in the interview as moral people of their non-contact with a biological parent. Kelly's and Rachel's accounts of breaking contact with their mothers highlighted an engrained sense of moral obligation to these (vulnerable) parents. Notably, to counter potential suggestions that she had abandoned her mother, Kelly emphasised that their non-contact had not been her choice, since her mother had thrown her out. The exceptional nature of Rachel's metaphor of 'breaking the chains' further suggests that there were few discourses readily available to these young people to justify the transgression of not maintaining contact with an often vulnerable and dependent parent despite the harm this relationship had brought them, or to paper over this gaping hole in a coherent family narrative.

These findings suggest that in the contemporary cultural context, it is difficult for young people whose lives cannot match up to expectations of relatively normal family and associated caring practices not to feel a sense of loss or of being undermined personally and morally by this absence from their lives. The embodied ideal of 'the family' presents difficulties for or, in Gillis's words, 'inflicts real pain on those who do not conform' to it (1996, p 238). As suggested, the data presented in this chapter may therefore be usefully analysed in terms of the degree of presence or absence of such expected caring practices within some families or of the difficulties of displaying a coherent family in certain circumstances. However, it is also argued that analysing such data exclusively through notions of 'practices' or 'display' may run the risk of losing something significant from what the young people said and how they said it. As Smart (2007, p 45) puts it, such 'tidy' conceptual approaches can 'flatten' data, downplaying messiness and ambivalence and the haunting power of cultural ideals of family; experiences that were reflected, for example, in some of the respondents' accounts of anger and shame, as well as their moral dilemmas over contact with parents. Smart suggests a 'toolbox' of concepts ('memory', 'imaginary', 'biography', 'relationality' and 'embeddedness') through which to explore the different socially constructed aspects of this messy, positive, negative and ambivalent emotional life. A further concept to consider here is that of 'belonging' (May, 2011) for the way it can encompass strong negative and positive emotions and sensory and spatial experiences around relationships, including feeling 'othered' by a sense of not belonging. The author is currently engaged in a project exploring the sensory and spatial construction of belonging (positive, negative or ambivalent) with young people not living with their biological parents.[3] Finally, while avoiding the further stigmatisation of young people and their parents living in the circumstances discussed in this chapter through the reinforcement of discourses of 'proper' family is an important concern, it is hoped that such sociological work may filter back into a policy discussion supportive of interventions that incorporate young people's perceptions and experiences of those difficult relationships.

Notes

[1] The research was funded by the Joseph Rowntree Foundation.

[2] A fuller discussion of some of the issues raised in this chapter is contained in the latter article.

[3] This Economic and Social Research Council-funded project is entitled Young People Creating Belonging: spaces, sounds and sight (RES-061-25-0501).

References

ACMD (Advisory Council on the Misuse of Drugs) (2003) *Hidden harm: responding to the needs of children of problem drug users*, London: Advisory Council on the Misuse of Drugs.

ACMD (2007) *Hidden harm three years on: realities, challenges and opportunities*, London: Advisory Council on the Misuse of Drugs.

Backett-Milburn, K., Wilson, S., Bancroft, A. and Cunningham-Burley, S. (2008) 'Challenging childhoods: young people's accounts of "getting by" in families with substance use problems', *Childhood*, vol 15, no 4, pp 461–79.

Bancroft, A., Wilson, S., Cunningham-Burley, S., Backett-Milburn, K. and Masters, H. (2004) *Parental drug and alcohol misuse: resilience and transition among young people*, York and Bristol: Joseph Rowntree Foundation and The Policy Press.

Bauman, Z. (2003) *Liquid love: on the frailty of human bonds*, Cambridge: Polity.

Beck-Gernsheim, E. (1998) 'On the way to a post-familial family', *Theory, Culture and Society*, vol 15, nos 3/4, pp 53–70.

Charles, N., Aull Davies, C. and Harris, C. (2008) *Families in transition: social change, family formation and kin relationships*, Bristol: The Policy Press.

Duncan, S. and Edwards, R. (1999) *Lone mothers, paid work and gendered moral rationalities*, Basingstoke: Macmillan.

Finch, J. (2007) 'Displaying families', *Sociology*, vol 41, no 1, pp 65–81.

Gillies, V., Ribbens McCarthy, J. and Holland, J. (2001) *Pulling together, pulling apart*, London: Family Policy Studies Centre and Joseph Rowntree Foundation.

Gilligan, R. (2003) *Promoting children's resilience: some reflections*, Glasgow: Centre for the Child and Society.

Gillis, J. (1996) *A world of their own making. A history of myth and ritual in family life*, Oxford: Oxford University Press.

Gross, N. (2005) 'The detraditionalization of intimacy reconsidered', *Sociological Theory*, vol 23, pp 286–311.

Houmøller, K., Bernays, S., Wilson, S. and Rhodes, T. (2011) *Juggling harms: coping with parental substance misuse*, London: Department of Health.

Illouz, E. (2007) *Cold intimacies: the making of emotional capitalism*, Cambridge: Polity Press.

Manning, V., Best, D., Faulkner, N. and Titherington, E. (2009) 'New estimates of the number of children living with substance misusing parents: results from the UK national household surveys', *BMC Public Health*, vol 9, p 377.

Mason, J. (2008) 'Tangible affinities and the real life fascination of kinship', *Sociology*, vol 42, no 1, pp 29–45.

Mason, J. and Tipper, B. (2008) 'Being related: how children create and define kinship', *Childhood*, vol 15, no 4, pp 441–60.

May, V. (2011) 'Self, belonging and social change', *Sociology*, vol 45, no 3, pp 363–79.

Morgan, D. (1996) *Family connections*, Cambridge: Polity.

Newman, T. and Blackburn, S. (2002) *Transitions in the lives of children and young people: resilience factors*, Edinburgh: Scottish Executive.

O'Brien, M., Alldred, P. and Jones, D. (1996) 'Children's constructions of family and kinship', in J. Brannen and M. O'Brien (eds) *Children in families: research and policy*, London: Falmer Press, pp 84–100.

Ribbens McCarthy, J., Edwards, R. and Gillies, V. (2000) 'Moral tales of the child and the adult: narratives of contemporary family lives under changing circumstances', *Sociology*, vol 34, no 4, pp 785–804.

Smart, C. (2007) *Personal life*, Cambridge: Polity.

Strathern, M. (1992) *After nature: English kinship in the late twentieth century*, Cambridge: Cambridge University Press.

Weeks, J., Donovan, C. and Heaphy, B. (1999) 'Everyday experiments: narratives of non-heterosexual relationships', in E. Silva and C. Smart (eds) *The new family?*, London: Sage, pp 83–99.

Wilson, S., Cunningham-Burley, S., Bancroft, A., Backett-Milburn, K. and Masters, H. (2007) 'Young people, biographical narratives and the life grid: young people's accounts of parental substance use', *Qualitative Research*, vol 7, no 1, pp 137–53.

Wilson, S., Cunningham-Burley, S., Bancroft, A. and Backett-Milburn, K. (2012) 'The consequences of love: young people and family practices in difficult circumstances', *Sociological Review*, vol 60, no 1, pp 110–28.

The trouble with siblings: some psychosocial thoughts about sisters, aggression and femininity

Helen Lucey

Introduction

On a recent visit to see my aunt Joan, who was celebrating her 100th birthday, we were talking about one of her younger sisters, Bina, now 98 years old, who had gone to live in a nursing home. "She was always able to make friends easily", said Joan, "as early as I can remember. I was never like that." And not for the first time, Joan went on to tell me how Bina, as a newcomer to the single-room rural Irish primary school that the older Joan had spent the previous two years establishing her school friendships in, "breezed in full of life and everyone seemed to love her. All my friends were around her and after that it seemed like none of the girls were a bit bothered about me." Although I had heard this story before, I was still moved and amazed by the enduring and contradictory feelings this elderly woman had about her sister: the sense of being robbed of something that was hers; the outrage and sadness of displacement by another; the affection, aggression and dependency. "I often used to give her a wallop", Joan continued, "She could talk to anyone whereas I was a bit shy. It was always great fun to go to a dance with Bina." Deeply felt questions of identity wove around Joan's relationship with the woman who would always remain her younger sister, although she was nearly 100 years old herself.

In this chapter, I want to take a psychoanalytically informed psychosocial approach to think a bit more deeply about trouble between siblings, and to focus in particular on aggression and conflict between sisters.[1] I will draw on work from psychoanalytic theorists including Sigmund Freud, Melanie Klein, Joan Riviere and Donald Winnicott, contemporary psychoanalytic thinkers whose focus is on relationships and relating (Bollas, 1987; Layton, 2008), and current research in the growing field of sibling studies (Dunn and Munn, 1986; Edwards et al, 2006; Punch, 2008) to locate aggression as central in relationships and in relating – with the self and with others. This will, in part, take in the highly influential Freudian idea that aggression and violence between siblings arises because they are always and inevitably rivalrous. A frequent finding in current sibling research is that conflict and aggression are dominant features of everyday, mundane interaction for all children (Duncan, 1999; Hensman Kettery and Emery, 2006). And other research tells us that for some children and young people, the levels of bullying and other maltreatment in families, including sexual abuse, cast a very dark shadow indeed (Hardy, 2001; Hooper, 2011). But I will also consider other lines of thought that are more to do with 'ordinary' love and hate; that place both as central to the development of the human psyche and, crucially, to issues of self, identity and subjectivity. This approach can help us to think about the important place of aggression in sisters' struggles not only to develop their own unique identity in the face of their sameness, or, as Juliet Mitchell (2003) calls it, their seriality, but also with the challenges of dependency, the uses and abuses of one's own aggression, and the problem of loving *and* hating the same person or people. In most families, sibling relationships are characterised by flows of love and hate (Punch, 2008), and it is this kind of ordinary aggression and hatred that I focus on here.

In family contexts, especially as children, girls are members of groups that, although they may be considered as lateral peer groups, are also as prone to the effects of power, status and hierarchy as any vertical one, living as they do in shared, often close spaces. In this context, the edges of one's self may be blurred with another not only by legal, social and biological definitions, but also by the power of conscious and unconscious identifications. We can also be certain that it is in the highly charged emotional context of early family relationships that we learn not only how to love and nurture, but also how to hurt and hate.

Aggression is an elusive and contradictory concept. It can refer to aggressive or violent bodily acts as well as internal thoughts and feelings. It is certainly implicated in destruction and harm, the domination of others, and the desire to control. Most research on sibling aggression is framed in this way and tends to rely on measurements of verbal or physical violence (Perlman et al, 2009). But it is also mobilised creatively, to protect the self and others, to fight for a good cause, to pursue ideals and goals. While some aggression is socially endorsed, as in competitive sports, war and business, other aggression is taboo, reviled and punishable.

In a psychoanalytically informed discussion of aggression, the focus need not be confined to physical manifestations of aggression in 'real' acts, but can equally 'find expression in phantasy behaviour intended to harm other people, or to destroy, humiliate or constrain them' (Laplanche and Pontalis, 1973, p 17). Thus, aggression and hate are also located in the mental realm, 'in a developmental progression, in particular emphasising the development of mind, separation, individuation, the capacity for thinking and especially thinking about feeling' (Mizen and Morris, 2007, p xi). This view places aggression as central to the human condition – in contrast to violence, which, although undoubtedly widespread, is not inborn, preordained or unavoidable in either men or women.

The psychosocial perspective that I take is also a strongly relational one, in that it views the boundary between self and other as often blurred, so that the line between the one who feels aggressed and the aggressor (the 'done to' and the 'doer') is often unclear. That is, 'In the mess of psychic states that are part of how our realities are made up, categories bleed'.[2]

I will discuss data from a qualitative study of children and young people's sibling relationships (see Edwards et al, 2006),[3] and focus on some of the ways that aggression and violence between siblings is linked to issues of differentiation and identification. This takes me to a discussion of love and hate not as opposites of one another, but as deeply connected, and as deeply involved in the business of interdependency and intersubjectivity.

Ordinary aggression and ordinary femininity

There is a tendency in psychology for sibling research to focus on problems, and psychoanalysts writing about siblings have most often based their work on material gathered in clinical contexts with clients who are experiencing crisis in their emotional lives (Bank and Kahn, 1982; Lewin, 2004). In sociology, research on 'problem' girls and women, alongside the pathologisation of female aggressivity and violence, means that more ordinary forms of the phenomena of hate, hostility and aggression tend to be overlooked (Bollas, 1987).

The focus of the research that yielded the data for this chapter was relationships, not problems, with groups of siblings recruited through random sampling techniques, snowballing and by advertising the project in schools and leisure centres. The sisters in our study were 'ordinary' girls and young women from 'ordinary' families; just the kind of girls and young women who are invisible in most accounts of female aggression (Burman et al, 2001).

However, we step onto shifting ground when trying to think about girls' aggression as ordinary when the notion that it is an indicator of an abnormal and malformed femininity (Burman et al, 2001) is a persistent and powerful one in popular and academic discourses. This is in contrast to understandings of masculine aggression, which tend to view it, however problematically, as a normal aspect of masculinity (Hall, 2002). Several writers have noted that because these understandings are based on findings from enquiries that focus on boys, which are then extrapolated to girls, it leaves us with a narrow analytical lexis to understand female violence without recourse to notions of feminine pathology (Lloyd, 1995; Blackman and Walkerdine, 2001).

It is also hard to focus on girls' aggression when girls and women are the victims of escalating male violence in families, schools and in personal relationships with boys and men (HM Government, 2009). Feminists, quite rightly, have concentrated on the problem of male domination of girls and women, revealing its shocking extent and asserting strong links between male sexuality, dominance and sexual abuse, including the sexual abuse of children (for an overview, see McCarry, 2007). But if we think about sisters, it is often the case that the random accident of birth, family break-up, the forming of new families and new sibling groups mean that girls can be in a position to hold much power, as older sisters, over younger children. In the shared, intimate and private spaces of the family, girls may have many opportunities to dominate, exploit, abuse and humiliate other girls and boys.

A psychoanalytic view of aggression

Freud's thinking about siblings was dominated by two main ideas: first, that older children may feel displaced in relation to the mother by the arrival of a younger sibling; and, second, that they are bitter rivals in the Oedipal conflict. A lively debate about Freud's legacy to contemporary psychoanalytic and psychosocial understandings of siblings has recently ensued (Coles, 2003; Mitchell, 2003; Rustin, 2007; Lucey, 2010). For example, Prophecy Coles' (2003) Kleinian-inspired work challenges the notion that sibling relationships are always rooted in hostility and, instead, emphasises the possibilities of love between siblings. In terms of thinking about sisters and aggression, the universalism of Freud's assertion that all sibling relationships of whatever sex are dominated by hatred and hostility actually opens up a rare space in which girls' aggression, as sisters, is considered normal!

Bollas notes that in Freud's instinct-based theory, love was connected to the impulse to obtain all things pleasurable (Freud, 1920). Hate, on the other hand, had two potential functions: to rid the ego, through expulsion or destruction, of anything that caused unpleasant and uncomfortable feelings; and to restore the ego to a previous state. However, it was Melanie Klein who really began the business of taking love and hate as seriously as was needed (see Klein, 1988). Although Klein retained Freud's conceptualisation of drives, one of her most important *departures* from Freud was her theorisation of hate as a more primitive emotion than love, and therefore the predecessor to love. She and her collaborator Joan Riviere (Klein and Riviere, 1937) maintained that there exists in the human psyche from birth an inherent struggle between love and hate. Intense impulses of love and aggression are felt towards the first object, the mother, because the breast that brings the blissful quenching of hunger and thirst must inevitably disappoint and become the source of craving and frustration. Thus, both loving and hating fantasies attach themselves to the important objects in the infant's life so that 'feelings of love and tendencies to reparation develop in connection with aggressive impulses and in spite of them' (Klein and Riviere, 1937, p 57).

Riviere's (1937) discussion of the likely triggers to aggression is useful for my consideration of siblings because she puts issues of dependency at the heart of aggressive impulses. She identifies a sense of loss or an attack on the self as a primary instigator of aggression and highlights how loss and a profound sense of pain can arise in relation to an unfulfilled desire. This links desire to needs and, therefore, to dependence on others to fulfil them. Now, with an other that is not under direct and permanent control of the self, the possibility that desires and needs may remain unfulfilled is an ever-present spectre.

Klein's ideas about the potential and proximity of love and hate as unconscious emotional forces have subsequently been exploited and developed in various strands of psychoanalysis. She has provided a foundational assumption that love and hate are the two main elements out of which we build ourselves and relationships with others and that *both* involve aggression. Here, love and hate are not opposites of one another; instead, they share some of the same unconscious, emotional ground.

In the following extracts from case studies of two groups of siblings, I will focus on the sisters in the groups to explore how aggression between them arose in response to issues of identity: in particular, of establishing an identity of one's own; of being independent in the face of one's own and others' dependency; and of desire, need, exclusion and appropriation.

Identity theft

While psychoanalytic and psychological accounts have tended to put rivalry at the core of sibling conflict, research on adolescent siblings finds that issues of individuation and differentiation are the main spurs to conflict (Raffaelli, 1992). To establish some measure of separation from a sister or brother inevitably involves mobilising aggression, both conscious and unconscious, towards the sibling. This is particularly so when there are unconscious confusions between self and other among siblings. The idea of territory wars and also of identity theft are useful for thinking about the 16-year-old Asian British Mirvat's struggle to be separate from her 11-year-old sister Parveen: "it's as if she didn't have a personality of her own, so everything I was, she was as well. And it was quite annoying because then I wasn't really me, I was just what she wants" (Mirvat, age 17).

Fantasies of sameness or merging with another may be effective in helping us to maintain a sense of security (Kohut, 1971). Unconsciously dissolving self–other boundaries can also be marshalled as a defence against unbearable feelings of difference. But this undifferentiated state of mind is bound to end in tears. If the fantasy of sameness is not one that the object of the fantasy can collude in, then s/he is likely to put up identity borders where the subject wishes there were none, and identity wars and border skirmishes are likely to ensue. In the face of these kinds of wishes (that may not be consciously known by the sibling who holds the wish), many adolescent sisters aggressively exclude their younger sisters and brothers in order to forge their own, differentiated identity. This exclusion is then just as often experienced as an aggressive act by the younger child, as with Parveen:

> She has her friends who always come over. And I think she tries to be different when her friends are over. She's not nice to me at all. She always shoves me out of her room and is more horrible to me while her friends are over. (Parveen, age 11)

A frequently told story in this study is the exclusion of younger siblings by older ones, with older sisters and brothers asserting their individuality through exclusionary behaviours and practices that are also sometimes intended to hurt and humiliate: for instance, Parveen says that Mirvat "asks me to walk behind her when she's with her friends, and stuff like that". Younger siblings, although they can be treated very badly in these ways, often continue to 'look up' admiringly and enviously towards older siblings and attempt to connect with them. From the perspective of the older sister, however, this kind of admiration can feel like an aggressive intrusion upon the self. Here, Mirvat again expresses how appropriating she feels Parveen can be:

> every couple of weekends one of my friends will come over, and she's determined to hang around and listen to what we are saying and talk the way we are talking, do what we do. And it gets really annoying sometimes, because my friends are saying 'I want to spend time with you this weekend'. And then they have to modify everything again to fit in with the little sister. And all I try and tell her is 'Parveen, when my friends come over you don't come and sit and stare at us, you have to go and find your own thing'. But she doesn't have things to do. She doesn't have any hobbies of her own, because she's always copying me. (Mirvat, age 17)

The urge to dissolve barriers between self and other can be a powerful one. Magagna (2007, p, 51), in her account of psychotherapeutic work with an identical twin sister, describes well the frustration, rage and sorrow of becoming a unique, separate person when a large part of the self is to be found in the other. This is useful for understanding what happens in non-twin sibling relationships when one or both siblings attempt to go their own way and develop separate identities. While Mirvat eagerly anticipated going away to university "far enough away that I'd have to stay there because I think I need to get away for a bit", Parveen dreaded the empty space filled with the "nothing" that she fantasised her sisters' absence would create:

> I don't think it will be nice at all [when Mirvat goes away to university]. When she's on trips we are all depressed and there's nothing to do. So I won't like it when she leaves for university. It will be horrible. (Parveen, age 11)

Merging, mirroring and fusing have their defensive functions in that they may protect the subject from the full knowledge of their precarious dependency on others and the endless potential for disappointment that this necessarily entails. It may involve envy of what the other possesses and the self wishes to destroy because of it. It certainly has its aggressive elements and may summon a forceful occupation, appropriation or even obliteration of the other's subjectivity. There may be elements of all of these things in siblings' relationships.

Sisters, secrets and exclusion

In the Morris family, a white British working-class family, territory wars were rife and fierce among all four siblings – Tracey (age 14), Marcie (age 12), Andy (age 10) and Patrick (age 16) – but in particular between Tracey and Marcie. They all borrowed or took one another's possessions without asking and lost and broke them without contrition or reparation. Rules about personal space were constantly made and transgressed. There were lots of fights – mostly shouting and occasionally physical, where things got thrown and people were hit. When more positive feelings did arise and were acted upon, they could not be sustained for very long and quickly seemed to break down:

> Well, every brother or sister fights no matter what happens. But say, like, if a brother or sister was to, like, be really, really generous and everything, then that wouldn't really be normal, because brothers and sisters naturally fight, it comes naturally. (Marcie, age 12)

There was a sense in this sibling group that they would like things to be better, but that everyone was such a disappointment and an embarrassment that the idea that they were connected was a very difficult one. Tracey and Marcie were ready to tell tales on each other at the drop of a hat. Marcie was especially adept in underhand techniques to invade and exact harm on her older sister: sneaking into her room and "going through her stuff" and listening "to all of her conversations on the phone", actions that Riviere (1937, p 15) refers to as 'insidious and indirect expressions of hate and aggression': "I spy on her when she's on the phone … it's like, what she says on the phone and everything, like if she says something my mum doesn't know, I just go and tell my mum" (Marcie, age 12).

Marcie fully expected to get found out and for there to be a row, but was prepared for this. When I asked Marcie "What's that all about?" she said she didn't know except that she just liked "getting people into trouble" (Tracey, age 14). This reminds me of a comment from one of the young siblings in Samantha Punch's study who said: "You can do nasty things to your brothers and sisters without a reason … you can just tease them if you're bored' (2008, p 336). But there is something in here about being excluded as well. Tracey pointedly excludes her younger sister, who wants to be included by Tracey when she is with her friends, either in the house or elsewhere. Marcie secretively 'listens in' on Tracey's conversations in an effort to get what is denied to her, but uses this in an enviously destructive way, by exposing Tracey's secrets to her mum. In a paranoid way, however, Marcie's own projected aggression, in the form of prying and telling tales, finds its way back to persecute her:

> No, I go to a different school to Tracey, because I didn't want to go to the same school as her, because she's my sister and like, if she knew

my secrets she'd go around telling all my friends and everything, and stuff like that. (Marcie, age 12)

Marcie clearly got some satisfaction from provoking the rage of her older sister and this resonates with Bank and Kahn's (1982, p 197) argument that in many forms of sibling aggression, the 'payoff' is internal, 'having to do with a forbidden satisfaction or the fulfilment of a deeper emotional need'. These needs include the need for constancy, the need to be recognised by others as subjects with our own desires worthy of fulfilment, the need to be thought well of and the need to be loved. Aggression is one of many ways of actively relating; it requires relational contact in some form, because the sibling towards whom hatred and anger is felt is considered someone important enough to make this form of destructive emotional connection with. Marcie's 'insidious' acts of aggression towards Tracey were effective in this way because they forced Tracey to take notice of her and to interact with her, albeit in a way that produced more difficulty.

Bollas's (1987, p 118) question, 'When a person hates, is it always true that he wishes to destroy?', is relevant here. He discusses the idea that hate is not only born out of a desire to destroy the object, but sometimes in order to conserve it, even though the consequences may be destructive. In this scenario, rather than hate being the opposite of love, it becomes a replacement or substitute for it:

> What this person dreads most of all is the indifference of the hated object, so he wants the other person to retaliate. He can't bear, literally, to be ignored or dismissed by the object. So not being seen is a great fear in all of this. (Bollas, 1987, p 118)

The challenges of desire, need and dependency are powerfully invoked in families, and not just vertically between parents and children, but also laterally between sisters and sisters and their brothers. Different kinds of defences can be mounted to manage the anxiety of dependency, including an illusion of an independent liberty (Riviere, 1937) and the assertion of difference and disconnection from those we are dependent upon through projective processes. But the more intimate the situation, the more difficult this is, as the one that we want to destroy may also be the same one who is 'greatly loved and desired' (Riviere, 1937, p 14).

Building on Klein's work, Winnicott (1936) connected ideas about love and hate to the transitional object – a position that could often be occupied by siblings. Here, symbolisation, and the notion that one object can stand for another, is crucial. So it is that the same special soft toy that is cuddled and cherished by the child, can also be beaten or mutilated by her, symbolising both aggression and love towards the mother. A normative theme across sibling studies, including the narratives of the siblings who took part in this study, is that to some extent they are required to and are able to *suffer* and *withstand* the attack of older and younger sisters and brothers in the relative privacy of the home. In this way, they become transitional objects, like the toy that does not desert you when you are mean to it or destroy it in fantasy. This allows us to 'imagine a form of hate which is positive: that intensely concentrated, aggressive use of a transitional object, which is founded on the infant's knowledge and gratitude that the object will survive' (Bollas, 1987, p 119).

Conclusion

In this chapter, I have tried to think about girls and aggression in the very particular context of sibling relationships by using an analytic lens that draws on ideas from psychoanalytic thinking. The work of Klein and Riviere, Winnicott, and Bollas gives us a way of thinking about the links between love and hate in relating to the self and to others. This is valuable because it does not depend on doing away entirely with a feminist emphasis on connection and creation in feminine identities, or shutting off love from hate, hate from love, and hate from the 'ordinarily' feminine. Nor does it rely on an exclusively Freudian understanding of sibling relationships as always and inevitably rivalrous. Rather, it allows for the consideration of girls' and women's aggression as a necessary and productive element of their psychosocial lives. In this relational light, where aggression holds a central place, and therefore must be given its proper due, it need not be something to be disavowed, or something that must be contained and carried by others, particularly men. Girls and women need to know about their own potential to hate and their own wishes to destroy, just as much as they need to know about love. My contention is that one of the perfect places to think about this is in sibling relationships.

Notes
[1] There are a number of relevant perspectives and literatures in sociology and psychology on girls' violence and aggression that I do not have the space to consider in this chapter (see Brown and Gilligan, 1992; Campbell, 1993; Besag, 2006; Duncan and Owen-Smith, 2006; Underwood, 2003).

[2] The quote is from the comment of an anonymous reviewer of an earlier version of this chapter.

[3] The 'Sibling practices: children's understandings and experiences' study was funded by the Economic and Social Research Council and conducted within the Families and Social Capital Research Group located at London South Bank University, UK.

References

Bank, S. and Kahn, S. (1982) *The sibling bond*, New York, NY: Basic Books.

Besag, V.E. (2006) *Understanding girls' friendships, fights and feuds: a practical approach to girls' bullying*, Milton Keynes: Open University Press.

Blackman, L. and Walkerdine, V. (2001) *Mass hysteria: critical psychology and media studies*, London: Palgrave.

Bollas, C. (1987) *The shadow of the object: psychoanalysis of the unthought known*, London: Free Association Books.

Brown, L.M. and Gilligan, C. (1992) *Meeting at the crossroads: women's psychology and girls' development*, Cambridge, MA: Harvard University Press.

Burman, M.J., Batchelor, S.A. and Brown, J.A. (2001) 'Researching girls and violence: facing the dilemmas of fieldwork', *British Journal of Criminology*, vol 41, pp 443–59.

Campbell, A. (1993) *Men, women and aggression*, New York, NY: Basic Books.

Coles, P. (2003) *The importance of sibling relationships in psychoanalysis*, London: Karnac Books.

Duncan, R.D. (1999) 'Peer and sibling aggression: an investigation of intra- and extra-familial bullying', *Journal of Interpersonal Violence*, vol 14, no 8, pp 871–86.

Duncan, L. and Owen-Smith, A. (2006) 'Powerlessness and the use of indirect aggression in friendships', *Sex Roles*, vol 55, pp 493–502.

Dunn, J. and Munn, P. (1986) 'Sibling quarrels and maternal intervention: individual differences in understanding and aggression', *Journal of Child Psychology and Psychiatry*, vol 27, no 5, pp 583–95.

Edwards, R., Hadfield, L., Lucey, H. and Mauthner, M. (2006) *Sibling identity and relationships: sisters and brothers*, London: Routledge, Taylor & Francis.

Freud, S. (1920) *'Beyond the pleasure principle'. The standard edition of the complete psychological works of Sigmund Freud, Volume XVIII (1920–1922)*.

Hall, S. (2002) 'Daubing the dredges of fury: men, violence and the piety of the hegemonic masculinity thesis', *Theoretical Criminology*, vol 6, no 1, pp 35–61.

Hardy, M.S. (2001) 'Physical aggression and sexual behavior among siblings: a retrospective study', *Journal of Family Violence*, vol 16, no 3, pp 255–68.

Hensman Kettrey, H. and Emery, B.C. (2006) 'The discourse of sibling violence', *Journal of Family Violence*, vol 21, pp 407–16.

HM Government (2009) *Together we can end violence against women and girls: a strategy*, London: Home Office.

Hooper, C.A. (2011) 'Child maltreatment', in J. Bradshaw (ed) *The well-being of children in the UK* (3rd edn), Bristol: The Policy Press.

Klein, M. (1988) *Love, guilt and reparation and other works 1921–1945*, London: Virago.

Klein, M. and Riviere, J. (1937) *Love, hate and reparation*, London: The Hogarth Press.

Kohut, H. (1971) *The analysis of the self*, New York, NY: International Universities Press.

Laplanche, J. and Pontalis, J.-B. (1973) *The language of psychoanalysis*, London: Karnac Books.

Layton, L. (2008) 'Relational thinking: from culture to couch and couch to culture', in S. Clarke, N. Hahn and P. Hoggett (eds) *Object relations and social relations: the implications of the relational turn in psychoanalysis*, London: Karnac.

Lewin, V. (2004) *The twin in the transference*, London: Whurr.

Lloyd, A. (1995) *Doubly deviant, doubly damned: society's treatment of violent women*, Harmondsworth: Penguin Books.

Lucey, H. (2010) 'Sisters' stories: a psychosocial perspective on families, peers and social class in resistance and conformity to education', *Gender and Education*, vol 22, no 4, pp 447–62.

Magagna, J. (2007) 'Transformation: from twin to individual', *Journal of Child Psychotherapy*, vol 33, no 1, pp 51–69.

McCarry, M. (2007) 'Masculinity studies and male violence: critique or collusion?', *Women's Studies International Forum*, vol 30, no 5, pp 404–15.

Mitchell, J. (2003) *Siblings, sex and violence*, Cambridge: Polity Press.

Mizen, R. and Morris, M. (2007) *On aggression and violence: an analytic perspective*, Basingstoke: Palgrave Macmillan.

Perlman, M., Ross, H. and Garfinkel, D. (2009) 'Consistent patterns of interaction in young children's conflicts with their siblings', *International Journal of Behavioral Development*, vol 33, no 6, pp 504–15.

Punch, S. (2008) '"You can do nasty things to your brothers and sisters without a reason": siblings' backstage behaviour', *Children and Society*, vol 22, pp 333–44.

Raffaelli, M. (1992) 'Sibling conflict in early adolescence', *Journal of Marriage and the Family*, vol 54, no 3, pp 652–73.

Riviere, J. (1937) 'Hate, greed and aggression', in M. Klein and J. Riviere (eds) *Love, hate and reparation*, London: Hogarth.

Rustin, M. (2007) 'Taking account of siblings – a view from child psychotherapy', *Journal of Child Psychotherapy*, vol 33, no 1, pp 21–35.

Underwood, M.K. (2003) *Social aggression among girls*, New York, NY: Guilford Press.

Winnicott, D.W. (1936) 'Transitional objects and transitional phenomena', in D.W. Winnicott (ed) *Through paediatrics to psychoanalysis*, London: Karnac Books.

CHAPTER FIFTEEN

Children and family transitions: contact and togetherness

Hayley Davies

In the global North, the issue of children's contact with parents following parental separation and divorce has been much discussed as a social, political and legal concern, and as a key site for contemporary family negotiations. The issue draws into focus, both at a societal and family level, the question of who counts as family and kin, the obligations ascribed to parent–child relationships, and, specifically, the expectations of the appropriate frequency and quality of contact time between non-resident parents, usually fathers, and their children (Hogan et al, 2003; Natalier and Hewitt, 2010). Negotiations around contact also take place at a micro-level, in the form of family practices in which children participate.

Typically, sociological research on children's contact with family members focuses on children's perspectives on their post-separation and post-divorce contact with their parents (Wade and Smart, 2002; Hogan et al, 2003; Moxnes, 2003a, 2003b). This research shows that parental separation and divorce are increasingly becoming part of the ordinary experience of childhood. Despite the ordinariness of these experiences, international large-scale findings suggest that separation and divorce cause notable, but often short-term, distress for the majority of children (Fomby and Cherlin, 2007; Elliott and Vaitilingam, 2008; Coleman and Glenn, 2010). For some children and young people, longer-term consequences include a negative impact on their educational success and well-being into adulthood (Fomby and Cherlin, 2007; Elliott and Vaitilingam, 2008; Coleman and Glenn, 2010). Longer-term troubles are more likely where conflict between parents continues post-separation, where parent–child relationships are poor (which may include lack of communication with children over the decision to separate and lack of contact with a non-resident parent afterwards), where are multiple transitions in family formation, where mothers' mental health suffers and where the family live in poverty (Hawthorne et al, 2003; Coleman and Glenn, 2010). Despite the normality of separation and divorce for children in the North, children's experiences of these processes remain troubling, although the extent of these troubles depends upon a complex mixture of circumstances, and support from grandparents, siblings and friends may all protect from long-term harm.

Children's own accounts of contact following separation and divorce often demonstrate a desire to re-establish a sense of normality, and to feel like a family once again. On occasion, children envisage re-establishing family life through imagining taking action to reunite separated parents or to attempt to break up new parental partnerships (Smart et al, 2001; Wade and Smart, 2002). Research in this area also suggests that children are often strategic, deploying a range of skills to navigate the emotional course of parental separation, divorce and re-partnering (Smart et al, 2001; Wade and Smart, 2002; Robinson et al, 2003). For example, children may use diversionary tactics to avoid thinking about their family problems or vent their feelings through emotional expression, writing a diary or seeking a confidant to talk through a problem with, which often involves assessing who would be trustworthy and maintain their confidence (Wade and Smart, 2002; Robinson et al, 2003). In seeking out ways of dealing with these family troubles, children challenge the often-tacit assumption that family troubles are adult troubles, and children reveal themselves to take up, and take issue with, matters such as contact time.

Building upon this and wider research into children's roles within the family and children's contributions to family decision-making (Morrow, 1999; Smart et al, 2001; Brannen and Heptinstall, 2003; Neale, 2002; Smith et al, 2003), in this chapter, I will first discuss the opportunities available to children for challenging and negotiating with their parents on their existing contact arrangements. I will go on to explore the ways in which children respond pragmatically to losing everyday contact with family members through finding new ways of being and feeling like a family, and achieving a sense of family togetherness (Christensen, 2002).

Researching children's constructions of family and close relationships

The chapter is based on the accounts of children who participated in an Economic and Social Research Council-funded study (PTA030-2003-01291) into children's constructions of family and close relationships (see Davies, 2008, 2011, 2012). This qualitative school-based field study was undertaken during 2006/7, within the context of a small Midlands state primary school (England) located in a relatively disadvantaged socio-economic area. Twenty-four boys and girls aged 8–10 opted into the study; the majority were white British (20) and a minority were British and of South Asian descent (four). While the project was focused on children's 'ordinary' family lives rather than their experiences of divorce or separation, these children had experienced 'multiple family transitions' (Flowerdew and Neale, 2003); there were a number of children who had experienced separation and/or divorce ($N = 16$), the death of a parent ($N = 2$) and a parent re-partnering ($N = 13$), and had acquired half- and/or step-siblings ($N = 13$) and/or had a non-resident sibling or parent ($N = 15$). These experiences of family fluidity, and children's shifting perspectives on their family contact time, were captured over a period of 18 months through research conversations with children in school, paired interview discussions, drawing and writing activities on the theme of 'my family', and visits to children's family homes.

Family contact: sites and circumstances of children's negotiations

Loss of contact, or very minimal contact, with a parent or sibling served as a key focus for a number of children in discussing their family lives and experiences not only in the interviews, but more broadly in the research conversations I shared with the children in school. While there were very few children who had entirely lost contact with parents following parental separation, there were two children who provided accounts of a long-term loss of contact with their fathers, and these accounts are discussed here as they illuminate children's agency in renegotiating contact. These children discussed their assumption of responsibility for making contact with their fathers, conveying both their active intent to make contact and their role in negotiating contact arrangements and subsequently, for one of the children, bringing about new family living arrangements.

In discussing his family in an interview, Kevin explained that his mother and father had separated. Previously, Kevin had told me that he and his brother had shared contact with their respective fathers in the year prior to this research, but that he and his brother had, at the time of the interview, lost contact with their fathers. Kevin attributed his loss of contact to his father repeatedly re-partnering.

Kevin appeared to know very little about his father, providing details such as his name and his former job, details that denoted a somewhat distant father–son relationship. Kevin said:

Kevin:	And my dad's called James and I don't know where he lives now.
Hayley:	Did you ever meet him?
Kevin:	Yeah. I'm gonna try and get my dad's phone number or summat.
Hayley:	Would you like to talk to him then?
Kevin:	Yeah.
Hayley:	What would you say?
Kevin:	[Shrugs]. By the way, he hasn't gave me all the toys and stuff he left in his caravan that I had for my birthdays and stuff … I don't think he took any of his stuff. Well, he must have took some clothes and stuff. (Interview with Kevin and Eve)

Kevin's account clearly shows that he wanted to make contact with his father, that his loss of contact with his father represented unfinished business and that there was little preparation for, or consultation about, his father leaving and discontinuing contact, as was also the case for other children in this study. While Kevin perceives himself as able to contact his father, his lack of contact details may represent a significant hurdle.

In contrast to Kevin, Bridget conveyed that she had shared no contact with her father between the ages of two and seven, and that she had initiated a dialogue with her mother about making contact with her father, from whom she had been estranged. Bridget said: "I didn't see my dad for five years from when I was two till when I was seven and then *I wanted to* start seeing him so my mum phoned him up" (interview with Bridget and Cara, emphasis added).

In this case, Bridget's requests to her mother had demonstrated considerable agency on her part and had, in the longer term, resulted in a significant change in her family relationships. At the time of the interview, Bridget was being co-parented by her mother and father and shared regular contact with her paternal grandparents, whom she had not previously known. Bridget had half-siblings from her father's previous relationship with whom she wanted to be in contact; she had asked her father if she could meet them, although he had made no promises. Bridget's changes to her family contact arrangements were brought about as a consequence of her mother taking her wishes seriously, and her parents' agreement and cooperation around this contact. While children's accounts of their agency in negotiating contact with their parents provides insights into children's potential role in family decision-making, this agency, if interrogated, is nearly always contingent on adult family members being willing and able to help children. This willingness, while dependent on a range of micro-influences such as the parents' relationship with one another, may also be shaped by cultural ideas about children's role in family democracy (Jensen and McKee, 2003).

Like Bridget, other children in the study shared no contact, or very little contact, with their non-resident step- and half-siblings. For those children with non-resident half-siblings, there was a longing and an expectation that they should know and see their half-siblings (see Davies, 2012). The children in this study who had lost contact with non-resident step- and half-siblings with whom they had formerly developed close relationships were virtually powerless to change their contact arrangements with these siblings. There were a number of factors that prevented children from even mentioning to parents that they were dissatisfied with their contact arrangements. In one case, a child conveyed that her desire to see her step-siblings would upset her stepfather who was not permitted to see his children either. For other children, parents' acrimonious relationships, physical distance and/or limited economic resources to meet the costs of visiting siblings served to prevent these visits taking place. Children faced additional challenges in gaining access to their valued step- and half-siblings to the ones they faced in securing contact with their parents, as this sibling contact relied upon the agreement and cooperation not of two parents, but often of two sets of parents, frequently with limited economic and temporal resources.

Family togetherness: maintaining contact and connectedness

Of the children who had experienced parental separation or divorce in this study, many shared once-weekly contact with their non-resident parents, during which time they attempted to work towards creating a sense of family togetherness and family cohesion through simply being and sharing in activities together. David described how his parents, who had separated over a year previously at the time of the interview, maintained a notion of family togetherness by going on family day trips and spending time together. David said: "My mum and my dad, they still get on with each other and they do spend some time with me and my sister … it's like we're in the middle of a family" (interview with David and Trusha).

David suggests that, for him, it felt as though he and his sister were in the middle of a family because his parents got along well enough to continue spending time together *as a family*, even though they were separated. David and his sister were the people who united this family. There were a number of accounts similar to David's. For example, Kayla lived with her father, her stepmother and her three half-siblings. Kayla's mother was often invited to join them on their family day trips, which Kayla valued greatly. In addition to these family day trips, Kayla indicated that there were other ways in which she and her mother maintained their close relationship:

> Ever since I started living at my dad's, she's [mum's] always like, been there for me. Like she's always called on the phone to say 'Hello', and ask how I am, and what I've got that's new and what's been happening. (Interview with Kayla and Tanisha)

For Kayla, her mother's interest in her daily life became particularly important after they were living apart. Even though her mother was not there to witness first-hand what was happening in her life, she was nevertheless sharing in Kayla's experiences by showing interest and 'being there' over the telephone. 'Being there' does not require the physical presence of family members; it is a quality of 'ongoing and lasting relationships', a quality of time, which may be particularly significant in families such as David's and Kayla's where family time is subject to redistribution following significant family transitions (Christensen, 2002, p 83). It is clear that where daily contact was not possible, children worked with their family members to find new ways of being in touch, being a family and maintaining important family connections.

For children who spent time or lived across households, their experience and satisfaction with contact arrangements was not necessarily the same in both homes and families. Kayla's account of her resident family is testament to this. Kayla had made an attempt to reorganise her family's time in favour of spending more time 'together', as she explains in the following:

Kayla:	Well, I like to do things like that with my family. I want to do things together more. Once I made a plan in my room of things we can do together.
Hayley:	What was the plan for?
Kayla:	I wanted us to do more things together instead of my dad sleeping on the sofa all the time and my stepmum working all the time too.
Hayley:	Did you show them?
Kayla:	Yeah. I went downstairs and showed them [the plan] and they said "We're not doing any of this. No way."
Hayley:	So they didn't listen to you?
Kayla:	No. I wanted us all to do more things together, but they didn't. (Interview with Kayla and Tanisha)

Kayla's account reveals her desire to *have a say* in how she and her family could enjoy some time together, and her inclination to *plan this time*; both of which are resonant of the 'qualities of time' valued by children (Christensen, 2002, p 81). For Kayla, it was not necessarily the amount of time spent together that was significant to her, but rather what this time entailed. Kayla's conversations with her mother about 'how she is' and 'what's been happening' demonstrate her mother's engagement with, attentiveness to and interest in Kayla, which were highly valued. Kayla's time with her father and her stepmother was dominated by the routines of family life: the work schedules of these working parents and the temporal organisation of care of Kayla's three younger siblings, who were aged five years, two years and nine months old. The pressures placed upon her father and stepmother and their limited temporal resources meant that they could not compete with the time offered by Kayla's mother, who was single and could provide Kayla with one-to-one undivided attention, as well as peace and quiet away from the rabble of a busy and overcrowded home.

Children were generally very sympathetic to and flexible about the constraints of family life post-separation/divorce and participated in seeking out ways of feeling connected to non-resident family members. Key ways of communicating with family members included telephone or Skype calls, text messages and instant messenger. Children also regarded keeping photographs as a significant visual substitute for the everyday face-to-face contact important in close family relationships. In this example, Cara is discussing her father keeping photographs of her. Cara visited her father, who lived with his partner and his two stepdaughters, on alternate weekends. Cara was consistent in her representation of her relationship with her father; the time that she spent with him was recounted as uneventful and boring, and she felt that he was largely uninterested in her.

When drawing her family, Cara noted:

> It's really unfair 'cause dad hasn't got a picture of me although he's married to a different woman. Her name's Jenny, I've told you about her before. In his bedroom, he's only got a couple of photos. *Even though he doesn't live with me no more, he wouldn't have a photo* and Jenny won't let him. 'Cause I'm not related to her, she doesn't want one. Even though my dad likes looking at pictures of her children, every time I've offered dad a picture of me, he says 'Jenny won't let me.' It's not his house, you see. (Interview with Cara and Bridget, Cara's emphasis)

Small gestures such as keeping a photograph of a child were regarded as key ways in which children reported maintaining family connections and a sense of togetherness, and these were invested with meaning. As in the example of Kayla, parents showing an interest in children and their day-to-day lives were ways in which non-resident parents, in particular, could sustain their connections with a child. For Cara, her father having a photograph of her, especially considering "he doesn't live with" her any more, was one way in which he could see her and how she looks; Cara mentioned the importance of these photos being contemporary photos, photos of her 'now'. Photographs offer a way of tracking a child's developmental progress, their changing appearances and height (James, 2000) and for Cara, they were a means by which her father could show that he valued their relationship; keeping photos is a key way of 'displaying' to loved ones, as well as to other 'relevant observers', the value that is attributed to that family relationship (Finch, 2007).

Conclusion

In this chapter, I have provided children's accounts of contact with family members following parental separation and divorce. The perspectives discussed here suggest that children find losing contact or a lack of contact in family relationships that they value a problematic and distressing element of parental separation and divorce. Conversely, children's irregular or uncertain contact with family members could also be a source of distress (see Davies, 2012).

The findings in this chapter show that children take up opportunities to attempt to bring about change in their family contact arrangements and family time together, but that these negotiations take place in a context in which parents' cooperation, not only with their child, but also with their former, and sometimes new partner, is essential. This parental cooperation relies on amicable and communicative parental relationships, and on parents having access to temporal and economic resources to facilitate visits or more family time together. As in other research, children who remained powerless to change their contact arrangements with family members found this experience troubling (Hawthorne et al, 2003).

Following parental separation and divorce, children recognise a need to be flexible about how their relationships are conducted, and they actively look for other ways to be and feel like a family and to create a sense of family togetherness. I have argued elsewhere (Davies, 2012) that face-to-face contact is significant to children in maintaining their relationships, but where this is not possible, children such as Kayla, David and Cara point to ways in which they feel that there is, or could be, continuity in their relationships with their parents. These ways include regular telephone contact and parents keeping photographs of children to remind them that they are valued. In looking for ways to sustain their relationships, children were actively contributing to reshaping ways of being a family that are meaningful, and which work for them and their family members.

References

Brannen, J. and Heptinstall, E. (2003) 'Concepts of care and children's contribution to family life', in J. Brannen and P. Moss (eds) *Rethinking children's care*, Buckingham: Open University Press, pp 185–97.

Christensen, P. (2002) 'Why more "quality time" is not on the top of children's lists: the "qualities of time" for children', *Children and Society*, vol 16, pp 77–88.

Coleman, L. and Glenn, F. (2010) 'The varied impact of couple relationship breakdown on children: implications for practice and policy', *Children and Society*, vol 24, pp 238–49.

Davies, H. (2008) 'Reflexivity in research practice: informed consent with children at school and at home', *Sociological Research Online*, vol 84, no 1.

Davies, H. (2011) 'Sharing surnames: children, family and kinship', *Sociology*, vol 45, no 4, pp 554–69.

Davies, H. (2012) 'Affinities, seeing and feeling like-family: exploring why children value face-to-face contact', *Childhood*, vol 19, no 1, pp 8–23.

Elliott, J. and Vaitilingam, R. (eds) (2008) *Now we are 50: key findings from the National Child Development Study*, London: The Centre for Longitudinal Studies.

Finch, J. (2007) 'Displaying families', *Sociology*, vol 41, no 1, pp 65–81.

Flowerdew, J. and Neale, B. (2003) 'Trying to stay apace: children with multiple challenges in their post-divorce family lives', *Childhood*, vol 10, no 2, pp 147–61.

Fomby, P. and Cherlin, A. (2007) 'Family instability and child well-being', *American Sociological Review*, vol 72, pp 181–204.

Hawthorne, J., Jessop, J., Pryor, J. and Richards, M. (2003) *Supporting children through family change: a review of interventions and services for children of divorcing and separating parents*, York: Joseph Rowntree Foundation.

Hogan, D., Halpenny, A.M. and Greene, S. (2003) 'Change and continuity after parental separation: children's experiences of family transitions in Ireland', *Childhood*, vol 10, no 2, pp 163–80.

James, A. (2000) 'Embodied being(s): understanding the self and the body in childhood', in A. Prout (ed) *The body, childhood and society*, Basingstoke: Macmillan, pp 19–37.

Jensen, A.M. and McKee, L. (2003) 'Introduction: theorizing childhood and family change', in A.M Jensen and L. McKee (eds) *Children and the changing family: between transformation and negotiation*, London: RoutledgeFalmer, pp 1–14.

Morrow, V. (1999) '"We are people too": children's and young people's perspectives on children's rights and decision-making in England', *International Journal of Children's Rights*, vol 7, pp 149–70.

Moxnes, K. (2003a) 'Risk factors in divorce: perceptions by the children involved', *Childhood*, vol 10, no 2, pp 131–46.

Moxnes, K. (2003b) 'Children coping with parental divorce: what helps, what hurts?', in A. Jensen and L. McKee (eds) *Children and the changing family: between transformation and negotiation*, London: RoutledgeFalmer, pp 90–104.

Natalier, K. and Hewitt, B. (2010) '"It's not just about the money": non-resident fathers' perspectives on paying child support', *Sociology*, vol 44, no 3, pp 489–505.

Neale, B. (2002) 'Dialogues with children: children, divorce and citizenship', *Childhood*, vol 9, no 4, pp 455–75.

Robinson, M., Butler, I., Scanlan, L., Douglas, G. and Murch, M. (2003) 'Children's experiences of their parents' divorce', in A.M. Jensen and L. McKee (eds) *Children and the changing family: between transformation and negotiation*, London: Routledge Falmer, pp 76–89.

Smart, C., Neale, B. and Wade, A. (2001) *The changing experience of childhood: families and divorce*, Cambridge: Polity.

Smith, A., Taylor, N. and Tapp, P. (2003) 'Rethinking children's involvement in decision-making after parental separation', *Childhood*, vol 10, no 2, pp 201–16.

Wade, A. and Smart, C. (2002) *Facing family change: children's circumstances, strategies and resources*, York: Joseph Rowntree Foundation/York Publishing Services.

TROUBLES AND TRANSITIONS ACROSS SPACE AND CULTURE

Introduction to Part Four

Jane Ribbens McCarthy

People have migrated around the globe for centuries, but there are new contexts for such migration in the contemporary world – not least, the advent of telecommunications and air travel, and the rise of women's migration as part of global care chains (Ehrenreich and Hochschild, 2003; Yeates, 2009) – with variable significance for the family lives of children and young people. In Part Four, issues of family change, transitions and troubles (including ill-health) across different global spaces and cultures are centralised, with chapters focusing on peoples from developing worlds, or the global South (including Africa, the Indian subcontinent and South America), as well as migrants on the edges of Europeanness. Issues of material resources and global inequalities loom large, but there is also evidence of a form of cultural inequality, through which Western understandings and discourses of childhood and family life may become dominant, almost hegemonic, through their incorporation into international legislation and the work of aid agencies (Boyden, 1997; Holzscheiter, 2010). These chapters demonstrate how some of these broad issues are manifest in the troubles of particular young people's family lives, in particular contexts, across space and culture. All the chapters bring young people's own perspectives into view, whether explicitly or implicitly – as in the discussion of forced marriage, which, by definition, entails resistance to an actual or proposed marriage.

Umut Erel's focus is on the experiences of Kurdish and Turkish migrants to London, drawing on the concept of 'generation work' to highlight the creation of a 'third space' between different generations of migrant family members, with young people actively negotiating and managing such processes. In this space, language is key, not just as a means of communication, but also as a symbol and metaphor for cultural differences, imbued with varied emotions. Rather than framing these young people's experiences through the widely used notion of 'cultural conflict', Erel draws out the complexity of their migration experiences and positioning, which cannot easily be categorised as troubled or not.

Across the world in South America, Maria Claudia Duque-Páramo explores the varied experiences of families in which children remain in the country of origin – in this case, Colombia – while one or more of their parents move abroad for work. This chapter teases out the diversity of perspectives between different family members, and between different sections of society, the media and some researchers, entailing a complex clash between more positive and more negative perspectives on parents' migratory decisions. A further underpinning dilemma, which the parents are not materially able to resolve in their home country, concerns ideals around the desirability of the co-resident nuclear family and also of an affluent childhood. At the same time, older indigenous cultural expectations may see some level of pain as a normal part of life, and, similarly, separation may be understood through long-standing cultural practices.

In the following chapter, by Elaine Chase and June Statham, young people experience the reverse situation, where they migrate to the UK without other family members. As well as bringing with them troubled memories of traumatic experiences from the past, troubles in the present include isolation, loss of family, emotional and spiritual concerns, and what might be termed 'external' factors and systems. With regard to the latter, it is the UK legal and administrative processes that may be associated with a severely troubling position for these young people, incurring the stigma of the 'asylum-seeker' label and an overwhelming uncertainty about whether or not they will be accepted as a UK resident (also a key concern for many of the young people in Evans' chapter). In these circumstances, the young people's accounts convey their struggle to cope with a loss of ontological security, expressing their desire to recover a sense of belonging and a level of predictability and routine. Education emerges as a significant source of hope for a potential trajectory of better times ahead, along with a sense of belonging as a more immediate benefit, and thus a sense of purpose and narrative continuity.

Ruth Evans' work also includes young people who have migrated to the UK, as well as those living in East Africa, but in both cases, ill-health is a potential (but not inevitable) source of troubles, in terms of family members affected by HIV and AIDS. Again, longer-standing cultural practices may be significant, in this case, in terms of expectations of children's participation in caring activities in African families; consequently, caring per se may not necessarily be seen as troubling even in these circumstances of significant health issues. In these family relationships, Evans conveys the complexity of the emotions and multiple meanings and directions of care between parents with HIV and their children, with some scope for perceiving some benefits from their troubles. Like the families in Colombia, however, the clash of African and Western expectations of childhood may become troublesome, especially if the young people move to the UK. Throughout all these experiences, however, Evans points to the importance of wider structural, cultural and material issues.

Cultural expectations are central to the topic of the concluding chapter in Part Four, by Peter Keogh and colleagues, which concerns forced marriage. In the UK context, forced marriage is seen as a source of family trouble that is unacceptable and illegal, but Keogh and colleagues suggest that it may be poorly understood by professionals. This chapter provides a detailed account of work to estimate the prevalence of reported (leaving aside unreported) cases of actual or threatened forced marriage, conveying important insights – and associated conundrums – into the difficulties of constructing such statistics. The chapter thus highlights how such estimates are the result of social processes that are difficult to ascertain, demonstrating the difficulties of producing the sorts of robust and generalisable data on which to build policy responses.

In many respects, then, Part Four of the book highlights some of the methodological issues discussed by Rutter and Francis in their chapters in Part One, while also building strongly on the chapters by Korbin and Fink. Unsurprisingly perhaps, material resources are a key element in several of the studies in this part (Duque-Páramo; Chase and Statham; Evans), constituting a strong factor in shaping whether changes become transformed into troubles. At the same time, the complexity of such transformation, and the process of how change comes to be experienced as trouble, is manifested in several ways, including the diversity of perspectives involved between different family members and between different sections of society (Duque-Páramo), and the ambivalences and subtleties of associated emotions. Several chapters point to the mixed implications of the changes experienced by the research participants, with benefits and losses at both emotional and practical levels (Duque-Páramo; Erel; Evans) and the subtlety of the directionality of care in circumstances of ill-health (Evans).

In some of these studies, however, the extremity of traumatic experiences recounted (or hinted at, as too difficult to speak) leaves little room for doubting their distressing negative impact on the lives of those concerned (Chase and Statham; Keogh et al). This may or may not be recognised by state services and systems, although from another perspective, it is also apparent that the state and professionals themselves may struggle to know how to respond to some troubles associated with cultural differences, with even basic prevalence information being extremely difficult to ascertain (Keogh et al).

As well as movement across geographical space, many of these chapters also draw our attention to the significance of trajectories of change, in terms of sudden and critical disruptions (Evans; Chase and Statham), and how individual responses to change are rooted in the histories of particular relationships (Duque-Páramo). Where change is experienced through a series of major traumas and unanticipated events, the loss of any sense of predictability can lead to an experience of chaos (Chase and Statham), leaving young people desperately struggling to work out how to deal with the past, and build for the future – a profoundly difficult challenge where citizenship status is lacking. At the same time, the sense of belonging may also be crucial to other young people experiencing the impact of migration in somewhat less traumatic circumstances (Erel). The significance of young people's own active agency in seeking to repair changes that have become sources of trouble is, thus, a theme that runs through many of these chapters (Erel; Evans; Chase and Statham), while Duque-Páramo stresses the importance of understanding the specific contexts and histories of particular relationships for managing change and minimising the troubles that may arise with change.

A key point to emerge from this part is the possibility that pain itself may be seen as inevitable and normal in some cultural contexts (Duque-Páramo; Chase and Statham), something that cannot be avoided or left in the past. This suggests the possibility of recognising pain and troubles as common to the human condition, with such recognition itself constituting a cultural resource in dealing with changes associated with varying and complex experiences of trouble. This is an issue we will return to in the concluding chapter to the book.

References

Boyden, J. (1997) 'Childhood and the policy makers: a comparative perspective on the globalisation of childhood', in A. James and A. Prout (eds) *Constructing and reconstructing childhood: contemporary issues in the sociological study of childhood*, Lewes: Falmer.

Ehrenreich, B. and Hochschild, A.R. (2003) *Global woman: nannies, maids and sex workers in the new economy*, London: Granta Publications.

Holzscheiter, A. (2010) *Children's rights in international politics: the transformative power of discourse*, Basingstoke: Palgrave Macmillan.

Yeates, N. (2009) *Globalizing care economies and migrant workers*, Basingstoke: Palgrave Macmillan.

CHAPTER SIXTEEN

'Troubling' or 'ordinary'? Children's views on migration and intergenerational ethnic identities

Umut Erel

Migration leads to experiences of discontinuity for families as they make sense of the differing societal circumstances and norms of the societies of origin and residence. Members of the migrant family face the challenge of integrating diverse experiences into a renewed sense of belonging both within the family and the wider society of residence. In the process of migration, family members elaborate new meanings and ways of being a 'mother', 'daughter', 'father', 'sister' and so on. The members of migrant families may have diverse linguistic and cultural competences. At times, children may have different notions of ethnic identity from those of their parents, and, in these circumstances, parents are challenged to question their own ethnic identification. These dynamic and fluid processes are often overlooked in representations of migrant families as either dysfunctional or steeped in 'tradition' (cf Erel, 2002; Kraler, 2010). Indeed, the experience of migration is often assumed to be troubling, both for individual family members and for the composition of the family.

This chapter explores how the experience of migration and settlement in the UK is constituted as 'troubling' or 'ordinary' through a focus on children's narratives, exploring the ways in which they complicate notions that migration troubles intergenerational ethnic identities. While differences in ethnic identification can certainly be troubling for some migrant families, here I explore how children engage in 'generation work' (Inowlocki, 1995). This 'generation work' consists of mutual efforts of migrants to discursively construct continuity between family members, despite their different experiences of migration. This is an important part of coping with these troubles.

During the 1970s and 1980s, a key explanation for the 'failed' integration of migrant young people was the so-called culture or generation clash. This assumed that parental attitudes and orientations towards a presumed culture of the homeland prevented young people from integrating. This has been critiqued for relying on a simplistic view of culture and family, failing to consider their dynamic and negotiated qualities. However, social policy and public debate in the UK has recently delegitimised multiculturalist notions of ethnic plurality; instead, increasingly legitimating new forms of assimilationism (Back et al, 2002). In this context, the migrant family 'is increasingly seen as an obstacle to integration – as a site characterised by patriarchal relationships and illiberal practices and traditions such as arranged and forced marriages' (Kraler, 2010). This is increasingly rendering migrant parents, and in particular mothers, responsible for what is perceived as the failed integration of the young generation of migrants (cf Hinsliff, 2002).

Women's role in ethnic and national projects is often conceptualised as upholding a static, immutable cultural essence of the national or ethnic group (Apitzsch, 1996; Mosse, 1985), with mothers socialising children into the ethnic group and transmitting ethnically specific values. This emphasises mothers' role in constructing intergenerational continuity (Anthias and Yuval-Davis, 1992). Yet, migration can also open up new ways of living family relations (Ganga, 2007; Tsolidis, 2001), and the transmission of ethnically specific values can entail a transformation of ethnicity (Fischer, 1986; Inowlocki, 1995; Lutz, 1998). Inowlocki (1995) argues that the loss of intergenerationally constituted identity through migration can lead to a crisis in the migrant family, where family members of different generations do not share the same cultural reference points or social norms, and where communication about this topic is not possible, potentially leading to a crisis in how family members view the intergenerational continuity of the family's cultural identity. Inowlocki coins the term 'generation work' to refer to the negotiation and the reflection on change within the family that may resolve this crisis. Generation work, thus, is the familial effort of making sense of the rupture and discontinuity of identity and meaning. Family members of different generations engage in dialogue to understand each other's experiences of migration, each other's cultural and social reference points and the meanings attached to these. These diverse experiences and meanings need to be discursively integrated into a liveable notion of self and family. In the process of doing generation work, family members elaborate new meanings of ethnic and cultural identity, of shared, as well as distinct, aspects of family members' identification with particular ethnic identities and cultural practices.

In the following discussion, I draw on data from a small research project undertaken in 2008 that explored the citizenship practices, belonging and participation of 15 pairs of migrant mothers and their children aged 12–18 in London. The sample was diverse in terms of family forms, class and educational background but focused on Polish, Turkish and Kurdish migrants. These groups were chosen because there is little research about families from new migrant groups who are categorised as 'white' (Phoenix and Husain, 2007). They represent different relations with Europeanness, with Polish migrants having just joined the European Union, while Kurdish and Turkish migrants are seen as just outside or at the boundary of geographical, cultural, religious and political notions of Europeanness. In the following, I present extracts from two interviews with Turkish and Kurdish children to show the complexities of their generation work. In the case of migrants from Turkey in London, ethnic diversity is a culturally and politically significant characteristic, more so than among migrants from Poland. However, the largest group consists of Kurdish refugees who arrived in large numbers from the late 1980s, although there are also students, business people, labour migrants and those who arrived through family reunification. They are geographically concentrated in London and economically concentrated in small ethnic businesses in retail and catering. Migrants from Turkey in the UK are estimated to number between 54,000 and 150,000 (King et al, 2008, pp 9–11). Migrants from Turkey have been largely 'invisible' in policy discourse, although they have experienced forms of racialisation mainly through their classification as refugees and as Muslim (Enneli et al, 2005; Erel, 2009).

Dilek: translating cultural difference

Dilek is a 12-year-old girl who lives with her mother in North London, where she was born. Her parents have recently separated. Her mother, Hayal, works as a hairdresser in a salon with many Turkish and Kurdish clients. She works long hours and Dilek spends a lot of time at the salon after school and at the weekends. Dilek and her mother have a very strong bond, but both feel rather socially isolated in London and miss Hayal's family in Turkey.

Doing research with migrants from Turkey in London, it is striking that when asked about the problems they experience in London, lack of English language is one of the first and most important topics they elaborate (cf Enneli et al, 2005). For this reason, different feelings associated with different languages were an important theme in the interviews:

Interviewer:	Do you feel differently when you speak English or Turkish?
Dilek:	No, there is no difference for me. It sounds the same to me. I am used to speaking English with certain people and Turkish with certain people … but I got used to it because it has been many years and speaking two languages sounds very normal to me.

Dilek is confident in using both English and Turkish. Dilek realises that her mother's English is not as good as her own, and she feels that her mother is more attached to Turkey:

Dilek:	She was in Turkey before and she was born in Turkey, so she feels she is more Turkish than me…. She is more attached to Turkey. She goes to Turkey two or three times a year. Incidentally, I speak English with her in Turkey.

Interviewer:	Can you give an example of a situation where you feel your mother might have felt differently from you?
Dilek:	When my mother speaks English, I say, "Yes, she is definitely English" but sometimes I feel she will never be like English. She makes me confused because she does not speak English at home and I see that she speaks [English] with her customers. Sometimes, she makes me speak English with her so that she can improve her spoken English.

Dilek acknowledges both differences and similarities between herself and her mother. While Dilek points out differences in their use of language, this is a way of speaking about wider issues of cultural difference. Dilek emphasises that she is proud of her mother for improving her English by attending college and practising at work. Dilek's point about speaking English with her mother when they are in Turkey on holiday, though they mostly do not speak English when they are at home, suggests that language use is not always designed to 'fit in' with the wider social environment. Perhaps Dilek looks to her mother for reassurance when she is in the culturally and socially different environment of Turkey through the use of the English language, with which Dilek is familiar. This suggests that the use of language between mother and daughter may be as much, or perhaps more, about creating emotional and social closeness as it is about shared linguistic proficiency.

Dilek, like many migrant young people, sometimes interprets for her mother. While Dilek says she is happy about being able to help her mother, she also experiences anger when she finds this goes beyond her own linguistic capacities. However, she forcefully rejects any suggestion by the interviewer that she might feel embarrassed by her mother's limited English:

> Definitely not at all. It is not funny either. There are some mums and they cannot speak at all. It is not funny. Some mums can't speak at all. They are not working and stay at home all day.

Dilek here refers to her experience of helping to translate for other mothers in her neighbourhood. She gives examples of witnessing how workmen or council representatives treated these women condescendingly because they didn't speak English. Dilek felt bad for these mothers and offered help: "I was very angry. I intervened and translated". This language-brokering makes her proud for being able to be helpful. Yet, these situations also confront her with uncomfortable feelings of anger, although Dilek does not elaborate on who she is angry with. I would interpret this as an emotion that arises at times when she realises the helplessness of the mothers she interprets for.

While acknowledging different degrees of attachment to Turkey and different language skills, Dilek foregrounds the commonalities with her mother. Even when she herself has difficulties understanding her mother's heavily accented English, she points out that they find ways of 'translating' and understanding each other. In their separate interviews, both Dilek and her mother emphasise that they are very close to each other and communicate well. The notion of 'translation' highlights that the differences between mother and daughter do not only concern different linguistic abilities, there are also cultural and social differences between them. Yet, rather than see these differences as insurmountable, the notion of 'translation' allows us to think about ways of bridging these differences (Bhabha, 1994).

However, when Dilek referred to her language-brokering for other migrant mothers, this highlights that the success of translation depends on the hierarchical relationship between the speakers of different languages. As the public and policymakers increasingly concur in expecting that migrants living in the UK should learn English in order to fully participate and access services, the onus on bridging the linguistic gap is placed on the migrant. Their languages are seen as less relevant, and the speakers of Turkish in this case are disempowered. Speaking English, on the other hand, is seen as the norm. It is not expected that the council workers will display knowledge of the various languages spoken by migrants in the locality. The onus of translation is thus placed on the speaker of the less powerful language. Translation, thus, always also encompasses a negotiation of socially constructed power relationships (Gutiérrez Rodríguez, 2010). Thus, Dilek's vehement rejection of 'making fun' of the insufficient English language skills of some mothers shows her awareness that not everybody is willing to accommodate linguistic differences.

When institutions in the society of residence are unwilling to accommodate translated culture, they do not value the in-between identification of migrant families like Dilek's. It is this view that one shared language and culture should be the norm within families that leads to a view of migrant families as 'troubled' rather than 'ordinary'.

Sevda: becoming a Londoner: a way to claim Kurdishness

Sevda is an 18-year-old student. She lives with her mother, father and two younger siblings in North London. Her mother is a stay-at-home mother while her father works in catering. Sevda's account foregrounds her Kurdish identity. Indeed, she strongly politicises her Kurdish ethnic identity and uses it to thematise other aspects, such as her plans for her future and her interest in politics, which delineates her own gendered identity from that of her mother, whom she sees as not political. Kurds are an ethnic minority in Turkey and cannot freely express their allegiance to Kurdishness in public for fear of stigmatisation or persecution (cf van Bruinessen, 2000). Her mother, Suna, emphasised in her interview that while living in Turkey, she had to conceal her Kurdish identity from their predominantly Turkish neighbours. Like Dilek, Sevda discusses her ethnic identification through the example of language. She emphasised the feelings attached to speaking different languages:

> When I speak Kurdish, I feel very natural.... I do not know why, but I feel happy and I enjoy it more when I speak Kurdish. Turkish is just an instrument to communicate with others.... I feel different when I speak English. I feel I am someone standing on the England side. I feel very modern and interesting. I speak English with people on the street or at school.... If we talk about Kurdish, of course everything changes. This is my mother tongue. I feel and own this language.

While speaking English connotes being 'modern and interesting', speaking Kurdish evokes feelings of home, allowing her a sense of ownership. Turkish on the other hand, the only official language in Turkey, does not reverberate emotionally for her. For Sevda, as for many other Kurdish interviewees from Turkey, migration is not simply about navigating cultural and ethnic attachments between the country of origin and the country of residence. Migration has enabled Kurdish migrants from Turkey to London to express publicly their Kurdish ethnic identity, and to speak Kurdish without fear of the reprisals they might encounter in Turkey. In this case, migration has served to overcome ethnic and political family troubles.

While Sevda thinks that she shares an ethnic identification with her mother, she nonetheless emphasises that there are also differences:

Interviewer:	Can you give an example of a situation where you feel your mother might have felt differently from you?
Sevda:	I think she is a mother. That is why she thinks she has to be like that [ie focused on providing care]. I think the only thing my mother cares about is her children to be healthy and be educated. Still, she is attached to her identity. For example, due to recent incidents in Turkey in terms of the Kurdish issue, she comments on the news while watching television. She defends Kurds. I am getting to know my mother more and more. I am so surprised sometimes when I learn her thoughts about the Kurdish issue.

Thus, Sevda sees her own identification as Kurdish as more explicitly political and views her mother as more narrowly focused on the well-being of her family. At the time of the interview, the violent conflict between the Turkish state and Kurdish guerrillas was at a peak and Sevda expresses her surprise when she realises that her mother engages with such news, and expresses strong political views. Sevda is more inclined to construct intergenerational continuity with her father. She aspires to emulate his explicit political involvement in the Kurdish national liberation movement. Her mother, on the other hand, in Sevda's eyes, is clearly tied to the domestic sphere, implicitly marking out an intergenerational difference that cuts across gender in the ways in which mother and daughter give meaning to their identity as Kurdish. Her mother's care for Kurdish identity in the domestic sphere contrasts with how Sevda mobilises the idea of her Kurdish identity, to propel herself into the public sphere of politics, study and career aspirations:

Sevda: In fact, I am a Kurd and I should have a country and my own rights as a Kurd. I think this situation made me stronger and I am more ambitious. You look at the world from a different perspective.

Interviewer: Can you give examples?

Sevda: I want to display my success. When I look at my surroundings, I cannot see anyone academic. I want to be successful.

Sevda strategically links her politicised Kurdish identity with her personal academic and professional project. By claiming a space in public, she implies that she is claiming a public recognition for the Kurdish identity, which, in her view, is denied political recognition in the absence of a nation-state. In this complex way, Sevda at once strengthens the intergenerational bond with her mother and father by constructing a common ethnic identity. With her father, she shares a political project of striving for an independent Kurdish nation-state; with her mother, she shares an emphasis on Kurdish language and tradition. Emphasising these commonalities and projecting her professional projects in the name of displaying Kurdish success helps Sevda pre-empt any possible critique of her independence through education. Elsewhere, she stresses that her parents are strict about monitoring and controlling her movements, not allowing her to socialise with non-Kurds outside school, as they fear she might adapt to the sexually more open norms of other British peers. While she is explicit about the intergenerational continuity of ethnic identification as Kurdish, Sevda implicitly breaks with the intergenerational continuity of a gendered Kurdish identity. She is ambitious and seeks to realise her professional dreams, while she views her mother's life as revolving around domestic responsibilities.

Conclusion

How can these stories enhance our understanding of migrant families as 'ordinary', 'troubled' or 'troubling'? First of all, they complicate the notion that an intergenerational divergence of ethnic identification is automatically problematic for migrant families. While these families may experience troubles, these are not necessarily related to intergenerationally divergent ethnic identifications between family members. These troubles can take a number of forms, and, as we saw in Sevda's case, migration may also alleviate some family troubles, such as the experience of ethnic discrimination.

Second, the case studies show that differences in ethnic identification can be reconciled. Differences of culture or language are not necessarily insurmountable. As family members can translate different languages, they can also translate different cultural meanings and reference points. Culture is a system of making meaning; it can be translated across ethnic boundaries. Culture can form new spaces of identification, rather than simply reproducing bounded ethnic identifications (Hall, 1990; Bhabha, 1994). Dilek's story shows how this notion of 'translation' can be part of 'generation work' for constructing a shared family identification across differences of ethnic, cultural and linguistic resources.

Third, Sevda's story highlights that the notion of ethnic identity cannot be reduced to a dichotomy of country of origin versus country of settlement. Instead, migrants relate to multiple ethnic identities, in the country of origin and also in the country of residence. Indeed, Sevda's case highlights that transnational mobility can enable migrants to claim ethnic identities, such as the Kurdish identity, that have been stigmatised, marginalised or even criminalised in the country of origin.

Fourth, Sevda's story also highlights that ethnic identifications are formed in intersections with other social identities. In this case, Sevda pursues divergent projects of femininity from her mother. Sevda seeks out a place in the public realm of employment and politics, in contrast to her mother's femininity, which is organised around care and domestic work. Nonetheless, Sevda constructs a shared allegiance to Kurdishness as an intergenerationally shared project.

Finally, Sevda's strategic use of Kurdishness to justify her educational and career projects, as well as Dilek's emphasis of her closeness to her mother, show the importance of the social imagination in constructing identities (Yuval-Davis, 2006). Both case studies show how migrant children negotiate different cultural resources and different ways of interpreting ethnic identification within the family by engaging in the generation work of constructing translated meanings for a shared intergenerational ethnic identification. Researchers and policymakers need to be aware of these complexities and recognise children's engagement in generation work, which might otherwise be lost in a generalised notion of troubling intergenerational differences.

References

Anthias, F. and Yuval-Davis, N. (1992) *Racialised boundaries*, London: Routledge.

Apitzsch, U. (1996) 'Frauen in der Migration', *Frauen in der Einen Welt*, vol 1, pp 9–25.

Back, L., Keith, M., Khan, A., Shukra K. and Solomos, J. (2002) 'The return of assimilationism: race, multiculturalism and New Labour', *Sociological Research Online*, vol 7, no 2, <http://www.socresonline.org.uk/7/2/back.html> Accessed 12/12/12

Bhabha, H.K. (1994) *The location of culture*, London: Routledge.

Enneli, P., Modood, T. and Bradley, H. (2005) 'Young Turks and Kurds: a set of "invisible" disadvantaged groups'. Available at: http://www.jrf.org.uk/sites/files/jrf/185935274x.pdf

Erel, U. (2002) 'Re-conceptualising motherhood: experiences of some migrant women from Turkey in Germany', in D.F. Bryceson and U. Vuorola (eds) *The transnational family: global European networks and new frontiers*, Oxford: Berg.

Erel, U. (2009) *Migrant women transforming citizenship. Lifestories from Germany and Britain*, Aldershott: Ashgate.

Fischer, M.J. (1986) 'Ethnicity and the post-modern arts of memory', in J. Clifford and G.E. Marcus (eds) *Writing culture. The poetics and politics of ethnography*, London: University of California Press.

Ganga, D. (2007) 'Breaking with tradition through cultural continuity: gender and generation in a migratory setting', *Migration Letters*, vol 4, pp 41–52.

Gutiérrez Rodríguez, E. (2010) *Migration, domestic work and affect: a decolonial approach on value and the feminization of labour*, New York, NY: Routledge.

Hall, S. (1990) 'Cultural identity and diaspora', in J. Rutherford (ed) *Identity, community, culture, difference*, London: Lawrence and Wishart.

Hinsliff, G. (2002) 'Speak English at home, Blunkett tells British Asians', *The Observer* 15 September 2002.

Inowlocki, L. (1995) 'Traditionsbildung und intergenerationale Kommuniktion zwischen Müttern und Töchtern in jüdischen Familien', in W. Fischer-Rosenthal and P. Ahlheit (eds) *Biographien in Deutschland*, Opladen: Westdeutscher Verlag.

King, R., Thomson, M. Mai, N. and Keles, Y. (2008) 'Turks' in London: problems of definition and the partial relevance of policy', *Journal of Immigrant and Refugee Studies*, vol 6, pp 423–34.

Kraler, A. (2010) *Final report civic stratification, gender and family migration policies in Europe*, Vienna: International Centre for Migration Policy Development.

Lutz, H. (1998) 'Migration als soziales Erbe. Biographische Verläufe bei Migrantinnen der ersten und zweiten Generation in den Niederlanden', in M. Calloni, B. Dausien and M. Friese (eds) *Migration, Biographie, Geschlecht*, Bremen: Werkstattberichte des IBL, 38-61.

Mosse, G. (1985) *Nationalism and sexuality: respectability and abnormal sexuality in modern Europe*, New York, NY: Howard Fertig.

Phoenix, A. and Husain, F. (2007) *Parenting and ethnicity*, York: Joseph Rowntree Foundation.

Tsolidis, G. (2001) 'The role of the maternal in diasporic cultural reproduction – Australia, Canada and Greece', *Social Semiotics*, vol 11, pp 193–208.

Van Bruinessen, M. (2000) 'Transnational aspects of the Kurdish question', working paper, Robert Schuman Centre for Advanced Studies, European University Institute, Florence.

Yuval-Davis, N. (2006) 'Belonging and the politics of belonging', *Patterns of Prejudice*, vol 40, pp 196–213.

CHAPTER SEVENTEEN

Colombian families dealing with parents' international migration

Maria Claudia Duque-Páramo

Introduction

International parental migration is perceived in diverse and contradictory ways by different family members, whose experiences of what is 'normal' and 'troubling' are shaped by both local cultural traditions and global social and economic forces. This chapter, based on fieldwork conducted in four cities in Colombia, raises issues about pain as a 'normal' experience of families living in circumstances of separation related to migration; both parents and children assume that pain is the normal price they have to pay for succeeding, searching for a better life and economic progress. Yet, there are differences in their narratives: while parents focus on their role as providers, children focus on the experience of separation. It points to the impact of wider attitudes, for example, as manifested through the media, and an ideological clash between the desirability of a nuclear family household and how a particular version of (affluent) childhood is meant to happen, and what parents can do when they are unable to meet both of these ideals.

The family members' voices talk about diverse and sometimes contradictory and troubling experiences. While most children perceive separation as a sad and stressful experience that, with time, they become used to, some remain angry and resentful for a long time. Beyond their economic role, both parents and children assign remittances a broader meaning as an emotional bond; thus, the failure of the parent in sending remittances is often a factor in determining feelings of abandonment and resentment in the child. There are also gender differences around the perception of troubles and normality for the parent who migrates.

Children and international parental migration

Children are actors in global processes (Stephens, 1995; Scheper-Hughes and Sargent, 1998); like other family members, they are agents in migratory practices and experiences, albeit within generational and gendered hierarchies of family power. In their interactions with parents, siblings, peers, carers and other relatives, they construct cultural and personal realities; they face change, separation and suffering through various kinds of personal and social trouble. In doing so, they also have expectations about, and enjoy some of the benefits of, migration. In the international context, they can migrate with their families, stay in the country of origin or migrate independently (Whitehead and Hashim, 2005); they can also be returnees (Potter, 2005).

In the context of transnational migration, children's lives are shaped by powers and forces that are both local and global. Globalisation, lack of employment opportunities in the countries of origin and the increased demand for carers in destination countries are shaping the increases in international women's migration (Sørensen, 2005; Alcalá et al, 2006; Pérez Orozco, 2009; United Nations, 2009). Ideals about desirable childhoods are motivating mothers' migration (Horton, 2008) and it is also argued that ideologies about the nuclear family may shape feelings of loneliness and sadness among children whose parents have emigrated (Coe, 2010). Yet, children are not passive participants in this process; they shape parents' decisions and, in some cases, may define local and global realities as receivers of remittances and decision-makers of their spending (Zapata Martínez, 2009). It is well evidenced that the education, health, clothing and nutrition of their children are important motivating factors for parents to migrate, even if doing so means enduring certain sacrifices when they are away from home (Hondagneu-Sotelo and Avila, 1997; Orellana et al, 2001; International Organization for Migration et al, 2010).

In the context of the inequalities of globalisation, migration of one or both parents has emerged as a growing family strategy against poverty (Cortés, 2007) and as a means for parents to find employment so as to give their families the benefits they cannot provide in the home country (D'Emilio et al, 2007). As discussed elsewhere (Duque-Páramo, 2012), besides resulting in positive and negative impacts (Whitehead and Hashim, 2005; Cortés, 2007, 2008), parents' migration is a reality that produces several contradictory reactions among different social actors. In Colombia, along with the rise of migratory processes and the increased number of migrant women, particularly in regions with higher migratory rates, international parental migration has emerged as a phenomenon that draws the attention of diverse segments of society, among whom the parents' migration, but particularly the mother's migration, is viewed in quite negative ways. These contradictory perspectives are also expressed in academic language, where scholars tend to use two concepts: children left behind and parental migration. While *children left behind* reflects the parents' behaviour and may be interpreted in a negative way for the children as being separated or abandoned, *parental migration* is a concept that reflects the children's experience and may be interpreted as positive parental mobility for the good of the children and the family.

As with Eastern European commentators (News.scotsman.com, 2009; Bezzi, 2010) and other Latin American countries (Agencias de Noticias, 2008), in Colombia, some voices from the media, and some researchers studying families, complain that migration-related separation is causing family rupture, dysfunctional families and abandoned children (Ministerio de la Protección et al, 2007; López Montaño, 2009). Children receiving remittances are sometimes stereotyped as lazy, problematic, spoiled and dangerous for the society, and their emigrant mothers or fathers as bad parents (A.P. Sección Economía, 2007; Redacción, 2007). Yet, the blame falls more harshly on the mothers – who, by tradition, are the ones who play the greatest role in the care of their children. In contrast, some current research does not focus on separation per se, but rather interprets changes and continuities as positive from the perspective of the members of transnational families and the emergence of new types of families (Sørensen, 2005; Parella, 2007).

Beyond the binary view of the positive or the negative effects of parents' migration, other scholars have focused on understanding the complexities of separation related to parents' migration through studying the experiences, circumstances and perspectives of different family members (Suárez-Orozco et al, 2002; Dreby, 2010). Although physical separation is a common experience for all family members, the narratives and the meanings that children give to the experience of living apart can be quite different from the narratives of the migrant parents (Schmalzbauer, 2004; Coe, 2008; Madianou and Miller, 2011).

Methods

In Colombia, some representatives of the media and academia are working on understanding children's perspectives and the multiple realities of Colombian transnational families (Puyana et al, 2009; Sarmiento, 2009; Zorro, 2009; Duque-Páramo et al, 2010). In this context, and assuming that it is necessary to develop research and actions that support children whose parents have migrated and their families, during 2009 and 2010, we conducted[1] a mixed-methods, quantitative–qualitative study about the experiences and health situation of children living with parental migration in three Colombian cities that have a high migratory index: Bogotá (the capital) and Apia and Santuario, two towns located at the department of Risaralda. The research was designed to understand the children's and family members' experiences, comprehending and challenging stereotypes, identifying health and emotional problems, and developing actions and interventions that might improve children's, migrants' and their families' lives. After approaching children with one or both parents living abroad through the school system, we followed a detailed consent process with each child and primary carers. Besides promoting autonomy, privacy, anonymity and confidentiality, the informed consent process worked as a tool for building trust and quality of the data.[2]

The quantitative objectives aimed to characterise and measure the health situation of the children living with parental migration, based on the concept of the Social Determinants of Health. There were 186 completed questionnaires (Bogotá: 60; Apía: 31; and Santuario: 95). In Apia and Santuario, the surveys were conducted by a pollster whom we had contracted, and in Bogotá, by nursing students who also developed their theses based on the project. The qualitative objectives aimed to understand the participants' experiences of the parents' migration, their daily lives and their health situation. With these purposes, I conducted short-term fieldwork in the three sites and interviewed 20 children in Bogotá, 19 in Santuario and 10 in Apía. With them, we also conducted group sessions using drawings as a way for them to share their experiences. Using a similar instrument to the one we used with children, we interviewed 15 parents living abroad; from them, we also interviewed two mothers and three fathers living in Spain, Venezuela and the US. The surveys and the interviews with those living abroad were conducted through the phone and the Internet. We also interviewed some key informants in the three cities: schoolteachers, psychologists, fathers who migrated and returned because their children got sick, a journalist, and school principals.

Based on that study and on five individual and five group interviews, I conducted short-term fieldwork in 2008 in Pereira, the capital of Risaralda, and again in 2011.[3] This chapter focuses on discussing the diverse perspectives of children, mothers, fathers and carers about experiences of normality and troubles related to parental migration and separation. Like the images of several photos of the same objects but with a singular focus from each one, the different voices and perspectives between family members on how they experience separation and what constitute troubles or normality reveal the joys, the silent sufferings, the justifications they make and the complexities of the realities they live.

Parents' migration: a normal and painful separation

The predominant problematic and negative perceptions of international parental migration among some prestigious Colombian social actors, such as schoolteachers, researchers or journalists (Duque-Páramo, 2012), contrast with the voices of the family members. Children, parents and carers tend to normalise one or both parents' migration as a typical and expected adult behaviour that responds effectively to shared implicit desires and family goals, such as a better life, a better future and satisfying aspirations and needs for food, clothing, housing, health and education, that otherwise would be unavailable in the unequal and restricted economic Colombian context. In this respect, participants' accounts and perspectives of parents' migration are closely related to other widespread and similar long-standing cultural practices of child mobility, such as *child circulation*, *child shifting* and *child fostering*. In the Caribbean (Suárez-Orozco et al, 2002), sub-Saharan Africa (Bigombe and Khadiagala, 2003) and the Andean region (Leinaweaver, 2007), it is common to send children to live temporarily or even permanently within other households generally of extended family members, relatives or neighbours. The reasons for this practice vary, but are usually related to family hardship and the parents' wish to provide the child with better educational or life opportunities. These practices normalise children's separation from their parents, since they are not viewed as deviant and 'no stigma is attached to its occurrence' (Suárez-Orozco et al, 2002).

Besides regarding parental migration as normal, children, parents and carers speak about it as a painful but not always problematic experience. Yet, there are differences in their narratives. Migrant parents tend to focus their accounts on ideals of the united family, the primacy of their economic motives, their role as parents and the economic pressures that led them to migrate. Both mothers and fathers privilege their roles as providers over other dimensions of child–rearing. In this sense, migration is not understood as a free individual decision, but rather is presented as the only way that fathers could be good providers and mothers good carers. For example, pushed by economic reasons and against his mother's and siblings' advice, Jaime[4] decided to travel to Spain:

> At that time, I was desperate, I was in a desperate anxiety to get a job and make money. Then, a brother's friend told me: 'Let's go, let's go, my sister lives in the Canary Islands'; I said: 'No, no, no, I'm not able to leave my family', but he convinced me in a week.

Parents and carers who stay in the country of origin express somewhat different views. If the mother is the one who stays, she generally assumes the entire responsibility of raising and caring for children and dealing with the issues of everyday home life, while the migrant father provides economically through remittances. But if the one who stays is the father, very often a woman from either the maternal or the paternal family *helps* by assuming the maternal role. When neither parent stays with their children, grandmothers and aunts are the main carers. In the context of traditional patriarchal families, it is expected that women should assume the responsibility of taking care of men and children whose wives/mothers are abroad. Although carers usually focused on the difficulties and the uncertainties of their roles – for example, as grandmothers having once again to raise young children – they also talked about emotional pain from two causes: separation from their adult children when they migrate; and then missing their grandchildren when, after years of taking care of them, they also migrate to reunite with their parents.

Colombian children's experiences and feelings about parental migration and separation are not homogeneous and may depend on particular circumstances, such as which parent has migrated, the characteristics of the carers and the family, the age of the child, and the support that the schools and the broader social context can provide. Although children's accounts are diverse and sometimes ambivalent and contradictory, most of their talk about separation focused on enduring family bonds and the joys of remittances and gifts, and about living within normal families that include a wide diversity of types: mother and siblings; grandmother, siblings and cousins; grandparents and siblings; among others. They talk about feeling supported and cared for by parents, carers and other relatives, about missing the migrant parent and feeling sad sometimes, and about continuities and strong communication with the migrant parent over distance. The conversation of three children in Santuario about how to explain to a close friend the parent's decision to live in another country shows the diversity of perspectives:

Girl 1:	My parents are leaving … that's it.
Girl 2:	I would tell only to my best friend with a bit of sadness.
Boy:	Both sadness and joy. Sadness because it is painful his leaving and who knows when I'll see him again; and joy because he is going to achieve a new future for the family and he is going to do whatever he wants to.

Julián Andrés was nine years old when his father went to work in Venezuela in 2008; by the time of the interview in December 2010, he was very happy because his father was returning for good, in a couple of weeks. When he explains his drawing (Drawing 1), he recognises that his father's migration has meant contradictory feelings: "I drew the angry snake and the happy deer because I felt both things when my father left to Venezuela."

Drawing 1

Related to the political and expressive value that children represent (Scheper-Hughes and Sargent, 1998), Colombian children tend to understand migration as a sacrifice that their parents make for their well-being and for the good of the whole family. In response to this sacrifice, they as children are expected to behave well, get good grades, take care of younger siblings when necessary, enjoy the gifts, be strong – meaning not being sad and not crying – and share the sacrifice that their parents make when they work abroad. Julián Andrés says that children help to support their migrant parents:

> When they behave well at school, with mom, and everywhere, so he is told good things about me. My dad gets very happy because he knows that I behave good and, of course, I'm glad that he is doing well at work.

They express some satisfaction at the thought that their parents are making these sacrifices for their future, for their education and to be able to send them gifts and increase their opportunities as consumers (Scheper-Hughes and Sargent, 1998).

When parents' migration becomes troubling

Like others who have studied children's experiences of migration-related separation (Suárez-Orozco et al, 2002; Jones, 2007), we found that Colombian children can be troubled by the emotional pain related to separation itself and to the stress of living apart for an extended period of time. Their words and drawings reflect their sadness; they sometimes weep out of deep anger and resentment. Suffering and emotional pain are more intense around the time when the parent leaves and generally decrease with time as the child gets used to the separation. The intensity of emotional pain may depend upon the previous relationship with the migrant parent or on the expectations or idealisations the child has about reunification. For example, children who talked about having a previous close relationship with the migrant parent generally recalled farewell and separation as very painful and hard experiences, but also highlighted how they still keep strong by means of continued communication with their parents. In contrast, some children who either were very little when the parent migrated or who had already experienced separation from that parent even during their lives in Colombia tended to point out two different perspectives: some expressed disappointment, limited communication, lack of interest and indifference to the migrant parent; and others, even with limited communication and few realistic possibilities of reunion, talked about their strong desire to achieve what might be seen as a kind of idealised reunion. In this sense, the extent of the *troubles* is context-specific, since it varies with the relationship between the parent and the child and the circumstances of the parents' migration.

Variable perspectives are presented by these girls in a group interview, talking about their feelings related to their parents' migration and explaining their drawings:

Girl 1:	It makes me very happy when he brings me gifts and when he comes back. You know that he will come back some day and you will see him again.

Girl 2:   It's normal for me. Since he left when I was very little, I haven't shared anything with him, and I live with my mom, then, for me is normal.

Girl 3:   I got very sad because I've always shared a lot with her and I love her very much.

Girl 4:   The title of my drawing [see Drawing 2] is 'The nicest family'." One day this family was sunbathing and they proposed not to separate ever and live together forever … I haven't met my father, but I drew him, my mother and me. I chat with him through the internet.

Drawing 2

Most children feel supported by their families and say that they lead normal lives, but some are regarded by teachers or carers as having problems or being problematic. In the interviews, some kept silent, gave brief answers, expressed deep regret and discouragement, or complained of infrequent and unsatisfactory communication with the parent living abroad.

Some others expressed rage because the migrant parent – who may have other children where he/she lives – does not send enough remittances. Besides their economic importance, the following children find it problematic being without the bond that remittances represent, particularly when the migrant parent has other children in Spain:

Boy 1:   My dad is careless, he doesn't send me money and calls me very little. I need glasses for reading, they cost $40.00. He hasn't sent the money.

Boy 2: Maybe he doesn't have money …

Boy 1: [loud and ironically] Sure … and he has my little brother in Spain like a king.

In contrast to children's perspectives, for migrant parents, troubles mainly emerge from the economic woes that first pushed their emigration and that are then the cause of painful worries in the country of destination. They urgently need to find employment and send money back home in order to repay the loans they took on for their travel and to provide for their children and other family members they support. They talked about facing discrimination, xenophobia, social exclusion and sometimes exploitation in the countries to which they migrated. Adaptation and cultural shock may also be troubling for parents: many of their accounts include health problems related to stress, missing Colombian food, poor sleep, lack of recreation and missing the presence and support of their families.

Generally, fathers talked about missing other adults – wives and mothers – and did not include children in their accounts of the persons they miss and need. Some fathers even find children's attachment to them to be problematic. For example, after a hostile divorce, Carlos decided to migrate to Spain eight years ago and left his children, a boy and a girl, in Santuario. Four years ago, he married a Colombian woman in Spain; he keeps in touch with his children by phone and the Internet, but he is puzzled trying to understand his children's attachment to him:

> I have a problem with my children, is worst with the boy, with the youngest. He is mad for coming to live with me here. I don't know why since I haven't lived with him that much. Maybe it is because of the calls and the internet. I try to visit them every year, but I haven't been there in the last three years. This is causing me many troubles. He tries to blackmail me.

In contrast, mothers' narratives tended to focus on the emotional pain and despair they felt for leaving and living apart from their children. Other gender differences include fathers' greater focus on their role as providers and mothers' worries about communication and maintaining bonds with their children. The mothers tend to seek family reunification and they send gifts as a mean to fill the gap caused by their absence. In January 2010, Carolina was very happy because, in December 2009, her son was reunited with her and her Spanish husband:

> I'm very happy and he is also happy. I hadn't seen him for three years; he was living with my parents. I did my best effort to bring him and contracted a lawyer. Living apart is a hard sacrifice that one does for succeeding and for the child, but it costs a lot. One says, 'Since I don't have his caresses, one is comforted by sending him money, so he can buy whatever he wants.' But now he is here with me.

Some parents find their children's expressions of emotional pain and sadness to be particularly difficult; sometimes they do not allow their children to go with them to the airport and either parents or carers ask children to be brave, not to cry and to be strong. Besides, since many parents have issues with money and/or documentation, children's emotional pain, sadness or school problems are usually not great enough reasons for parents to return. Only when his son exhibited marked signs of depression, did Jaime, who was happily living in Spain, decide to return to Colombia; although he was divorced, he had to return because his son's mother was in Canada still paying off the travel loan and had no chance to return:

> I had to return because of my son. My wife left him with her mother when she went to Canada. He was very bad psychologically, he cried, didn't eat, didn't sleep. The psychologist said if he stayed more time without a parent he would have died from sadness and pain. I came back to live with him and he became normal again, to study, to eat and to sleep well.

In the extensive literature on the impacts of parental migration, few studies focus on the carers' experiences and troubles (Goodman and Rao, 2007; Help Age International Moldova, 2008). Children's narratives about being cared for reflect the support carers provide, but carers are often invisible and their work and sufferings are not always recognised, such as loneliness, worries related to child-rearing, difficulties in exerting authority and fears of not receiving enough money or punctual remittances. In contrast, accounts from other people, such as teachers, school principals and even researchers, assume that children's problems are related to a lack of discipline and love, and affirm ideas about carers who are more interested in remittances than in caring for children or considering their responsibility for children's risk-taking behaviour.

Conclusion

Parental migration means separation for all family members. They live diverse experiences and circumstances and have different and sometimes contradictory perspectives about their family troubles. In contrast, most of the research about parental migration conducted around the world focuses on either the effects of remittances on a limited range of dimensions of children's lives – education and health – or in documenting its impacts on children's rights. Based on the diversity and complexities of the experiences of children, parents and carers in Colombia, I strongly recommend the development and implementation of policies based on the lived experiences of family members and their different perspectives about the issues that they face.

Notes

[1] The research was funded by the Pontificia Universidad Javeriana. Daniel Gonzalo Eslava and María Belén Jaimes were the co-researchers who conducted the quantitative component of the research.

[2] We sent a printed report to all participants, their families, teachers and other people who supported the fieldwork in schools, local and regional government, and health institutions.

[3] The main purpose of the interviews I conducted with children in February 2011 was to discuss with them the report and obtain feedback and validity.

[4] All the names of the participants, children and adults, are pseudonyms – most chosen by them.

References

Agencias de Noticias Fides (2008). Defensoría: 482 familias sufren maltratos debido a la migración. *Agencia de Noticias Fides* August 21. Newspaper Article Retrieved 26-09-2008 , from http://www.noticiasfides.com/print/454922

Alcalá, M.J., Leidl, P., Deligiorgis, D., Brachman, P., Boumenchal, Z. and Chaljub, M. (2006) *State of the world population. A passage to hope. Women and international migration*, New York, NY: United Nations Population Fund, UNFPA.

A.P., Sección Economía (2007). Remesas emperezan a jóvenes. *El Tiempo.* June 3. Newspaper Article Retrieved 03-06-2007, from http://www.eltiempo.com/archivo/documento/MAM-2516583

Bezzi, C. (2010). White Orphans, the enlargement's children. Osservatorio Balcani e Caucaso. Retrieved 29-01-2011, from http://www.balcanicaucaso.org/eng/Regions-and-countries/Romania/White-Orphans-the-enlargement-s-children

Bigombe, B. and Khadiagala, G.M. (2003) 'Major trends affecting families in Sub-Saharan Africa', in *Major trends affecting families: A background document.* Report for United Nations, Department of Economic and Social Affairs, Division for Social Policy and Development, Program on the Family. Retrieved 31-10-2011 from http://social.un.org/index/LinkClick.aspx?fileticket=3VvV_mL8oMw%3d&tabid=282.

Coe, C. (2010) 'How children feel about their parents' migration', in C. Coe, R.R. Reynolds, D.A. Boehm, J.M. Hess and H. Rae-Espinoza (eds) *Everyday ruptures: children, youth, and migration in global perspective*, Nashville, TN: Vanderbilt University Press.

Coe, G. (2008) 'The structuring of feeling in Ghanaian transnational families', *City and Society*, vol 20, pp 222–50.

Cortés, R. (2007) *Remittances and children's rights: An overview of academic and policy literature*, Working Paper. Unicef. Division of Policy and Planning. Retrieved 16-05-2009, from http://www.unicef.org/socialpolicy/index_45552.html

Cortés, R. (2008) *Children and women left behind in labor sending countries: an appraisal of social risks,* Working Paper. Unicef. Division of Policy and Practice. Retrieved 18-10-2010, from http://www.unicef.org/socialpolicy/files/Children_and_women_left_behind%283%29.pdf

D'Emilio, A.L., Cordero, B., Bainvel, B., Skoog, C., Comini, D., Gough, J. and Kilbane, T. (2007) *The impact of international migration: Children left behind in selected countries of Latin America and the Caribbean,* Working Paper. Unicef. Division of Policy and Planning. Retrieved 09-06-2010, from http://www.unicef.org/socialpolicy/index_46050.html

Dreby, J. (2010) *Divided by borders. Mexican migrants and their children,* Berkeley and Los Angeles, CA: University of California Press.

Duque-Páramo, M.C. (2012) 'Parental migration in Colombia: children's voices in national and international perspectives', *Journal of Latin American and Caribbean Anthropology,* vol 17, no 3, pp 472–92.

Duque-Páramo, M.C., Eslava Albarracín, D.G. and Jaimes Zanabria, M.B. (2010) *Análisis preliminar. Experiencias y situación de salud de niñas y niños viviendo migración parental en Bogotá y dos municipios de Risaralda y de sus madres y/o padres migrantes,* Bogotá: Pontificia Universidad Javeriana.

Goodman, M.R. and Rao, S.P. (2007) 'Grandparents raising grandchildren in a US–Mexico border community', *Qualitative Health Research,* vol 17, pp 1117–36.

Help Age International Moldova (2008) 'Grandparents and grandchildren: impact of migration in Moldova', in UNICEF HAIM (ed) *HAI/UNICEF project – findings and recommendations,* Chisinau, Moldova: Help Age International Moldova.

Hondagneu-Sotelo, P. and Avila, E. (1997) 'I'm here but I'm there. The meanings of Latina transnational motherhood', *Gender and Society,* vol 11, pp 548–71.

Horton, S. (2008) 'Consuming childhood: "lost" and "ideal" childhoods as a motivation for migration', *Anthropological Quarterly,* vol 81, pp 925–43.

IOM (International Organization for Migration) (2009) *Unió de Pagesos, Unión Europea, & Solidaris, Pagesos* (Temporary and circular labour migration experiences, challenges and opportunities) IOM Series of Research into Migration. No 2. Retrieved 18-01-2011, from http://www.upf.edu/gritim/_pdf/Temporary_and_Circular_Labour_Migration_Experiencesx_Challenges_and_Opportunities.pdf

Jones, A. (2007) 'Child-centred methodology: children's experiences of separation through migration: the case of Trinidad and Tobago', in Bruun, S.S.A.L. (ed) *Focus on children in migration – from a European research and method perspective,* Warsaw, Poland: Save the Children, Sweden.

Leinaweaver, J.B. (2007) 'On moving children: the social implications of Andean child circulation', *American Ethnologist,* vol 34, pp 163–80.

López Montaño, L.M. (2009) *Niños y niñas ante la migración internacional del padre o de la madre. Eje Cafetero Colombiano.* Paper presented at the Seminario Andino: Niñez, Familia y Migraciones. Situación actual, tensiones y perspectivas, Bogotá, April 16.

Madianou, M. and Miller, D. (2011) 'Mobile phone parenting: reconfiguring relationships between Filipina migrant mothers and their left-behind children', *New Media and Society*, vol 13, pp 457–70.

Ministerio de la Protección, S., Instituto Colombiano De Bienestar, F. and Aesco. (2007) Informe final sobre el resultado de la investigación "Grado de vulneración de los derechos de los niños usuarios de los Hogares Infantiles y Comunitarios del Instituto Colombiano de Bienestar Familiar en Dosquebradas quienes tienen uno o ambos progenitores en el exterior del país" (pp 106). Pereira: Ministerio de la Protección Social and Instituto Colombiano de Bienestar Familiar.

News.scotsman.com (2009) '"Strawberry orphans" driven to despair by their migrant mothers', 21 February.

Orellana, M.F., Thorne, B., Chee, A., Lam, W.S.E. and Lees, L.H. (2001) 'Transnational childhoods: the participation of children in processes of family migration', *Social Problems*, vol 48, pp 572–91.

Parella, S. (2007) 'Los vínculos afectivos y de cuidado en las familias transnacionales. Migrantes ecuatorianos y peruanos en España', *Migraciones Internacionales*, vol 4, pp 151–88.

Pérez Orozco, A. (2009) 'Global perspectives on the social organization of care in times of crisis: assessing the situation', in U.N. INSTRAW (ed) *Gender, migration and development series. Working paper 6*, Santo Domingo, Dominican Republic: United Nations International Research and Training Institute for the Advancement of Women (INSTRAW).

Potter, R.B. (2005) '"Young, gifted and back": second-generation transnational return migrants to the Caribbean', *Progress in Development Studies*, vol 5, pp 213–36.

Puyana, Y., Motoa, J. and Viviel, A. (2009) *Entre aquí y allá. Las familias colombianas transnacionales*, Bogotá: Editorial Códice LTDA.

Redacción J. (2007) Decenas de colombianos que migran al exterior son padres que no responden por sus hijos. *El Tiempo.* November 12. Newspaper Article Retrieved 12-11-2007, from http://www.eltiempo.com/archivo/documento/CMS-3812649

Sarmiento, J. (Director) (2009) La migración parental. *En Familia.* [Radio]. Bogotá: Caracol Radio. Retrieved 04-04-2010 from http://www.caracol.com.co/blog.aspx?id=897100

Scheper-Hughes, N. and Sargent, C.F. (1998) *Small wars: the cultural politics of childhood,* Berkeley, CA: University of California Press.

Schmalzbauer, L. (2004) 'Searching for wages and mothering from afar: the case of Honduran transnational families', *Journal of Marriage and Family. Special Issue: International Perspectives on Families and Social Change*, vol 66, pp 1317–31.

Sørensen, N.N. (2005) *Transnational family life across the Atlantic: The experience of Colombian and Dominican migrants in Europe*, Paper presented at the Migration and Domestic Work in a Global Perspective, Wassenar, The Netherlands. Retrieved 12-06-2009 from http://www.grupochorlavi.org/webchorlavi/migraciones2006/bibliografia/G%C3%A9nero/sorensen.pdf

Stephens, S. (1995) *Children and the politics of culture*, Princeton, NJ: Princeton University Press.

Suárez-Orozco, C., Todorova, I.L.G. and Louie, J. (2002) 'Making up for lost time: the experience of separation and reunification among immigrant families', *Family Process*, vol 41, pp 625–43.

United Nations and UN-Instraw (2009) Synopsis of the virtual discussion 'Global Care Chains', *Series Virtual Discussion "Gender, Migration and Development"* Retrieved 26-11-2009, from http://www.un-instraw.org/view-document-details/733-synopsis-of-the-second-virtual-discussion.html

Whitehead, A. and Hashim, I. (2005) 'Children and migration', Background paper for DFID Migration Team.

Zapata Martínez, A. (2009) 'Familia transnacional y remesas: padres y madres migrantes', *Revista Latinoamericana de Ciencias Sociales Niñez y Juventud*, vol 7, pp 1749–69.

Zorro, J.F. (2009) La niñez, familia y migración [Radio]. Colombia: Oxígeno de Caracol. Pereira 1300 AM.

CHAPTER EIGHTEEN

Families left behind: unaccompanied young people seeking asylum in the UK

Elaine Chase and June Statham

Introduction

Every year, several thousand children and young people arrive in the UK to seek asylum without the care or support of parents or other family members and more such claims are made in the UK than anywhere else in Europe (European Migration Network, 2012). In 2009, for example, 2,990 asylum applications (just over 12% of all those registered in the UK) were from unaccompanied asylum-seeking children and young people claiming to be under the age of 18 (Home Office, 2010). Of these, only 11% were granted asylum, 16% were refused and the remainder (73%) were awarded discretionary leave, mostly until they reached the age of 17-and-a-half years old.[1] Hence, the majority of young people arriving unaccompanied into the UK in search of asylum are judged not to meet the criteria of 'persecution', as defined within the United Nations Refugee Convention (1951), and consequently have no clear sense of how long they will be able to remain here.

This chapter considers the experiences of a sample of young people who arrived independently to seek asylum in the UK, having left families behind at some point in their journey. It traces the extreme turmoil and upheaval they experienced, often accompanied by the accumulated loss of loved ones, family and friends over time, and the consequent troubles that ensued for them. Central to young people's narratives, however, was what we have interpreted here as the notion of *ontological security* (Giddens, 1991): a sense that irrespective of upheaval and trauma, what helped mitigate the difficulties they encountered was an ability to reconstitute the predictability and routine of life and to envisage a future for themselves. We go on to show how their subsequent interactions with structures, systems and social environments once they arrived worked in contrasting ways to both re-establish and undermine young people's sense of ontological security and well-being.

Methodology

This research was conducted as part of a UK Department of Health-funded study into the factors affecting the emotional well-being of children and young people seeking asylum on their own in the UK and the implications for policy and practice. The qualitative interviews were carried out between January and July 2007, with a purposive sample of 54 unaccompanied children and young people accommodated (or previously accommodated) by local authorities in London. Young people were accessed via a combination of specialist social work teams working with young people seeking asylum in and leaving care and a number of voluntary organisations with a remit to support unaccompanied young people. The sample comprised 29 girls and young women and 25 boys and young men, from 18 different countries. The age range at the time of interview was 11–23 years (15 of whom were 11–16 years old; 21 were 17–18 years old; 16 were 19–21 years old; and two were aged 23 years old). All participants had previously arrived unaccompanied in the UK as children seeking asylum (under the age of 18 years old).

An inductive methodology based on the grounded theory approach (Glaser and Strauss, 1967) was adopted. Throughout the in-depth interviews, young people were encouraged to talk openly about their lives and well-being in an integrated way (see, eg, Aggleton et al, 1998). They were asked to think about two broad questions: first, the things that made them feel happy since arriving in the UK; and, second, the things that made them feel sad or created difficulties for them. Researchers often met with young people on more than one occasion and all young people were offered the opportunity to have an interpreter present at the interview (although only three young women who spoke Mandarin opted to do so). A topic guide was used to draw out key aspects of young people's lives and experiences and helped to ensure that comparative data were generated. Once all data from the research interviews had been transcribed, an inductive thematic analysis was conducted.

Findings

The troubles

Those young people who spoke of the circumstances surrounding their departure from their countries of origin (or the country in which they were living prior to their journey to the UK), for the most part claimed that the decision for them to leave had been taken by a significant adult in their lives – usually a relative or close family friend. This same adult had usually secured and organised their transit. In the majority of cases, an intermediary or agent was paid a fee to transport them, and many reported having no prior knowledge of where they would travel to or by what means. Aliya[2] talked of how at the age of 13, she had to leave her home in Somalia and travel to the border of Kenya. She lived there for two years with her mother (her father had died when she was very young), while her brothers and sisters remained in Somalia. When war escalated in Somalia, her mother decided that Aliya should leave the country, a decision that Aliya herself regretted:

> I mean, she [mother] wanted a better life for me but I wish that whatever the hardship, I would stay with her. Because you can come to Europe but you are on your own … you have no one to share it with. But if you are in a war or something, you've got your mother. I mean you've got that mother thing, she won't let you die or something.

Varying degrees of violence underpinned young people's narratives of why they had left their own countries. Many had been beaten or tortured themselves, others had witnessed others being beaten, tortured or killed. Others still, particularly those who were very young, appeared to have been removed from potential danger before they encountered them first-hand. While trauma was experienced in its different forms prior to their departure, it was also frequently encountered throughout their journeys. Some had made long arduous trips, spending days on end in the backs of lorries without food or water; others spoke of being beaten and maltreated or just simply terrified by the uncertainty about where they would end up. On her journey into Kenya to stay with relatives, Aliya said she was arrested. At that point in her narrative she faltered and said: "I don't want to remember … I mean so many horrible things have happened to me."

Young people's journeys were all unique, some had travelled directly from their original countries; others, such as Claude from Burundi and Nadine from Rwanda, had left their countries at the ages of five and six, respectively. Originally in the company of family members, they had spent years in a series of refugee camps, circumstances construing to separate them from their families along the way. The cumulative sense of loss that many young people felt stemmed from a combination of: their sense of detachment from family, friends and community; the death and disappearance of loved ones; and missing the lives and security that they had once enjoyed.

Their arrival in the UK was for many also a shock, particularly those who were older and were treated with suspicion and mistrust by the officials they came into contact with. Many spoke of the disconcerting label of 'asylum-seeker' and how this served to brand them both within and outside the asylum system. Within the system, they described being constantly scrutinised and monitored (see Chase, 2009); outside, they were acutely aware of the generalised stigma that the label evoked (see also Lynn and Lea, 2003; McDonald and Billings, 2007; Morris, 2009). Maryam, from Iran, commented:

> What really bothers me is the name 'asylum-seeker'. Whenever I have problems, it always comes back to the fact that I am an asylum-seeker. Maybe it's just me, but anything I come across, whenever I'm depressed

or I can't do something, or I think I'm not sociable – it's because I'm an asylum–seeker.

The impact on self

The impact of the vicissitudes described by young people were multiple and complex. Their inner turmoil and troubles became manifest in diverse ways and they collectively described a full range of emotional health problems from difficulties with sleeping, nightmares and anxieties, through to acute and chronic depression, attempted suicide and, in some cases, periods of severe mental illness requiring hospitalisation.

Missing family members and either grieving their loss (if they had died) or constantly wondering about whether or not they were alive was a common theme. While a few young people from Afghanistan had some contact with extended family members in the UK, general anxieties about what was still happening in their home countries and whether remaining family members were safe were common for most others. Even those young people who knew where their family members were, missed them a great deal. Zemar, aged 21 and having arrived from Afghanistan at the age of 17, reflected:

> not seeing my family is the most shocking thing. I know that even when I grow so old, and my eyebrows turn white, I will still picture my mum you know – that warmth that you feel is unprecedented, it is unmatchable – you can never match that with anything.

Consequently, young people frequently described feelings of loneliness, detachment and isolation, and 'feeling alone', 'having no one', 'having no family' or seeking replacements for family – 'God is my family now' – were terms commonly used by young people. These feelings were often hidden from others and only emerged some time into the interviews, when young people felt safe enough to open up. Some described the solitude of crying alone behind closed doors, or not sharing their distress with anyone.

Acute anxiety emerged as a recurrent theme; Ibrahim's account of his troubled mind typically illustrated the commonly expressed notion of 'thinking too much' – about things that had happened, about life back home, about their fears and insecurity, or about what might happen to them depending on the outcome of their asylum applications – "the brain is, you know, small because it is thinking, thinking, finished … there is no power there".

Finding a way forward

The ability of refugee and asylum-seeking young people to weather the adversity and upheaval that they have faced has been previously noted (see, eg, Wallin and Ahlstrom, 2005; Bash and Zezlina-Phillips, 2006; Rutter, 2006; Hodes et al, 2008).

Similarly, young people in the current study talked of the various ways they found to cope with the emotional and spiritual troubles resulting from their experiences.

Several had been given access to medical or therapeutic interventions to deal with their immediate symptoms of anxiety, depression and trauma. These variably took the form of medication, counselling or psychiatric intervention, some effective (according to the young people) in alleviating symptoms, others not. Several young people were particularly sceptical about the use of antidepressants, believing this to be a misplaced focus on the 'mind', whereas, as Mahamat from Chad neatly expressed it, he felt "a sickness of the heart … not of the mind". Similarly, while some who had experienced counselling spoke of its therapeutic benefit, many others deliberately rejected the suggestion that they should see a counsellor, associating it with a label of insanity or with what they saw as an illogical fixation on the past when what they wanted to do more than anything was to focus on the future. Others saw no point in talking about what had happened since it did not make it go away. Mahlet, from Ethiopia, explained:

> I think the counsellor thinks that if you are speaking it, it just goes away but it doesn't … it's not in your mouth and like you took it out – it's inside in your heart … so you can't take it out. I just told you now but it's still inside me … I got it in here [motions to her heart], it doesn't go out.

What was most striking from young people's accounts, however, was the ways in which they almost universally spoke of the need to re-establish order, structure and routine to their lives and to bracket the past and move forward to a future. The sense of routine could most notably be found in learning and education. When asked what had helped them deal with much of the previous upheaval they had encountered, 'college', 'school', 'learning' were repeatedly highlighted by young people as being fundamentally important. Learning provided structure to the day, developed new skills and allowed them to consider a future. Malashu, aged 17 from Eritrea, commented: "I like learning because it makes me think of the future and forget the past".

Moreover, when Nanu, also from Eritrea, was asked what had helped her to cope with some of the extreme events she had described, she spoke of the various ways in which college had helped her:

> For me, the better things that helped me is that I go to college … that help me a lot. I used to concentrate on my study and forget everything. I just want to be someone for me and my son…. I don't want to live this life every year. I want to change something in my life…. When I stay at home, all the thing I think about is family, myself and what I have been through with these problems. But now I have college I think, 'What am I going to do next year? What is my progress now?'

Outside of school or college, routine was sustained for many through regularly attending the church, mosque or temple. Young women, in particular, frequently described attending several church services and being involved with other church-related activities, such as the choir or youth group. Religion and faith in God provided solace and safety. Claude, from Burundi, described it as his alternative to counselling:

> I trust my belief in God in everything which I do. When you believe, you don't really feel lonely. I feel like when I go to church I listen to music, some prayer, I just feel like me. I forget everything – it's my counselling, isn't it?

An important strategy for many young people in dealing with their 'troubles' was to find new ways to belong, something that was achieved to varying degrees. Those below the age of 16 tended to be placed initially in foster care, where they frequently spoke of the strong bonds and attachments they had developed with their surrogate families. Other placements were less successful and several young people either described having experienced a number of placement moves or that they never really felt a part of the family in which they were living. Other young people were placed together in supported accommodation and here girls and young women, in particular, spoke of developing very close bonds with each other, through which they derived extensive support. The sense of shared troubles brought them together, although many still spoke of how they were cautious about how much detail of the past they could share with even their closest friends.

Nanu, from Eritrea, had arrived in the UK aged 16 and pregnant (as a result of being raped) and went on to have her child. At least eight other young people in the study had become pregnant or fathered a child since arriving in the UK. While having a baby or becoming a parent had different associations for the young people we spoke with, the role of parenthood in helping to recreate a sense of belonging, hope and purpose in life was commonly expressed. Mireille, from Cameroon, neatly illustrates this point:

> Before, I didn't have anything. I used to live just like that, without knowing what was going to happen. I don't know what's happened to my dad, mum. I don't know where they are, but I have my baby now. Now I feel I have something to do, I am important to someone. I have to feed him and take him to the park. Before I used to live like that, I would eat because I had to.

Continuing troubles

Despite the efforts that young people made to re-establish their lives and the successes they achieved in doing so, most continued to be haunted by uncertainties about their immigration status, which would ultimately dictate their future. Apart from a small minority who had been granted refugee status in the UK, this left the majority in a state of proverbial limbo, a state most acutely felt by those who were nearing or beyond the age of 18 years old. The constant anxieties about the future destabilised young people and left them feeling insecure. Life was unpredictable and uncertain and they lived with the constant fear of being returned to countries from which they felt dislocated, of having their dreams and aspirations curtailed and of reliving the extreme upheaval and trauma that they had previously experienced. There was little doubt from the analysis of young people's accounts that such uncertainty exacerbated other mental health difficulties and left some very unwell. At the time of the research, Rakeb, aged 21 from Eritrea, was having to consider the imminent prospect of deportation. She visited her psychiatrist on a weekly basis, lived in a hostel with her young son with vouchers for food and no recourse to public funds. She reflected on how she had no clear sense of belonging or family ties anywhere and saw no future for herself:

> I do not belong to this country, I have been here for four years. I do not belong in Ethiopia, I do not belong in Eritrea. I do not belong to England.... If you ask me 'Where is your home?', I don't know 'cos I was born in [name of place in Eritrea], I am Eritrean. I used to live in Ethiopia. I don't know my country... I can't speak my language – I speak Ethiopian language. If I go to Ethiopia, they say that the British government have agreement with Ethiopian government and they will not harass us or anything. But I don't want to go there, because I don't have anybody there ... I don't have family.

Conclusions

For Giddens (1991), ontological security stems from a sense of order and continuity to life, which in turn gives life meaning. Conversely, chaos and disruption threaten our sense of ontological security and create a state of anxiety. When events occur that are not consistent with the routine of an individual's life – such as turmoil, upheaval, trauma, unexpected disruption – the routine and the trust in the predictability of life is broken.

Ontological security is sustained, however, through the acquisition of biological, material and psychosocial resources that enable us to perceive life as being consistent, structured and understandable. The young people in the current study spoke to varying extents of the past traumas they had encountered. They talked in detail about the impact of these events on their lives and their sense of self and also about what helped them to cope and re-establish a sense of belonging and normality in their lives. The pervasive allusions to their need for ontological security and how it was rooted in the interpersonal connections and the routine they could establish were striking. Educational opportunities, their faith in God, friends, surrogate families and community, as well as creating their own families through parenthood, were all important factors in helping them acquire such security.

Yet, repeatedly, young people spoke of what undermined their security – a combination of their haunting pasts, the structures and systems they had to deal with, and the insidious stigma they faced as 'asylum-seekers'. For almost all young people, these day-to-day difficulties were surpassed, however, by their overriding anxieties surrounding the lack of certainty about the future as a result of their immigration status.

While previous research has highlighted the importance of resilience in coping with adversity and troubles, what we have highlighted here is that resilience alone does not fully engage with the structural factors beyond an individual's control. For young people seeking asylum to leave behind the troubles of the past and to begin to lead normal lives, they require something more than resilience. Analysis of the accounts of the young people in the study suggests that ontological security requires: an ability to sustain a biographical narrative; a sense of belonging and attachment; a belief that life has routine, predictability and will offer security into the future; and a capability to carve out a realistic life plan. While, arguably, the difficulties they have encountered may become less traumatic over time, their ability to capture the security of a 'normal life' is jeopardised by systems and structures that engage with young people seeking asylum as other than 'normal'. For this reason, their lives are likely to remain troubled.

Notes

[1] Prior to the introduction of the New Asylum Model (2007), discretionary leave was normally awarded for three years or until the young person reached 18 years of age.

[2] All the names of the young people participating in the study have been changed.

References

Aggleton, P., Whitty, G., Knight, A., Prayle, D., Warwick, I., and Rivers, K. (1998) 'Promoting young people's health: the health concerns and needs of young people', *Health Education*, vol 98, no 6, pp 213–19.

Bash, L. and Zezlina-Phillips, E. (2006) 'Identity, boundary and schooling: perspectives on the experiences and perceptions of refugee children', *Intercultural Education*, vol 17, no 1, pp 113–28.

Chase, E. (2009) 'Agency and silence: young people seeking asylum alone in the UK', *British Journal of Social Work*, vol 40, no 7, pp 2050–68.

European Migration Network (2012) *EMN Inform: Migration and International Protection Statistics, 2009*. Available at http://emn.intrasoft-intl.com/html/index.html (accessed 1 October 2012).

Giddens, A. (1991) *Modernity and self-identity: self and society in the late modern age*, Cambridge: Polity Press.

Glaser, B. and Strauss, A. (1967) *The discovery of grounded theory: strategies for qualitative research*, Chicago, IL: Aldine Publishing Company.

Hodes, M., Jagdev, D., Chandra, N. and Cunniff, A. (2008) 'Risk and resilience for psychological distress amongst unaccompanied asylum seeking adolescents', *Journal of Child Psychology and Psychiatry*, vol 48, no 7, pp 723–32.

Home Office (2010) *Quarterly statistical supplementary tables October–December 2009*, London: Home Office. Available at: www.homeoffice.gov.uk/rds/pdfs10/immiq409supp.xls (accessed 30 August 2011).

Lynn, N. and Lea, S. (2003) 'A phantom menace and the new apartheid: the social construction of asylum-seekers in the United Kingdom', *Discourse and Society*, vol 14, no 4, pp 425–52.

McDonald, I. and Billings, P. (2007) 'The treatment of asylum seekers in the UK', *Journal of Social Welfare and Family Law*, vol 29, no 1, pp 49–65.

Morris, L. (2009) 'Civic stratification and the cosmopolitan ideal', *European Societies*, vol 11, no 4, pp 603–24.

Rutter, J. (2006) *Refugee children in the UK*, Berkshire: Open University Press.

UNHCR (1951) Convention and Protocol Relating to the Status of Refugees. Geneva: UN High Commission for Refugees.

Wallin, A. and Ahlstrom, G. (2005) 'Unaccompanied young adult refugees in Sweden, experiences of their life situation and wellbeing: a qualitative follow-up study', *Ethnicity and Health*, vol 10, no 2, pp 129–44.

CHAPTER NINETEEN

Young people's caring relations and transitions within families affected by HIV

Ruth Evans

Introduction

This chapter provides insight into young people's caring relations and transitions within what is often considered a particularly 'troubling' familial context in both the global North and South: living with HIV. I analyse the findings from two qualitative studies of young people's caring roles in families affected by HIV in the UK, Tanzania and Uganda from the perspective of a feminist ethics of care, emotion work and life course transitions.

Since the 1990s, research in the global North has documented the roles and responsibilities that children undertake within families and the negative (and sometimes positive) outcomes that caring for a parent with an impairment or chronic illness may have on their education, health and emotional well-being, leisure activities, social lives, and transitions to 'independent adulthood' (Aldridge and Becker, 2003). This has resulted in growing policy and practice recognition of 'young carers' as a social category, and such children in the UK now have specific legal rights both as 'children' and as 'carers' (Becker, 2007). Despite the significant attention focused on young carers in social policy and research, young people's roles in caring for family members affected by HIV are often invisible, due to the stigma surrounding HIV. This means that parents are reluctant to disclose their status to others and seek to ensure that their care needs are met within the family, increasing the reliance on children. The groups most affected by HIV in the UK are men who have sex with men of all ethnicities and 'African-born' heterosexual men and women from countries with a high prevalence of HIV (HPA, 2010). For African migrants in the UK, living with HIV is exacerbated by restrictive immigration and asylum policies, differential entitlements to healthcare and welfare support, racial discrimination, and wider processes of social exclusion that are detrimental to the well-being of migrant families (Doyal and Anderson, 2005).

In communities affected by the HIV epidemic in Eastern and Southern Africa, young people are increasingly relied on to provide care for chronically ill parents and relatives (Robson et al, 2006), including siblings, elderly grandparents and other community members who have experienced the loss of their usual carers (Evans, 2005; Skovdal, 2011). The caring activities that young people undertake for family members with HIV broadly correspond to the care work of young people caring for parents/relatives with other impairments and illnesses globally (Evans and Becker, 2009). However, the stigma surrounding HIV, fluctuations in the illness trajectory and its life-limiting nature can result in considerable emotional distress, uncertainty and isolation (Evans and Thomas, 2009). Furthermore, the loss of the most economically active 'middle generation' has resulted in a growing number of child- and youth-headed households, where orphaned young people care for their younger siblings without a co-resident adult relative, and grandparent-headed households, where young people may care for siblings and elderly grandparents.

The first study discussed in this chapter was based on in-depth interviews with 33 young people with caring responsibilities (aged 9–23), 33 parents/ relatives living with HIV and 27 support workers in Tanzania and the UK.[1] The majority of the UK families interviewed were recent migrants and refugees of black African ethnicity from Uganda, Tanzania, Malawi, Zimbabwe, South Africa and Somalia, although a small number of British families of white, Asian and black African ethnicities also participated. The second study was based on interviews and participatory workshops with 14 orphaned young people (aged 12–23) caring for their siblings in youth-headed households, 18 of their siblings and 39 non-governmental organisation (NGO) staff and community members in Tanzania and Uganda.[2] Following an overview of the theoretical perspectives used to interpret the data, I discuss young people's disposition to care, transitions and changing familial relations in the context of HIV.

Theoretical perspectives

The feminist ethics of care literature has called for greater recognition of human vulnerability and the varying (inter)dependencies that characterise social relations, cultural values and arrangements for the provision of care over the life course (Tronto, 1993; Kittay, 1999). Care is understood as an ongoing process of 'maintaining, continuing or repairing the world', which is both a disposition and a practice (Tronto, 1993, p 104). Four core ethical values emerge from Tronto's (1993, pp 131–6) phases of caregiving: *attentiveness*, which is being attentive to the needs of others; *responsibility*, which is 'embedded in implicit cultural practices'; *competence* to provide good care, which includes the availability of adequate resources; and *responsiveness* of the care-receiver to the care, that is, seeking to understand the needs of others by considering 'the other's position as that other expresses it'. Care is understood as both particular and universal; what is considered 'adequate care' and who is responsible for the phases of 'taking care' and 'care-giving' vary in different places (and across time), while care is regarded as a universal aspect of human life. Care-giving and care-receiving can be regarded as a series of negotiated interdependencies between different actors (Kittay, 1999), rather than as fixed roles or periods in an individual's life course.

Care is also imbued with multiple, often contradictory, emotions, which are bound up with power relations (Bondi, 2008). Studies reveal the importance of the context and meanings invested in a particular location or space in understanding people's emotional well-being. Hochschild's (1979) notion of 'emotion work' is useful in conceptualising how 'carers' and those who are 'cared for' seek to manage, shape and suppress their emotions. She argues that there is often a discrepancy between what one feels and what one wants to feel, and those involved in care work try to eliminate this discrepancy by 'working on' their feelings.

Alongside these perspectives on care and emotions, I draw on recent literature on youth transitions and the life course to interpret young people's experiences. Research has highlighted the ways that young people's choices are both 'individualised' and highly 'structured' (Bowlby et al, 1998). Young people negotiate increasingly prolonged and diverse pathways in their transitions to 'independent adulthood' in both the global North and South (Valentine, 2003; Christiansen et al, 2006). Age can be regarded as an ongoing process of 'social becoming', rather than in terms of chronological time or developmental stage. This raises the question of how moments, events and periods of change in individuals' lives should best be understood (Hörschelmann, 2011). Events may represent 'rites of passage' in the life course and may constitute population groups and inscribe social meanings through time (Bailey, 2009). Thompson et al's (2002) notion of 'critical moments' is useful in conceptualising how young people recognise and respond to significant events in their lives. While young people may 'speak the language of individual choice, control and agency', the authors suggest that the personal and cultural resources that young people are able to draw on in response to such 'critical moments' are shaped by social and economic environments, structures and processes (Thompson et al, 2002, p 351). I draw on these understandings of youth transitions, moments and events in the life course to interpret how young people negotiate parental illness and death in different contexts and manage changing familial roles and responsibilities over time.

Young people's disposition to care

Previous research has revealed that the reasons why a particular child becomes a carer within the family at a particular time are complex and vary according to the context (Becker et al, 1998). Children, families and communities in Eastern and Southern Africa are generally regarded as having reciprocal responsibilities to provide care and support for the younger and older generations according to an implicit intergenerational contract (Collard, 2000). Thus, expectations of 'normal' familial responsibilities often differ from dominant norms in the global North. However, parental ill health or death, combined with a lack of alternative support in families affected by HIV, means that young people are called on to fulfil significant familial responsibilities to care and provide for older and younger generations at a much younger age than would usually be expected (Van Blerk and Ansell, 2007).

Most young people in both studies started taking on greater caring responsibilities when they were aged 10 years old or older. The assumption of a more significant caring role was linked to events surrounding parental ill health and a growing need for care and/or disclosure of HIV status, parental death, migration (both internal and international) and changing household composition. The narratives of young people who had experienced bereavement in both studies suggest that parental death represented a 'critical moment' that resulted in a significant biographical disruption, both emotionally and in terms of bringing about changes in family circumstances and residential location. Many orphaned young people heading households in Tanzania and Uganda associated the loss of a parent with the commencement of their caring role. For most of these young people, the loss of their parent was due to AIDS-related illness and death; for some, it was related to their mother's migration for work or to receive care from a relative, which was followed by news of her ill health and eventual death away from home. A parent's death in these circumstances can be seen as reaffirming young people's role in caring for their siblings, making their status as a youth-headed household seem more permanent. For many young people in the UK and several in Tanzania, the assumption of a caring role for a parent was linked to the disclosure of their parent's HIV status. For others, caring was seen as a gradual process associated with their parent's deteriorating ill health and growing care needs, rather than related to a particular event or moment in time. Some orphaned young people caring for their siblings had previously commenced their caring trajectories when their parent became ill. Parental death represented a change in the focus of their care work and generational relations within the household, from providing intensive nursing care for their parent alongside other household tasks, to heading the household, earning an income and supervising their younger siblings. Thus, the events surrounding a parent's deteriorating health, disclosure of their status and parental death represented 'critical moments' that had a significant impact on young people's emotional well-being and current and future caring responsibilities.

Many African young people in Tanzania, Uganda and the UK saw their caring roles as 'normal' and part of their moral duty to provide for their parent/siblings. Many drew on their religious faith in making sense of their need to care for family members and saw their faith as a source of strength and consolation as they struggled to perform their care work with very limited resources and little access to formal or informal support. June (aged 18, Tanzania) said:

> I feel quite normal because this is my mother, I can't abandon her, I thank God for everything and pray that God gives me the strength to persevere until the end. I can't walk away from my responsibility, because she's my mother.

Many eldest siblings who had been orphaned also regarded caring and providing for their siblings as a moral duty. This was often closely aligned to a desire and sense of obligation to fulfil their late parents' wishes that the siblings should look after each other after their parents' death. However, some siblings articulated the assumption of responsibility to head the household in terms of a choice to stay with their siblings and live independently in their inherited parental home, rather than with relatives or neighbours. As Rickson (aged 19, Tanzania) explained:

> I started [caring for my siblings] because my father died, then our mother died. Therefore, we were left alone. I had to think, 'Should we go and start living with neighbours or friends?' I got that courage to say that we will take care of ourselves.

Such narratives were underpinned by concerns about 'property-grabbing' and orphaned young people's desire to safeguard inherited assets (such as farm land and property) from unscrupulous relatives or neighbours (Evans, 2011a). Thus, young people's well-being and survival was tied up with the collective unit they sought to protect.

In many African societies, children are trained to contribute to the household's social reproductive work from an early age, with boys and girls undertaking different household and caring tasks according to a traditional gendered division of labour (Katz, 1993). Notions of 'normal' expectations of domestic and caring responsibilities are shaped by dominant gender and generational relations. A mother with HIV from Uganda living in the UK, for example, commented on her daughter's caring responsibilities:

> She comes from a culture where they're expected to do bits and pieces in the house, so I don't think it has affected her. I think she feels those are the norms and values of her being a female child and an African child, those are the things which we take as acceptable.

In contrast, boys in Tanzania who undertook domestic and caring tasks that transgressed gender norms commented on how they were ridiculed and stigmatised by their peers and other relatives, which had negative impacts on their emotional well-being.

Changing familial relations and 'emotion work'

Research with families affected by HIV has shown that caring relations are often characterised by reciprocity, interdependence and close emotional connections, as well as tensions, 'emotion work' and, sometimes, the exploitation of adult–child power relations, in terms of denying children's inheritance rights, verbal abuse and neglect (Evans and Becker, 2009; Evans and Thomas, 2009). Most mothers and children in Tanzania and the UK reported that HIV-related illness and caring had strengthened loving relationships within the family. The unpredictable, fluctuating nature of HIV-related illness and its emotional effects meant that both children and parents/relatives gave and received emotional support, advice and guidance at different times. Caring relations in Tronto's (1993) 'care-giving' and 'care-receiving' phases were characterised by interdependence, reciprocity and the ethical value of 'responsiveness'. This challenges simplistic understandings of care as a one-way process in which parents with a chronic illness are seen as 'dependent' on children and assumptions are made about parents' lack of capacity to care for their children (Evans and Atim, 2011).

Close, interdependent relations were also evident in households headed by siblings and grandparents in Tanzania and Uganda. Siblings expressed a strong sense of solidarity and commitment to look after each other, especially following negative experiences of harassment, property-grabbing or ostracism from others in the community. Tumaini (aged 19) identified positive and negative aspects of living with his younger siblings: "I feel good because we comfort each other about everything. We feel bad when we're harassed." This illustrates the importance of close family ties and group cohesion for the household's survival as a collective unit.

Nevertheless, hierarchies of age, gender and birth order were enacted through unequal, sometimes conflictual, relations between siblings within the social space of the household. When younger siblings misbehaved or did not respect elder siblings, the latter sometimes needed outside help to resolve arguments and conflict. While several siblings were proud of their role in heading the household, they expressed ambivalence about having to take on a parenting role for their siblings while they still considered themselves to be a young person (Evans, 2011a). As Juma (age 16, Tanzania) commented:

> You see, us, we didn't want to be adults, but we had to be adults because of the things that happened with our parents. We would still like to be able to do the things we used to. To be able to play and laugh with our friends, but my life is really a struggle and when I need help, I don't have an adult who I can ask. It's not as though I wanted to live on my own. Any problems that you have, you have to know how to deal with them. I have to be like both mother and father.

This suggests that the usual intergenerational contract has been fractured in youth-headed households, since the parental generation is missing and young people have to try to compensate for the loss of their parents and take on the roles of "both mother and father" towards their younger siblings.

Similar contradictions were evident in parent–child relationships in both African and British contexts. While many mothers with HIV thought that caring enabled children to gain useful life skills as part of their informal education in the family and community, they felt 'sad' that children had to take on these responsibilities at a young age. Such perspectives draw on dominant Western understandings of childhood as a period in which children are free from responsibilities and are 'dependent' on their parents (Such and Walker, 2004). 'African' and 'Western' discourses of childhood coexisted in some mothers' narratives, resulting in feelings of guilt and regret that could be difficult to reconcile. Although Patience, a mother with HIV in Tanzania, was happy that her son (aged 10) was helping her and her extended family, she said that she felt "awful" about his responsibilities due to his young age and the extent of his care work: "It hurts him I know. It is too much work for a boy of his age." She felt that her son had changed since he had started caring for her: "he has a lot of responsibilities at such a tender age, he thinks about important issues". Such contradictory discourses were particularly evident in families in the UK, where young people's caring roles deviated from dominant understandings of a 'normal' childhood. Several young people (those of British and African backgrounds) living in the UK felt 'different' to their peers due to their caring roles, which could result in isolation and withdrawal from social activities and cause tensions between children and parents (Evans, 2011b).

Despite tensions in some families, many young people felt that their caring role had made them 'stronger' and more emotionally mature. The life-limiting nature of their parent's illness and the vulnerability of their younger siblings, however, limited the reciprocity of emotional support. Young people caring for parents with HIV felt that they needed to regulate and manage their emotions to avoid their parent becoming worried or stressed, as they knew this could make their illness worse (Evans and Thomas, 2009). Young people heading households did not feel that they could turn to their younger siblings for emotional support, and several lacked opportunities to share their feelings with others. In Tanzania, as part of a participatory workshop, siblings identified loneliness and the need to suppress their feelings as some of the worst aspects of heading the household: "I feel lonely when I see my friends being brought up by their parents" and "I'm forced to be happy all the time, even though I'm sad".

Several parents expressed their concerns about the emotional impacts of disclosure of their HIV status and of care work on their children. Flomina, a mother with HIV in Tanzania, commented on the closeness of her relationship with Saumu, her daughter (aged 13). However, she thought that Saumu had become more withdrawn and her educational attainment had decreased since the disclosure of her mother's and younger brother's HIV status and the assumption of a caring role. Indeed, some parents sought to hide pain and other symptoms of the illness, engaging in 'emotion work' in order to protect their children from the emotional impacts of HIV.

For African migrants in the UK, living with HIV was heightened by the uncertainty caused by their insecure immigration status. Fear of deportation was linked to the potential loss of access to life-prolonging medication. This could lead to further isolation and marginalisation from potential sources of support for both parents and children (Evans, 2011b). Alice (aged 17, from Tanzania, with insecure immigration status in the UK), for example, commented:

> Getting visa is something that has changed me and my mum's life, especially my mum's as she was so depressed, confused, stressed and I really felt helpless by the time we had refusal because I didn't know what to do to help and this really stressed me a lot. And I used to pretend I was happy so as to just be strong for my mum, yes.

Alice's and others' narratives suggest that events related to gaining more secure immigration status, such as being granted a visa or indefinite leave to remain in the UK, may represent more significant 'critical moments' in young people's lives than the 'troubles' associated with assuming a caring role or dealing with the ongoing emotional pressures associated with a parent's chronic life-limiting illness.

Conclusion

Research with families affected by HIV in Tanzania, Uganda and the UK suggests that young people's 'disposition' to care for parents with HIV and orphaned siblings is related to a complex range of factors, including:

- existing emotional connections and kinship relations, co-residence, gender, sibling birth order, and power dynamics within the family;
- sociocultural understandings of childhood, gender roles and intergenerational relations;
- fear of, and direct experiences of, stigma, ostracism and exploitation by the extended family and community and a lack of alternative support; and
- the broader landscape of care, comprising the socio-economic and political context, welfare regime, policies and entitlements to social protection, and formal health and care support.

Young people's experiences suggest that parental illness, migration and death, rather than the assumption of a caring role within the family per se, represent 'critical moments' that have a major influence on their present well-being and future life trajectories. Many young people saw their caring roles as 'normal', articulating this as an expression of their love for their parent/siblings and the need to fulfil expected familial responsibilities when alternative support was lacking. Young people and parents associated care-giving with a number of positive outcomes, such as strengthening family relations, fostering emotional maturity and developing life skills. Care-giving often led to close, interdependent relations and mutual emotional support. This challenges assumptions about the one-way nature of 'care-giving' and dominant representations in the media, policy and research that young care-giving represents an inherently 'troubling' familial situation. Thus, it is exploitation, vulnerability and (lack of) resources beyond the household that contribute significantly to troubles, rather than young care-giving per se.

As Korbin (Chapter Two, this volume) cautions, it is important not to confuse 'culture' with family troubles, or to interpret a perceived 'trouble' (in this case, young care-giving) as a cultural issue. While young people's contributions to the household's domestic and care work may be regarded as potentially problematic according to dominant 'Western' cultural norms of childhood (and more culturally accepted in 'African' contexts), the picture that emerges of caring relations and responsibilities within the family is far more complex and ambiguous than such a binary interpretation. Parents and young people in the UK, Tanzania and Uganda were aware that young people's caring responsibilities were not 'normal', since they went beyond usual expectations of age, gender and intergenerational relations. They recognised that care-giving could have negative impacts on young people's emotional and physical well-being, education, social lives and future life course transitions. Some also expressed unease that young people had to provide care for a parent or had to 'parent' their younger siblings while they were still young. This coexistence of individualist and communitarian family values linked to dominant 'Western' and 'African' discourses of childhood caused tensions and emotional pressures within families.

Although the critical moments in young people's lives were associated with individual experiences surrounding parental illness, migration and loss, their ability to negotiate these events was highly structured and depended on the resources and support they were able to draw on in different sociocultural and welfare contexts. Young people assuming caring roles that challenge gender and/or generational relations are often positioned as 'deviant' according to global and local norms of childhood and marginalised by the wider family and community (Evans, 2011a, 2011b). Thus, rather than the care work itself being 'troubling', it was the social attitudes and stigma associated with HIV, young people's roles in providing cross-generational, and sometimes cross-gendered, care and the lack of alternative support that they and those they cared for found problematic. For African migrant families in the UK, HIV and young care-giving were exacerbated by pressures linked to immigration and asylum policies, which were often viewed by both mothers and young people as much more 'troubling' than chronic illness and the need for care. The research thus reveals the importance of analysing wider structural inequalities, the availability of material and emotional resources, and gender and generational relations in particular cultural contexts when conceptualising the vulnerability of young carers and family members affected by HIV.

Acknowledgements

I wish to thank all the participants in the two studies for sharing their experiences, Saul Becker for his support and the Economic and Social Research Council, Royal Geographical Society (with the Institute of British Geographers) and the University of Reading for funding the research. I am also grateful to Jane Ribbens McCarthy, in particular, and Carol-Ann Hooper and Val Gillies, for their helpful feedback.

Notes

[1] The research on children caring for parents with HIV in Tanzania and the UK was led by Saul Becker and Ruth Evans, University of Nottingham, UK, and funded by the Economic and Social Research Council, UK 2006-2007, grant number RES-000-22-1732-A. For further information, see Evans and Becker (2009).

[2] The research on young people caring for siblings in youth-headed households in Tanzania and Uganda was funded by the University of Reading and by a Royal Geographical Society

(with the Institute of British Geographers) Small Grant 2009. For further information, see Evans (2011a).

References

Aldridge, J. and Becker, S. (2003) *Children caring for parents with mental illness: perspectives of young carers, parents and professionals*, Bristol: The Policy Press.

Bailey, A. (2009) 'Population geography: lifecourse matters', *Progress in Human Geography*, vol 33, no 3, pp 40–418.

Becker, S. (2007) 'Global perspectives on children's unpaid caregiving in the family: research and policy on "young carers" in the UK, Australia, the USA and sub-Saharan Africa', *Global Social Policy*, vol 7, no 1, pp 23–50.

Becker, S., Aldridge, J. and Dearden, C. (1998) *Young carers and their families*, Oxford: Blackwell Science.

Bondi, L. (2008) 'On the relational dynamics of caring: a psychotherapeutic approach to emotional and power dimensions of women's care work', *Gender, Place and Culture*, vol 15, no 3, pp 249–65.

Bowlby, S., Lloyd-Evans, S. and Mohammad, R. (1998) 'The workplace. Becoming a paid worker: images and identity', in T. Skelton and G. Valentine (eds) *Cool places: geographies of youth cultures*, London: Routledge, pp 229–48.

Christiansen, C., Utas, M. and Vigh, H. (eds) (2006) *Navigating youth generating adulthood: Social becoming in an African context*, Uppsala: Nordiska Afrikainstitutet.

Collard, D. (2000) 'Generational transfers and the generational bargain', *Journal of International Development*, vol 12, pp 453–62.

Doyal L. and Anderson, J. (2005) '"My fear is to fall in love again …": how HIV-positive African women survive in London', *Social Science and Medicine*, vol 60, pp 1729–38.

Evans, R. (2005) 'Social networks, migration and care in Tanzania: caregivers' and children's resilience in coping with HIV/AIDS', *Journal of Children and Poverty*, vol 11, no 2, pp 111–29.

Evans, R. (2011a) '"We are managing our own lives …": life transitions and care in sibling-headed households affected by AIDS in Tanzania and Uganda', *Area*, vol 43, no 4, pp 384–96.

Evans, R. (2011b) 'Young caregiving and HIV in the UK: caring relationships and mobilities in African migrant families', *Population, Space and Place*, vol 17, no 4, pp 338–60.

Evans, R. and Atim, A. (2011) 'Care, disability and HIV in East Africa: diverging or interconnected concepts and practices?', *Third World Quarterly*, vol 32, no 8, pp 1437–54.

Evans, R. and Becker, S. (2009) *Children caring for parents and relatives with HIV and AIDS: global issues and policy responses*, Bristol: The Policy Press.

Evans, R. and Thomas, F. (2009) 'Emotional interactions and an ethic of care: caring relations in families affected by HIV and AIDS', *Emotions, Space and Society*, vol 2, pp 111–19.

HPA (Health Protection Agency) (2010) *HIV in the United Kingdom: 2010 report*, London: Health Protection Agency, Centre for Infections. Available at: www.hpa.org.uk/hivuk2010 (accessed 14 September 2011).

Hochschild, A. (1979) 'Emotion work, feeling rules and social structure', *American Journal of Sociology*, vol 85, no 3, pp 551–75.

Hörschelmann, K. (2011) 'Theorising life transitions: geographical perspectives', *Area*, vol 43, no 4, pp 378–83.

Katz, C. (1993) 'Growing circles/closing circles: limits on the spaces of knowing in rural Sudan and US cities', in C. Katz and J. Monk (eds) *Full circles: geographies of women over the life course*, London: Routledge, pp 88–106.

Kittay, E.F. (1999) *Love's labor: essays on women, equality and dependency*, New York, NY: Routledge.

Robson, E., Ansell, N., Huber, U.S., Gould, W.T. S. and van Blerk, L. (2006) 'Young caregivers in the context of the HIV/AIDS pandemic in sub-Saharan Africa', *Population, Space and Place*, vol 12, pp 93–111.

Skovdal, M. (2011) 'Examining the trajectories of children providing care for adults in rural Kenya: implications for service delivery', *Children and Youth Services Review*, vol 33, pp 1262–9.

Such, E. and Walker, R. (2004) 'Being responsible and responsible beings: children's understanding of responsibility', *Children and Society*, vol 18, pp 231–42.

Thompson, R., Bell, R., Holland, J., Henderson, S., McGrellis, S. and Sharpe, S. (2002) (2002) 'Critical moments: choice, chance and opportunity in young people's narratives of transition', *Sociology*, vol 36, no 2, pp 335–54.

Tronto, J. (1993) *Moral boundaries: a political argument for an ethic of care*, London and New York, NY: Routledge.

Valentine, G. (2003) 'Boundary crossings: transitions from childhood to adulthood', *Children's Geographies*, vol 1, no 1, pp 37–52.

Van Blerk, L. and Ansell, N. (2007) 'Alternative strategies for care giving in the context of AIDS in Southern Africa: complex strategies for care', *Journal of International Development*, vol 19, pp 865–84.

CHAPTER TWENTY

Estimating the prevalence of forced marriage in England

Peter Keogh, Anne Kazimirski, Susan Purdon and Ruth Maisey

Background

A forced marriage (FM) has been defined in the UK as 'a marriage conducted without the valid consent of both parties, where duress is a factor' (Home Office, 2000, p 4). The Court of Appeal clarified that duress is: 'whether the mind of the applicant has been overborne, howsoever that was caused' (Magill and Lee, 2008, p 8). FM is therefore a marriage in which one or both spouses do not (or, in the case of some vulnerable adults, cannot) consent to the marriage and duress is involved. Duress can include physical, psychological, financial, sexual and emotional pressure. FM is therefore distinct from arranged marriage, as in an arranged marriage the family will take the lead in arranging the match but the couples have a choice as to whether to proceed.

Previous research suggests that the majority of FMs involve a young female victim, and take place among South Asian communities, such as the Pakistani, Bangladeshi and Indian communities. However, it has been shown that young men can also be victims of FM, and that FMs take place among other minority communities too, especially from Africa, the Middle East and parts of Eastern Europe (Khanum, 2008).

To develop responses to FM, we must seek to describe in full how and why family members seek to control the kinds of relationships young people make and the intimate behaviours they engage in. On the one hand, FM seeks to prevent 'unsuitable' relationships (eg relationships outside ethnic, cultural, religious or caste groups) or behaviours and identities (including perceived promiscuity, or being gay, lesbian, bisexual or transgender). On the other hand, it ensures 'desirable' alliances, such as those that are materially advantageous to the family (eg those that ensure that land, property and wealth remain within a family, or that family members from abroad can migrate to the UK as spouses). Other desirable alliances may be those that ensure care for a vulnerable parent (the young person being married into a family with the express purpose of providing care or support for elderly parents), or, indeed, to maintain the position of a vulnerable young person (eg a child with learning disabilities may be 'married off' in order to ensure their own continued care within a family).

The abuses associated with FM are greater than the marriage itself (Home Affairs Select Committee, 2008; Khanum, 2008; Kazimirski et al, 2009). First, FM forms part of a range of practices that restrict the potential of young people generally. For example, families will often withdraw their daughters from education in the belief that if daughters become educated, men from the same ethnic or religious group, especially those brought up abroad, will refuse to marry them. Second, FM can be seen as a form of 'honour'-based violence, which occurs in communities where the concepts of honour and shame are bound up with the expected behaviour of families and individuals, particularly that of women (Home Affairs Select Committee, 2008). The term 'honour-based violence' refers to crimes of violence, which include assault, imprisonment and murder, where the person is being punished by their family or their community. Victims are punished for actually or allegedly undermining what the family or community believes to be the correct code of behaviour. In transgressing this code, the person is perceived to have shown that they have not been properly controlled by their family and this is seen to 'shame' or 'dishonour' the family (FMU, 2008).

However, FMs do not necessarily involve physical violence. Victims of FM can be placed under pressure from many family members besides their parents, such as siblings and extended family. The types and forms of abuse by which a victim of FM may be harmed are wide-ranging and may include physical, sexual or psychological abuse as well as financial or material neglect (Brandon and Hafez, 2008).

FM is troubling because, unlike other forms of domestic abuse, it is not a question of one perpetrator and one victim, nor, indeed, is it a symptom of dysfunction within a single relationship (husband and wife, parent and child etc). Rather, it generally involves multiple members, multiple generations and, indeed, diasporic family members acting in concert against one or two of their own kinship networks. Moreover, it involves the (ab)use of culturally acceptable marital customs (such as arranged marriages) to limit the rights and liberties of individuals in fundamental ways. As FMs serve a range of wider social and cultural purposes within families and communities, tackling it risks being seen to call into question the values of entire communities, rather than those of one individual within a relationship. Such fears have inhibited social care and other professionals in detecting, reporting and dealing with cases in the past.

However, another significant impediment to detecting and responding to FM lies in the fact that it resists being encompassed within any one social care professional or disciplinary discourse. Our own research on FM (Kazimirski et al, 2009) describes 'framings' of FM within three professional discourses. Domestic violence (DV) discourses describe it as a type of abuse or violence within families and point towards a legal response involving a perpetrator and a victim. The victim is to be removed from the situation and legal remedy sought. Child protection (CP) discourses understand FM in terms of the need to protect vulnerable children from the impact of familial dysfunction. This framing also involves the intervention of the state, often to remove the victim, but with the ultimate aim of rehabilitating the family unit. Finally, communitarian discourses construct FM as a human rights issue, where it is understood in terms of negative cultural practices that limit the freedom, rights and welfare of the individual. This framing calls for interventions that empower the individual to resist these forms of abuse, and work with communities to ensure that negative cultural practices that lead to abuses of human rights are made unacceptable.

However, all of these framings are insufficient mainly because FM is neither confined to the couple relationship (as is often the case with DV), nor the parental relationship (as is the case with CP discourses), nor to relationships within and between communities (as in the communitarian framing). Rather, it traverses a wide range of relationships both within and outside of the family. Hence, these multiple framings allow scope for variation in responses to FM and, indeed, for cases of FM to fall through the gaps between these three different approaches.

In recent years, the Home Affairs Select Committee (2008) report, the government response, the Forced Marriage Unit's (FMU's[1]) statutory guidance on FM (FMU, 2008) and the media have created a much higher level of awareness about FM in the UK than ever before. In addition, the Forced Marriage (Civil Protection) Act 2007 has added to this momentum. The elevation of the FMU's guidance to a Code of Practice in November 2008 aimed to make local authorities (LAs) and statutory agencies more alert to their obligations regarding FM. Multi-agency steering groups are increasingly being set up in LA areas, linked to Domestic Abuse Forums, to deal with issues of FM, child protection, cross-agency training, information–sharing, risk assessment and standardised ways of record–keeping and monitoring. However, the same reports have highlighted a lack of robust, clear and consistent data.

Gathering robust data on FM in order to generate an estimate of prevalence presents major challenges. By far the most preferable approach would involve a very large-scale general population survey with sufficient sample numbers from minority ethnic groups for robust prevalence estimation. The sensitivity of the issue would, nevertheless, generate particular challenges for data collection, the accepted best method in most similar surveys being face–to–face interviews with respondent self-completion for the most sensitive questions. This approach is likely to be further undermined by language and literacy considerations in some of the key populations at risk for FM. This leaves researchers and policymakers alike without firm evidence about the extent of this particular source of family troubles.

Consequently, as part of a larger study on responses to FM (Kazimirski et al, 2009), we were asked to produce a best estimate of the profile and prevalence of reported cases of FM in England, built up through analysis of the cases that are known to voluntary or statutory organisations. Given the limitations of the information available to inform sampling, as well as of the time and budget available for the study, the aim was to generate a broad, general estimate (rather than precise, statistically significant estimates).

Method/approach

Our aim was to generate an estimate based on data collected from local and national organisations that encounter cases of FM, rather than a population survey. Using population data and data from the FMU, we purposively sampled all English LAs in order to yield a sample of 10 LAs showing appropriate variation across the following two dimensions: prevalence of cases of FM reported to the FMU (low, medium and high) and varying minority ethnic populations. We then constructed a profile of each of the LAs in our sample, yielding all statutory and voluntary agencies in each LA. Organisations were identified through a combination of desk research and snowballing (agencies were asked to identify other local agencies working with victims). Each agency was sent a short questionnaire that asked about the number of victims the organisation had dealt with in 2008 and collected socio-demographic profile data on victims. These were accompanied by telephone follow-up calls offering assistance in filling out the questionnaire. In total, data from 58 organisations were collected. Although this represents only half of the organisations contacted, inspection of the non-responding organisations suggests that these were mostly small organisations that would have encountered very few cases of FM, if any. A similar data collection questionnaire was also sent to national organisations that might encounter cases of FM. These questionnaires similarly collected information on the number of cases that each organisation had encountered over 2008 as well as data on the profile of those cases.

The definition of FM used throughout this exercise was quite broad, covering any incident where an individual feels that they have been coerced or might be coerced into marrying someone against their will. However, since agencies have different methods of collecting and storing data, the accuracy with which they were able to recall all of the cases that they had encountered across the year is likely to vary. Furthermore, this approach only collected information about *reported* cases of FM, and it is likely that there are many victims who have not come to the attention of any agencies or professionals. These 'hidden' cases are not included in our estimates. As such, the profile of *all* cases of FM may differ from those reported here if particular groups of people are less likely to report FM than others, and the total number of cases of FM across England is very likely to be higher than the estimate of reported cases provided here.

We look first at the profile of reported FM cases in the 10 LAs that were involved in the data-collection exercise.[2] We then move on to estimate the national prevalence of cases known to local and national organisations, based on an extrapolation from the number of cases known to local organisations within nine of the LAs (too few responses were received from one of the 10 LAs for the prevalence estimate to be robust), plus the cases known to national organisations.

Profile of FM

As can be seen from Table 20.1, the majority of FM cases reported in the 10 LAs originated within Asian communities (97%) and among Pakistani families in particular (72%). This reflects the data regarding country of origin held by the FMU for the cases that have come to their attention, where, in 2008, 64% of cases related to Pakistani victims, 15% related to Bangladeshi victims and 8% related to Indian victims.[3]

Information on whether the cases encountered by organisations related to threats of FM or actual FM was less comprehensively recorded, being unknown for 48% of cases. Nevertheless, the information available suggests that where this was known, just under two thirds of cases related to threats of FM compared to just over one third that related to actual FM (see Table 20.2).[4]

Table 20.3 shows that the overwhelming majority of cases reported within the LA prevalence exercise involved female victims: 96% being female and only 4% being male. This represents a smaller proportion of male cases than reported by both the FMU and Karma Nirvana[5] (the two largest national organisations providing support to victims of FM), whose proportions of male cases in 2008 were 14% and 43%, respectively.[6] These differences in the gender of those reporting FM to local versus national agencies is striking and worthy of further investigation. Respondents in qualitative interviews reported elsewhere (Kazimirski et al, 2009) suggest that young men may experience greater felt stigma around being

Table 20.1: Ethnicity of FM cases in 10 LAs

	Total %
White	+
Black	
African	1
Caribbean	1
Other	0
Asian	
Pakistani	72
Bangladeshi	13
Indian	9
Other	3
Mixed race	0
Other ethnicity	1
Base	*750*

Notes: Base: cases of FM reported in LA data-collection exercise. In 23% of cases, ethnicity was unknown (excluded from the base). + denotes a percentage less than 0.5%.

Table 20.2: Nature of FM cases (marriages that had taken place versus threats of marriage) in 10 LAs

	Total %
Marriages that had taken place	38
Threats of marriage	62
Base	*512*

Notes: Base: cases of FM reported in LA data-collection exercise. In 48% of cases, the nature of the case was unknown (excluded from the base).

Table 20.3: Gender of FM cases in 10 LAs

	Total %
Female	96
Male	4
Base	*796*

Notes: Base: cases of FM reported in LA data-collection exercise. In 19% of cases, gender was unknown (excluded from the base).

the victim of FM and may therefore be more reticent to report their situation to local agencies where their identity might become known more easily within local communities. Whether or not this is the case, these disparities point to a clear demand for services among male victims that may not currently be met at the local level.

Within local organisations, 41% of the reported cases involved minors, that is, children aged under 18 (14% were under 16 and 26% were aged 16–17),[7] 40% involved adults aged 18–23 and 20% involved adults aged 24 or over (see Table 20.4). This represents a greater proportion of minors than encountered by the FMU, as only 29% of the FMU cases related to minors.[8] As in the case of gender, these marked differences in the age profile of local reports versus those of national agencies is striking and certainly worth further investigation. It may reflect differences in knowledge and access to different agencies depending on age or perhaps differences in approaches of professionals dealing with cases (with younger cases being less likely to be reported on to the FMU).

Finally, we can see in Table 20.5 that most of the cases of FM encountered by local organisations involved victims with UK citizenship (85%) and only 15% involved victims who were not UK citizens.[9]

Table 20.4: Age of FM cases in 10 LAs

	Total %
Under 16	14
16–17	26
18–23	40
24 or over	20
Base	*643*

Notes: Base: cases of FM reported in LA data-collection exercise. In 34% of cases, age was unknown (excluded from the base).

Table 20.5: Citizenship of FM cases in 10 LAs

	Total %
UK citizen	85
Not UK citizen	15
Base 651	*796*

Notes: Base: cases of FM reported in LA data-collection exercise. In 34% of cases, citizenship was unknown (excluded from the base).

Prevalence of FM

The data on the number of FM cases encountered by local organisations within the 10 LAs, and by Karma Nirvana and the FMU, has been used to estimate the national prevalence of the *reported* cases of FM in England. Our estimate is that the national prevalence of reported cases in 2008 was between 5,000 and 8,000 cases (of either actual FM or the threat of FM). We describe how we reached this estimate in the following.

FM cases known to local organisations

To estimate the number of FM cases known to local organisations, we first conducted analysis that looked at the relationship between the number of cases of FM reported in each LA involved in the data-collection exercise and the size of the population within that LA. Given the high prevalence of FM cases among Asian communities, we looked at these relationships separately for the ethnic groups with the highest prevalence of FM. This meant that we looked at the relationship within five groups:

- Asian Pakistani
- Asian Bangladeshi
- Asian Indian
- Other Asian
- Other non-white ethnic groups[10]

This analysis was conducted on nine LAs because while the response from local organisations was generally adequate, too few responses were received from one of the 10 LAs for the prevalence estimate to be robust. These nine local authorities reported 970 cases of FM, which, as mentioned earlier, includes the threat of FM as well as actual FM. The findings showed statistically significant relationships across LAs between the number of cases of FM among each ethnic group and the population size of that ethnic group.[11] Therefore, based on this data, the estimated rates of FM among the different minority ethnic populations considered are shown in Table 20.6.[12] Assuming that these rates apply across England,[13] this would mean that, across the country, *local* organisations encountered approximately 4,000 cases of FM in 2008.

Table 20.6: Rates of FM in different populations, and cases of FM known to local organisations

	Rate in population per 100,000	Size of population	Cases of FM
Asian Pakistani	360	706,539	2,541
Asian Bangladeshi	308	275,394	848
Asian Indian	50	1,028,546	514
Asian other	3	237,810	7
Other non-white ethnic groups	1	2,211,181	15
Total		4,459,470	3,925

Note: Base: cases of FM reported in LA data-collection exercise.

FM cases known to national organisations

The largest national agencies providing support to victims of FM are Karma Nirvana and the FMU. The number of cases they encountered in 2008 can be found in Table 20.7, which also shows the estimate of the gender breakdown of their cases.

Table 20.7: Cases of FM known to national agencies

Gender	Cases of FM	
	Karma Nirvana (N)	The FMU[a] (N)
Female	1,250	1,400
Male	950	225
Total	2,200	1,625

Note: [a] For the FMU data, the gender is only known for 1,470 cases, but the gender breakdown has been scaled up here to the total number of enquiries received by the FMU.

Given the widely different gender profile of cases encountered by local and national organisations, it was apparent that some FM cases are likely to be known only to national organisations. Thus, in seeking to generate an estimate of the cases known to both local and national agencies, it is not plausible to assume that the national cases are all counted within local estimates. Instead, the national cases need to be added to the local cases, at least to some degree.

Estimating a maximum

To estimate the maximum number of reported FM cases from the data presented earlier, we make the most generous possible assumption that all the cases reported to us by local and national organisations are completely independent of each other (ie every case is known to just one organisation). This scenario is unlikely, but if it were true, the number of FM cases would be the sum of all the cases reported locally and nationally, as presented in Table 20.8. Thus, the maximum number of FM cases reported in 2008 was in the region of 8,000.

Table 20.8: Maximum number of cases

Gender	Cases of FM			
	Local estimate (N)	Karma Nirvana (N)	The FMU (N)	Total
Female	3,775	1,250	1,400	6,425
Male	150	950	225	1,325
Total	3,925	2,200	1,625	7,750

Estimating a minimum

To estimate the minimum number of reported FM cases from the data presented earlier, we would need to assume that the cases reported by these organisations are not all independent and that there is some degree of double-counting. Some information on the extent of double-counting was available from the data–collection questionnaires returned by local agencies, who were asked to estimate the number of their cases they thought were known to other agencies. On aggregate, they reported that this applied to 26% of cases. This information is not available for cases reported by Karma Nirvana or the FMU.

The most cautious, but unlikely, assumption would be that the extent of double-counting is extremely high. First, all the cases that local organisations indicated were known to other organisations could be excluded (assuming that these are known either to other local organisations or to national organisations); excluding these cases would leave just the cases that were only known to a single local organisation. Second, with regard to the national organisations, complete overlap between Karma Nirvana and the FMU could be assumed, and the highest number of *women* reported by either organisation (which was reported by the FMU) could be added to the highest number of *men* reported by either organisation (which was reported by Karma Nirvana). Table 20.9 presents the numbers associated with these assumptions, and the total.[14] Based on these assumptions, the minimum number of FM cases reported in 2008 was in the region of 5,000.

Table 20.9: Minimum number of cases

	Cases of FM			
Gender	Local estimate (N)	Karma Nirvana (N)	The FMU (N)	Total
Female	2,800	–	1,400	4,200
Male	125	950	–	1,075
Total	2,925	950	1,400	5,275

Summary

This chapter describes an estimate of the profile and prevalence of reported cases of FM in England. While FM is not exclusively an issue for Asian communities, 97% of those seeking advice or help relating to FM from organisations were identified as Asian. Although the majority of victims that seek advice or support from local and national agencies are women between the ages of 18 and 23, the sample included a substantial (and likely under-reported) proportion of men and it is worth remembering that up to 40% of the sample were 18 years old or younger when they sought help.

In terms of national prevalence across England, as reported at the start of this chapter, our estimate is that between 5,000 and 8,000 cases (of either actual FM or the threat of FM) were reported in 2008. It is unlikely that the actual number falls at one extreme or the other, as the extent of double-counting is unlikely to be so high that the minimum estimate applies, and the extent of double-counting is unlikely to be so low that the maximum estimate applies. However, it is important to bear in mind that this analysis is based only on FM cases that were known to voluntary or statutory organisations, and we have no means within this study of estimating the number or profile of cases of FM that do not come to the attention of any organisation. Such cases *may* represent a substantial proportion of the total number of FM cases in England, and their profile may potentially be very different.

Our estimate does show that, *at a national level*, FM is currently going under-reported, with many more cases being seen at a local level than national figures would suggest. In order to develop appropriate responses, collecting meaningful data on the nature and scale of this problem is essential. However, it is highly unlikely that this will be achieved through population surveys (because of sampling and reporting difficulties). The development of data-collection protocols for LAs (either through the careful modification of current DV or CP protocols and/or the increased involvement of a broader range of agencies in active data collection) to inform their FM response would go some way to redressing this lack of data. Until data collection is improved, it is unlikely that either national or local responses will be sufficient to address the scale of this problem.

What is undoubtedly a major obstacle to the collection of robust data around FM is the fact that it is a problem that is hard to define in terms of single sets of actions or perpetrators. Moreover, it remains insufficiently understood by social care and other professionals. This lack of understanding is likely to impact on the capacity to recognise and report cases of FM. The disparity between local and national reporting, both in terms of overall magnitude and also in terms of differences in the gender and ages of cases, is an indication either that FM is likely to be understood differently depending on the perspective of who is doing the recording and/or that different groups of victims alert different professional groups. Further qualitative research is necessary to investigate these disparities properly. What is clear from this research is that the scale of FM, however it is understood, is greater than the available national data sets show.

Acknowledgements

This research was funded by the (then) Department for Children, Schools and Families (DCSF), with the support of the Forced Marriage Unit (FMU). It was carried out by the authors while all employed at or by the National Centre for Social Research (NatCen).

Notes

[1] The FMU is a joint initiative between the Home Office and the Foreign and Commonwealth Office. It provides direct support to victims, advice and support to practitioners, and leads on government policy. The FMU receives reports of individual cases of FMU through calls to a single national helpline.

[2] The profile of these cases is presented while recognising that there may well be some double-reporting, with individuals featuring on more than one return.

[3] Based on 1,427 cases (which includes enquiries from professionals and victims as well as cases where the FMU provided assistance).

[4] This information is not available on FMU cases, so no comparison is possible.

[5] Karma Nirvana is a national charity that offers a helpline to potential victims of FM.

[6] FMU data is based on 1,470 cases (which includes enquiries from professionals and victims as well as cases where the FMU provided assistance). In 9% of cases, gender was unknown (excluded from the base). Karma Nirvana data is based on 2,200 cases.

[7] The percentages of the components do not add up to the total because of rounding.

[8] Based on 1,071 cases (which includes enquiries from professionals and victims as well as cases where the FMU provided assistance). In 34% of cases, age was unknown (excluded from the base).

[9] This information is not available on FMU cases, so no comparison is possible.

[10] White individuals were not included in the analysis because only one case was reported among this ethnic group.

[11] The relationships were significant for the Asian Pakistani, Asian Bangladeshi and Asian Indian groups.

[12] These rates represent the regression coefficients from a weighted linear regression analysis of LAs, where the dependent variable was the number of local cases of FM within an ethnic group, and the independent variable was the local population of individuals in that ethnic group.

[13.] For instance, that the rates apply equally to LAs with a small minority ethnic population as well as to those with a large minority ethnic population, and to areas with different socio-economic profiles to the LAs involved in the data-collection exercise.

[14] The rationale for adding the highest number of women and men reported by each organisation is that this represents the minimum number of female and male cases known to national organisations. For instance, since Karma Nirvana know about 950 male cases of FM, there must be at least 950 known at the national level. The assumption of complete overlap between Karma Nirvana and the FMU would assume that the 225 male cases known to the FMU are already included within the 950 known to Karma Nirvana, which is why they have not been added separately to the total.

References

Brandon, J, and Hafez, S. (2008) *Crimes of the community: honour based violence in the UK*, London: Civitas.

FMU (Forced Marriage Unit) (2008) *The right to choose: multi-agency statutory guidance for dealing with forced marriage*, London: FMU.

Home Affairs Select Committee (2008) *Domestic violence, forced marriage and 'honour'-based violence*, London: House of Commons.

Home Office (2000) *A choice by right: the report of the Working Group on Forced Marriage*, London: Home Office.

Kazimirski, A., Keogh, P., Kumari, V., Smith, R., Gowland,S., Purdon, S. and Khanum, N. (2009) *Forced marriage: prevalence and service response*, London: DCSF.

Khanum, N. (2008) *Forced marriage, family cohesion and community engagement*, Luton: Equality in Diversity.

Magill, C. and Lee, V. (2008) *CPS pilot on forced marriage and so-called 'honour' crime – findings*, London: CPS.

WORKING WITH FAMILIES

Introduction to Part Five

Carol-Ann Hooper

Families come into contact with state agencies in a range of contexts – from before their children's birth and throughout their childhoods – and the impacts of public policy and family members' interactions with professionals on their troubles have been evident in many chapters. This part brings into focus: the ways families are worked with in different national contexts (see the chapter by Boddy); the potential and limitations of some key current policy developments in Anglophone countries in relation to the growth of parenting education programmes (see the chapter by Churchill and Clarke) and the increased attention to fathers' roles (see the chapter by Featherstone); and the kinds of theoretical, moral and philosophical thinking needed to work with families in trouble, to build resilience (see the chapter by Vetere), to protect children at risk (see the chapter by Forsberg) and to reflect critically on the meanings-in-context of family members' experiences and the values informing intervention (see the chapter by Ribbens McCarthy). Themes from previous chapters reappear here, especially the issue of contested definitions and practices (see the chapters by Churchill and Clarke and by Forsberg) and of the uncertain boundary between the ordinary and the harmful (see the chapters by Featherstone; Forsberg; Ribbens McCarthy).

Since the mid-1990s, growing critiques of the child protection systems developed to respond to family troubles in the UK and other Anglophone countries, which prioritise the identification of children at risk within highly proceduralised approaches (see, eg, Lonne et al, 2009), have led a number of researchers to look to other countries and learn from alternative approaches (Heatherington et al, 1997; Freymond and Cameron, 2006; Covell and Howe, 2009). Janet Boddy's chapter draws on two studies conducted across European countries, based on interviews with professional stakeholders and expert reviews, to explore similarities and differences in the way support for families is positioned within wider policy frameworks, and the ways specific approaches reflect both different countries' assumptions about the relationship between families and the state and their broader approaches to social welfare. Her analysis contrasts the assumed divide between ordinary and troubled families implicit in the way services are organised in the UK with continental European countries where institutionalised rights to support for all children and/or families, and a more professionalised holistic approach to family support embedded within universal services, makes specialist help more easily accessible and 'trouble' less stigmatised. Harriet Churchill and Karen Clarke's chapter, by contrast, takes a local focus, discussing a group parenting programme for families with adolescent children, and its evaluation based on professionals' and parents' perspectives. Such standardised programmes have proliferated in the UK over the last decade or so and are likely to remain a feature of the policy landscape, despite their limitations as a response to the challenges of parenting in the context of complex family histories, social and economic deprivation and overstretched and rationed services. In practice, it is largely mothers who are worked with in this context, and while most found the programme helpful in some ways, their perspectives on their children's troubles were significantly different from those of the programme providers, locating responsibility for them in a much wider context than the parent/mother–child interaction that is the focus of such programmes.

The continuing reality of a gendered division of labour in parenting, and its taken-for-granted nature by services, means that women generally still play the central role in negotiating with services on behalf of children. In Anglophone countries, however, there have been growing efforts to engage fathers in welfare and education services and to promote their involvement with their children (alongside more limited attention to paternity and parental leave entitlements and the public provision of child care). Such developments emphasise fathers' role as resources for their children, while in other contexts, primarily child protection, fathers either remain invisible or are constructed largely as risks. Brid Featherstone's chapter charts these developments, highlighting: first, the complexities of contemporary family life and the fragmentation of fathering, and the reality of violence, abuse and the continued care-giving role of mothers, all of which tend to be ignored in 'fathers-as-resource' developments; and, second, increasing concerns both about unrealistic expectations of mothers where fathers are not engaged and about constructing fathers only as risks in the child protection arena, where more holistic, flexible and responsive approaches are beginning to emerge, although they remain controversial.

Working with couples, and with parents and children together, requires careful judgements about safety where there is a history of conflict, violence and abuse. Arlene Vetere, however, gives an account of how a systemic approach, informed by attachment theory and the importance of narrative, can help individuals and families to cope with and grow through trauma and adversity, to the benefit of both adults and children. While resilience is often defined in individual terms, it is clear that the availability of supportive close relationships plays a central part in its development, so working directly with family relationships, while remaining sensitive to the influence on them of their social context (including material inequalities and cultural diversity), to enhance the quality of interaction and thus the support available for all family members has much potential. Vetere's approach is based on her work as a systemic family psychotherapist at a domestic violence project, although it is relevant to a wide range of situations.

Where families are troubled by divorce/separation, the courts' role in ordering contact may override some family members' preferences about ongoing relationships – the supervised contact meetings with non-resident parents that are the result are the focus of Hannele Forsberg's chapter. She draws on interviews with social workers in Finland involved in monitoring such meetings to reflect on the knowledge and concepts they need to do this highly complex and uncertain work ethically. While the courts work to the principle of 'the child's best interests' and in many cases contact may enable troubling situations to resolve somewhat, children under 12 years old commonly have little say over these decisions and may therefore be in situations that they do not want, and which are sometimes readily observable to be harmful, raising important questions for social workers about their role in implementing the courts' judgements. In the context of diverse and contested family practices, where dividing lines between the normal and the exceptional are not easily drawn, social work decision-making is inherently value-laden – more than knowledge of research findings, Forsberg argues, it requires the capacity for ongoing moral reasoning informed by dialogue with family members in a particular situation.

The inescapably moral nature of the issues at stake in considering family troubles are at the heart of the final chapter in this section, from Jane Ribbens McCarthy, who, having taken the lead on this project throughout, appropriately draws it to a close with a wide-ranging discussion drawing on sociology, philosophy, political theory and anthropology. Making meaning of family troubles is an existential challenge that faces all who experience them, and those meanings may be shaped by interpersonal, material and cultural contexts (including the available narratives for explaining suffering and the relative value placed on autonomy, community and/or divinity in different societies). Ribbens McCarthy explores the processes involved, highlighting the contestations that may arise over meaning between different participants and stakeholders, and then goes on to take up the challenge of debating whether, despite the particularity of meanings in contexts, any universalising principles can be brought to the task of setting boundaries between the 'normal' and the 'troubling' in family life. She considers four perspectives: a critical realist approach from sociology; an international legal approach framed as rights; an anthropological perspective on non-uniform universality; and a form of feminist philosophy framed as an ethic of care. She concludes that all have something to offer as reference points in necessarily ongoing debates, arguing for the usefulness of such explicit frameworks and providing clear grounds for dialogue focused on the gains and losses that may be associated with them, rather than for an uncritical adoption of any one framework or a single conclusive answer to the question.

Work with families is shaped by many influences, including: the balance between universal and targeted services; how and where lines are drawn between normal and troubling behaviour and the context-specific and political contestations over meaning that underlie this; the emphasis placed on different factors – individual, family, community, socio-economic – in understanding family troubles and its implications for attributing responsibility; gendered constructions of parental responsibility and age-differentiated constructions of childhood; the relative emphasis on maintaining family relationships and/or intervening to protect children from harm within them; the role and use of the legal system; the coherence or otherwise of the approaches of different agencies impinging on family life; and professional training (or lack thereof). While there is more use of coercion in the UK than formerly in relation to parental responsibility both for child protection and young people's troubling behaviour, and more also than in many other countries, interactions remain largely a negotiation between family members and professionals, although one shaped by the very different positions of power or powerlessness of the different actors involved. One recurring theme across the chapters in this part is the limitations of dichotomous thinking – centrally, the unhelpful dichotomy between 'normal' and 'troubled' families (see the chapter by Boddy) – and, hence, the creative potential for ways forward that are 'both/and': recognising teenagers as both troublesome and troubled (see the chapter by Churchill and Clarke), violent men as both perpetrators and fathers (see the chapter by Featherstone), and all family members as having both strengths and vulnerabilities (see the chapter by Vetere) – and combining 'insider' understanding with 'outsider' critique to locate the personal within its political and cultural context (see the chapter by Ribbens McCarthy).

Another recurring theme is the need for all services to be sensitive to change (both of form and process), diversity and complexity in contemporary family relationships, and to avoid assumptions, for example: equating father involvement with the birth father, who may not be the 'father' involved in the everyday practice of parenting (see the chapter by Featherstone); equating teenage bad behaviour with the mother's parenting, when her influence may be less than an absent father's or an ongoing peer group's (see the chapter by Churchill and Clarke); equating contact with non-resident fathers with the child's best interest, without paying due attention to the child's experience of the relationship (see the chapter by Forsberg); or equating childhood with the protection of innocence, to the extent that children may be denied some cultural resources that could contribute to resilience (see the chapter by Ribbens McCarthy). Finally, while Boddy is appropriately cautious about using cross-national research to conclude that other countries 'do it better', there is inspiration to be drawn from 'work with' families that aims to make that phrase a reality, enabling professionals to work democratically to co-create solutions with families, rather than offering or imposing a standardised approach or intervention.

References

Covell, K. and Howe, R.B. (2009) *Children, families and violence: challenges for children's rights*, London: Jessica Kingsley.

Freymond, N. and Cameron, G. (eds) (2006) *Towards positive systems of child and family welfare: international comparisons of child protection, family service and community caring systems*, Toronto: University of Toronto Press.

Hetherington, R., Cooper, A., Smith, P. and Wilford, G. (1997) *Protecting children: messages from Europe*, Lyme Regis: Russell House Publishing.

Lonne, B., Parton, N., Thompson, J. and Harries, M. (2009) *Reforming child protection*, London: Routledge.

CHAPTER TWENTY-ONE

European perspectives on parenting and family support

Janet Boddy

Support for parents and families has been a key aspect of policy across government departments in most European countries over recent years. The policy drivers for this emphasis also have some commonalities across countries, including concern with agendas of social inclusion (eg Hantrais, 2004). But there are also important differences between countries in the position of parental support relative to wider policy frameworks for children and families, and beyond that, to wider discourses about the rights of parents and children, and the role of the state in family life. For example, what do policymakers and service providers aim to do when they intervene with families and their 'troubles'? Do families have a right to support in dealing with the troubles they face? Or are policy and services designed to address aspects of family life that are troubling to the 'normal', as discussed earlier in this volume? How do such understandings of the purpose of support inform the design and delivery of parent and family support services?

This chapter considers these questions in the context of two studies commissioned by the UK government[1] and conducted in Europe. The studies examined policy and services in relation to 'mainstream' parenting and family support, and targeted support for families of young people where placement away from home is being planned or considered. In discussing these studies together, the chapter will examine continuities – and disjunctures – between 'universal' and 'targeted' services, considering both the conceptualisation of the work (in policy and practice) and its implementation.

The studies

Working at the 'edges' of care? (Boddy et al, 2008, 2009a)

Conducted in England, Denmark, France and Germany, this study was concerned with support for young people (aged 10–15 years old) and their families when placement away from home was being planned or considered. The study's title stems from a government policy document – the *Care matters* Green Paper (DfES 2006) – which coined the phrase 'at the edge of care' to refer to children in this situation. The research was concerned with policy, professional skills and practice, and sought to understand better the ways in which care entry can be prevented, or planned and supported. A related aim was to consider the role of social pedagogues and social pedagogy in the policies, theory and practice of this work: social pedagogy (alongside approaches such as *éducation spécialisé* in France) is the dominant theoretical discipline and professional qualification for direct work with children and families in many continental European countries, spanning a range of child and family services (see Cameron and Moss, 2011).

The practical intent of the *Edges of care* study coincided with a broader conceptual question about the purpose and use of public care in the countries studied. The research aimed to question whether a conceptual 'edge' of care exists in those countries, and to examine the implications of that understanding for work with young people and families and the role of social pedagogic theory and practice in that work.

Expert reports were commissioned from academics in the three continental countries,[2] and this was followed by interviews with 104 professionals across the four countries (including England). They included social care practitioners and managers, workers in related services such as mental health and youth work, and national policy advisers in each country.

International perspectives on parenting support: non-English language sources (Boddy et al, 2009b)

This study was based on expert reviews of parenting support in five European countries: Denmark, France, Germany, Italy and the Netherlands. The review was designed to extend existing knowledge beyond an earlier review of the English-language evidence entitled *What works in parenting support* (Moran et al, 2004). This earlier study had been confined to English-language literature, and its authors acknowledged that it was dominated by North American work. They noted that this material represented only part of an international picture of parental support, and highlighted the need to attend to non-English-language sources. For the *International perspectives* study, an initial scoping review of 12 non-English-language countries was conducted as a basis for selecting five European countries for in-depth review.[3] Subsequently, expert partners[4] were recruited to write knowledge synthesis reports for each country, describing policy, services and workforce, along with examples of interventions and any available evidence on effectiveness. In the final stage of the work, the English team, in consultation with expert partners, prepared the reviews for cross-country comparison and analysis of relevance to policy and practice development in England.

Parenting support in the context of child welfare

There exists a substantial literature on public policy across countries in relation to families (eg Hantrais, 2004), and it is beyond the scope of this chapter to try to replicate or summarise that body of work. However, it is important to recognise that parental and family support policy and services are located within a broader societal approach to social welfare.

'Ideal-types' of welfare regime

Esping-Andersen's (eg 1990) distinction between three broad 'ideal-types' of welfare regime provides a starting point for considering the context in which parental support policies operate. He distinguished between:

- 'neoliberal' regimes, including the UK, which seek to minimise the role of the state and to promote market solutions;
- 'social-democratic' welfare regimes, characteristic of Scandinavian countries, which are redistributive of wealth, in which the state assumes the greatest part of responsibility for welfare; and
- 'conservative' or 'corporativist' regimes, in countries including France, Italy and Germany, which fuse compulsory social insurance with subsidiarity traditions, emphasising social assistance rather than welfare rights.[5]

This typology has been rightly contested, for example, as lacking explanatory power (eg Arts and Gelissen, 2002), and there are, of course, differences between hypothetical models and the 'messy realities of real-life policies' (Jensen, 2008, p 151). There are also important differences between countries *within* this broad typology. For example, policy approaches to child and family welfare in Germany, France and Italy have many fundamental differences, as well as some commonalities (eg Hantrais, 2004).

Moreover, policy approaches are not constant. Esping-Andersen himself (2003) acknowledged that changes in population demography and in the global economy were prompting shifts in the three traditional models. Political change is also a factor. In England – historically, a neoliberal state – the previous New Labour government's preventive agenda in family policy introduced greater central direction, shifting towards a more statist discourse of 'progressive universalism' (eg DCSF, 2007). However, with subsequent political change following elections in 2010, English family policy has shifted back towards neoliberalism, with greater emphasis on targeting and an increased role for the private sector (eg Department for Work and Pensions and Department for Education, 2011). Regan and Robinson's (2004) observation – that the balance between universal and targeted remains one of the central tensions in English welfare – is no less relevant today. Despite the need to acknowledge dynamism and some blurring of boundaries between different models, aspects of Esping-Andersen's broad typology remain useful in considering policies and practices cross-nationally.

Dualistic and holistic systems

Hetherington and colleagues developed a typology of approaches to child and family welfare, which distinguished between 'holistic' and 'dualistic' systems (eg Katz and Hetherington, 2006). *Holistic systems*, they argue, 'promote early intervention and preventive work and there is an assumption that there should be a continuum of care' (Katz and Hetherington, 2006, p 432). A holistic approach has a strong focus on family support: protection of children from abuse is seen as one element of child welfare, but is not the dominant concern. Katz and Hetherington (2006, p 432) reported that Nordic and continental European countries commonly follow this pattern, but 'do not approach the task the same way'. Their different approaches can be understood in relation to Esping-Andersen's typology. In Nordic countries, the state assumes responsibility for delivering services (through local authorities) and there are few voluntary organisations involved. Strong traditions of subsidiarity in countries such as Germany imply a more minimal role for the state, with voluntary organisations (including those affiliated to the Church) as the predominant service providers. However, the distinction between statism and subsidiarity is not absolute. France provides an example of a mixed system of statism and subsidiarity, with elements of centralisation *and* decentralisation, and a strong role for local authority service delivery (eg Grevot, 2006).

Dualistic systems – which include most English-speaking systems – are described by Katz and Hetherington (2006, p 431) as focused on child protection and 'dominated by the need to prevent abuse and rescue children from abusive situations'. The dualism reflects a separation of systems for child protection from systems for family support. There is a further dualism in English child and family policy in the legal separation of youth justice and child welfare systems, although the conceptual distinction between the child as *victim* (troubled and in need of protection) and the child as *threat* (in need of control, correction and punishment) is rarely so tidy in practice (Goldson, 2007).

The state and family life

In English policy and services, discussions about parenting and family support are located within a broader debate about the appropriate role for the state in family life – and, therefore, about families' rights to state support, alongside their responsibilities. Writing about the Home Office in the 1940s, Cunningham (2006, p 233) observed:

> [According to the government] in the 1940s ... 'hard-working families' remained the bedrock of the state, the place where children should be brought up. Parents were now frequently reminded of their responsibilities, as well as of their rights, but wherever the emphasis lay, few doubted it was they who should make decisions for their children.

Cunningham's description of a minimal role for the state in family life is consistent with Hantrais's (2004, p 140) observation that the UK is often presented in cross–national analysis as an example of a country with 'an implicit, neutral, underdeveloped or negative family policy, in the sense that governments have gone so far as to reject the idea that family policy should be identified as a specific policy domain'. Among the countries in the research described here, only England does not have a legal constitution. In Italy, France and Germany, the family as a unit is protected within the constitution, and – critically in relation to parental support – these constitutions include statements about the state's responsibility to support and/or protect the family unit. Thus, for example, the German Basic Law sets out principles of protection for families, and parents have a right, in law, to help with upbringing (*Hilfe zur Erziehung*).[6] In France, too, the reference of the Civil Code to the '*absolutisme*' of parental authority has meant that the predominant approach to parental support was emancipatory, focused on enabling parents to meet their responsibilities, and undertaken with the voluntary participation of the parents. In Italy, there are legal requirements[7] for services to provide 'essential levels of care' (*livelli essenziali di assistenza*), including a requirement to support parental responsibilities.

The Danish and Dutch constitutional laws, in making no explicit reference to families, present a contrast to this emphasis. The Danish constitution does, however, specify the rights of children (eg in access to education), an emphasis shared with other Scandinavian countries such as Finland (see Hantrais, 2004). This emphasis on the rights of children as citizens is also evident in more recent Danish policy, which stipulates that all citizens have a right to support from the state. More specifically, the Service Act 1998 requires that support for families (and hence parents) is embedded within universal practice in local authorities. Consequently, mainstream parental support is conceived as an integral part of health, child care and education provision. The ethos of the Danish approach was summed up by a national politician, interviewed in the *Edges of care* study: "Children's welfare and education [in the broadest sense] are a common responsibility — it's everybody's, it's a responsibility for society."

What are the implications of these broad policy framings for the design and delivery of parent support services? There were many similarities between the six countries (including England) in specific policy agendas related to parental support. Parental and family support was accorded high priority in all the countries in the two studies, with common policy priorities such as social inclusion, enabling mothers to work and the recognition of changing family forms (often in the context of increased rates of parental separation and divorce). However, the countries also differed – from England and from each other – in approaches to both 'mainstream' and 'targeted' support.

Approaches to parental support

Before going on to reflect on commonalities and differences in approaches to parental and family support, two key caveats demand consideration. First, the purpose of such comparison is not to say that one way is 'better', but rather to consider the potential for shared learning between countries. Cross-national comparison can stimulate the development of new approaches, but it can also prompt us to question our hidden assumptions – for example, about how we understand 'what works' or what is 'effective' in supporting families. Both studies were commissioned to inform English policy and service development, and the discussion presented here is informed by that agenda.

Second, policy and services in all the countries, in both studies, are decentralised to some degree. This makes it unwise to seek to generalise *within* countries. It is impossible to say, for example, 'Germany is like this …'. Indeed, as noted earlier, Germany has a highly decentralised federal structure that emphasises local determination and non-statutory (voluntary sector) service provision. Similarly, in Italy, while service frameworks are broadly defined by national legislation, Canali (2008) noted considerable local variation in the extent of service development in different regions of the country.

With those caveats in mind, analysis of themes emerging from the two studies highlight two key, interrelated points with relevance for our understanding of support for troubled families in an English context, and these shall be considered in turn:

- First, different service models in each country had implications for the targeting and accessibility of support.
- Second, countries varied in the extent to which interventions followed structured evidence-based programmes, and this in turn appeared to be associated with:
  - the professionalisation and specialisation of the workforce; and
  - the theoretical base for the work, and particularly the influence of social pedagogic theory.

Targeting and accessibility

Compared to England, the other five countries in the two studies all had less sharply defined boundaries between mainstream and specialist parental support provision. This blurring of the boundaries between universal and targeted support was most evident in Denmark, typically classified as a universalist Scandinavian welfare regime. Danish legislation – and the Service Act 1998 in particular – emphasises continuity between universally accessible and targeted provision, within a 'single-stringed' (*enstrenget*) system. Continuity is, of course, also a principle of English integrated children's services (eg CWDC, 2007). The difference lies in emphasis, and in the way in which Danish services were framed to enable that continuity.

In Denmark, principles of continuity and accessibility are at least partly addressed by embedding parental support in services that are universally (or almost universally) used – such as schools and early childhood education and care settings. Of Danish children, 90% use some form of local authority child care,[8] including early childhood and out-of-school provision, and child care workers play a key role in the provision of mainstream parental support. This was illustrated by the comments of an early years pedagogue interviewed on the topic by Korintus and Moss (2004, p 72):

> The parents actually use us a great deal, so when it comes to the parents right here, then we are very important, first of all because we take care of their children but also with regard to confusion and despair in day-to-day life. 'What are we doing wrong? How can we do better? How do you do it?' In this context they ask us for advice the same as they would ask a nurse for advice, so they use us a great deal in the upbringing of their child.

Danish parents automatically 'access' this kind of support if their child attends the setting – without any requirement for assessment, referral or formal identification of 'need'. Of course, in England and other countries, universal service providers often play a key role in the early identification of needs and the activation of additional support. The distinctive feature of Danish practice is that there is no onward referral to a separate professional or service – it is the worker *within* the universal setting (eg the pedagogue) who is delivering the support. There is no distinct service threshold to cross. Arguably, this active role for early years workers in parenting support in Denmark is also possible because of their greater professionalisation (early years workers are commonly qualified as pedagogues, to Bachelor's degree level[9]), in contrast to the English early years workforce.

Another key framework for family support in Denmark was also seen (in similar forms) in the Netherlands, Italy and Germany: the 'Family House'[10] model. These settings varied across countries, of course, but they shared two important commonalities:

- They were staffed by highly qualified multi-professional teams, including psychologists, pedagogues, social workers and/or healthcare professionals. In some Italian Family Counselling Centres, lawyers also formed part of the team (eg advising in relation to parental separation and divorce).
- These centres – and the same staff within the centres – provide both targeted child and family welfare interventions and universally accessible support.

The development of integrated working in England means that services such as Children's Centres often have multidisciplinary staff teams, with involvement of specialist professionals such as social workers or psychologists (eg Myers et al, 2004). Nonetheless, high thresholds for specialist services such as child mental health, educational psychology or children's social services mean that specialists such as social workers have tended to occupy 'a somewhat marginal role' in English early intervention services (Parton, 2009, p 68). It remains unusual for psychologists and social workers to have a direct role in the delivery of mainstream services.

In contrast, the Family House model in other countries embeds specialist expertise *within* a universally accessible service, minimising the need for onward referral and blurring the boundary between universal and targeted support. In the Netherlands, Youth and Family Centres provide specialist targeted support – including case coordination for children with significant or complex needs (disabilities or social care needs) – alongside general parental support and advice. In Danish Family Houses, psychologists offer therapeutic intervention with families (who may be referred or may self-refer), as well as drop-in counselling and advice services. In one of the Danish city case studies in the *Edges of care* study, it was reported that each family was entitled to eight open-access counselling sessions at a Family House before any statutory assessment was required. If further support was mandated as a result of statutory assessment, it could be delivered by the same professional within the same setting as before – ensuring the *estrenget* continuity principle.

These frameworks present an interesting contrast for an English audience, accustomed to sharp boundaries that govern access to specialist professional support. They illustrate the potential for service frameworks to blur the boundaries between specialist and mainstream provision; integrating services not only across *agencies*, but across *levels of need*.

Professionalisation

Examples of specialist support embedded within universal services highlight another important finding from the studies: the extent of professionalisation (and of professional differentiation) among those carrying out direct work with families. Care work in England has long struggled with low qualifications and low professional status. Apart from schoolteaching, graduate professionals, such as social workers, are in a minority, and direct work with children and families tends to be delegated to those with low-level vocational qualifications, or to unqualified staff (eg Brannen et al, 2007; Cowley et al, 2007; Simon et al, 2008). Elsewhere in Europe, Bachelors degree-level or three-year vocational qualifications in (social) pedagogy or similar disciplines (eg *éducation spécialisé* in France) are the predominant qualifications for direct work with children and families, including parent and family support (eg Korintus and Moss, 2004; Petrie et al, 2006; Boddy et al, 2008, 2009b).

It is important to note, however, that pedagogues (or their equivalents) were not the only graduate professionals involved in the support for parents and families. One of the most striking features of the workforce in the five countries involved in the two studies was the extent of professional differentiation among staff doing the work, either through inter-agency working or through multidisciplinary teams. Professionals included pedagogues, but also psychologists, social workers, lawyers and family mediators, and medically qualified staff including maternity and public health nurses and doctors.

Theoretical approaches

The study countries differed in their theoretical approaches to parent and family support, and particularly in the extent to which they had implemented, and prioritised, formal parenting programmes. Such programmes were most widely used in Germany and the Netherlands. The Netherlands, in particular, placed a similar emphasis to England on formal evaluation, supported by the role of the Netherlands Youth Institute in promoting the implementation of evidence-based interventions.[11] Standardised programmes were also promoted in Denmark, on a central government website,[12] but Danielsen's (2008) review indicated that they were not commonly used in practice. Canali's (2008) and Milova's (2008) reviews of Italy and France, respectively, found very little use of standardised interventions, although both described group meetings. In these countries, as in Denmark, there was also a strong emphasis on approaches to support tailored to the family that was the focus of the intervention. Such interventions were delivered through individual or group work in Family Houses (or equivalents), or in home-based support, an approach that was also found in Germany and, to a lesser extent, in the Netherlands.

Arguably, variation between countries in the use of parenting programmes reflected a distinction between 'top-down' and 'bottom-up' approaches to parenting support – between standardised evidence-based theory-led programmes and approaches that were primarily parent- or family-led. This distinction could be seen to imply that parent- or family-led approaches are not theoretically based. However, the research suggested that this was not the case. Rather, models of intervention in the five non-English-language countries were drawing on different theoretical bases than English-language parenting programmes.

Parental support in Germany and Denmark was often explicitly based in social pedagogic theory, perhaps reflecting the key role of social pedagogues in delivering such support. In Germany, Garbers (2008) highlighted the social pedagogic concept of a *Resourcenorientierung* – a resource-orientation, based on the identification and development of parental competencies – as a key theme underpinning a range of parental and family support services, including standardised programmes *and* less structured counselling services. That underpinning principle was also central to Danish models of intervention, such as the Parental Guidance Programme – a relationships- and resource-oriented intervention, first developed in Norway in 1985.

Social pedagogic theory also emphasises attention to the individual (or individual family) through the concept of *Lebensweltorientierung* (Thiersch, 1995, 1997;

cited in Colla et al, 2006). Literally meaning 'life–world' orientation, this can also be thought of as an 'everyday world orientation'. It requires that intervention should support the individual's resources in relation to their everyday world, their individual situation and problems, and the social context in which they live – a situated and reflexive perspective that does not sit easily with standardised or manualised approaches to support.

At the same time, social pedagogic theory emphasises democratic approaches. Sünker (2007, p 242) discussed the potential of 'pedagogical work' to become 'a crucial basis for democratisation processes that aim for the democratisation of all areas of life'. In the present context, this interpretation of pedagogical work implies that the distinction between theory-led (top–down) and parent-led (bottom–up) approaches is a false dichotomy, since democratic practice should be both theoretically informed and client-led. Similarly, while writing in a different pedagogic tradition, the Brazilian theorist Paolo Freire (1993 [1970], p 51) argued for 'co-intentional' practice, achieved through 'common reflection and action'.

Social pedagogy was, of course, not the only theoretical influence on parental support identified in the present study. In France, the psychoanalyst Françoise Dolto's 'Maison Verte' approach has been highly influential in work with children and families (Milova, 2008; Hall et al, 2009). The central tenet of Dolto's approach – relational work between professionals, children and parents together – is not based in social pedagogic theory, but there are clear parallels with social pedagogy's emphasis on relationships (Boddy, 2011). A French éducateur, interviewed for the *Edges of care* study, said that his role was to work with relationships ("*travailler avec des relations*"). Writing about Germany, Garbers (2008) also described models of family education that were informed by psychoanalytic theorists, including Rudolf Dreikurs and Alfred Adler, and by Carl Rogers's person-centred approach.

Our research also identified an emphasis on family-oriented models of support across the countries in the two studies; an approach that is specified in law in Denmark, Germany and Italy. In Danish law, the *helhedsprincip* (unity principle) specifies that intervention should address the whole family (and not merely its component parts). Similarly, in Italy, legislation sets out the concept of a *care pathway* (*percorso assistenziale*), concerned with the well-being of the family as a whole. In German law and service provision, parenting support is encompassed within 'family education' (*Familienbildung*), and targeted support for parents *and* children – including placement of the child – is framed in legislation as help with upbringing (*Hilfe zur Erziehung*), one measure of which is social pedagogic family support (*Sozialpädagogischefamilienhilfe*).

This emphasis on family-oriented and relational approaches raises a theoretical question about the nature of 'parenting' support. One finding to emerge from the research reported here was the apparent absence of an equivalent word for 'parenting' in the non-English languages. Thus, in France, for example, the term '*soutien à la parentalité*' refers to support for parent*hood*: there is no equivalent verb 'to parent' ('*parent-er*'). Similarly, other countries refer to support for 'upbringing' or 'education' (eg *Erziehung* or *Bildung* in German; éducation in French; *Opvoeding* in Dutch) or, more generally, to support for parents or families. The *Oxford English Dictionary*[13] attributes the etymology of the verb 'to parent' in English to a US self-help book, *How to parent*, written by Fitzhugh Dodson in 1973. While not wishing to over-interpret terminological differences across countries, they appear to indicate different theoretical constructions of parenthood, and hence of parental support. Parent*ing* implies individual behaviour that can be taught. Behaviour towards a child is clearly one fundamental component of the parent–child relationship, but, arguably, a broader, ecological theoretical frame is necessary to capture the complex, dynamic and dyadic nature of that relationship, and to understand how that relationship is situated within the family system and broader social networks (eg Kuczynski, 2003; Moran et al, 2004; Bronfennbrenner, 2005).

Conclusions

In opening this discussion, both similarities and differences were noted across the six countries (including England) in their social and demographic contexts for policy and services in relation to support. It was also argued that the comparisons presented here are not evaluative: no one country's approach is 'best', nor can it be assumed that the approaches described here would 'work' in an English context. Nevertheless, common themes emerge across the two studies that offer useful challenges to common assumptions within English approaches to parenting and family support.

First, the blurring of boundaries between 'universal' and targeted or specialist services explicitly challenges the English neoliberal dualism between services for 'ordinary' and 'troubled' families. This in itself is troubling to English approaches to family policy and family support, because it implies a greater role for the state, an incursion into family life. In Denmark, the state has a legislated duty to share families' responsibilities for the upbringing of children; in the other countries we studied, constitutional law specifies families' rights, including rights to support or 'help with upbringing'. Support is not only offered because it is *preventive* or *corrective* of problems (although those are also legitimate objectives for work with families), but because the state has a duty to the family and the child.

Second is a question about understanding effectiveness. While there was less emphasis on formal outcome evaluations in the study countries than in England, there was no evidence that family support services were less developed or less fully theorised. Rather, it appears that different approaches to support require different understandings of effectiveness (Boddy et al, 2011). Less standardised approaches are less readily amenable to quasi-experimental evaluation designs. The historical dominance of social pedagogic theory (or equivalent disciplines) in the countries we studied appears to have given rise to models of support that are designed to be theory-led *and* family-led: situated, relational and democratic. Within this context, a programmatic assessment of effectiveness ('Does this work for most families?') has limited utility. It is more meaningful to ask, 'Does this work for *this* family?'

Thus, looking across the two studies reported here, we can see differences of perspective about how best to approach support for parents and families. Writing about the English-language literature, Smith (2010) criticised the dominance of problem-focused deficit models of parenting; at the same time, English-language policy and academic literature on parenting support emphasises standardised approaches (eg Moran et al, 2004; Allen, 2011). Deficit-focused research and programmatic approaches to support are both consistent with the emphasis of neoliberal welfare regimes on targeted intervention. The very model of evaluation that is seen as the gold standard – the randomised controlled trial – is a methodology originally designed to gauge the effectiveness of medical *treatment* (Medical Research Council, 2008). To evaluate parenting support within this paradigm draws a conceptual equivalence with medical intervention, which seeks to be 'corrective' or 'preventive' of problems. Family-led or democratic approaches do not sit easily with this idea of intervention as a standardised expert 'treatment', because they imply that the solution must be co-created – found *with* the family.

So, what does the research reported here offer to the development of policy and services for so-called 'troubled' families in England? Social pedagogic approaches have commonalities with other long-standing English (and UK) traditions, including models of emancipatory social work or informal education (eg Jeffs and Smith, 2005; Banks, 2006). Like social pedagogic theories, these approaches emphasise partnership-working, listening and dialogue. These areas of common ground between UK and continental European approaches offer a potentially valuable basis for moving beyond dominant 'corrective' conceptualisations of parenting support. They imply an emancipatory conceptualisation that spans universal and targeted support, helping families with the common, diverse *and* unique troubles that they face.

Acknowledgements

The research presented in this chapter was carried out in conjunction with colleagues at the Thomas Coram Research Unit, Institute of Education, including: June Statham, Pat Petrie, Susan McQuail, Marjorie Smith, Deborah Ghate, Hanan Hauari and Valerie Wigfall.

Notes

[1] Policy and services for children and families differ between UK countries. The research on which this chapter is based was commissioned by the UK government to inform English policy and services, and equivalence with other UK countries' policy approaches cannot be assumed.

[2] Inge Danielsen (Denmark); Michael Tetzer and Herbert Colla (Germany); and Mihai Dinu-Gheorghiu, Lucette Labache and Chantal David (France).

[3] Countries were selected on the basis of availability of information, as well as indications that support services for parents were sufficiently developed for there to be potential for

cross-national learning. This latter criterion included considerations of translatability to an English context, for example, in terms of service frameworks and population demographics.

[4] Inge Danielsen (Denmark); Cinzia Canali (Italy); Marion Flett (Netherlands); Simon Garbers (Germany); and Helene Milova (France).

[5] Subsidiarity implies a limited role for the state, with an emphasis on local determination, low threshold support services and non-statutory service provision.

[6] Basic Law (Grundgesetz) of 1949; Sozialgesetzbuch (SGB) Achtes Buch (VIII) Kinder- und Jugendhilfe; KJHG; 1991.

[7] Law No. 328/2000.

[8] Information from 'Clearing House Colombia country profiles, Denmark' (2004). Available at: http://www.childpolicyintl.org/countries/denmark.html

[9] Pedagogues in Denmark, with a common generalist professional Bachelors qualification, work across a wide variety of universal and targeted services. According to Børne- og Ungdomspædagogernes Landsforbund, the national trade union and professional association for pedagogues, pedagogues work in services including:

* universal services for children below compulsory school age (day nurseries, day-care centres, pre-school classes) and for school-aged children (recreation centres, school-based leisure time facilities, after-school clubs);

* targeted services for children and families with identified needs (including residential care, foster care, child welfare services and child and youth psychiatric services);

* services for disabled children, young people and adults; and

* services for adults with social problems (homelessness, substance abuse, mental disorders), and child and youth psychiatric services (information from: http://www.bupl.dk/english/pedagogy_in_dk?OpenDocument; see also Petrie et al, 2006).

[10] 'Family Houses' in Denmark; 'Youth and Family Centres' in the Netherlands'; 'Family Centres' and 'Family Consultation Centres' in Italy; and 'Counselling Centres' in Germany.

[11] See: http://www.nederlandsjeugdinstituut.nl/youthpolicy/docs/pdf/Database_of_effective_youth_interventions.pdf (accessed 18 October 2011).

[12] See http://www.socialstyrelsen.dk/born-og-unge/evidensbaserede-programmer (accessed 4 December 2012).

[13] See OED Online. Available at: http://www.oed.com (accessed 30 September 2011).

References

Allen, G. (2011) *Early intervention: the next steps*, London: Department for Work and Pensions.

Arts, W.A. and Gelissen, J. (2002) 'Three worlds of welfare capitalism or more? A state-of-the-art report', *Journal of European Social Policy*, vol 12, pp 137–58.

Banks, S. (2006) *Ethics and values in social work* (3rd edn), Basingstoke: Palgrave MacMillan.

Boddy, J. (2011) 'The supportive relationship', in C. Cameron and P. Moss (eds) *Social pedagogy and working with children: Engaging with children in care*, London: Jessica Kingsley.

Boddy, J., McQuail, S., Owen, C., Petrie, P. and Statham, J. (2008) 'Supporting families of young people entering public care: European models', final unpublished report to Department for Children Schools and Families, London: Institute of Education.

Boddy, J., McQuail, S., Owen, C., Petrie, P. and Statham, J. (2009a) *Working at the 'edges' of care? European models of support for young people and families*, DCSF Research Brief DCSF-RBX-09-07, Nottingham: DCSF.

Boddy, J., Statham, J., Smith, M., Ghate, D., Wigfall, V., Hauari, H., Canali, C., Danielsen, I., Flett, M., Garbers, S. and Milova, H. (2009b) *International perspectives on parenting support: non-English language sources*, DCSF Research Report DCSF-RR114, Nottingham: DCSF.

Boddy, J., Smith, M. and Statham, J. (2011) 'Support for parents and families: cross national perspectives on "what works"', *Ethics and Education*, vol 6, no 2, pp 181–95.

Brannen, J., Brockmann, M., Mooney, A. and Statham, J. (2007) *Coming to care: the work and family lives of workers caring for vulnerable children*, Bristol: The Policy Press.

Bronfenbrenner, U. (2005) *Making human beings human. Bioecological perspectives on human development*, London: Sage.

Cameron, C. and Moss, P. (eds) (2011) *Social pedagogy and working with children: engaging with children in care*, London: Jessica Kingsley.

Canali, C. (2008) 'Parenting support in Italy', unpublished project report for International Perspectives on Parenting Support, Padova, Fondazione Zancan.

Colla, H.E., Tetzer, M., Jansen, A., Renk, F. and Sieburg, J. (2006) 'Supporting families of young people entering public care: European models', unpublished report on Germany for Supporting Families of Young People Entering Public Care: European Models, Lüneburg, Institüt für Sozialpädagogik, Universität Lüneburg.

Cowley, S., Caan, W., Dowling, S. and Weir, H. (2007) 'What do health visitors do? A national survey of activities and service organisation', *Public Health*, vol 121, pp 869–79.

Cunningham, H. (2006) *The invention of childhood*, London: BBC Books.

CWDC (Children's Workforce Development Council) (2007) *Common Assessment Framework for Children and Young People: managers' guide*, Leeds: CWDC.

Danielsen, I. (2008) 'Parenting support in Denmark', unpublished report for International Perspectives on Parenting Support project, Copenhagen: Københavns Socialpædagogiske Seminarium.

DCSF(Department for Children, Schools and Families) (2007) *The children's plan. Building brighter futures*, Nottingham: DCSF.

Department for Work and Pensions and Department for Education (2011) *A new approach to child poverty: tackling the causes of disadvantage and transforming families' lives*, London: HM Government.

DfES (Department for Education and Skills) (2006) *Care matters: transforming the lives of children and young people in care*, London: HMSO.

Esping-Andersen, G. (1990) *The three worlds of welfare capitalism*, Cambridge: Polity Press.

Esping-Andersen, G. (2003) 'Towards the good society, once again?', paper presented at 'Social Security in a Long Life Society, 4th International Research Conference on Social Security', International Social Security Association, Antwerp.

Freire, P. (1993 [1970]) *Pedagogy of the oppressed*, London: Penguin.

Garbers, S. (2008) 'Parenting support in Germany', unpublished report for International Perspectives on Parenting Support project, Lüneberg, Institüt für Sozialpädagogik, Universität Lüneberg.

Goldson, B. (2007) 'Child protection and the "Juvenile Secure Estate" in England and Wales: controversies, complexities and concerns', in M. Hill, A. Lockyer and F. Stone (eds) *Youth justice and child protection*, London: Jessica Kingsley.

Grevot, A. (2006) 'The plight of paternalism in French child welfare and protective policies and practices', in N. Freymond and G. Cameron (eds) *Towards positive systems of child and family welfare*, Toronto: University of Toronto Press.

Hall, G., Hivernel, F. and Morgan, S. (2009) *Theory and practice in child psychoanalysis. An introduction to the work of Françoise Dolto*, London: Karnac.

Hantrais, L. (2004) *Family policy matters. Responding to family change in Europe*, Bristol: The Policy Press.

Jeffs, T. and Smith, M.K. (2005) *Informal education – conversation, democracy and learning*, Nottingham: Educational Heretics Press.

Jensen, C. (2008) 'Worlds of welfare services and transfers', *Journal of European Social Policy*, vol 18, no 2, pp 151–62.

Katz, I. and Hetherington, R. (2006) 'Co-operating and communicating: a European perspective on integrating services for children', *Child Abuse Review*, vol 15, pp 429–39.

Korintus, M. and Moss, P. (2004) *Work with young children: a case study of Denmark, Hungary and Spain. Care work in Europe: current understandings and future directions. Workpackage 7 consolidated report*, London: Thomas Coram Research Unit, Institute of Education.

Kuczynski, L. (2003) *Handbook of dynamics in parent–child relations*, Thousand Oaks, CA: Sage.

Medical Research Council (2008) *Developing and evaluating complex interventions: new guidance*, London: MRC.

Milova, H. (2008) 'Parenting support in France', unpublished report for International Perspectives on Parenting Support project, Paris, University of Paris X, Nanterre.

Moran, P., Ghate, D. and Van der Merwe, A. (2004) *What works in parenting support: a review of the international evidence*, DfES Research Report DfES RR574, Nottingham: DfES.

Myers, P., Barnes, J. and Brodie, I. (2004) *Partnership working in Sure Start local programmes: synthesis of early findings from local programme evaluations*, London: Sure Start Unit.

Parton, N. (2009) 'From Seebohm to Think Family: reflections on 40 years of policy change of statutory children's social work in England', *Child and Family Social Work*, vol 14, pp 68–78.

Petrie, P., Boddy, J., Cameron, C. and Wigfall, V. (2006) *Working with children in care: European perspectives*, Maidenhead: Open University Press.

Regan, S. and Robinson, P. (2004) 'Loud and clear. An open and persistent poverty strategy', in IPPR (Institute for Public Policy Research), Social Market Foundation, Policy Exchange, Scottish Council Foundation and Institute of Welsh Affairs (eds) *Overcoming disadvantage. An agenda for the next 20 years*, York: Joseph Rowntree Foundation.

Simon, A., Owen, C., Moss, P., Petrie, P., Cameron, C., Potts, P. and Wigfall, V. (2008) *Working together: volume 1. Secondary analysis of the Labour Force Survey to map the numbers and characteristics of occupations working within social care, childcare, nursing and education*, DCSF Research Report TCRU-01-08, Nottingham: DCSF.

Smith, M. (2010) 'Good parenting. Making a difference', *Early Human Development*, vol 86, pp 689–93.

Sünker, H. (2007) 'Globalization, democratic education (Bildung), educating for democracy', paper presented at the 'Oxford Mini-Conference on Critical Pedagogy: The Possibility/Impossibility of a New Critical language in Education – Critical Theory and Critical Pedagogy Facing Globalizing Capitalism'. Available at: http://construct.haifa.ac.il/~ilangz/oxford2007/indexoxs.html

What supports resilient coping among family members? A systemic practitioner's perspective

Arlene Vetere

Introduction: learning from practice, linking to theory

What helps family members develop shared, supportive and constructive ways of responding to life events, both expected and unexpected? This chapter will explore how their relational and social context supports the development of resilient coping in a family/kin group. Individual definitions of resilience speak of the ability to bounce back in the face of adversity and overcome life challenges (Rutter, 1999). Joseph and Linley (2008) write of the potential we as individuals hold for post-traumatic growth. Resilience is not about invulnerability or untested capacity to cope. Interestingly, much of the research on the development of individual resilience posits the importance of others, as sources of support and esteem, or the importance of other activities and contexts that support competence, again often involving others (Rutter, 1999). In my therapeutic practice, I am keen to identify and strengthen key interactional processes that support resourcefulness in the couple or family group, in the face of trials, tribulations and too much uncertainty (Smith, 1999). Thus, for me, resilience becomes a concept of 'within and between' – the formulation of a set of hypotheses both about what supports resilient coping in individuals and what leads to a shared set of beliefs about, and practices of, resilient coping in the family group. Families will be defined here either as the resident household group, which may span a number of generations, with legal, birth and/or psychological ties, and/or as the 'problem-determined system', that is, that group of people with intimate emotional connections organised around particular psychological dilemmas and problems in living. This sometimes includes non-resident members, such as life partners and ex-spouses, and the boundaries may change over time.

To put my thinking about family resilience into context, I am a clinical psychologist and a systemic family psychotherapist and for the past 16 years, I have co-directed a domestic violence project where we work therapeutically with both victims and perpetrators of violence, in all its forms, within any family relationship, for example, siblings, parents and children (of any age), couples, older people and their carers, and so on (Cooper and Vetere, 2005). In trying to understand the complexity of interpersonal violence – the reasons for hurting the people we love, interactions and beliefs that maintain violence, strategies for survival, resourcefulness, commitment and coping, shame, guilt and suffering, and ways of ending the violence – I have learned that an integrated theoretical position most helps me be of help to others.

This kind of work is not appropriate in all situations involving family violence. We put safety first and our safety methodology includes an exploration of the capacity and the wish to change, and the ability to take responsibility for behaviour that harms others. If we are faced with a person's resolute refusal to take responsibility for their behaviour, constant blaming of others and lack of empathic appreciation of the impact of their behaviour, and possibly a desire to actively harm others, we do not proceed with relational therapeutic work. A legal or forensic response may be more appropriate. Our major models of psychotherapy are concerned with arousal and affect regulation and the development of compassion and empathy, so we need to see some willingness to take responsibility and to recognise the relational consequences of behaviour.

In working with family violence, we try not to confuse explanation of violence with responsibility for violence, nor to let explanation elide responsibility. As a systemic psychotherapist, I use ideas of pattern and process to help understand how violence begins and is maintained (Goldner et al, 1999). As a clinical psychologist, I use Bowlby's attachment theory to help me understand the intersect of power and control in relationships on the one hand, with passion and commitment on the other (Bowlby, 1988, Dallos and Vetere, 2009). And, as both a clinical psychologist and a systemic psychotherapist, I am interested in narrative development as a skill – specifically, under what relational circumstances do children learn to give an integrated, coherent account of themselves and their experiences, and under what circumstances do people achieve a resolved balance in the aftermath of trauma (Crittenden, 1998).

The integration of attachment theory with systemic theory and practice and narrative theory provides the platform for exploring the complexity of family violence, and the long-term effects of living with fear in relationships – intergenerational trauma (where abuse is carried on down the generations), continuous trauma (where family members are constantly exposed to predictable and unpredictable violent events, such as with domestic abuse) and developmental trauma (where children are living in fear and their psychological development is compromised) (van der Kolk et al, 1996). Safety and protection are of primary importance in our work. We find attachment theory attractive because it does not pathologise dependency in relationships; rather, it conceptualises autonomy and dependency as complementary processes in close relationships. In other words, I am helped to 'know my own mind' and develop my reflective abilities when I feel safe, and when I can trust and know that I can turn to others for help and comfort in the face of threat and danger. Thus, interpersonal resourcefulness and a sense of felt security in relationships are built with (mostly) predictable experiences of accessibility and responsiveness in our key relationships. This fits with my systemic bias, to seek out strengths and resources in individuals' repertoires of responses, and within family groups. This bias does not put me at risk of ignoring or minimising distress, either personal or relational, or its impact on individuals and their relationships because the basic systemic premise is dialectical, for example, the dynamic relationship between stability and change in our relationships, or between strengths and needs, opportunities and constraints, and so on. Systemic supervision would have these dialectics in focus.

Relational resilience and family coping

From a family systems perspective, we can see coping in families as a developmental process over time. In systemic practice with families, we are interested in the context that supports constructive, cooperative and resilient coping – when family members see and experience each other as empathically responsive and accessible, in both how they seek and give help. Following Bowlby, Mary Ainsworth (1989) defined the healthy family in terms of the availability and the consistency of care; thus, felt by all as a sense of security. This way of thinking was further developed in the family systems field by a number of researchers and scholar practitioners, such as Byng-Hall (1995), Crittenden (1998), Flaskas (2002), Johnson (2002), Dallos and Vetere (2009), Pocock (2010), among others.

If it can be said that as individuals we develop, over time, strategies of coping and response styles in the face of interpersonal threat, or attachment threat, or actual loss, rejection and abandonment, then we can think systemically of how children and adults in families, or couples, may mutually influence one another's response styles in feedback loops, governed by unspoken 'rules' of what it is safe to talk about, and expectations of one's own and others' behaviour. Bowlby (1988) wrote about the development of internal working models, or templates for how relationships work, and the associated development of beliefs about ourselves and others in terms of care and care-giving, that is: 'Am I deserving of others' care and attention?' and 'Are others deserving of my care and attention?' From a systemic perspective, attachment relationships are both interconnected and nested, for example, the developing relationship between a mother and infant may be supported emotionally by the relationship between the mother and father, and their relationships with their parents; similarly, in the developing relationship between two gay parents and their adoptive child, the emotional and practical support of grandparents can be significant to a healthy adjustment.

Froma Walsh (2006) has developed a family resilience framework to help understand how family groups withstand trauma and adversity and how they can emerge strengthened and more resourceful. Her framework brings together theory, research and practice and focuses on endurance and growth in response to crisis and challenge. When distressed family groups are struggling to survive, it is important to affirm their potential for repair and growth. By way of illustration, Nugent and Parkes' (1993) study of social work crisis intervention in the state of

Florida showed that families whose youth were in crisis with the law and at high risk of harm were more likely to stay together as a group when offered two family meetings, and that offering five meetings made that outcome twice more likely.

Jordan (1994) has put forward a definition of relational resilience as supported vulnerability, mutual empathic involvement, relational confidence and relational awareness. This complements Walsh's ideas (see earlier) that effective family processes for reducing stress and vulnerability and fostering healing and growth in the face of adversity are found in family belief systems, organisational patterns, the family's capability for communication and shared problem-solving. These are all fundamental tenets of a family systems approach to understanding learning and development in family groups.

Coping and resilience are often defined in individual terms, as capacities and as potentials. Here, though, we are interested more in group functioning and whether we can talk of resilient coping among a group of family members – for a couple, for parents and children, and for household and kin groups. Thus, the context for resilient coping in the group would involve analysis and understanding of group interaction, along with consideration of factors external to the group, but impacting on the group.

One approach to the deconstruction of context for resilient coping would be to consider the meanings at different specified levels of contextual understanding, for example: the behavioural events and episodes; the relationships within which they occur; the beliefs about these events held individually, collectively and historically; and the social and political discourses that might influence understanding and action (Burnham, 1986). These levels of context can be said to have mutual influence. So, for example, some political views, delivered in political speeches, about lone mothers being responsible for the unlawful behaviour of adolescent sons could act as a constraint to a mother. She may be struggling to help her son stay in school, to help him interact effectively with his teachers and to do so herself, and to encourage him to be reflective about his choice of wayward friends. The constraint could be to her sense of authority as a parent, to speak for her son and to speak with him, with a consequent and discouraging sense of failure for herself as a mother.

A systemic approach to formulation: adaptation, coping and power

When an individual, interpersonal or family difficulty is distressing, and requires an adaptive response from family members, a systemic approach to the formulation of the problem covers five domains of understanding that can be integrated to provide a map of how best to intervene and support family members' efforts to manage: the nature and definition of the problem; problem-maintaining patterns within the family and community; ideas and beliefs about the problem held individually and collectively; emotions and attachments, both in the here and now, and in the past; and the social, cultural and political context that both supports and constrains functioning and well-being (Vetere and Dallos, 2003). The domains are:

1. *The problem.* What is the nature of the problem? Is it seen as individual or interpersonal? That is, is it seen as a property of the person ('He has misbehaved'; 'He is defiant') or as a relationship issue within and beyond the family ('We do not get on'; 'We do not listen to each other')? What is the history of the development of the problem? Has the definition of the problem changed over time? What solutions have been tried? Did some work? If yes, why? If not, why not? Do people give themselves credit for trying to solve the problem? Has the attempted solution to the problem become the problem?

2. *Problem-maintaining patterns.* Is there a pattern to the problem? That is, do arguments and disagreements follow the same course? Is problem behaviour reinforced? Do people take sides in loyalty conflicts that prevent resolution? How are wider kin and communities involved in the conflict? Is it difficult to discuss the problem when people have calmed down for fear of starting the argument again? Is a pattern of blame and counter–blame maintaining hurt feelings and preventing calm discussion and resolution? And so on.

3. *Ideas and beliefs about the problem.* What ideas are held about the causes of the problem, and possible solutions that have implications for action, for example, an act of God, individual responsibility and so on? Are intentionality and impact confused together? How are disagreements about the cause, nature and solution to the problem discussed, negotiated and managed? Do family members see themselves and others as resourceful, reliable and trustworthy? Are there gender scripts held separately and collectively, for example, ideas about masculinity and what boys and young men are expected to do, or not do, such as 'Boys don't cry'? Who is able to challenge gendered ideas about boys' and girls' development? Are these scripts protective?

4. *Emotions and attachments.* How does the problem impact on relationships and how do relationships impact on the problem? Does the problem bring people closer or drive them apart? Is it emotionally safe to confide and seek help from others? Are some feelings discouraged or encouraged? Are there family 'rules' that proscribe what can be talked about, with whom and how? Who can challenge these rules? Who were these rules made to protect?

5. *The wider social context.* What social, economic and political conditions are the family members living in? What social, financial and practical resources do they have access to? Is access to resources and power bases of influence either gendered or determined by social class and privilege? To what extent do wider social divisions and processes constrain people, for example, what is the impact on family members' functioning and well-being of living in poverty, or with social exclusion, bullying, discrimination or oppression? Have the family recently migrated and is social support less available? Are the family members part of a minority cultural group and less likely to access services for fear of being misunderstood, or their family values not being appreciated by members of the majority group? These considerations are one of the strengths of the systemic approach to working with culture and context – for example, the different ways that the balance between autonomy and family connectedness

can be seen at different times in a family lifecycle, or within and across different cultural groupings.

This is not an exhaustive list, but gives a flavour of how understanding and unpacking both the intra-familial and extra-familial context of relationships and resources can help provide an integrated road map to the development of resilient responding and recovery. Such an 'unpacking' demands a safe environment in which family members can take emotional risks in the face of exposure, vulnerability and strong emotions. Such a safe environment can be created with the help of a trusted person or professional therapist, who creates a secure base for problem-solving, emotional accessibility and responsiveness among family members.

Attachment as representational

It could be argued that psychotherapies of all theoretical persuasions strive to help people become more reflective, that is, to think about their own thinking, feelings, decisions and actions. If people are overly preoccupied with their emotional states or actively dismissing of the significance of their emotions, psychotherapy tries to help people achieve a more balanced relationship between these two extremes of coping. The active conditions for reflection often involve a sense of felt safety and calm, so it can be safer to contemplate fearful responses, or abusive intentions, to make oneself emotionally vulnerable, and to integrate memories across all representational systems.

Memory researchers suggest that we hold memories about our lives and our relationships in separate systems, for example: a) procedural memory, for how we remember to do things, like riding a bicycle, or having an argument; b) sensory memory, for what things feel, look, smell and taste like, and how we have been touched, held and comforted; c) semantic memory, for our ideas, beliefs and attitudes; d) episodic memory, for sequences of events and experiences; and e) integrative memory, for when we draw on all our memory systems to describe and explain our experiences and to reflect on feelings, thoughts, decisions and actions (Tulving, 1987).

The capacity for integration strengthens and supports our ability to give a good narrative account of ourselves and our experiences. The systemic or relational psychotherapies support such integration, but focus more on how feelings and thoughts of safety are co-constructed in relationships, and how family members can stay attuned and responsive to one another while enacting and re-enacting difficult moments in therapy. As a result of earlier adverse experiences in relationships, family members may have learned to overly rely on one or more of the representational memory systems (eg sensory or semantic), and have less experience of integrated thought, that is, meta-communication, meta-cognition or reflective self-functioning (depending on the therapeutic orientation and theoretical language!). At times of stress, family members may become overwhelmed emotionally, or may dismiss or deactivate their emotional responses, and operate primarily within one representational system, thus reducing manoeuvrability, creativity and their ability to problem-solve. If we can bring forth a more integrated set of memories and responses, it helps us think about our choices and actions at very difficult moments and at very challenging times.

Resilience as relational co-construction

We can find some help in moving the discussion of resilience from an individual level to the level of relational co-construction in the work of Mikulincer (2006). In Mikulincer's research, he and his colleagues explore the relationship between self-reported feelings of felt security in close relationships and psychological factors, such as:

1. Affect regulation – experienced as more balanced, less subject to extremes of emotional responsiveness.
2. Communication style – clearer, coherent and more reflective, aids problem-solving.
3. Sense of self – more elaborated, not overly reliant on single definitions of self.
4. Support-seeking – more likely to see others as helpful and to turn to others for support.
5. Information-processing – more able to deal with complex information, and to be less preoccupied by one's emotional state.

If we think about these individual factors systemically – a) in terms of how a safe relationship context supports the development of the factors just mentioned; b) how in a relationship itself, these capacities can be strengthened and developed further; and, importantly, c) how earlier adverse experiences that may lead to a lack of trust in others can be challenged and changed to become earned relationship security – we can see how close relationships can form the context for resilient coping and, importantly, can give rise to resilient coping. Thus, resilience can also be seen as an interactional process over time, within and between relationships.

An example from practice: couples work, trauma and narratives of healing

In the following example of therapeutic work with a couple, we can see how individual coping strategies, developed over time in family of origin experiences, can be reworked in a mutually supportive and co-constructed manner to achieve a better fit with the couple's needs at this time. The couples work started first, and then ran in parallel with work with them as parents and as a family, to address the impact of past experiences on the children's development and their development as a family. The family/parental work will be reported briefly at the end of the description of the work with the couple. The couples work addressed both their childhood experiences and their current relationship.

Sam and Jim are in their mid-30s, are married and have a son aged four years old. They live with Sam's son aged 10 years old, born in her previous marriage. Both boys have regular contact with her ex-husband, and Sam reports that her relationship with her ex-husband is reasonable and cooperative. (Sam and Jim have given permission for this description but details have been changed.)

Jim's family (mother, father, younger brother by five years) migrated to the South of the UK from the North when he was 11 years old for economic reasons, leaving extended family behind. One year later, Jim's father died suddenly and unexpectedly. According to Jim, his mother "went under the duvet" in her grief, and at the age of 12, Jim found himself in the position of having to look after his younger brother, both practically and emotionally. As Jim's mother recovered the threads of her life, Jim described how he maintained his role as carer of his younger brother and how he and his mother ran the household together. Now, in his employment, Jim has responsibility for the well-being of a large team of workers.

Sam's family is local. She has two younger sisters and her parents are alive, as is her maternal grandmother. Sam describes being sexually abused by her maternal grandfather during her later childhood and early teenage years. She thinks that he did not abuse her sisters and she believes she protected her sisters "by taking it". Sam married in her early 20s and she and her husband were part of a friendship group that worked hard during the week and drank hard at the weekends. It was in this context of alcohol misuse that Sam started to experience flashbacks of the sexual abuse, and her marriage to her first husband came to an end. Jim was part of this friendship group and as Sam's problem with alcohol use escalated, he helped her with practical and emotional support, looked after her son and encouraged her to attend the local alcohol counselling service. Their romance developed in this context and they married.

Sam used the alcohol counselling sessions well and became abstinent of alcohol, but as her reliance on alcohol diminished, her feelings of anxiety increased, particularly as sensory embodied memory, that is, her 'throat feeling' – a constriction in her throat when she remembered the earlier abuse. Her alcohol counsellor suggested that she meet a cognitive behavioural therapist (CBT) for help with managing anxiety and processing the trauma memories. Sam worked hard with her CBT and, in this context, decided to disclose her grandfather's sexual abuse to her parents and sisters. Her mother frankly disbelieved her. Her father was uncertain, but told her, as her grandfather was now dead, not to disturb her grandmother with this information. Her middle sister believed her, but her younger sister did not. Sam was sorely disappointed with and hurt by this response, but reflected that perhaps her own mother had been sexually abused as a child. Jim supported Sam during these disclosures and comforted her when she was not believed. Jim believes Sam in what she says of her past experience.

During the CBT sessions, Sam spoke of her behaviour a few years previously – behaviour for which she was deeply ashamed. Apparently, while her romance with Jim was developing, and they were night-clubbing and she was drinking to excess, she would flirt with other men in front of Jim, and kiss them. If Jim said that it was time to go home, she would protest and drunkenly beat him in front of others. Sam did not remember all these occasions, but Jim and the friendship group did. The CBT recommended couples therapy to address these hurts in their relationship. Jim agreed to attend couples therapy for this reason, and also for help as a man, when he and his wife wanted sex, in how to manage the occasional frightening flashback for Sam. Jim's fear of upsetting his wife further led to him being very tentative in their sexual relationship.

Our systemic therapy focused on understanding the nature of the attachment injuries and resolving them, helping jointly with the flashbacks and their sexual relationship, supporting Jim in asking for care and comfort in his own right, helping Sam to feel deserving of care, and supporting Sam in facing her shame and walking through it, so that together the couple could develop a joint narrative of how they healed their relationship (Johnson, 2002). The couples therapy also considered their relationship as parents, the emotional needs of their children and any effect of the earlier drinking problems on their children's psychological development. The context for these discussions needed to feel safe for both of them, so that they could be helped to stay responsive and accessible while the other was exploring their feelings, intentions, hopes and sense of vulnerability. The therapy supported emotional risk-taking so that their sense of trust and intimacy deepened. Jim had learned over the years that the safest and most self-protective way to respond to attachment threat and abandonment was to deactivate his emotional responses, as if to persuade himself that he was alright. This strategy had helped him survive but had not encouraged reflection on his own emotional needs, such as his need for comfort and reassurance at times of anxiety. Similarly, Sam had struggled to learn to understand and manage her own emotional responses in the confused and confusing context of intra-familial sexual abuse and lack of protection. In situations of high anxiety, aroused by the perception of attachment threat, she remained overwhelmed by her feelings and unable to think clearly about her own and others' needs.

Sam and Jim worked hard in the couples therapy and managed to stay empathically attuned to their own and each other's needs, with support, encouragement and understanding. The therapy was complicated by trauma and took nearly 30 meetings in all. Together, they developed a compassionate understanding of the impact of the past on the present, offered and accepted forgiveness, and recommitted to their relationship. Jim managed to develop a more balanced coping strategy, where he was less reliant on deactivating his emotional responses and became bolder about speaking about his need for comfort and reassurance, in turning to Sam and others for help, and in believing that he was entitled to care and being looked after. Sam developed her ability to stay calmer in difficult moments, and to continue to think and reflect even when she was upset.

Sam turned her trauma memories into bad memories, whereby she had more control of what she remembered and when she remembered; thus, the memories lost the power to overwhelm and terrify her. Both of them used an integration of their representational systems at the end of therapy as they talked about what they had achieved for themselves, each other and their children.

At all times during the couples work, we kept the needs of the children in mind, but it was not until the couples work was well under way and we were sure that both parents were paying attention to safety that we met them with their children. The younger son was born when Sam was well into recovery, so the focus for him was on supporting his relationship with his half-brother, and helping all three parents work cooperatively around his needs. However, the older son had experienced some disruption to his care prior to Sam's recovery, and the two men, his birth father and stepfather, had cooperated in his care then, and now. The work supported Sam in processing her feelings of shame and sense of failure around her care of her older son at earlier times, and supporting and strengthening their relationship through shared activities and open talking. The weave of couples meetings with family meetings, with consultation with the birth father, developed fully near the end of the therapeutic process. We held a few follow-up review sessions for both the couple and the family at their request.

Conclusion

In my view, one of the bigger mistakes made in the history of our adult mental health services is to see family members as a hindrance or part of the problem, to the exclusion of seeing them as a resource or part of the solution. We may say that some family groups do overly struggle in the face of adversity, or simply have too much to deal with, or may stay locked in an endless cycle of blame and recrimination. Although the development of psychological distress and psychiatric problems may be seen in a contextual light, most services deal with individuals in isolation from their social networks and their many social roles, offering individualised treatments away from the contexts that may be maintaining or causing the problems, and that may hold the seeds of the solution. A systemic approach would recruit family members into the work, and see them as a resource, to both assist in managing and solving problems, and to help them all cope in ways that support family members, rather than inadvertently making their difficulties worse. Clearly, we are not talking about circumstances of intended abuse. However, if we consider social isolation to be potentially traumatising, we might critically evaluate our professional therapeutic practices to see how we can actualise the potential for enhanced understanding and compassion, growth and resourcefulness, in family groups, however they are variably defined by individuals, and what we might do to support these key processes between people.

References

Ainsworth, M. (1989) 'Attachments beyond intimacy', *American Psychologist*, vol 44, pp 709–16.

Bowlby, J. (1988) *A secure base: parent–child attachment and healthy human development*, New York, NY: Basic Books.

Burnham, J. (1986) *Family therapy: first steps towards a systemic approach*, London: Routledge.

Byng-Hall, J. (1995) *Rewriting family scripts*, New York, NY: Guilford.

Cooper, J. and Vetere, A. (2005) *Domestic violence and family safety: working systemically with violence in family relationships*, Chichester: Wiley.

Crittenden, P. (1998) 'Truth, error, omission, distortion and deception: the application of attachment theory to the assessment and treatment of psychological disorder', in M. Dollinger and L. DiLalla (eds) *Assessment and intervention across the lifespan*, London: Lawrence Erlbaum.

Dallos, R. and Vetere, A. (2009) *Systemic therapy and attachment narratives: applications across a range of clinical settings*, London: Routledge.

Flaskas, C. (2002) *Family therapy beyond postmodernism: practice challenges theory*, London: Brunner-Routledge.

Goldner, V., Penn, P., Sheinberg, M. and Walker, G. (1999) 'Love and violence: gender paradoxes of volatile attachments', *Family Process*, vol 29, pp 343–64.

Johnson, S. (2002) *Emotionally focused couple therapy with trauma survivors: strengthening attachment bonds*, New York, NY: Guilford.

Jordan, J. (1994) 'Relational resilience', in J. Jordan, M. Walker and L. Hurtling (eds) *The complexity of connection*, New York, NY: Guilford Press, pp 28–46.

Joseph, S. and Linley, P. (2008) *Trauma, recovery and growth: positive psychology perspectives on posttraumatic growth*, Hoeboken, NJ: Wiley.

Mikulincer, M. (2006) 'Attachment, caregiving and sex within romantic relationships: a behavioural systems perspective', in M. Mikulincer and G. Goodman (eds) *Dynamics of romantic love: attachment, caregiving and sex*, New York, NY: Guilford.

Pocock, D. (2010) 'Emotions as ecosystemic adaptations', *Journal of Family Therapy*, vol 32, pp 362–78.

Rutter, M. (1999) 'Resilience concepts and findings: implications for family therapy', *Journal of Family Therapy*, vol 21, pp 119–44.

Smith, G. (1999) 'Therapist reflections', *Journal of Family Therapy*, vol 21, pp 154–8.

Tulving, E. (1987) 'Multiple memory systems and consciousness', *Human Neurobiology*, vol 6, pp 67–80.

Van der Kolk, B., McFarlane, A. and Weisath, L. (eds) (1996) *Traumatic stress: the effects of overwhelming experience on mind, body and society*, New York, NY: Guilford.

Vetere, A. and Dallos, R. (2003) *Working systemically with families: formulation, intervention and evaluation*, London: Karnac.

Walsh, F. (2006) *Strengthening family resilience*, New York, NY: Guilford.

CHAPTER TWENTY-THREE

Troubled and troublesome teens: mothers' and professionals' understandings of parenting teenagers and teenage troubles

Harriet Churchill and Karen Clarke

Introduction

Many Organisation for Economic Co-operation and Development (OECD) countries have increased investment in parenting education (Churchill and Clarke, 2010). Focusing on UK developments, this chapter examines the policy and practice aims of one type of provision: group parenting programmes targeted at families with adolescent children. Drawing on the findings of a local programme evaluation, it contrasts policy, programme and service-user concerns about young people, parenting and families. While the discussion highlights the benefits participants gained from taking part in the parenting programme, it illustrates the limited way the programme engaged with and addressed parental concerns and young people's support needs. These limitations, it is argued, are related to tensions between a policy and programme focus on young people as troublesome to others (a problem to be addressed via parenting interventions), in contrast to the participants' sense of their own and their children's 'troubles'. The chapter initially considers the policy context and describes the local programme and evaluation study. It then turns to contrast programme and service-user perspectives, ending with reflections on wider policy and programme implications.

The policy context

The social consequences of 'poor parenting' became major policy issues under the former Labour government (1997–2010). Over three terms in office, these concerns led to significant investment in parenting education initiatives. Labour developed a spectrum of provision, with a substantial role for group parenting programmes. Consistent with its emphasis on evidence-based policy, Labour stressed the importance of using parenting programmes that had been subject to rigorous evaluation. Two influential programmes were the Australian Triple P programmes and the Webster Stratton programmes developed in the US – which have proved popular forms of provision (Churchill and Clarke, 2010).

These programmes use social learning theory and behavioural interventions to promote 'authoritative parenting', which is seen as the most desirable parenting style (Churchill and Clarke, 2010). In practice, most programmes served parents of pre-school children, but Labour also invested in provision for parents of adolescents, funded as part of policies to address youth anti-social behaviour and offending. Controversially, Labour introduced measures – Parenting Orders (POs) and Parenting Contracts (PCs) – that directed parents to engage with parenting programmes (sometimes in combination with other services) to address concerns about youth offending, anti-social behaviour and school attendance (see Churchill and Clarke, 2010). Despite the public spending cuts introduced by the current Conservative–Liberal Democrat government, it is clear that extending the use of parenting interventions remains an important policy preoccupation (HM Government, 2011).

The parenting programme and local evaluation

The parenting course was developed by the Educational Psychology Service (EPS) of a large northern English city with high levels of child poverty, educational underachievement and youth offending. In 2006, the city council received Children's Fund[1] support to deliver targeted interventions to address youth crime and anti-social behaviour. The EPS designed a group parenting course for parents of 'pre-teens and younger teens', drawing on the Webster Stratton parenting programmes for the parents of younger children.

The programme consisted of eight two-hour sessions (see Box 23.1) delivered weekly by two Webster Stratton-trained parenting practitioners, working with groups of six to 10 parents. Consistent with the evidence base informing this approach, the course drew on theories of adolescent development, cognitive behavioural therapy and positive child behaviour management. The parenting course included sessions that considered parent–youth interactions, parental understandings and emotions about their teenager's behaviour, positive communication strategies, parental disciplining and boundary-setting, and parental praise for teenagers. Social learning theories informed the weekly use of group discussion, role-play scenarios, videos and practical 'learn by doing' tasks.

The original target group was self-referring parents struggling in their relationships with children who were starting secondary school or in their early teen years. Consistent with its funding through the 'reducing crime and disorder' strand of the Children's Fund, the aim of the programme was early intervention in what the psychologist who devised the programme described as 'late onset conduct disorders'.[2] However, due to demand and insufficient alternative provision, the course also served parents with more severe problems and those with older teenage children, including parents who were required to attend under a PO and PC or were referred by a variety of professionals. After 15 months of delivery, EPS commissioned us to carry out a pilot programme evaluation. In collaboration with the practitioners involved, we designed a multi-method study involving participants who had attended the course between September 2006 and December 2007. The main elements of the study were: a postal survey of participants; qualitative interviews with participants some six to 12 months after they had completed the course; analysis of data from a number of standardised measures of parenting style; and parents' assessment of young people's psychological well-being[3] collected by the course trainers at the start and end of the parenting course (see Clarke and Churchill, 2012). This chapter draws on data from the qualitative interviews.

Box 23.1: The parenting course weekly sessions

Week 1: Introductory session

Week 2: Strong feelings: how not to murder your teen

Week 3: Time and talk 1: ending the shouting match

Week 4: Time and talk 2: communicating and problem-solving

Week 5: Praise and reward: more carrot and less stick!

Week 6: Clear limits: let's take charge!

Week 7: Ignore and sanctions: say what you mean and mean what you say

Week 8: Celebratory session: putting it all together – look at what we've achieved

---

We conducted 23 semi-structured interviews with participants recruited through the postal questionnaire or through a follow-up reunion of parents. The interviews covered: reasons for attending the parenting course; access routes; parents' concerns; their experiences of taking part; and their perceptions of changes following the courses. Interviews lasted between 45 minutes and an hour, and generally took place at the participant's home. All but two of the interviews were recorded with the permission of the interviewee. Interviews were transcribed, anonymised and thematically coded and analysed.

The EPS attempted to recruit fathers and minority ethnic parents to the programme but the majority of participants were women and of white British ethnic background. These characteristics were mirrored in our interview sample (see Table 23.1). Four men completed the postal survey, although none volunteered to be interviewed. None of the parents interviewed had been subject to a PO or PC. However, many had significant problems, and had been recommended to attend by children's services or youth offending professionals. All had completed the course and, thus, were likely to have relatively positive views of it.

Table 23.1: Characteristics of interview sample

Ethnicity	White British	21
	Other	2
Relationship to child	Mother	18
	Foster mother	2
	Grandmother	3
Family status	Lone parent/grandparent	13
	Married/cohabiting/civil partnership	7
	Step-family	3

In reanalysing the evaluation data for this chapter, we sought to examine the participants' narratives of youth 'troubles', 'maternal troubles' and 'family troubles' and compare these with the assumptions contained in the parenting programme about 'normal teenage troubles' and 'troublesome teenagers'. The latter were identified through discussions with local authority personnel responsible for local parenting education provision, an interview with the psychologist who devised the programme and the programme content.

'Normal' teenage troubles

Some participants attended the parenting course for advice about the teenage years in anticipation of problems they perceived as part of the normal difficulties of adolescence. Sadie was concerned about her 12-year-old daughter's "mood swings and temper", which had recently become more "volatile, conflictual and challenging". Sadie associated this with the transition to secondary school and "hormonal changes" in early adolescence, but was also worried about whether her daughter's "moods" were normal or symptomatic of more serious problems, perhaps unhappiness at school or home:

> My daughter and I would get into arguments and a slinging match. I would be picking her up from school wondering, 'Oh what mood is she in today?' It was really, really stressful. I went on the parenting course because I wanted to be able to cope better with Naomi's moods. I wanted to know how to deal with it better.

Mothers were rarely merely concerned with mother–adolescent relationships. Several were concerned about the levels of conflict between siblings in the home. Jackie had three teenagers living at home. She felt that heightened family conflict was common in the teenage years when "anything you said, anything trivial, can turn into an argument":

> My middle son [aged 10] would just explode over anything. He was thinking everyone was on his back. He was thinking, 'Well, I will act all big like the older ones.' And he was getting into arguments with the older ones too.

Negotiating teenagers' growing independence was also an issue. There were a number of 'risky' behaviours or risks to young people that mothers worried about, such as alcohol use, drug use, anti-social behaviour, sexual relations, detrimental peer pressure, young people staying out too late at night and young people's safety.

Participants differed on significant issues such as what age children should be allowed to do certain things or the degree to which infrequent or low-level alcohol use was acceptable and 'normal' for teenagers. Two mothers commented on how their own parenting styles differed from their view of mainstream British culture. One mother, who was South African and had moved to the city a few years earlier, felt that her background meant she had different expectations for younger teens. Another, a practising Muslim, contrasted her views on teenage sexual relationships and on drinking alcohol with those of other parents:

> I think the way that we raise our children is quite strict compared to other people.... 'Cos they were talking about sex, things like that, but my children have not gone into that yet. Because for us they know if they want to have a girlfriend, they have to tell us.... We don't go out and smoke.... We're quite open about that. We say drugs are bad, we don't drink alcohol.... We always say they have to respect elders.... Our family values are different from the other person.

Other participants were concerned about achieving an appropriate balance between teenagers' social activities and the risks these might pose to their well-being or schoolwork. Issues of emotional and personal well-being were at the forefront of many maternal concerns.

These accounts of 'normal' teenage troubles were informed by mothers' reflections on their own experiences of growing up. Some women emphasised new social risks for young people; others pointed to continuities in lived experiences or more progressive aspects of social change, such as the greater mutual openness of parents and teenagers about issues such as family relationships, feelings, sexual orientation, bullying or personal problems. However, some felt that there had been changes that undermined parental authority, made teenagers' lives more risky and insecure, and increased parental anxiety. For example, Kim felt that it was now harder for parents to "provide moral boundaries and guidance" as "teenagers were too empowered", "family and school discipline" was less effective and TV programmes and the Internet were influential. She talked about the power of peer pressure and teenagers' ease of access to drugs and alcohol – with the latter issue requiring tougher regulation:

> When they are teenagers, peer pressure is so much stronger and alcohol and drugs are so readily available. When I was younger, if you wanted to buy alcohol, it was a lot of money. But now cider is less than a pound. My view is that the drinking and smoking age should be raised.

Sarah, a mother who worked as a professional within children's services, felt that young people were "more open and aware of their rights". Rather than young people facing new risks, she thought that some risks had become more pervasive:

> Teenagers are more open in a way and will talk about things. And they are more aware of their rights. But there is more bullying or at least it seems to be getting more severe maybe. The drugs are also a bigger issue than they were. Criminal behaviour has always existed too – but the severity and the age group – a younger age group is getting more severe in their behaviour.

For the three grandmothers who were interviewed, an important motivation for attending the course was to seek advice on contemporary teenage troubles and, as Vera stated, "top up on parenting skills", in recognition of perceived generational divides.

These women were engaging in the kinds of reflective, responsible and preventive thinking encouraged by parenting education policies. Many reported learning useful parenting and communication strategies on the course, and receiving valuable reassurance and support, although there was little focus in the programme on many of the issues previously highlighted. The psychologist who designed the parenting course referred to this group as the "worried well". Their 'normal' troubles were not intended to be the focus of the programme. Rather, it was parents whose teenagers were troublesome in some way who were the primary target group.

Troublesome young people

The policy aim of the parenting course was primarily to teach parents how to interact with their children in such a way as to manage their behaviour and prevent children from becoming troublesome to others, truanting from school and, as a consequence, failing to achieve educationally. The problem was constructed as one of 'conduct disorder', which is to be 'ordered' and controlled by better communication, by appropriate regimes of praise and reward, and imposing sanctions and adult limits (see Box 23.1). Thus, the focus was on behaviours that are problematic or harmful to others (externalising behaviours), in contrast to internalising behaviours, such as depression, anxiety or eating disorders, which are directed against the self (Achenbach, 1982).

Many of the participants, therefore, attended the course due to concerns about 'troublesome youth'. They had generally been recommended to attend by a member of the Youth Offending Team (YOT) because of their child's engagement with the YOT. It was often not until this occurred that mothers got access to a service that responded to troublesome behaviour, which had been going on for some time. Debbie described the difficulties she had had with her two younger daughters, aged 16 and 14:

> I had both of them not going to school, it was a stress, it really was a stress on my head, so that's why I went there, and with the attitude and kicking the walls and everything, doors and stuff like that.

Kim described how her son would "get into real rages and anger and violence, my house would be completely trashed". Later she described how her older son had:

> trashed rooms with no regard to his own safety and he's attacked his brother and on the flip side, then his brother, now getting older, has then physically attacked him to the degree he did it with a bike chain, a huge bike chain.

A number of other mothers and grandmothers described experiences where after some involvement with different services, such as the police, social services and mental health services, they felt that they had been left to cope with serious violence at home with little or no support. Margaret's son, aged 15, had been "constantly in trouble with the police", including stealing from cars and robbery with a fake firearm, but the trouble he gave his parents was a more hidden problem:

> I mean he broke our bedroom door, we have a Yale lock on and we have a big padlock on because we keep all the valuables in there 'cos we've gone through five digital cameras, a laptop, numerous amount of money. I mean I sleep with my purse under my pillow because he used to creep into the bedroom at night and he'd take money out of my purse so that's the only way to stop that.

She described her efforts to get help:

> It's so hard when you're doing everything you can and, we've done, I mean, we've been everywhere! We had a social worker; they've closed the case 'cos they said there's nothing they can do. We've had family intervention team. Because Matthew won't engage with them, they closed the case, nothing they can do.

Mothers in this situation were caught in a dilemma. On the one hand, they were desperate for help and, on the other hand, they were afraid of being judged a 'bad mother' if they attended a parenting course because of the problems they were experiencing. Mary said that she had not told her friends or family about attending the course: "when you say, 'Oh I'm on parenting group', they look at you, you think they're looking at you, saying, 'Oh she's a bad mother' or something".

Several participants believed that going on a parenting course involved being identified as a bad parent. Kim said: "At one stage I thought to myself, 'Why am I going on it?' Because I think I'm a good parent." She had a clear sense that the categorisation into 'good parent/bad parent' was not a helpful way to understand the dynamics of parent–child relationships, and that young people's behaviour could not be understood as a simple outcome of how she had conducted herself as a mother:

> I deem myself to be a good parent as such and I've always had boundaries and I've always had y'know discipline and understanding and talking, but when their dad left, it was just like a light switch came on and everything that they were never allowed to do, they were now gonna do, smoke, take drugs, drink, stay out.

The parenting course dealt exclusively with the dyadic relationship between parent (in practice, mother/grandmother) and child, and with helping parents develop techniques of communication, positive reward for good behaviour and the maintenance of firm boundaries. The focus of the course on this dyadic relationship essentially constructed parenting as occurring in an abstract space where other relationships and practical, material and social factors are filtered out. However, the mothers' accounts indicated for them that the reality of their lives with troublesome teenage children was very different.

In most cases, women were coping with their troublesome teenage child on their own, either as a lone parent or because their partner was unable or unwilling to be as involved. Sometimes, this was because of their partner's work commitments. Many mothers felt that they had a qualitatively different relationship with their children from that which fathers (or stepfathers) had. Anne, a single mother, described the difference in her daughter's relationship with her two parents:

> She'll talk to me more, her personal – oh, I mean, well, she'll talk to me about different things. I mean, she sees me every day, she doesn't see him every day and she might tell me things … I know a bit more about her friends and stuff like that whereas she's not so personal with him, you know.

This closer relationship also made her more emotionally vulnerable to her daughter:

[I]t's a bit easier for him 'cos he doesn't live with her. I live with her and she's very different with him than what she is with me … she knows how to push me, she knows what buttons to press.

Even when the parents were not separated, it was often the mother who bore the brunt of the child's difficult behaviour, with the father playing a much more limited role. From participants' accounts, the gendered division of responsibility for children between the parents was not an issue that was addressed in the course, but seemed rather to be accepted as part of the context in which mothers had to operate. Women themselves felt that fathers had neither the time nor the inclination to discuss parenting problems in a group context.

One consequence of fathers' relative lack of engagement and mothers' anxieties about being judged a bad mother, combined with the emotional and practical difficulties of coping with very difficult behaviour by their teenage children, was that women were often very isolated, and this added further to their distress and feelings of desperation. The parenting course was helpful in reducing this isolation and providing a space in which mothers could talk about the difficulties they were experiencing and, through hearing about others' experiences, feel that they were not alone. This was a valued aspect of the course for all the women in the study, and for some, whose problems were very severe, it was the principal benefit they derived from attending the course. Margaret commented:

They did once say to me, 'There isn't an awful lot I can say to you is there?' And I said, 'No, but I enjoy coming because I'm getting the chance to say what I'm, what's going on, I'm listening to other people'…. And it was, it's an awful thing to say, but it was an outing. It was away from here and away from [son].

However, with few fathers involved in the course, these benefits were not extended to them and there was little engagement with fathers', partners' or other family members' 'troubles' and concerns.

Many of the mothers believed that they had learned valuable skills through the course, around communication in particular, and support to change their parenting style. They were equally clear, however, that these changes in their style of interaction were unlikely to change their troublesome teenagers' behaviour and that they were struggling against a whole range of influences in the wider environment. In particular, peer influence was a significant problem that they felt they could do little about: "It's the group, he hangs around with a gang of lads and it's the group he's hanging around with, erm they range from 14 up to 20. And none of them go to school so they're all wandering about' (Margaret). The ideal solution for Margaret would have been to move house: "if we could afford to move tomorrow, I would do".

Bullying and repeated truancy from school were other issues that the mothers sometimes reported as problems they found difficult to 'solve'. In general, mothers understood their children's troublesome behaviour as stemming from a number of different influences and experiences, including family 'troubles'. Furthermore, in many cases, this troublesome behaviour was understood as a response to troubling experiences, sometimes many years earlier. These are discussed in the following section.

Troubled young people

In describing the family circumstances that had led them to attend the parenting course, several mothers described a history of abusive relationships, which had had a significant effect on their children. Kim's husband had been violent towards her and physically and emotionally abusive towards their two sons – the latter of which she stated that she was unaware of at the time. Their release from his abuse when it was eventually revealed, and he left the home, had precipitated the sons' violent and self-harming behaviour, but the trauma they had suffered was such that it was difficult to address and repair:

> The biggest problem we had is all three of us, we're all dealing with our own issues so it was hard to deal with anybody else's, so I tended to get angry quite a lot of the time if, if violence kicked off.

Mothers also identified the troubling effects of illness for teenage children, either directly or indirectly because of the attention needed by another family member. Several teenage children had long-term health problems, which their mothers saw as having psychological effects that contributed to difficult behaviour. Debbie described the effects of her daughter's disability on their relationship:

> She's been in, in and out of hospital … having operations since she was six. She's got scoliosis, curvature of the spine you see so, so she's had, missed out on a load of schooling and stuff and after so many years, I started to put my foot down and because I put my foot down, she doesn't like it, you see, so – cos she's always got her own way, cos I didn't know what else I could do with her, do you know what I mean?

In several cases, maternal concerns about their child's behaviour had been dismissed in earlier contact with services. Cathy described her health visitor's response when she asked for help, when her son was two: "he really, he did have behaviour problems but there was nobody to help me. I asked my health visitor and she went, 'Oh he'll grow out of it don't worry' and I thought 'Oh I hope this kid does.'"

Even when children's troubled behaviours led to a referral to appropriate services, this might not help if the child refused to engage. This was an issue for Debbie, whose 14- and 16-year-old daughters had been referred to a clinic for children and adolescents:

they go to [clinical psychology service], it's a psychiatrist place sort of thing, you know, where they can talk and stuff.... But they don't really open out to him you see, that's the only problem, they don't open out.... They, like, say 'Oh, everything's alright', when it's not alright.

Jane's son also did not want to engage with the family intervention team: "We was working with family intervention team as a family but the child that we needed the help with wasn't getting involved."

Despite the intention of the EPS that the parenting course should be for parents with mild to moderate parenting problems emerging in early adolescence, it was clear from the accounts of the majority of the 23 women we interviewed that many of them had been struggling for years with very difficult behaviour on the part of one or more children. The behaviour was troublesome to others, and it was this that led services to recommend the course to the mother, but the problematic behaviour was also understood by mothers as a consequence of experiences that had been or continued to be troubling for their child. The parenting course allowed them to share these experiences with others who had had similar difficulties, but it did not attempt to address some of these more fundamental issues. Its approach, focusing on communication and behavioural management as matters of technique, was one-dimensional. The wider family dynamics and the relationship of the family and the teenage child to very significant aspects of the wider environment – neighbourhood and school – were not included, and this limited what it could achieve. As one mother put it: "I was thinking at the time, it's a great course but it doesn't, you know, it doesn't go on, it doesn't go deep enough into this, that and the other."

Conclusion

Parenting courses for families with adolescents have been introduced in Britain as part of a broader set of policies to address behaviour that is socially problematic in a variety of ways: anti-social behaviour, criminal behaviour or truanting from school. They are premised on the assumption that 'parenting' is a matter of managing behaviour through appropriate systems of reward and punishment, and that with the right techniques, behaviour that is troubling to others, or threatens to become so in the future, can be brought under control. The delivery of such courses through group sessions over a relatively short period of time (eight to 12 weeks) implies that such techniques are straightforward to learn and that the social learning involved in group delivery is an effective way to teach the skills required. The parenting course for the parents of young adolescents examined in this chapter had been designed to offer an intervention at the point of transition to secondary school, identifying this as a significant moment in the development of parent–child relations.

Many of the women who had completed the course had found aspects of it useful and reassuring, normalising some of the difficulties they were experiencing in their relationship with their teenage child. However, it is also clear that their understanding of the troubles they faced as mothers/grandmothers differed in important ways from the ideas that informed the course design – and those of the most widely used standardised parenting programmes, such as Triple P or Webster Stratton. Implicit in the content and approach of the course was the assumption that the origins of difficult adolescent behaviour can be localised in both time and place, and that troublesome behaviour can be changed by maternal implementation of a set of techniques at home. The focus on the parent/mother–child dyad as the key site for change in order to change young people's behaviour excluded consideration of the difficulties that arose from the wider social and material environment in which families lived. The concern with behaviour marginalised maternal worries about their adolescent child's more general well-being and their ability successfully to navigate the wider social environment. A number of mothers/grandmothers who were dealing with very difficult behaviour understood this as a manifestation of long-standing problems, which were not a simple matter of inadequate parenting, but had their origins in both difficult family relationships, health problems and the wider social environment. The parenting course was unable to address these more profound and complex issues, or even acknowledge their significance. While these other troubling factors remain unacknowledged, parenting education will continue to carry the implication of parental (maternal) blame for the troubles others experience from teenagers. Further, when parenting education programmes fail to acknowledge the complexity of 'family troubles' and effectively collaborate with other family and youth services – or when there is insufficient availability of a wider range of specialist support services – opportunities are missed to help mothers and families to access help and advice that may enable them to support young people better.

Notes

[1] The Children's Fund was part of the Labour government's strategy to reduce social exclusion. It ran from 2000 to 2008 at a total cost of £960 million. It provided funds for preventive services for children aged five to 13 at risk of social exclusion and whose needs were not covered by existing statutory services (Pinnock and Evans, 2008).

[2] 'Conduct disorder' refers to 'one of three subclasses of disruptive behaviour disorder of children' that has been correlated with adult criminality and anti-social behaviour. It has been differentiated into early onset and late onset, the latter referring to the absence of characteristic criteria before the age of 10 (Coid, 2004, pp 49–50).

[3] Three measures were used: the Strengths and Difficulties Questionnaire (SDQ) (Goodman, 1997); the Conflict Behaviour Questionnaire (CBQ) (Prinz et al, 1979); and the Parenting Scale (Adolescents) (Arnold et al, 1993).

References

Achenbach, T.M. (1982) *Developmental psychopathology*, New York, NY: John Wiley and Sons.

Arnold, D.S., O'Leary, S.G., Wolff, L.S. and Acker, M.M. (1993) 'The parenting scale: a measure of dysfunctional parenting in discipline situations', *Psychological Assessment*, vol 5, no 2, pp 137–44.

Churchill, H. and Clarke, K. (2010) 'Investing in parenting education: a critical review of policy and provision in England', *Social Policy and Society*, vol 9, no 1, pp 39–53.

Clarke, K. and Churchill, H. (2012) '"A chance to stand back": parenting programmes for parents of adolescents', *Children and Society*, vol 26, no 4, pp 316–27.

Coid, J. (2004) 'Formulating strategies for the primary prevention of adult anti-social behaviour: "High risk" or "population" strategies?', in D. Farrington and J. Coid (eds) *Early prevention of adult anti-social behaviour*, Cambridge: CUP.

Goodman, R. (1997) 'The strengths and difficulties questionnaire: a research note', *Journal of Child Psychology and Psychiatry*, vol 38, no 5, pp 581–6.

HM Government (2011) *A new approach to child poverty: tackling the causes of disadvantage and transforming family lives*, Cm 8061, London: Crown Copyright.

Pinnock, K. and Evans, R. (2008) 'Developing responsive preventative practices: key messages from children's and families' experiences of the Children's Fund', *Children and Society*, vol 22, no 2, pp 86–98.

Prinz, R.J., Foster, S.L., Kent, R.N. and O'Leary, K.D. (1979) 'Multivariate assessment of conflict in distressed and non-distressed parent–adolescent dyads', *Journal of Applied Behavior Analysis*, vol 12, no 4, pp 691–700.

CHAPTER TWENTY-FOUR

Contested family practices and moral reasoning: updating concepts for working with family-related social problems

Hannele Forsberg

This chapter focuses on complex, ambiguous and ethically charged problem situations with children and families, which it is partly the responsibility of social work to resolve. The focus is mainly on the special challenges that such situations give to professionals, although, in all probability, the problematic situations that are discussed here are much more demanding to the family members involved. The ultimate goal is to discuss the need for developing new conceptual angles to overcome some of the current difficulties with the conventional conceptualisations of 'family problems' in the context of social work, particularly from the Finnish perspective. New conceptual approaches are needed because of the increasing pluralism and complexity of family practices and values, which sometimes makes the distinction between what is ordinary and what is exceptional far from clear.

The chapter is divided into three sections. In the first, I discuss briefly the conventional orientation of social work with regard to family problem situations and the need to rework and elaborate it in the context of complex, uncertain, ethically demanding troubling situations. Second, as an example of a special and deeply challenging conflict situation, I will examine supervised meetings between children and non-resident parents, designed to ensure the continuity of family contact. This example allows me to concretise the moral and remedial dimensions of work with family troubles. I interpret these dimensions as hints of the (ultimate) boundaries of a normal and looked-for family. Third, I will argue that because the situations are ethically arresting and new and previous information and experience are of little help, this work with 'family change' becomes more deeply challenging and different. I propose that the conscious integration of moral reasoning as part of professional expertise — and, thus, expanding the concept of knowledge — may help us to realise the boundaries of our expertise and the need for new knowledge, and to form an appropriate direction for our actions.

From family problems towards contested family practices

In theoretical debates on social work, change-oriented work with families is usually approached in the framework of the research tradition concerning various family problems. In this tradition, family problems are sometimes located inside the family as interpersonal problems, and sometimes as problems stemming from broader societal factors, such as economic depression, unemployment and cutbacks in social benefits. Attempts are also made to anticipate and prevent family problems, for example, by means of risk identification. Approaches based on previous knowledge are, however, often inadequate and see phenomena as too simplified when the problem situation at hand is difficult, contested and ethically challenging. In the same way, newer traditions that rely on an unlimited relativism and focus on the interpretive nature of family problems, seeing problems as more relative phenomena linked to time, place, speaker position and mutual negotiation, may fail to address the challenge of ethical responsibility inherent in these situations.

Instead of 'family problems' typically spoken of in traditional social work debate, I draw on the idea of 'family practices' presented by David Morgan (1996, 2011). By family practices, I refer to decisions that concern family life and are implemented by both ordinary people and professionals in their daily practices (Morgan, 1999, pp 18–19). I propose the concept *contested family practices* for referring to family practices that are special, difficult, considered ethically charged and conflict-ridden for one reason or another, and for which there exist no clear-cut answers known in advance. The first part of the concept, 'contestedness', refers to a disagreement on the nature or task of family relationships or on the expectations or rights associated with them. It arises out of conflicts of interest between family members or conflicting interpretations of family relationships embraced by cultures, legislation or professionals. The concept is characterised by fragmentation, different angles and lack of objectivity – the view depends on from whose viewpoint it is looked at. There may be several normative structures concerning families, they may overlap and conflict with each other, and so the content of the contestedness is not always easy to define. 'Practices', in turn, refers to the fact that family relationships are 'not just' interpersonal relationships, but simultaneously also cultural conceptions and institutional practices (Forsberg and Pösö, 2009, pp 149–50). It is important to capture and examine simultaneously the family relationships and the social structures that mediate the contestedness associated with them.

The increasing liberalisation and proliferation of the values associated with families also challenge us to redefine the concepts vis-a-vis family situations interpreted as problematic. Current Western societies are habitually characterised by increasing pluralism and tolerance of multiple family values and practices. It has been suggested that instead of universal societal norms, the everyday negotiations of values by ordinary people (or professionals and family individuals) have come to hold a central position in the solving of family conflicts (eg Morgan, 1996, 2011; Lewis, 2001; Smart, 2004). An example of this is divorce legislation, which has become more neutral. Neither party is any longer defined as guilty; rather, divorce is seen as the private choice of the spouses. Consequently, many researchers have pointed out that the external morals of family relationships, based on social rules, have increasingly been replaced by new, inductive ethics. Nevertheless, although coupledom is no longer regulated by external norms, the same is not true for the parent–child relationship (Lewis, 2001, pp 87–94; cf Ribbens McCarthy et al, 2000). Carol Smart (2004) writes of these phenomena in the context of divorce and post-divorce family life: people have to make decisions about how to act, how to relate, how to prioritise, how to safeguard their children and how to balance and reconstruct family living. The changing nature of family life pushes people to negotiate new moral principles, and this, in turn, is generating new ways of 'doing' family life. Families have more 'choices' about which relationships to sustain, but it is these very choices that demand the reflexivity that is part of the emergent moral code identified (Smart, 2004).

The supervised meetings[1] to be discussed later – on the basis of retrospective accounts of the social care workers involved in them[2] – are an example of a contested family practice. They are an institutional practice that takes a stand on, changes and modifies the relationships between family members. In the background there is a disagreement on how family members should maintain their mutual contacts. Supervised meetings concern a very special group of parents undergoing divorce/separation: "Normal is not a word you'd use to describe what they have", is how one of the supervisors expressed it. These workers define certain aspects of the meetings as highly confusing and contested. In this context, I will discuss the moral and remedial dimensions of the meetings on the basis of accounts from professionals who supervised them. In addition to lawyers and psychologists, social workers play an important part in this work. The municipal social workers arrange supervised meetings according to court orders related to divorce situations, and also play a part in assessing the success of the meetings on the basis of information received from the supervisors. In child welfare situations, the municipal social workers may independently restrict meetings on child welfare grounds. In certain situations, the social worker may team up with the supervisor at the meetings.

Deeply challenging conflict situations: supervised contacts

This nine-year-old boy is not motivated to meet with his father, he refuses to come. We need to work hard to get him to agree to a meeting. It makes you wonder whose interest it serves that these meetings are set up. The child vomits, has stomach ache and headache. He's afraid, you can see it as soon as he arrives, that he's just about panicking. The father has a restraining order with regard to his family because of violence. The court has decided that the father may meet his child three times a week under supervision. The mother tells us that she has had to persuade the child at home as best she can. The father's lawyer stresses that the court order must not be opposed. The family clinic where the boy has therapy because of his symptoms, has recommended that the meetings should be stopped. And it does feel

> pretty bad when still, after 13 supervised meetings, the child's reaction
> towards his father is the same. (Supervisor)

The divorcing family in the example is not an instance of the modern ideal of negotiation and private choice of the divorce solution best suited to their needs – personal 'good practices'. Because of their conflict, the parents resort to the morals of societal rules. The supervisor's description shows the range of the actors involved, with conflicting angles and interests, and a power hierarchy between them. We are dealing with contested family practices here. The viewpoints of father, mother and child are mutually conflicting. In addition, the solutions proposed by the professionals, all appealing to the child's best interest, stress different things. Professional practices often strongly rely on and appeal to law and judicial practice and existing psychological and psychiatric expert knowledge. In contrast, moral conflicts are ignored at the outset through the stress laid on moral principles typical of liberal rational values, or individual autonomy and rights (cf Haste, 1998; Forsberg and Vagli, 2006).

The principal moral justification for supervised meetings is based on the interpretation of what is the child's best interest (Auvinen and Kaivosoja, 2003). Thus, maintaining contact with the non-resident parent is seen as an instance of this even when parenting is 'deviant' in one way or another. The child's best interest is a universal moral code based on the principle of justice. However, the idea of the child's best interest falls apart when the logic of the meetings is evaluated locally and close by.

First, despite the conflict inherent in situations like the case outlined earlier, the workers' experience is that most supervised meetings work reasonably well in the long run. The child may be confused, even fearful, during the early meetings, but with several meetings, they become more acceptable to the child. At least momentarily, it is possible to observe that the child is happy and pleased at meeting the parent. The supervisors' active support measures, which they resort to from time to time, are important in this sense. The parents may also change and their problem situation may become less acute. In such situations, the supervised meetings ultimately become successful from the child's point of view (Forsberg and Pösö, 2008). The conflict is resolved. In this way, over time, even difficult parental relationships may be 'normalised' and the problematic situation may 'return to normal'.

Second, some of the meetings continue to be problematic and highly confusing. They cause continual uncertainty in the contact worker as to what really is in the child's best interest. The prevailing conceptual framework, which dictates that family contact should be supported because of the child's best interest, is not working. In such circumstances, the professionals repeatedly ask whether it is right for them to support such situations:

> I've been wondering as to what would be wisest in this situation.
> We've got a family where the mother comes to meet her little son,

and she has behaved violently towards him at home. And the boy has been scared to death about seeing his mother. He goes to therapy. He is in foster care. And then these meetings are arranged by force, since the mother wants them. The boy has said clearly that 'I don't want to – I'm frightened'. So you wonder where the child's voice has got to, my goodness, he's made to come by force. Like if we're supposed to look after the child's best interest, and the child is, after all, eight or nine – this boy I mean – and he says 'No', then surely he has some sort of sense, I mean he ought to be heard. (Supervisor)

In asking whether it is right to support this activity, the professionals also inquire as to the justification and grounds of institutional activity. The questions activate moral debate, and open up both the possibility of moral reasoning and negotiation regarding the norms for family relationships implemented in supervised meetings. This could be described as hints on the (ultimate) boundaries of normal and looked-for family relationships and the special challenges of professional work at the boundaries.

Moral reasoning is activated when the professionals are alerted to the characteristics of supervised meetings that involve moral dilemmas. Some of the interviewees had become resigned to the fact that "there is nothing you can do about it, the court order must be obeyed". They had recognised the moral dilemma, but handed over the responsibility to other authorities. Although the activity appears confusing and even wrong in a moral sense, it was interpreted as conforming to the law and not discussed further.

However, the process may also involve taking responsibility for situations with a moral dilemma, as well as reflecting on whether some action is needed. The supervisors' retrospective accounts describe explicit means of assuming responsibility in unexpected/unpredicted situations, which can be interpreted as morally debatable and potentially harmful from the child's viewpoint. These include: a) interrupting a meeting; b) arranging meetings less frequently; and c), in some cases, refusing to continue arranging the meetings:

But indeed, we have had to interrupt a meeting a few times. The children have been so weepy that we've had to. They have begun to, begun to cry terribly and sort of wanted to leave and then we've interrupted the meeting. (Supervisor)

The court has decided that the father is entitled to meet the child three times a week. We considered that it could not be more than once a week, absolutely. Simply because the children would have to travel too often over too long distances to come to the meetings. (Supervisor)

I'm reminded of a parent with mental illness who had behaved in a threatening way with a knife even earlier. Things went so that there was a violent attack against the person who was bringing the child in. After that, we decided that we no longer arrange the meetings. The matter was then taken to court and we gave a statement about why we have stopped them [supervised meetings]. It was the first time for, after this experience, to comment that it may not be in the child's best interest to continue the meetings. (Supervisor)

The 'quality criteria' for the family tie between parent and child after a divorce or separation supported by societal means are broad and flexible from the viewpoint of supervised meetings. The concept of 'normal' is interpreted liberally in this context. In exceptional cases, a child's strong objections may temporarily suspend the meetings, but it is more likely that the meetings are cancelled because the non-resident parent forgets or is unable to attend due to being ill. It is only when a child is 12 years old (age mentioned in law) that his/her opinions are considered weighty enough to be taken into account in arranging the meetings; children over this age are actually quite rarely seen in supervised meetings (see Forsberg and Pösö, 2008). The supervisors may also intervene in what the parents say or do if they think it is harmful to the child. The boundary of 'normal' is encountered in situations where the supervisors end up stopping the meetings on their own initiative; in doing so, they challenge the a priori interpretation that the parental tie should be maintained 'even by force' as being in the child's best interest. These situations come up when a parent is violent enough to assault someone in connection with a meeting. In addition, some of the units arranging supervised meetings systematically refuse to arrange supervised meetings when they know there is proven incest between parent and child.

Moral reasoning: navigation in exceptional situations

The narrow and mechanical concept of knowledge underlying the traditional orientation of experts overlooks value issues on what is good and bad, right and wrong. Ethics, however, directs attention to uncertainty: it underlines the importance of continuously pondering on right and wrong, good and bad (Venkula, 2005, p 34). The moral reasoning activated in the accounts of professionals involved with supervised meetings is connected with the knowledge/competence needed in problem-solving situations that are a priori complex and ambiguous. At the same time, moral reasoning highlights the need to revise ways of action. The importance of putting into words this angle and preparing a discursive space for it has recently and repeatedly been taken up in international debate on social work with children and families (eg Lonne et al, 2009, pp 114–30). Activity of the type of moral reasoning is believed to provide professionals with a deeper ongoing capacity for action.

The special nature of supervised meetings and the ethically arresting quality of situations associated with them, their newness and the lack of previous knowledge and experience make this work with 'family change' more deeply challenging and different. In the 1960s, it was still generally thought that a child's contact with a parent living elsewhere and grappling with a severe alcohol problem, for instance, are not necessarily good for the child. Now that "aggressive, delusional, manipulative parents, missing meetings and blaming each other", common descriptors given by supervisors, can meet their children under supervision by professionals, we are facing a new situation in which previous experience or general expert knowledge on post–divorce parenting is not necessarily of much help. The question of how to respond best to such a difference requires the conscious integration of moral reasoning as part of professional expertise. This orientation may alert us to the boundaries of expertise, the need for new knowledge and the need to formulate an appropriate direction in ethically challenging situations when a clear direction is impossible to identify otherwise.

When supervised meetings were first instituted, the underlying thought was that the supervisors should only supervise and not really intervene in the meetings. When the workers' moral reasoning was taken seriously in the studied meeting practices, one of the things noticed was that in addition to the general norm on the continuity of post–divorce parenting, we need interpretive frameworks related to special situations. For example, as Janet R. Johnston (2001) suggests, the fear that some children express towards the non–resident parent in these situations may be due to previous experiences of violence and abuse, and therefore some of the children can only settle down when they no longer need to meet the parent. From the viewpoint of such a trauma framework, it is justified to be sensitive in recognising the special situations where forcing the children to attend supervised meetings is not in their best interest.

Knowledge that informs professional activity is often equated with technical–rational scientific knowledge applied to practical problem situations. Nevertheless, the professionals' activity in practical situations cannot be wholly reduced to such knowledge. In practice, family problems are not manifested to the workers in the same way as they are manifested as research information, often being vague, 'messy' and contested. In such situations, knowledge is often tacit and implicit, and it grows out of the dialogue among those involved. The dialogue also helps to clarify and make evident the special nature and uncertainty of the situation and eventual value conflicts. This interactive knowledge lives and proliferates thanks to reflection during activity, and it is more flexible and application–oriented than technical–rational knowledge (Schön, 1983, 1987; Parton and O'Byrne, 2000, p 32).

As a result of the group discussions held with the supervisors in the course of the study, the practices of different units became known and shared by the workers and contributed to mutual reflection. At the same time, activity was developed in a new direction: new recommendations were drawn up to specify the nature of work with supervised meetings further. Among other things, the recommendations stipulate zero tolerance towards violent behaviour during the meetings.

The education of professionals working with family problems relies largely on teaching a combination of research-based knowledge and practical skills. It is not enough to provide unambiguous rules and informational content; in addition, practice with complex problem situations should be included. In this respect, moral reasoning is essential. Recognising family changes is an unavoidable part of the contextual understanding of the concept of moral reasoning (St. John, 2009, pp xiv–xix).

Concluding remarks

I have discussed complex, ambiguous and ethically challenging family problem situations encountered in social work. My ultimate interest lies in the conceptual tools needed to do challenging specialist work. The existing approaches to family problems, based on previous knowledge, are often inadequate and oversimplifying when dealing with a new kind of complex and mutually conflicting viewpoints. I use the concept 'contested family practices' for such situations. Supervised meetings between children and their non-resident parents have been considered as a case example of the interpretive frameworks related to the normality/exceptionality of a family undergoing changes because of divorce/separation. The practices in supervised meetings bring out the predominance of the Western 'pro-contact' norm. In this sense, the negotiation of boundaries between what is normal and exceptional that takes place during the supervised meetings exemplifies something that is more general and widespread in the cultural rules and conceptions of modern society (cf Garfinkel, 1984). Norms on post-divorce parenting are being reproduced, but also challenged, and one forum in which they are negotiated is worker accounts of supervised meetings. A greater sensitivity to contested situations opens up a perspective on the workers' contextual moral reasoning and on the boundaries of what is normal in family relationships. At the same time, it is possible to capture the need for new knowledge and the grounds for appropriate activity to protect the most vulnerable party.

Acknowledgements
My work was supported by the Senior Scientist project funding of the Academy of Finland (2009/10).

Notes
[1] In Finland, a court may order the meetings between the child and the non-resident parent to be supervised if there are justified grounds for assuming that they constitute a risk to the child's safety (safety risks typically arise if the parent has serious mental disturbance or substance abuse problems or is violent, or if there is the risk that the child may be kidnapped) (Auvinen and Kaivosoja, 2003, p 28).

[2] The research data is based on group interviews with persons working at the meeting places provided by the Federation of Mother and Child Homes and Shelters in Finland (the largest provider of meeting place services in the country). The supervisors interviewed

(17) are all qualified social (care) workers. The group interviews were arranged in 2003 at a time when the meeting place activity was being developed by the Federation. The data is part of a larger research project, conducted with my colleague Tarja Pösö, on the best interest of the child in supervised meetings. Minor modification/changes have been made in the data extracts in order to protect the participants' anonymity.

References

Auvinen, M. and Kaivosoja, M. (2003) *Lapsen turvallisuus komplisoituneessa huoltoriidassa. Työryhmämuistioita,* (huoltoriidassa (The safety of the child in the complicated custody dispute) Helsinki: Sosiaali- ja terveysministeriö.

Forsberg, H. and Pösö, T. (2008) 'Ambiguous position of the child in supervised meetings', *Child and Family Social Work,* vol 13, no 1, pp 52–60.

Forsberg, H. and Pösö, T. (2009) 'Valvottujen tapaamisten näyttämö: vieraan ja perhesidoksen rajankäyntiä' ('The stage of the supervised meetings: negotiation of the boundaries of "tranger" and family unity'), in R. Jallinoja (ed) *Vieras perheessä,* Helsinki: Gaudeamus, pp 146–61.

Forsberg, H. and Vagli, Å. (2006) 'The social construction of emotions in child protection case-talk', *Qualitative Journal of Social Work,* vol 5, no 1, pp 9–31.

Garfinkel, H. (1984) *Studies in ethnometholodogy,* Cambridge: Polity Press.

Haste, H. (1998) 'Communitarianism and the social construction of morality', *Studies on Moral development and Education.* Available at: http://tigger.uic.edu/~lnucci/MoralEd/articles.html (accessed 10 March 2011).

Johnston, J.R. (2001) 'Rethinking parental alienation and redesigning parent–child access services for children who resist or refuse visitation', paper presented at the International Conference on Supervised Visitation, Munich, Germany, 9–10 July.

Lewis, J. (2001) *The end of marriage? Individualism and intimate relations?,* Cheltenham: Edward Elgar Publishing.

Lonne B., Parton N., Thomson J. and Harries, M. (2009) *Reforming child protection,* London and New York: Routledge.

Morgan, D. (1996) *Family connections: an introduction to family studies,* Cambridge: Polity Press.

Morgan, D. (1999) 'Risk and family practices: accounting for change and fluidity in family life', in E.B. Silva and C. Smart (eds) *The 'new' family,* London: Sage, pp 13–30.

Morgan, D. (2011) *Rethinking family practices,* Basingstoke: Palgrave Macmillan.

Parton, N. and O'Byrne, P. (2000) *Constructive social work,* Basingstoke: Palgrave Macmillan.

Ribbens McCarthy, J., Edwards, R. and Gillies, V. (2000) 'Moral tales of the child and the adult: narratives of contemporary family lives under changing circumstances', *Sociology,* vol 34, no 4, pp 785–803.

Schön, D. (1983) *The reflective practitioner: how professionals think in action,* New York, NY: Basic Books.

Schön, D. (1987) *Educating the reflective practitioner: toward a new design for teaching and learning in the professions*, San Francisco, CA: Jossey-Bass.

Smart, C. (2004) 'Changing landscapes of family life: rethinking divorce', *Social Policy and Society*, vol 3, no 4, pp 401–8.

St. John, E.P. (2009) *College organization and professional development. Integrating moral reasoning and reflective practice*, New York, NY: Routledge.

Venkula, J. (2005) *Epävarmuudesta ja varmuudesta (On the certainty and uncertainty)*, Helsinki: Kirjapaja.

CHAPTER TWENTY-FIVE

Working with fathers: risk or resource?

Brid Featherstone

Policies in relation to child support, contact post–divorce and separation, and the reconciliation of paid work and care responsibilities have emerged in many countries over the last decades, with particular implications for men as fathers. This chapter, however, is concerned with developments that seem a particular feature of Anglophone countries such as the US and the UK from the 1990s onwards (Featherstone, 2009), which have called upon practitioners in a variety of welfare and education services to engage fathers and promote their involvement with children. This project has incorporated social investment and moral underclass discourses and highlighted the role of parents and parenting in promoting better outcomes for children (primarily those seen as disadvantaged).

It will be argued that such policy calls have failed to address tensions around the status of fatherhood and changes in family forms and gender relationships, despite preceding decades witnessing a considerable transformation in these. Moreover, the construction is of fathers as resources, with the risks that might be posed by violent or abusive practices left unaddressed. Thus, a normalising project has been pursued that ignores troubling questions about fathering status or their practices in relation to care. In order to accomplish normalisation, use has been made of a very narrow physiologically informed literature, with a neglect of wider sociological interrogations of fathering practices or gender inequalities (see, eg, Doucet, 2006; Dermott, 2008). In contrast, in areas of welfare work such as those concerned with the protection of children, policies have invoked a gender-neutral language of parenting, while practices have appeared to ignore fathers or construct them as risks. Thus, while some men as fathers have been actively invited into families, others have disappeared or been asked to.

However, the risk–resource dichotomy has been troubled to some extent in the child protection arena recently, and this chapter will highlight developments over the last decade that have emerged around working with men, fathering practices and domestic violence. Historically, work with men in relation to domestic violence has operated on the basis of all men as risks and has been promoted by constituencies with strong links to women's organisations and the refuge movement. There have been ongoing critiques of singular explanations or approaches here. These critiques have also emerged in the work around fathering, as practitioners and researchers have engaged with understandings of men as fathers and carers as both troublesome and troubled (Rivett, 2010). Furthermore, the possibilities of working with fathers to move them from risk to resource has emerged (Ferguson and Hogan, 2004). The chapter reflects upon contemporary debates here, highlighting the apparent seductions of split thinking around fathers as risks or resources.

Background

The UK has historically adhered to a strong male breadwinner model, with the post-war welfare settlement locating the meeting of care needs within the private sphere and, in practice, with mothers. This settlement was to be subject to determined assault as part of a neoliberal project from the late 1970s onwards. As Culpitt (1999) notes, a neoliberal project successfully eclipsed the former moral imperatives of mutual obligation that sustained political support for welfare states.

From the 1970s onwards, there were considerable changes in family forms, with a growth in lone parents, an increase in non-resident fathers and, not surprisingly, given the adherence to neoliberalism, a growth in inequalities (Featherstone, 2004). Non-resident fathers became the lightening rod for tensions about changing families, particularly in the 1980s and 1990s, with anxieties expressed across the political spectrum. Child support legislation was introduced in the UK as in a range of countries, although its framing varied (see Lewis, 2002). This was linked to the differing balances drawn between providers of cash and care in differing welfare regimes. In some countries, where the dual-earner model was firmly established and where adult citizenship was tied to participation in the labour market, the focus was more on the care provided by fathers and part of the debate about achieving greater equality in the division of unpaid work as well as paid work. This was not the case in the UK, where the focus was on the burden non-resident fathers were seen to place on welfare budgets.

Alongside concerns about the burdens on the public purse as a result of non-resident fathers not supporting children financially, discourses in countries such as the UK and the US emerged in the 1990s locating non-resident fathers within an 'underclass', variously stressing men's fecklessness and/or the increased power attained by women as a result of the development of the welfare state. A key aspect of such discourses was a concern that boys were lacking male role models as a result of fathers' non-residence, which was assumed automatically to connote absence.

When New Labour came to power in 1997, their commitment to neoliberalism took on a different cast to that of the 'small state' conservatives and they developed an array of interventions to construct 'active citizens':

> The disadvantaged individual has come to be seen as potentially and ideally an active agent in the fabrication of their own existence. Those 'excluded' from the benefits of a life of choice and self-fulfilment are no longer merely the passive support of a set of social determinations: they are people whose self-responsibility and self-fulfilling aspirations have been deformed by the dependency culture, whose efforts at self-advancement have been frustrated for so long that they suffer from

'learned helplessness', whose self-esteem has been destroyed. And it thus follows, that they are to be assisted not through the ministrations of solicitous experts proffering support and benefit cheques, but through their engagement in a whole array of programmes for their ethical reconstruction as active citizens. (Rose, quoted in Culpitt, 1999, p 83)

Engaging fathers in the context of change and complexity

An array of developments ensued under New Labour. While concerns about 'absent' fathers were important in promoting a commitment to strengthening child support policies, concerns about male role models fed into and promoted practice developments. These were also influenced by a wider set of concerns in relation to improving outcomes for children from marginalised backgrounds. As has been well-rehearsed in the literature, New Labour's project around a 'social investment state' obliged considerable investment in services for children and parents. Sure Start was perhaps the classic example here, with an ambitious programme to construct the skilled, healthy and motivated citizens needed for the flexible economy of neoliberalism (Lister, 2006). Within this broader canvas, parents generally were called upon to realise their children's potential as future citizens and, in an unprecedented move, fathers were called upon explicitly as 'resources' for their children. It is important to note here that such developments were not accompanied by robust entitlements for fathers in relation to paternity leave or parental leave, and, indeed, the model of leave adopted promoted mothers as the primary care-givers for children, with fathers in a 'supporting' role (Dermott, 2008). Gender inequalities were reinforced by the failure to develop a universal system of public-funded or supported child care.

Supporting families: a consultation document (Home Office, 1998) was published in 1998 by a new Labour government elected in 1997 and, according to Jack Straw, the then Home Secretary, marked the first-ever government consultation document on the family. Here, a beginning rationale for developing service provision for men as fathers was outlined, which developed further momentum over the next decade. It noted that:

> Increasingly boys and young men *seem* to be having difficulty maturing into responsible citizens and fathers. Declining educational performance, loss of traditional 'male jobs', the growth of a 'laddish' antisocial culture, greater use of drugs, irresponsible teenage fatherhood, and the rising suicide rate *may* all show rising insecurity and uncertainty among young men. (Quoted in Featherstone, 2009, pp 139–40, emphasis added)

The tone was tentative rather than definitive in these sections. However, it then shifted, asserting definitively that fathers have a crucial role to play in their children's upbringing and their involvement can be particularly important to their sons. It noted that most organisations find it much more difficult to encourage fathers to participate in parenting support than mothers. This was to be one of the foci of future work and, indeed, a range of projects directed at fathers did receive funding the following year. This was not to be a one-off, but continued over the subsequent decade. Interestingly, despite the apparent emphasis on fathers providing role models for sons, very few were funded that only focused on this. However, an array of practice developments was funded, both as specialist initiatives and as part of wider projects such as Sure Start (see Featherstone, 2009).

The 'high point' of such developments might be argued to be the then Minister for Children Beverley Hughes' announcement of a 'Think Fathers' campaign in November 2008. This ordered all government departments to 'dad-proof' services, with an expectation from that being that fathers would be involved from birth through early years and schools. Hughes argued that everything was mother-dominated in public services, and that the benefits for children of fathers being involved in their early lives were considerable, not just for boys, although there was a particular effect with sons. Services needed to engage fathers because the relationship with the father was important for a boy's attainment, behaviour and emotional resilience (see Curtis, 2009).

What constructions of fatherhood, motherhood and childhood were practice initiatives predicated upon? Collier and Sheldon (2008) argue that debates about the future of fatherhood have become central to a range of conversations about the changing family, parenting and society. They deploy the idea of 'fragmentation' to describe how broad demographic shifts have led to a position in which genetic fathers have become increasingly 'split' across families. Divorce and separation have played a key role here, with fathers either parenting at a distance or not at all. Men who retain parental roles and responsibilities will, thus, typically do so while living in a different household, perhaps sharing the role of social father with the children's mother's new partner and, if they themselves have re-partnered, possibly living with and parenting the children of their new partner. This involves a very practical kind of fragmentation, where the work of fathering is shared between two or more men. The idea of fragmentation may also reflect aspects of the lived experience of parents themselves – parenting is packed into pockets of time (sometimes court-sanctioned pockets of time), but also fatherhood as a unified concept may no longer be meaningful in a context where there are distinctions between progenitor and carer. Indeed, Ives (2007) suggests the need for a division between causal, material and moral fatherhoods so that the morally meaningful fatherhood as carer can be distinguished from the less morally significant father as progenitor.

While a range of scholars have explored fragmentation within a variety of disciplinary and interdisciplinary contexts, the policy documents promoting practice initiatives under New Labour dealt with it in two ways. The dominant tendency was to ignore fragmentation and assume that fathers are birth fathers who are resident and available to be 'involved' with their children, if services are sufficiently sensitive and engage them. The other tendency was to acknowledge that fathers might be non-resident and demand that services actively engage them, thus involving practitioners in a reordering project irrespective of the wishes of those doing family in specific contexts. Thus, schools were asked to send letters about their children's progress to non-resident fathers and to invite them to school meetings under the Think Father campaign (see Featherstone, 2010). No mention was made of the possible implications for a social father or, indeed, for anyone else of such actions.

Essentially, there was a promotion of fatherhood as unified and anchored to birth. As the earlier quote from Hughes notes, there was a reliance on 'research evidence' to support father involvement in terms of children's outcomes. Many of the documents repeat each other, so let us take *Every parent matters* (Department for Education and Skills, 2007, p 6) as an exemplar of the arguments deployed:

> Research shows that where fathers have early involvement in a child's life there is a positive relationship to early educational attainment; there is an association with good parent–child relationships in adolescence; and children in separated families are protected from mental health problems.

However, the research evidence is not that straightforward. Pleck and Masciardelli (2004) found that in two-parent families with resident fathers, positive father involvement was of value to children. What counts as positive? O'Brien (2005) notes something of a consensus on this, stressing secure attachments and the need for parents to adopt an authoritative parenting style (however, for a critique of the latter from a perspective that takes ethnicity seriously see, Phoenix and Husain, 2007).

An important point missed out consistently in an array of policy documents, but stressed by researchers, is that all family relationships are interrelated and father involvement needs to be understood systemically (Lamb and Lewis, 2004). Moreover, the relationship between mother and father is of central significance and there is considerable evidence of adverse impacts upon children if it is characterised by violence and abuse. Promoting father involvement without acknowledging the importance of the mother's role and assessing their relationship is, therefore, problematic, and this recurs throughout the documents, leading to a consistent failure to discuss violent and abusive practices and a tendency to promote fathers as resources at the expense of recognising risks.

Indeed, fathers (birth fathers) were constructed as abstract figures parachuted in to read to their children (that is often the only concrete activity mentioned as an example of father involvement) and ensure, therefore, that they would have good outcomes. The dyadic focus on fathers and children obscured mothers' care giving work in a context where gendered inequalities persisted (Dermot, 2008).

Mothers were either invisible in the documents or constructed as ignorant of the benefits of father involvement for their children and needing to be educated. In terms of children, they were constructed passively and as outcomes. The notion of role models was deployed without any acknowledgement of the lack of research evidence to support the 'effectiveness' of role-modelling and the considerable literature that highlights the problems with social learning theory as a way of understanding how identities are developed within social practices (see, eg, Hicks, 2008).

A failure to engage with gender and embodiment, in particular, means that a curiously abstract picture was painted that was seriously out of kilter with the reality of men's bodies moving through what had hitherto been women's spaces. Doucet (2006), in her study of fathers as primary care-givers, makes the following key points: fathers spoke as embodied subjects in care-giving; the care of children is social and occurs not only between carer and cared-for, but also within larger sets of social relations, wherein it is perceived and judged; and particular venues, such as nurseries (historically, women–only spaces), draw attention to how space and embodiment constantly intersect. The fathers in her study spoke of feeling 'watched' and of anxiety about themselves as men engaging with children in specific spaces. Men's bodies are often marked as dangerous, especially in risk-averse societies, and there can be particular issues for men from different classes and ethnicities (Featherstone, 2009).

Overall, the decade-long promotion of service initiatives led to a literature on practice skills largely focused on technique, emphasising the need for differing and imaginative engagement strategies. There were limited attempts to interrogate the complexities of men's shifting identities as fathers and to locate father involvement in a wider canvas. It is of interest that in a lot of the documents, violent and abusive practices were ignored. However, there is one arena where this was not possible. In the next section, we explore the child protection arena.

Protecting children: fathers as invisible or as risks?

Alongside the array of new practice sites such as Sure Start, involving practitioners from a variety of backgrounds who were engaged in constructing the children of the future as productive and employable, other practices underwent considerable transformation. A command–and–control approach to social work in the arena of child protection led to a blizzard of initiatives emphasising e-communication, targets and timescales. The 'perfect storm' that ensued from such an emphasis on meeting targets within specific timescales and assuming technological fixes for interpersonal communication on sensitive and nuanced issues was exposed writ large with the death of Baby Peter Connolly, aged 17 months old, in 2007, a child who had been on the local authority's child protection register for the previous eight months, and seen 60 times by a range of agencies. However, in the storm raised by the exposure of how well and truly the audit tail was wagging the practice dog, some more long-standing issues about practices with men, including fathers, went unaddressed.

Baby Peter lived with his birth mother but had contact with his birth father. It transpired after his death that two other men were living in the flat, who were tried and convicted alongside the mother for his death. This case should have opened up discussion about the complexities of working with women's relationships with violent and/or dangerous men. It should also have raised issues about why Baby Peter's birth father was as invisible to services as the men who, it appeared, were hiding in the flat, with disastrous consequences. But it did not raise these issues. This fits within a long-standing pattern and is reflective of a culture where child abuse or protection scandals become focused on systems and procedures rather than on why children are hurt or abused and what might be happening in the adults' lives, relationships and psyches. It also reflects the 'failure' of a gendered analysis to be embedded in thinking about practice, as evident in the continued use of gender-neutral language.

Moreover, in a very limited discussion on the role of the men in the death of Baby Peter, the focus was on the dangers of 'stepfathers', producing a bifurcation between safe birth fathers and dangerous others, which is problematic (Revans, 2009). As Batchelor (2003) has pointed out, methodological problems are rife in the work looking at child abuse and step-parents. Not only is there inconsistency in the definitions of abuse used, but there are difficulties around the term step-parent: 'if abuse is attributed to a stepparent, was he or she a long-standing member of the child's household or one of several transient adults in that child's life?' (Batchelor, 2003, p 203). As she notes, men who have problems in forming close attachments and who have a history of violent relationships may have a series of relationships with vulnerable women, some (or many) of whom may be single parents. These men may come into contact with and abuse a series of children, any or all of whom may be classed as their stepchildren, regardless of whether they have taken on what may be considered to be a parenting role. Similarly, paedophiles may seek out and build relationships with single parents as a means of having ready access to children; their sexual abuse may figure in research as 'abuse by a step-parent'.

However, there has been some growth in developing interventions with men, who are fathers, and who are violent to women, and a limited growth in the associated literature (Harne, 2011). There are a number of differing and often tension-laden reasons for this. A significant development in the UK has been the recognition of domestic violence as a child protection issue. This has led to a considerable increase in referrals to child protection services (Featherstone and Peckover, 2007). While the majority of agency responses have tended to focus on the role of the mother in securing the protection and welfare of the children, there has been some recognition that such responses are unsustainable (in that domestically violent men may rejoin other families). A central imperative has been to improve the welfare of children. Children's services have turned to already-existing programmes designed to tackle men's violence and referred men to these or been involved in developing or promoting newer interventions.

A further development internationally is the increased emphasis in private law on the importance of fathers, even in cases involving domestic violence, retaining contact with their children post-separation and divorce (Harrison, 2006). This has prompted considerable concern among researchers and practitioners in the area of domestic violence. Indeed, Hester (2011) has noted that policies often appear to inhabit different planets, with encouragement to retain contact between fathers and their children on a different one to that seeking to tackle men's violence. The emphasis on contact has been central in reinforcing interventions that incorporate safety-planning for women and children.

An audit of contemporary practice interventions around fathering and domestic violence suggests that they come with different emphases and foci. Indeed, language is very important here, with some interventions starting from a focus on working with men as *perpetrators* and developing fathering inputs in that context, and others coming from what would seem a different tradition with more of a primary focus on them as *fathers* (Ashley, 2011).

In order to understand some of the contemporary differences and tensions, exploring the history is instructive. There is a considerable history of developing programmes that work with men who are violent to women in intimate relationships. These have usually been called *perpetrator* programmes and have their roots in both the therapeutic, anti-sexist men's movement and the women's refuge movement in the US (Featherstone et al, 2007). Historically, it is the latter that emerged to set standards for treatment and safety as a result of concerns that those which had a more therapeutic focus were in danger of excusing men's behaviour. Moreover, they were considered to be too isolated from mainstream services and, therefore, unable to ensure the safety of women and children (Rivett, 2010).

The Duluth programme emerged over time as the foremost programme reflecting a feminist perspective on the causes of violence as rooted in men's control and power over women in a patriarchal society and masculine socialisation practices (Pence and Paymar, 1993). It was, and is, designed to be embedded within a coordinated community response and is not supposed to be a stand-alone programme. It has its origins in community reaction to the murder of a woman in a specific locale. This history is of relevance in understanding the apparent high level of anxiety about moving away from a set format. Safety-planning for women and children is central. It consists of a set format where power, control and equality issues are systematically addressed and where cognitive behavioural therapies are used. This is the model that has been supported by UK governmental guidance and is the regulated programme for criminal justice settings. Practitioners within the field have created a charity called Respect to lay down standards of good practice and to accredit programmes.

Over the years, Duluth programmes have been subject to a number of criticisms. Their set format is considered to be too prescriptive and insufficiently sensitive to the differing needs of differing men attending programmes (Rivett, 2010). An allied critique has contested the underlying theoretical approach, as it assumes singular explanations for why men are violent (Gadd, 2004). A linked critique has contested the reliance on cognitive behavioural approaches and argued for psychosocial approaches that engage with unresolved childhood pain and trauma. A range of writers have suggested the importance of recognising that not all violent men are the same (Gondolf, 2002) and that not all violence is the same (Johnson, 1995). Moreover, it is argued that the role played by factors such as mental health difficulties and substance misuse needs more consideration than that found in Duluth (Rivett, 2010).

Moving towards seeing men as both troublesome and troubled has been an underpinning, if tension-ridden, imperative behind many of these critiques. The originating impulse of the Duluth model was to explain the violence in singular ways and to see any other explanation as part of men's attempts to excuse or minimise their behaviour. This reflects a tendency towards dichotomising approaches as if one level of description or explanation necessarily excludes another. However, there have always been those from within a feminist politics who have argued against this: 'To say that violence, domination, subordination and victimization are psychological does not mean they are not also material, moral or legal' (Goldner et al, 1990, p 345).

With the emergence of a more diverse set of constituencies in this area and the focus on fathering practices, the tensions have unsurprisingly continued, if not intensified. For example, an influential development from Canada has been the 'Caring Dads' programme (Scott and Crooks, 2004). The programme has a both/and philosophy. It relates to men as fathers and as abusers, it contains gender reflections and assumes men can change, and explores men's maltreatment of children generally. While the originators of the programme see it as having a 'fatherhood' focus *and* a 'perpetrator' focus, this is strongly contested by those who would emphasise the need to stress the identity of perpetrator as primary and the necessity of adopting the Duluth format (Respect, 2010).

As indicated, the tensions and anxieties here are linked to long-standing debates within feminist and pro-feminist scholarship and practice. They reflect the continued difficulties with moving away from dichotomising and splitting, especially in relation to understanding and working with men's violence. Highlighting the links between individual men's practices and wider cultural practices in a context of institutionalised power relations was, and is, extraordinarily important. However, it is also important to be alert to, and able to engage with, the variations in men's relationships with power and powerlessness and devise interventions that are responsive and flexible. It is of interest that it does seem possible to criticise 'one-size-fits-all' programmes in other arenas (eg parenting programmes) without the level of tension and anxiety that can attend critiques in the area of domestic violence.

Conclusion

Working with fathers emerged onto policy and practice agendas in the last decade in hitherto unprecedented ways. Overall, it is of interest to consider the differing splits between fathers as resources in one set of policy arenas and subsumed within the category of men as risks in another. Splits in understanding and construction have mapped onto splits in practising, and these have been highlighted when attempting to develop projects that cut across domains such as those concerned with domestic violence.

The fragmentation of fatherhood so apparent in the contemporary landscape has been denied or subject to reordering in the face of a valorisation of the role of birth fathers. Interesting, if tension-ridden, initiatives have emerged to destabilise risk–resource constructions.

References

Ashley, A. (2011) *Working with risky fathers*, London: Family Rights Group.

Batchelor, J. (2003) 'Working with family change; repartnering and stepfamily life', in M. Bell and K. Wilson (eds) *The practitioner's guide to working with families*, Basingstoke: Palgrave/Macmillan.

Collier, R. and Sheldon, S. (2008) *Fragmenting fatherhood: a socio-legal study*, Oxford and Portland, OR: Hart Publishing.

Culpitt, I. (1999) *Social policy and risk*, London: Sage.

Curtis, P. (2009) 'Family policies "dad-proofed" to give fathers bigger role – but no extra paternity leave', *Guardian*, 21 February.

Department for Education and Skills (2007) *Every parent matters*, London: The Stationery Office.

Dermott, E. (2008) *Intimate fatherhood*, London: Routledge.

Doucet, A. (2006) '"Estrogen-filled worlds": fathers as primary caregivers and embodiment', *The Sociological Review*, vol 54, no 4, pp 696–716.

Featherstone, B. (2004) *Family life and family support: a feminist analysis*, Basingstoke: Palgrave Macmillan.

Featherstone, B. (2009) *Contemporary fathering: theory, policy and practice*, Bristol: The Policy Press.

Featherstone, B. (2010) 'Engaging fathers – promoting gender equality?', in B. Featherstone, C.-A. Hooper, J. Scourfield and J. Taylor (eds) *Gender and child welfare in society*, Chichester: Wiley–Blackwell, pp 173–95.

Featherstone, B. and Peckover, S. (2007) 'Letting them get away with it: fathers, domestic violence and child protection', *Critical Social Policy*, vol 27, no 2, pp 181–203.

Featherstone, B., Rivett, M. and Scourfield, J. (2007) *Working with men in health and social care*, London: Sage.

Ferguson, H. and Hogan, F. (2004) *Strengthening families thorough fathers*, Dublin: Family Support Agency.

Gadd, D. (2004) '"Evidence led or policy led evidence": cognitive behavioural programmes for men who are violent towards women', *Criminal Justice*, vol 4, pp 173–97.

Goldner, V., Penn, P., Sheinberg, M. and Walker, G. (1990) 'Love and violence: gender paradoxes in volatile attachments', *Family Process*, vol 29, no 4, pp 343–64.

Gondolf, E. (2002) *Batterer intervention systems*, Thousand Oaks, CA: Sage.

Harne, L. (2011) *Violent fathering and the risks to children*, Bristol: The Policy Press.

Harrison, C. (2006) 'Dammed if you do and dammed if you don't? The contradictions between public and private law', in C. Humphreys and N. Stanley (eds) *Domestic violence and child protection: directions for good practice*, London: Jessica Kingsley.

Hester, M. (2011) 'The three planet model – towards an understanding of contradictions in approaches to women and children's safety in contexts of domestic violence', *British Journal of Social Work*, vol 41, pp 837–53.

Hicks, S. (2008) 'Gender role models …who needs 'em?', *Qualitative Social Work*, vol 7, no 1, pp 43–59.

Home Office (1998) *Supporting families: A consultation document*, www.homeoffice. gov.uk/vcu/suppfam.htm, accessed 1 September 1999.

Ives, J. (2007) 'Becoming a father/refusing fatherhood: how paternal responsibilities and rights are generated', DPhil thesis, University of Birmingham.

Johnson, M. (1995) 'Patriarchal terrorism and common couple violence: two forms of violence against women', *Journal of Marriage and the Family*, vol 57, pp 283–94.

Lamb, M.E. and Lewis, C. (2004) 'The development and significance of father–child relationships in two-parent families', in M.E. Lamb (ed) *The role of the father in child development* (4th edn), Chichester: Wiley, pp 272–307.

Lister, R. (2006) 'Children (but not women) first: New Labour, child welfare and gender', *Critical Social Policy*, vol 26, no 2, pp 315–36.

O'Brien, M. (2005) *Sharing caring: bringing fathers into the frame*, Norwich: University of East Anglia.

Pence, E. and Paymar, M. (1993) *Education groups for men who batter*, New York, NY: Springer.

Phoenix, A. and Husain F. (2007) *Parenting and ethnicity*, York: Joseph Rowntree Foundation.

Pleck, J.H. and Masciardelli, B. (2004) 'Parental involvement by US residential fathers: levels, sources and consequences', in M.E. Lamb (ed) *The role of the father in child development* (4th edn), Chichester: Wiley, pp 222–72.

Respect (2010) *Respect statement on Caring Dads programme*, http/www.respect. uk.net/data/filesrespect_position_on_the caring_dads_programme.pdf (accessed 27 February 2012).

Revans, L. (2009) 'Lurking in the shadows', *Community Care*, 9 April, pp 18–21.

Rivett, M. (2010) 'Working with violent male carers (fathers and step-fathers)', in B. Featherstone, C.-A. Hooper, J. Scourfield and J. Taylor (eds) *Gender and child welfare in society*, Chichester: Wiley, pp 195–223.

Scott, K. and Crooks, C. (2004) 'Effecting change in maltreating fathers', *Clinical Psychology; Science and Practice*, vol 11, pp 95–111.

CHAPTER TWENTY-SIX

What is at stake in family troubles?
Existential issues and value frameworks

Jane Ribbens McCarthy

Introduction

> Wherever one looks on the globe it appears that human beings want
> to be edified by their miseries. It is as if the desire to make suffering
> intelligible and to turn it to some advantage is one of those dignifying
> peculiarities of our species.... Human beings, unlike other living things,
> want to ... make their suffering intelligible, even as it is unwanted.
> (Shweder et al, 1997, p 119)

In this chapter, I ask the question of what is at stake in family troubles, and highlight
some key themes in responding, including: the moral issues of family living and
the care of children; existential issues of shared and variable human experiences of
troubles and suffering in relational lives and the challenges these pose, particularly
in relation to children; and cultural resources for dealing with such experiences.
And I further consider what help is available from philosophers and social scientists
for establishing any frameworks or guiding principles that can avoid a nihilistic
form of cultural relativism in defining family troubles, while remaining sensitive
to the diversities, ambiguities and complexities of the family lives of children and
young people in variable contexts. In this discussion, I seek to keep in mind how
children and young people actively construct meanings through which to make
sense of their everyday interactions and circumstances, but I also reflect on how
adults and social institutions shape the meanings of troubles in children's family
lives and the sorts of resources young people can marshal in order to make sense
of such troubles, and seek some degree of intelligibility in the process.

In considering the question of whether, and how far, troubles may be seen as a
'normal' part of children's changing family lives, we might consider how troubles
may come, for example, in the form of unwelcome changes and challenges (or
their absence), but also in the context of welcome changes that may nevertheless
pose challenges to previous daily normalities, and thus entail some degree or
form of loss (for consideration of the complexities of understanding changes in
children's family lives, see Ribbens McCarthy et al, Chapter One). Yet, it is also
clear that some changes may be more deeply disruptive than others, which, in itself,

raises difficult issues about when and how the changes in children's family lives move beyond a sense of challenge to become disruptive, traumatic and, perhaps, a source of suffering. How and when this occurs, how some parties involved may be more or less troubled than others, and the significance of power in shaping such processes has been the focus for discussions throughout this book. Contributors have discussed a wide range of family troubles, exploring the contestations that occur in particular family situations at specific historic and cultural moments, and demonstrating how far the significance and meaning of particular troubles may, thus, depend on the circumstances, resources and wider contexts in which experiences of family troubles are embedded. Along the way, different contributors have drawn on various conceptual tools and disciplinary frameworks to explore these issues, and how troubles may sometimes be appropriately understood as loss, trauma, abuse or oppression. In Chapter One, we also introduced various other conceptual tools, including expectations, vicissitudes, disappointment and suffering.

In recent years, there has been renewed sociological interest in the question of human suffering (BSA, 2012). This debate has demonstrated how the social sciences have much to offer through the application of social theory to some of the key issues of suffering and pain faced by a mediatised and globalised world. Veena Das (1997), for example, considers how early sociologists saw suffering as an important form of pedagogy that creates social bonding and, through that, society itself. More recently, the sociologist Ian Wilkinson argues that suffering can be understood as 'the cultural construction of the embodied experience of pain' (2005, p 44); he suggests that we fail to provide an adequate account of such experience, and thus continually engage in 'a cultural struggle to reconstitute a positive sense of meaning and purpose for self and society against the brute force of events in which they are violated and destroyed' (2005, p 45).

These debates have so far largely focused on the international dimensions of suffering, and the dynamics of such issues at a macro level. Building on these discussions, I seek to extend this debate to consider the experiences of people in their domestic and intimate relationships, and, in particular, in children's family lives. Indeed, Calhoun (2012) questions the sociological focus on the global dimensions of humanitarianism rather than lived experiences of suffering. In this chapter, then, I consider broad issues regarding the cultural struggles of meaning, in regard to changes and challenges, troubles and suffering, in the more directly interpersonal contexts of children's and young people's family lives. In doing so, I build on Kleinman and Kleinman's (1991) argument that suffering cannot be reduced to disease or cultural categories, since it entails a moral and existential interpersonal experience. In this discussion, I thus ask 'What is at stake in family troubles?'

Such existential issues, I suggest, are a pervasive feature of family lives generally. While some family troubles may stem from extraordinary events, crises and catastrophes, some may also occur through the mundane and everyday routines of family lives, which at first sight might hardly seem worthy of notice. But, in the very ordinariness and mundaneness of such everyday practices, major issues of politics, morality and the existential significance of human relationships of vulnerability, care and (inter)dependence are implicated. Family troubles thus highlight the pervasiveness and significance of conflict, violence, abuse and suffering, alongside the possibilities for human endurance, creativity, love and care, in the context of young people and their families. At the same time, besides being routinely enacted in children's everyday relationships, these mundane family practices and meanings occur as part of culture, while also constituting culture. In the process, people are inevitably grappling with the underlying existential and philosophical issues implicated in concrete interpersonal interactions and the normal family lives of children (Ribbens, 1994).

In approaching the troubles of the 'small' everyday worlds of children and their families, it is also important to incorporate attention to the large-scale patterning of troubles and suffering, both between and within particular societies. Structural issues of power, resources and inequalities are crucial, and, indeed, one of the most significant features for resilience in children's lives may well be their families' access to resources – such that one might say that 'affluence protects' (Ribbens McCarthy, 2006). At the same time, I suggest that the question of 'meaning' is core to any discussion of family troubles, and, at this point, it may be useful to explore this further. Later in the chapter, I will consider what is at stake in family troubles more directly – temporarily holding moral evaluations to one side – before concluding with an exploration of potential frameworks for thinking about how to understand and evaluate the complexities of troubling experiences in children's family lives.

The meanings and contexts of troubles

Across societies and across history, the experience and meanings of pain, violence and suffering may vary enormously. European Christian cultures, for example, at one time saw pain as having divine meaning (Dass, 1997; Wilkinson, 2012), and many cultures impose painful experiences on young people in the form of initiation rites that are seen as crucial to becoming a full person capable of dealing with the challenges and hardships of life (Jackson, 1989). During the Victorian era in England, however, suffering came to be seen as obnoxious, creating disgust at unnecessary and undeserved suffering (Davaid Roberts, 2002). Notably, it was also during this period that ideals of childhood as a protected time of innocence and nurturance became widespread and institutionalised (see also Ribbens McCarthy et al, Chapter One).

In considering how suffering entails a cultural struggle around meaning, it is apparent that outright conflicts may occur as different bodies seek to impose or contest particular meanings of pain and suffering. This can be seen even in the context of adult consensual sexual activities, on which others may impose definitions of illegality (as in the case of the gay men in the US who engaged in consensual sadomasochistic activities for which they were later jailed, discussed by Ray, 2011). In the context of the family lives and relationships of children and young people, such struggles may be writ even larger, in contentious conflicts about what may be in children's 'best interests', who has the power to determine these and when and how young people may be enabled to express and assert their own meanings and priorities. Furthermore, such debates may themselves presume some form of shared, institutionalised meanings of 'childhood' and 'youth'.

The importance of meanings is, of course, a long-standing concern of hermeneutic approaches to understanding social lives in general (sometimes referred to as an 'interpretivist', 'constructionist' or 'subjectivist' perspective; eg Houston, 2001). Such an approach draws attention to social beings as active participants in the construction and meanings of their social worlds, even while these must always be understood as intrinsically implanted in, as well as constitutive of, cultural and material worlds. Meanings are thus embedded in human lives in particular contexts, and are therefore most usefully understood as 'meanings-in-context' (Ribbens McCarthy et al, 2012). At the same time, while a focus on meanings draws attention to the ways in which people make sense of their lives in the circumstances in which they find themselves, some meanings become more systematised as institutionalised discourses, with powerful implications. Where this happens, other meanings within and between societies may be silenced or obscured because they fail to conform to the dominant sets of meanings – for example, in terms of (inter)national legal frameworks, or the operating assumptions of international aid agencies, or simply the power and reach of contemporary media (as discussed in Part Four).

The notion of 'meaning' itself, however, needs some explication, since it is a term that may be used by psychologists to refer to both 'meaning as comprehensibility and meaning as significance' (Janoff-Bulman and Frantz, 1997, quoted in Janoff-Bulman, 2004, p 33), while sociological usage may include further nuances around meaning as 'sense-making' or as 'purposefulness' (Ribbens McCarthy, 2006). Each of these understandings of meaning may be used to frame interventions, for example, through meaning-reconstruction in narrative-based therapy. But meaning as sense-making may also be used without such a therapeutic orientation, to understand the phenomenology of people's (including children's and young people's) experiences, which are seen to be framed and shaped by their ongoing search for meaning by which to 'make sense' of their lives and experiences in interactions with others.[1] Such a phenomenology provides a disciplinary and theoretical basis for exploring people's understandings and meanings on their own terms – which may be a crucial dimension also for more scientific approaches to understanding risk and resilience in children's family lives (Rutter, 1999, 2000). An emphasis on human meaning-making also helps to make visible the ways in which human endeavours may create 'bearable solutions' (Philip, 2010) for their personal family troubles, although young people's scope to pursue their own endeavours is structurally limited by generational inequalities and dependency, to varying degrees and in varying ways in different contexts. At the same time, then, it is important not to stray into celebrating such agency and creativity without paying attention to those features of inequalities and power – both structural and more immediately interpersonal – that may subvert such responses.

An emphasis on meaning also raises important questions about how to understand and research the meanings of others, whether within 'our' personal cultural milieu or in cultural contexts more distant from 'our own'. One of the important ways in which the meanings of children's family lives may be constructed and become powerful is through the assumptions underpinning professional discourses, but such frameworks may arguably reshape and empty out the moral and political aspects of experience and suffering. There are issues, then, about how far a term such as 'trauma', for example, may be tied to a lexicon of medical taxonomies with all the associated professional and institutional power, or can accommodate the everyday moral and existential experience of family members themselves. For these reasons, Kleinman and Kleinman (1991, p 293) suggest that

> local moral worlds ... could perhaps be more humanly rendered not as a representation of some other reality (one that we as experts possess special power over), but rather as evocation of close experience that stands for itself.

Such an ethnography of interpersonal experience, they argue, points towards a fundamental critique, exposing how experience is transformed within psychiatric categories. Indeed, more recent discussion of psychiatry in the context of multicultural worlds suggests the importance of teaching ethnography as part of a 'culturally competent' professional training in traumatology, including a 'critical analysis of the culture of mental health care and trauma' itself (Mattar, 2010, p 50).

At the same time, however, anthropology in general, and ethnography in particular, is not without its own controversies and long-standing debates about the knowledge claims produced. Kellehear (2009) thus suggests that experience-near categories may be interpreted and transformed through semiotic analyses that fail to stay close to everyday meanings and understandings. Indeed, Kleinman and Kleinman (1991, p 278) themselves call for dual lenses through which to 'interpret patterns of meaning within situations understood in experience-near categories', as well as to 'shift to the view from afar [in order to] abstract universalizing processes from the particularizing content of ethnopsychological meanings'. This call for multiple perspectives resonates with the sociological dilemma of how to develop appropriate links between first-order (ie everyday) and second-order (ie sociological) constructs (Schutz, 1954), or between folk understandings and professional discourses, as well as the anthropological distinction between emic and etic approaches (Denzin and Lincoln, 2005). The latter distinction prioritises an understanding of cultural meanings from the 'insider' perspective, but also calls for an analysis and critique from an 'outsider' perspective, a both/and perspective (Headland et al, 1990). While an emic approach thus seeks to stay close to experience-near categories, an etic approach requires a critical stance that considers both the circumstances in which these meanings are embedded as well as their consequences for social life in its broadest sense.

I will return later to such difficult issues of understanding and representing variable culturally framed meanings. But for now, from this position of multiple perspectives, I turn again to ask what is at stake in family troubles, exploring this question next in terms of existential issues and their associated moral identities, and cultural framings that may exacerbate family troubles or provide resources to help shape responses.

Existential and moral issues of family troubles

> Can there be a society without sadness? Can there be a culture without menace? Can the flow of experience … escape suffering? (Kleinman and Kleinman, 1991, p 293)

The presence of suffering in the world, particularly perhaps the suffering of children, points to the concerns of theodicy, that is, is there any existential meaning (particularly in terms of meaning-as-purpose) in suffering? What exactly does suffering entail, and what explanations are available for accounting for suffering and rendering it intelligible? Are there conditions of suffering that arise from general human experience, and, if so, are there also specific conditions of suffering that relate to the position of children and young people?

In Chapter One, we discussed various possible answers to this last question. Developmental psychology would certainly suggest an affirmative answer, although significant concerns may also be raised about the cultural specificity of its theoretical frameworks and empirical underpinnings (see also Korbin, Chapter Two). Attachment theory and trauma psychology are approaches that seek to identify universal features of children's experience that may be relevant, and Jamieson and Highet (Chapter Eleven, this volume) draw on sociological theories about the development of the self during childhood that may have cross-cultural purchase. The sociologist Giddens (1991) posits a need for ontological security and for some sort of workable model of the world that can provide a degree of predictability (also discussed in Chapter One; see also Chase and Statham, Chapter Eighteen) as a widespread feature of human experience. In this regard, phenomenologists have argued that children's early experiences of social life hold a particular status, since their first encounters with the world may always seem the most significant and 'real', simply because these are the primary experiences to which all other encounters will be secondary – even though this particular and primary set of encounters will be a matter of chance of birth and circumstance (Berger and Luckman, 1971). Such working models of the world (immediate and more distant) may formulate what people can expect of life, how to make sense of and evaluate their experiences, and how to respond appropriately.

In a similar vein, Shweder et al (1997) suggest that one way to render suffering intelligible is to trace its genesis to some 'order of reality', where one may point the finger at events and processes that can be held responsible as the cause. They use the expression 'causal ontology' to refer to a person's or people's ideas about the 'orders of reality responsible for suffering' (Shweder et al, 1997, p 121), and draw on anthropological work to suggest that there may be broadly identifiable variations in cultural understandings of such causal ontologies, most particularly: biomedical (medicine, physiology); interpersonal (sorcery, abuse, exploitation); and moral (transgressions, ethical failures). These three causal ontologies, they suggest, are the main three found around the world.

The biomedical causal ontology sees suffering as a material event to be controlled through material interventions. Scientific theodicy thus sees suffering as a material, not a moral, concern. 'It is as though suffering had no intelligible relation to any plot, except as a chaotic interruption' (Shweder et al, 1997, p 159), devoid of any existential meaning or purpose – which is, indeed, a central assertion in Kleinman and Kleinman's critique of medical science as an approach to suffering. This form of causal ontology resonates with an objectivist perspective on how to assess risk in the family lives of young people (Houston, 2001; see also Rutter, Chapter Four, this volume).

An interpersonal causal ontology sees suffering as victimisation, such that others are identified as responsible, an ontological framework that is often invoked to explain children's suffering. In European and New World societies, the suffering of children in their family lives may often be understood in terms of neglect, abuse or exploitation, thus drawing attention particularly to children's vulnerability and the associated power relations in which they find themselves. In this case, the perpetrator may be seen as damaged, sick or evil, while the child is seen as a victim. In contemporary Western cultures, this would seem to be the predominant positioning for children in both professional and everyday discourses, drawing on a view of children as 'natural innocents' (Ribbens, 1994). Yet, in other cultures or periods of history, children might, indeed, be seen as embodying an evil that must be contained, exorcised or subjugated (Montgomery, 2009), and echoes of this also persist in Western cultures (Ribbens, 1994; Robinson, 2010).

The ambiguous positioning of children in terms of good and evil also carries implications for a moral causal ontology, which sees suffering in terms of reaping what one sows – 'agents bear the primary responsibility for their own miseries' (Shweder et al, 1997, p 127). This opens up particular questions about the moral standing of children, who might be argued to have some level of moral *agency*, but are nevertheless overwhelmingly positioned in Western cultures as immature and, thus, outside of moral *accountability*. Instead, it is the relevant responsible adults who are likely to be held morally accountable for the character and behaviour of children in their care (Ribbens McCarthy et al, 2000), while legal systems struggle with the question of what chronological age is appropriate for treating young people as criminally accountable in their own right, with the ages of children's legal accountability varying greatly even between Western countries (Hazel, 2008).

These questions of causal ontology implicate major debates about how to understand agency in social life, and how this may vary across cultures, which, in turn, points to further issues about the tensions between seeing people as responsible for their own woes or as passive and dependent. Such debates become even more complex when considering individuals who are seen to have varying competencies, whether associated with age or otherwise. Furthermore, the time perspective may be crucial here, and individuals who may be positioned as victims of adverse experiences and upbringings during childhood may be regarded as villains as they get older. And chance may also play a significant role in determining whether a particular young person comes into contact with child protection services (positioned as a victim) or with youth justice systems (positioned as an offender). Such dilemmas may require an understanding of agency that goes beyond dualistic frameworks (Hooper, 2010; see also Ribbens McCarthy et al, Chapter One, this volume). In considering these dilemmas, Shweder et al (1997, p 163) suggest that:

> If we seem to suggest that some 'blame' be given back to sufferers, the critical point is not to say that they 'deserve punishment' but, rather, that they deserve to be made aware of whatever degree of personal control they may have over their own conditions.

Further, even in the absence of any satisfactory causal ontology by which to explain the origins of children's family troubles, I suggest that it may still be helpful to consider that people, including children, may have some agentic scope in how they *respond* to difficult experiences, an important element in theorising 'resilience'.

Such questions of agency, personhood and the source of troubles and suffering feed directly into moral considerations. And, as discussed earlier, such issues carry particular existential and moral dilemmas when it is children who are the potential victims or actors. Additionally, family relationships also carry potent moral meanings as particular culturally constructed sites for the experience of vulnerability and inequality as well as care and nurture. Family troubles may, thus, see the moral issues writ large, but everyday family lives may always see moral identities to be at stake, particularly in relation to the care and control of children (May, 2008).

Kleinman and Kleinman (1991, p 296) use the term 'local moral worlds' to refer to 'local contexts of experience ... networks or communities of bounded relationships where everyday life is transacted'. Such everyday social activities are moral because 'vital interests and values are at stake' (Kleinman and Kleinman, 1991, p 102), resonating with various forms of classical sociological theorising (eg Durkheim) and interactionist sociology (eg Goffman, 1963) that understand all social life as moral.[2] Some decades later, David Morgan (2011) suggested that there has been a particular ethical turn in family studies in the last 15 years or so, with increasing academic attention to the reflexive awareness of practical ethics in everyday family practices. Such considerations may be central to the 'moral tales' told about family lives, invoked through particular sorts of language, for example, around 'fairness' or 'selfishness' (Ribbens McCarthy et al, 2003). One aspect of this, Morgan suggests, is that families are seen as '*the source* of much, if not all, of our ethical understanding and practices' (Morgan, 2011, p 140, emphasis added) (as clearly seen to be apparent in the young people's struggles for a moral identity in Wilson's study of families affected by substance abuse, Chapter Thirteen). Morgan also sees a specific link between ethical issues and family change, since the key events of family lives are also the focus for much ethical discussion.

While Morgan makes these connections between families and ethical issues on the basis of recent British research in particular, the nature and content of ethical deliberations in 'local moral worlds' may, of course, vary widely. Fung et al (2004), for example, discuss how important listening correctly is for Taiwanese child-rearing, drawing on a Confucian perspective. In their detailed observational study, they show how parents – assiduous in their children's moral education – may explicitly and repeatedly narrate children as 'failed moral actors' (Fung et al, 2004, p 309) and transgressors in some past event, which may be evoked again by a present misdeed. The children themselves are expected to be attentive listeners, but may also construct their own moral meanings, with which they will sometimes resist their parents.

In order to explore such everyday moralities in context, Shweder et al (1997) undertook an analysis of ethical discourses apparent in interviews with residents in India in relation to certain specified social transgressions (of which almost 90% involved family relationships). From this analysis, they identified three main ethical discourses – of autonomy, community and divinity – each invoking differing understandings of the self. These three, they suggest, can be seen as the three 'goods' of social life around the world, although they may be expressed and prioritised in variable ways in different cultural contexts. The ethics of autonomy thus prioritises and values the individual, in which moral regulation centres on enhancing the self through increasing choice and personal liberty. An ethic of community, by contrast, positions the (in)dividual (Boddy, 1998) as a 'social person' (Ribbens McCarthy, 2012), and ethical priorities are formulated on the basis of 'the self as office holder ... one's role or station in life is intrinsic to one's identity and is part of a larger interdependent collective enterprise with a history and standing of its own' (Shweder et al, 1997, p 138).

The ethics of divinity is framed by a view of:

> the self as a spiritual entity connected to some sacred or natural order of things and as a responsible bearer of a legacy that is elevated and divine [with a desire to avoid] ... anything ... that is incommensurate with the nature of the spirit that joins the self to the divine ground of all things. (Shweder et al, 1997, pp 138–9)

Cultural variabilities may thus shape the moral identities at stake – for all ages – in family troubles, but may also provide variable resources not only for how to understand troubles and the meanings they hold for individuals and families, but also for how to respond.

Cultural resources for responding to troubles

As discussed in Chapter One, Michael Carrithers uses a rhetorical approach to culture to consider how vicissitudes may be seen to be a general feature of the human condition. He suggests that it is important to recognise people's rhetorical struggles, whatever their degree of sophistication, because:

> it is often in moments of difficulty – whether those moments arise and pass away swiftly or slowly – that rhetoric leads to the creation of culture, the fashioning of new instruments by which people are able to work out what to think and how to act, both individually and collectively. (Carrithers, 2009, p x)

This links again to the question of the existential issues posed by troubles and vicissitudes, and the ways in which new meanings may sometimes emerge in response to such troubles, for better or worse. But Carrithers' (2009, p 10) discussion also points to the possibility that rhetoric and culture may provide resources for mobilisation against vicissitudes, to 'move oneself and others to a common understanding and a common policy'. Such cultural struggles and reshaping of meanings may be found throughout human interactions, including the everyday family lives of children and young people.

Cultures may be understood as people's 'ways of living' (Chaudhary, 2004, p 34), formed, shaped and constantly mobile, in response to the circumstances in which they find themselves, particularly (as Carrithers suggests) in the face of difficulties. For most peoples, across history, such ways of living have involved a collective struggle to survive in situations where material resources may be few and threats to survival may be great. Indeed, many cultures across the globe and across history may suggest that pain and suffering are normal and even necessary – as seen in many faith traditions. But, as Craib (1994) argues, this may not be the case for the affluent in contemporary societies of the global North, where the basic struggle for physical survival has receded and, at the same time, expectations of pain and suffering as a 'normal' part of experience have become marginalised, with political struggles to effect progressive social change and a belief in modernity's capacity to advance knowledge and push back human encounters with suffering.

This may be seen, for example, in the contemporary sequestration of death (Stanley and Wise, 2011), since the end of life represents the ultimate failure of medicine and science to overcome the final frontier of death. From this perspective, a belief in constant progress as a result of scientific advances, seen as a key characteristic of the cultures of modernity, can be argued to have left people with few resources for understanding and responding to the vicissitudes of life. Craib (1994) thus draws our attention to the importance of disappointment as a deeply psychoanalytic concept, where disappointments are seen to be a profound and *inevitable* feature of human experience (see also Ribbens McCarthy et al, Chapter One). Indeed, one might suggest that disappointments are often the outcome of positive expectations that have failed to materialise. Craib argues powerfully that people living in affluent Western contexts do themselves and others a disservice by trying to hide from the inevitability of human disappointment, and push it beneath the surface – potentially, one might add, increasing children's risk of trauma (in Janoff-Bulman's [2004] terms, discussed in Chapter One). Similarly, although working within a different paradigm, Rutter (2006) suggests that there is some evidence of a 'steeling effect' that may occur where children who have coped with adversity in childhood are found to be more resilient in adulthood, although little is known about the circumstances underlying such an effect.

A cultural failure to equip people to deal with 'disappointments' and 'vicissitudes' may, arguably, be particularly apparent in relation to the family lives of children and young people. The everyday language of family is loaded with people's deepest desires for connection and care (Ribbens McCarthy, 2012), while institutionalised and commercialised ideas of childhood give rise to expectations of a time of innocence and freedom from responsibility – and from pain and suffering. Thus (as discussed in Chapter One), while some forms of change and challenge in children's lives may be expectable and desirable (such that the absence of such changes may be seen as troubling), other forms may be seen as major threats to the period of freedom and happiness that is the culturally designated constitution of childhood. It is, then, clear that cultures across the globe and across history offer different sorts of, more or less useful, resources for deployment in responding to troubles and vicissitudes in the family lives of children and young people. These may include cultural resources such as the hopes and expectations of life in general (and childhood in particular), as well as institutional, material and interpersonal resources for coping with challenging changes when they do arise. Nevertheless, it can be very difficult to see beyond the limits of one's 'own' taken-for-granted cultural assumptions to see how this is happening (a point I will return to later).

In relation to childhood bereavement, for example, thinking beyond a concept such as 'bereavement' may be a hard task for those of us from European and New World societies, as Jenny Hockey (2001) has pointed out in her discussion of how public mourning and private grief have been interpreted by anthropologists, with a focus on ritual in non-Western societies and a focus on emotion in Western societies, which may then be universalised. In Western academic discussions of bereavement in cross-cultural contexts, we find a widespread view that 'grief' is universal, such that its absence may implicitly be considered pathological. Furthermore, much of the existing research evidence outside Western contexts points to the implications of a significant death for somatic symptoms rather than for emotional responses (discussed in Ribbens McCarthy, 2011). A notion such as 'childhood bereavement' may, thus, powerfully juxtapose two particular Western notions – the innocence and victimhood of youth and the individual emotional response to death – in ways that present a profound rhetorical challenge to existing cultural assumptions of a proper childhood, which may also prevent attention being paid to the commonality of young people's widespread experiences of significant death in their lives (Harrison and Harrington, 2001).

Expectations and disappointments may, thus, be understood as fundamental human experiences, but the shaping of expectations is itself a feature of power struggles and moral debate, while the experience of disappointment may be closely tied to material resources as well as expectations. This discussion, then, poses the question of how far do 'we', in contemporary affluent societies, *create* problems for young people by expecting that life can be lived without troubles, and that childhood can be a time of protected innocence and nurturing? And, at the same time, how far do we export such problems writ large when this version of childhood becomes the global expectation, even where there is a notable absence of the material affluence required to underpin such a childhood (eg see Duque-Páramo, Chapter Seventeen)? Where such expectations are unfulfilled, this can mean a severe disruption to identity and a sense of being an outsider to how normal life 'should be'.

How can spaces be created for the construction of narratives and provision of cultural resources without stigma and pathologisation in times of trouble, to enable and sustain livable lives (Butler, discussed by Boesten, 2010), while also avoiding normalising troubles that should be challenged? It is notable that self-help groups, as social networks of people sharing a particular experience of trouble, offer an important resource for the maintaining or redefining of identities in ways that both name troubles and recognise strengths, resilience, recovery and so on. This was vividly conveyed by a presentation at the Colloquium from a group of women involved in different self-help groups who came together to voice their experiences across the 'normal' divisions of academia and everyday lives.

My discussion in this chapter so far has emphasised and explicated the ways in which meanings and cultural expectations, which work alongside and through policy frameworks (see, eg, Boddy, Chapter Twenty-one) and material resources, may be important dimensions of family troubles. It is clear that cultural interventions as well as policy change have an important place in responding to family troubles. Yet, an emphasis on meanings – sometimes, as mentioned earlier, associated with an interpretivist approach – is often seen to risk sliding into cultural relativism (although this is perhaps rather crudely understood), failing to provide any basis for taking action or intervening in the lives of vulnerable others. But, as Andrew Sayer (2011, p 239) puts it: 'It is one thing to reject relativism, but how far should we take pluralism?' My final discussion, then, turns to address such issues head-on.

Values and diversity in family troubles

I have argued in this chapter that an attention to (ever-changing) cultural diversities in understanding family troubles is crucial – as these are played out through the complexities and ambivalences of families and relationships and the specificities of local contexts. Yet, this leaves me with a core and troubling question: are there any universalising principles that are possible to assist in defining and responding to the family troubles of children and young people, and in setting the boundaries between acceptable, 'normal' and expectable changes and troubles on the one hand, and harmful and unacceptable changes and troubles on the other (even as we have sought to trouble such boundaries in this volume)? In considering this question, I will briefly consider in turn four particular perspectives: 1) a sociological discussion from Andrew Sayer about what matters to people, building on critical realism and drawing on the capabilities approach of Martha Nussbaum; 2) an anthropological discussion by Richard Shweder, using a framework of non-uniform universality; 3) an approach based on international law centred on the UN Convention on the Rights of the Child; and 4) a form of feminist philosophy towards an ethics of care. Associated with this core issue is the question of whether there are any limits to the plasticity of cultural variations, or some sort of bottom line where culture comes up against (human) nature – particularly the vulnerability and dependence of children – in ways that cannot be evaded or varied. While the usefulness of this question, posed in these terms, may itself be queried, each of the four perspectives also has something to say on this point. Each also invokes variable ideas of individual, self and personhood, which, in turn, carry implications for ideas of agency and causality that may, for example, variously position troubled young people as victims and/or as (failed) agents, to be pitied and/or blamed.

A sociological framework

Andrew Sayer's work is generally framed as taking a critical realist approach to sociology. In his book, *Why things matter to people* (Sayer, 2011), he argues that social science has neglected to understand people's normative orientation to their social worlds, and, hence, why anything matters to them. The result, he suggests, is that much of social science has an alienating character. Arguing that this represents the failure of modernist scientific approaches to consider values in social life – generally seen as falling outside of scientific and rational frameworks – he seeks to provide 'an account of human being' (Sayer, 2011, p 101) that also pays proper attention to human and cultural diversity, suggesting that critical approaches in social science can open up 'a space for public discussion of what constitutes well-being' (2011, p 7). Building on his critical realist framework, Sayer (2011, p 238) suggests that social science can argue for well-being and ill-being as 'objective states of being, and not merely as norms or preferences'. He thus asserts the recognition of a universal human nature, which can underpin general statements about human experiences that are better or worse, and, thus, 'some elements of a good life' (Sayer, 2011, p 112), although he also considers that people may sometimes benefit from suffering. As Sayer (2011, p 158) puts it: 'The intuitive distinction between good and bad, felt in the body as well as the consciousness, seems to be a difficult distinction to dispel'.[3] Taking this assertion as providing a claim for an objectivist conception of well-being, he also argues that this view is 'compatible with pluralism but not with relativism' (2011, p 135). His objectivist view thus opens the potential for stating that some cultural ideas about flourishing and suffering can be 'wrong'. Within this, he suggests that children have particular needs, to do with 'their physical and psychological constitution', and that their well-being requires a pluralist objectivism.

In developing this position, Sayer argues that vulnerability is as important for human life as capacities, while both vulnerabilities and capacities stem from attachments. Such broad aspects of the human condition facilitate all kinds of possibilities for human flourishing and suffering, although nature, Sayer argues, sets limits on cultural variability. The self is visceral, experienced through a 'symbolizing physiology.... [P]sychosomatic processes are transmitters and receivers of cultural codes ... [but also] cultural codes cannot make of each of us precisely what they will' (Sayer, 2011, p 293).

In thinking this position through into the moral dimensions of everyday lives and 'what matters to people', Sayer suggests that judgements about flourishing in practice cannot be avoided, and, in this regard, he introduces Martha Nussbaum's work on capabilities, that is, 'the ability of people to achieve a given functioning, should they choose it' (Sayer, 2011, p 234). This approach emphasises what people can do or be, as well as what they have, and offers a framework for thinking about well-being across cultures. While Sayer suggests that Nussbaum's list of human capabilities is useful, he is concerned that the list needs to be treated as always provisional, and open to 'inclusive cross-cultural assessment and revision' (Sayer, 2011, p 235). In this, account needs to be taken of how the capabilities approach gets applied in practice in unequal societies, since inequality carries significant implications for human flourishing. Consequently, the capabilities approach needs to be applied through 'ethnography, history, geography, and political and economic knowledge of the community' (Sayer, 2011, p 237), alongside a social and political analysis of why the potential for human capabilities in certain contexts is not met.

An anthropological framework

I discussed earlier the research of the anthropologist Richard Shweder and colleagues (1997) on cultural variabilities in forms of morality. More recently, Shweder (2012) has written directly about the issues around universalism and relativism, suggesting that both positions have been caricatured by others; on the one hand, as subjectivism (if this is what the person feels/thinks, then this makes it 'right'); and, on the other hand, objectivism (in determining moral truths it makes no difference what the person thinks/feels). At the same time, he also notes that there seems to be a universal tendency for all cultures to view their (culturally specific) moral judgements as having objective truth beyond individual or collective preferences. Yet, while this moral stance seems to be a universal phenomenon, the content of such moral judgements can vary enormously in ways that persist over generations.

At the same time, Shweder suggests, ethnographic work showing this variability is not the end of the discussion, that is, relativism is not the only conclusion to be drawn, but the beginning of the conversation. From an anti-objectivist point of view, he quotes Geertz's (2000) warning of the dangers of provincialism; relativists, Geertz suggests, are concerned that our perceptions, intellects and sympathies may be dulled, leading us to overvalue what is accepted to be (moral) truth in 'our own' particular societies, and our experiences within that (ie ethnocentrism). The counsel being offered here, then, is to avoid 'our unfortunate inclination to rush to judgement about others, especially when confronted with cultural differences that instantly flood and arouse us with unpleasant feelings' (Shweder, 2012, p 8).

Shweder (2012, p 9) thus proposes a hybrid relativist anthropological approach of 'moral universalism without the uniformity'. In their earlier empirical work (discussed earlier), Shweder and colleagues (1997) suggest that there are three main ethical discourses apparent around the globe – autonomy, community and divinity – each evoking different understandings of the self and relationships. Different cultures seem to emphasise one or other of the discourses: Hindu society emphasises community and divinity for example, while the US emphasises autonomy. Subordinate discourses may be backgrounded but persist in 'folk culture', so that these discourses cannot be categorically mapped onto particular societies in any simplistic way. Drawing on this framework, Shweder et al (1997, p 141) argue that there is a need for multiple discourses of morality to frame the complexity of human experience and suffering, in order to enhance the 'goods' of 'human dignity and self-esteem'. While the three 'big' moral discourses may be in conflict, '[a]n anti-dogmatic casuistry with multiple (but rationally limited) discursive resources may be the most effective method to meet the vicissitudes of human ethical experience' (Shweder et al, 1997, p 141).

A framework of international law

The introduction of human rights as a matter of international law occurred after the systematic state violence seen in the Second World War. Issues of cultural differences, and the extent to which rights are underpinned by a specifically Western understanding of the individual, were apparent from the beginning, with the (somewhat notorious) stance of the American Anthropology Association (AAA), which refused to support the UN Declaration. While the stance of the AAA changed some decades later, the underlying issues of cultural differences and meanings of individuality remain (Engle, 2002), even as the understandings of both terms have become more complex. In the context of international law particularly, 'culture' as a notion raises issues of how to respond to disagreements and differences between people said to belong to the same culture, as well as the need to take account of the fluidity and constant changeability of culture. And, as discussed in Chapter One, some European and New World scholars have become increasingly aware of the limited nature of Western concepts of 'the individual' to whom rights are attached. As Calhoun (2012) observes, human rights see people through a 'logic of equivalence' but people's lives are positioned through their connections and their 'solidary groups', which are not equivalent.

Some of these issues are intensified with regard to children's rights, since, as discussed earlier, it has been increasingly recognised that ideas of 'childhood' are both culturally and institutionally constructed, and also imbued with deeply felt imagery of what is evoked by 'the child'. The suffering child may, thus, be seen to represent much broader issues of war and famine, with childhood constructed as a 'zone of peace' (Vattachi, Deputy Director of UNICEF, 1986, quoted by Holzscheiter, 2010, p 162). The 1989 UN Convention on the Rights of the Child is, thus, a particularly potent arena for the negotiation of worldviews and moral reasoning.

The Convention was the outcome of decades of negotiation, and has been ratified by every country in the world, except Somalia and the USA, and, in this sense, has been a major achievement of international legislation. At the same time, it is also crucial to recognise that it is a legal framework (Montgomery, 2010), so does not include things that cannot be legislated for such as love and affection – although such issues are discussed in the general Preamble to the Convention. The Convention gives children distinct rights, covering: provision (food, housing education); protection (against abuse, exploitation); prevention (to guard against loss of rights); and participation (to have a say in decisions made on their behalf). Furthermore, 'the best interest of the child shall be a primary consideration' (Article 3). Holzscheiter (2010, p 161) suggests that, in the process of these developments, the child was constructed in a novel way, 'as subject of law rather than an object of kindness', such that the child was transformed 'from mute object to speaking subject with his or her own interests and a right to be involved in decisions' (Holzscheiter, 2010, p 16). Yet, while, at one level, the Convention represents a hegemonic understanding of the vulnerability and particular needs of children, at another level, the charge is again made that it reflects particular cultural views and understandings of children. This is seen to apply most particularly with regard to two areas: appropriate family and parental relationships; and the meaning and significance of age, immaturity and capacity.

In its original conception, the Convention was expected to centre on the responsibilities of organisations and governments, and the introduction of rights relating to their family lives and relationships was fiercely debated (Holzscheiter, 2010). There is, thus, much scope still for disagreements about the extent and duration of parental responsibilities and rights, and particularly with regard to the child's right to be heard and to participate in decisions. But the differences also go further, to include such questions as which parent has these rights and responsibilities (particularly in terms of male authority), and cross-generational issues such as the right of adults to perpetuate their cultural heritage (Shweder et al, 2012). In this regard, then, the Convention represents an assertion of a triangular relationship between the child, family and state.

> The Convention, for the first time in international law, establishes a direct relationship between the child and the State that challenges the presumption that parents have rights of ownership over the child. It renders the child visible as a subject of rights within the family. (Lansdown, 2005, p ix)

More fundamental still, however, is the question of the cultural construction of childhood, even with regard to when it begins and ends (Montgomery, 2010), and most particularly with regard to the right to participation. While chronological age is used as the upper limit of childhood (set at 18 years), the Convention is premised on the child's immaturity and 'evolving capacities', to enable participation as well as assert the need for protection. The question of context thus becomes crucial, given the evidence for 'the significance of experience, culture and parental support and expectations, in shaping competence' (Lansdown, 2005, p ix), and the relevance of particular contexts with regard to the risks and opportunities that may be at stake in decisions being made that are relevant to the well-being of the child.

A framework from the feminist ethics of care

While the human rights framework is criticised for centring on the notion of the autonomous individual detached from social context, feminist theorising and ethical philosophy of care puts situated relationships at its core (Tronto, 1993; Noddings, 2003). Theorising of 'care' was particularly associated with second-wave feminism in the later decades of 20th-century Western societies, and sought to explicate that what had seemed to be a 'natural' activity could be seen to be socially constructed – in much the same way that feminists theorised 'family' at this time. As with other aspects of feminist theorising about features of social experience that have been particularly associated with women's lives, there is a dilemma in how to describe and refer to care. Thus, in seeking to make women's lives and concerns more visible – personally, theoretically and politically – there is a struggle to identify differences in gendered experiences without essentialising them as biologically determined and, thus, inevitably demarcated by gender, and to value such differences while also keeping their costs in view.

Theorising of care has, thus, been sophisticated, nuanced and grounded, and, indeed, Sayer (2011) observes that feminist work on care is unusual in its close dialogue between empirical studies and philosophical normative writing. Theorising of care seeks to encompass both the labour and the emotions involved, and to consider how care straddles the (naturalised but political) public–private divide, and the complex divide between unpaid and paid activities. At the same time, while keeping the ambivalences of emotions in these differing contexts firmly in mind, the emphasis on care as labour centralises its embodied and material basis, and, thus, its situatedness in time and place. The dual focus on labour and emotion has been theorised in terms of caring for, and caring about, the other; thus, both an activity and a disposition.

At the core of theorising about care is a view of vulnerability and dependence as an inevitable part of human experience. At one level, this immediately draws attention to the significance of age and capacity with regard to the need for care, with care of dependent children potentially seen as the quintessential caring relationship (again evoking the view of childhood as a time of special vulnerability and need for protection), while care of the aged is also a core concern of social policy on care. Undoubtedly, issues of age and competence are implicated in concrete caring relationships, but theories of care also draw attention to dependence as a continuing feature of human experience across the life course, and, thus, of the human condition, even while power (both material and discursive) may be deployed in ways that mask this situation – hence the view of the child carer as anachronistic (see Evans, Chapter Nineteen, and Clarke and O'Dell, Chapter Six). Where circumstances thus cut across the view of childhood as a special time of dependence, there is the potential to reveal how the division between carer and cared-for is by no means clear-cut; the categorical distinction is exposed as misleading, such that the direction of care cannot be assumed. Caring is intrinsically about a relationship, with the perspective of the (supposedly) cared-for being crucial in the acceptance of care, and for confirming that it is, indeed, a relationship of care (Noddings, 2003; Slote, 2007).

In these ways, ambiguities and ambivalences are at the heart of care, including tensions between nurturance and (in)dependence, protection and control. Furthermore, by placing vulnerability and dependence at the centre of human experience, theorising of care fundamentally challenges the idea of the autonomous individual as a myth (Hollway, 2006), and, instead, highlights the notion of the relational individual (MacKenzie and Stoljar, 2000; Donchin, 2001), in which there is the potential to see how the interests of self and other may be mutually entwined (Ribbens McCarthy and Prokhovnik, under review). At the same time, feminist theorising of care has also been developed as a political project, linked to issues of inequalities (including the international inequalities involved with global care chains; see Duque Páramo, Chapter Seventeen), and also championed as a basis for rethinking citizenship (Sevenhuijsen, 1998) and political priorities (Williams, 2004). Thus, while theorising of care is grounded, not abstract, it nevertheless has the reach to encompass and link caring as relevant to specific groups, and caring as a politicised ethics of a shared human condition (Bendelow, 2012). Furthermore, Slote (2007, p 8), argues that an ethics of care based on empathy has the potential to encompass a 'truly human morality', which extends to incorporate care for distant others and provides a basis for justice and respect for autonomy.

Furthermore, feminist philosophers have sought to explicate the values and ethical reasoning associated with care, and their manifestation in affective and material relational processes and practices (Held, 2006). Such values include attentiveness, responsibility, trust, competence and responsiveness to human frailties.

Additionally, experiences of caring for children are theorised to be associated with a form of 'maternal thinking', entailing attention to preservation, nurturance and training (Ruddick, 1989). In these ways, the feminist theorising of care draws attention to values that offer a framework for exploring the needs and interests of all, including children, and their implications for political priorities as well as personal and family relationships.

In conclusion?

These four frameworks are offered as a basis for discussion, and others could undoubtedly be suggested. It is apparent that there are some threads that can be found in common between these frameworks, but there are also some fundamental differences of view, most particularly concerning ontological issues of the status of 'reality', and how far to centralise meanings. This raises fundamental philosophical issues of how far we choose to assert an underlying empirical and/or moral 'truth' that is present regardless of the human meanings entailed. And while some scholars and social scientists assert a realist or objectivist ontology of one sort or another, others may refuse such a possibility, asserting the inescapable significance of human meanings in all scientific endeavours. Some may work towards a position that might reconcile both, and others, again, may suggest the usefulness of a hybrid position, in which the chosen ontological stance may be determined strategically in light of the circumstances at the time (Alldred, 1998). Politically, for example, it may sometimes be useful to take a realist stance and adopt the role of knowledgeable 'expert' (even if with limitations) to give greater weight to statements made. And in terms of concrete practical actions and interventions, there comes a point at which decisions have to be made about which version of 'truth' is the one that serves 'our' purposes best and will, therefore, form the basis for action (for a particularly vivid and detailed example of a decision to intervene as an ethnographer in an incident of violence/justice she witnessed in a South African community, see Scheper-Hughes, 2004 [1995]). Each of us may ultimately decide how, when and where to assert our particular moral judgements, even as we may embrace the paradox of knowing that these are exactly that – a matter of judgement. So, in determining 'what serves us best', questions of value are inescapable in terms of desirable ends – which is the point at which frameworks such as those discussed earlier may be invoked. Such frameworks may then assist towards a *common* policy for action. In such a process, it will be important to consider what is gained and what is lost through each framework, what is made more visible and what is made more difficult to see.

With regard to Sayer's approach of critical realism and the application of a capabilities framework, there is much of interest for thinking about the family troubles of children and young people in varying cultural and material contexts, but I do not find all of Sayer's arguments convincing. Ultimately, if 'human nature' is always culturally entwined (as Sayer argues), and cultures vary, then it would seem that human being and flourishing is, for all intents and purposes, inevitably variable too (as Sayers himself accepts, although within limits). At the very least, even for attachment theories – which may look like a good candidate for an assertion of universal children's needs – the research base and the arguments are still in development (Barrett, 2006; as discussed in Chapter One), and I suggest it is crucial to remain open concerning the extent of cultural variability. Indeed, given Sayer's emphasis on the need for detailed ethnographic knowledge of particular communities, it is not clear that his 'objectivist' approach actually provides a basis for more than a strong assertion of (children's) needs rather than a tentative one.

Keeping open the space concerning cultural variability is at the core of Shweder's 'moral universalism without the uniformity'. I find this a compelling point, since it is extraordinarily difficult to see our own ethnocentrism – requiring a major leap of the imagination to even begin to appreciate how difficult it is to know what it is we do not know, and how it is that we do or do not know (Gressgård, 2010). This can be seen, for example, with regard to understandings and experiences of self, personhood and relationality (Ribbens McCarthy, 2012). Further, ethnocentrism may also be implicated in Western notions of science, thus risking a form of cultural imperialism in disguise (Haug, 2005). While I also find it helpful to have some sort of categories or models of morality (such as those offered by Shweder and colleagues [1997]) to think through and develop conversations, it is also always important to be open to revise, refine or transform the categories or models evoked in such conversations (Coates et al, 2006), and to recognise the dilemmas raised for cross-cultural and international social work (Gray, 2005; Yip, 2005).

A concern about disguised cultural imperialism also applies to the UN Convention on the Rights of the Child. There are, thus, debates about the extent to which non-Western perspectives were silenced as the Convention progressed to become international law (Holzscheiter, 2010), and questions of culture and context underlie arguments that the Convention is a further manifestation of power between the global North and South. From this point of view, the North wages a 'low intensity political warfare in which the South is cast as the villain, while the North's image is that of a paragon of morality and enlightenment' (Wallace, 2001, quoted by Montgomery, 2010, p 149) – although we might add that the reality may not live up to the image. As Shweder et al (2002, pp 13–14) put it:

> it is one step to unearth the particular cultural assumptions and potential imperialism behind the rhetoric of international human rights; then we have a choice among cultural practices rather than a collision between rights and culture. It is another step to acknowledge the variety and contestability of views about the flexibility of particular notions, such as children's best interests or freedom of choice, within the human rights world – and the variety and contestability of views about any given cultural practice that allegedly conflict with a human right.

Additionally, respect for, and acceptance of, a framework of rights can itself by argued to rest implicitly on empathy and care (Held, 2006; Slote, 2007). Issues of context and situated morality are central concerns for feminist theorising of care, alongside the explication of the values underpinning care and attention to potentially universal experiences of dependence. Developments and critiques of this work, however, have come from various perspectives, including post-colonial theory (Raghuram et al, 2009) and disability studies (Garland-Thomson, 2006). There have also been major debates about how far an ethics of care may be in tension with an ethics of justice, although some recent work in this area seeks to reconcile the politicised ethics of care and justice (Slote, 2007). From being somewhat marginalised at the turn of the 21st century, there has been a recent resurgence of academic work on care (Philip et al, 2012), reinvigorating its potential for thinking across many of the boundaries of conventional Western theorising and for contributing a generalisable framework that can yet encompass the specificities of particular contexts and relationships. There has also been an extensive literature developed about how such theorising of care may be relevant to professional child care practice (Parton, 2003).

The importance of context is also argued for in empirical research into children's understandings and experiences of well-being in varying communities (Camfield and Tafere, 2009; Camfield and Knowles, 2010). Indeed, the significance of local context and situated ethics can be seen to be a common thread that runs strongly through all four of the frameworks discussed earlier, particularly when abstract ideas, such as capabilities or rights, are thought through into, and out of, practices. Explicating the value positions and the assumptions about personhood and social life, I suggest, may generally provide a stronger basis for a common policy for action than claims to objective truths about suffering and evil, well-being and ill-being. And, while there is not likely to be any easy route to agreement, such frameworks may clarify what is at stake in different stances. Swheder et al (1997, p 165) thus advocate a 'casuaistic flexibility in ... moral discourse' in relation to suffering and well-being in particular situations.

In a similar vein, Goodale (2009) calls for an anthropology of ethical practice as a means of approaching the study of ethics in everyday life while also seeking to explicate and reflect upon the underlying values implicated in such practices, while Heintz (2009, p 2) has called for 'an anthropology of moralities that enables the recognition of the plurality and creativity of moral discourses all over the world and simultaneously keeps them in dialogue'.

The difficulties of such an enterprise are not to be underestimated, however, when the endeavour to communicate about meanings and truths may be undermined by the incommensurability of terms and ideas. Furthermore, even a responsible analysis of 'context sensitivity' 'runs the risk of reinstituting fixed metaphysical referents' (Gressgård, 2010, p 111) and, thus, freezing and reifying ideas of 'cultural difference'; yet, Gressgård argues, without some notion of cultural difference and multiculturalism, there is always a risk of leaving out what cannot be accommodated within prevailing discourses.

If we consider such arguments with regard to the language of childhood and youth, it becomes clear that different understandings of the early years of life, as these relate to different institutionalised structures and material circumstances, will carry variable implications, for example, for children's need for protection (from 'harm'), their rights to opportunities (for 'development') or their capacity for self-determination (as 'citizens' and 'social agents' in their own right). These are all terms and frameworks that have been implicated throughout the work reported in this volume, and found to be important and useful. At the same time, our deliberations may need to be open to the possibility that general changes in the circumstances of human lives may themselves lead to new meanings and new ideas of personhood, well-being, care and harm. The development of new welfare regimes outside of European and New World countries may, for example, lead to unexpected paradigm shifts in international debates on children's and young people's lives. And issues and experiences that highlight global interconnections of economics, health or ecology may perhaps moderate the Western ethics of autonomy towards the ethics of community and/or divinity (Shweder et al, 1997), or the ethics of autonomy may be increasingly harnessed around the world towards changes in the position of women and young people. In the process, vicissitudes may lead to rhetorical cultural struggles that have significant repercussions for expectations of children's family lives and the understanding of family troubles.

Acknowledgements
I would like to thank my fellow editors, Carol-Ann Hooper and Val Gillies, for their constructive feedback on this chapter. Responsibility for the content, however, is mine alone.

Notes
[1] The potential relevance of unconscious processes in shaping meanings that develop in interaction with others, and that thus constitute aspects of culture, is beyond the scope of my present discussion.

[2] There are, of course, further questions about how far the social sciences are themselves inevitably moral endeavours. Evens (2009), for example, argues that all anthropology is intrinsically ethical, since this is the only grounds for knowing both ourselves and others – even though such knowledge is always indeterminate.

[3] Haidt and Joseph (2004, pp 56, 61) argue that humans may 'come equipped' with an intuitive ethics, such that 'much of moral functioning is intuitive rather than deliberative … among our moral intuitions are as small number that are primitive and innate, or at least innately prepared', one of these being a response of compassion to suffering.

References

Alldred, P. (1998) 'Ethnography and discourse analysis: dilemmas in representing the voices of children', in J. Ribbens and R. Edwards (eds) *Feminist dilemmas in qualitative research: public knowledge and private lives*, London: Sage, pp 147–70.

Barrett, H. (2006) *Attachment and the perils of parenting*, London: National Parenting and Family Institute.

Bendelow, G. (2012) 'The caring response to suffering', Sociology, Suffering and Humanitarianism, Presidential seminar, British Sociological Association, 3 February, London.

Berger, P.L. and Luckmann, T. (1971) *The social construction of reality: a treatise in the sociology of knowledge*, Harmondsworth: Penguin.

Boddy, J. (1998) 'Afterword: embodying ethnography', in M. Lambek and A. Strathern (eds) *Bodies and persons: comparative perspectives from Africa and Melanesia*, Cambridge: Cambridge University Press, pp 252–73.

Boesten, J. (2010) *Inequality, normative violence and liveable life: Judith Butler and Peruvian Reality*, POLIS Working Papers: Working Paper No 1, Leeds: University of Leeds.

BSA (British Sociological Association) (2012) 'Suffering, sociology and humanitarianism', Presidential seminar, London, 3 February.

Calhoun, C. (2012) 'Human suffering and humanitarian response', Sociology, Suffering and Humanitarianism, Presidential seminar, British Sociological Association, 3 February, London.

Camfield, L. and Tafere, Y. (2009) 'No, living well does not mean being rich': diverse understandings of well-being among 11–13-year-old children in three Ethiopian communities, *Journal of Children and Poverty*, vol 15, no 2, pp 119–38.

Camfield, L. and Knowles, C. (2010) 'Supporting children and young people in a changing world', *Journal of International Development*, vol 22, pp 1055–63.

Carrithers, M. (2009) 'Introduction', in M. Carrithers (ed) *Culture, rhetoric and the vicissitudes of life*, New York, NY: Berghahn Books, pp 1–17.

Chaudhary, N. (2004) *Listening to culture: constructing reality from everyday talk*, New Delhi: Sage.

Coates, J., Gray, M. and Hetherington, H. (2006) 'An "ecospiritual" perspective: finally, a place for indigenous approaches', *British Journal of Social Work*, vol 36, pp 381–99.

Craib, I. (1994) *The importance of disappointment*, London: Routledge.

Das, V. (1997) 'Sufferings, theodicies, disciplinary practices, appropriations', *International Social Sciences Journal*, vol 154, pp 563–72.

Davaid Roberts, F. (2002) *The social conscience of the early Victorians*, Stanford, CA: Stanford University Press.

Denzin, N. and Lincoln, Y. (2005) 'Introduction: the discipline and practice of qualitative research', in N. Denzin and Y. Lincoln (eds) *The Sage handbook of qualitative research,* Thousand Oaks, CA: Sage, pp 1–42.

Donchin, A. (2001) 'Understanding autonomy relationally: toward a reconfiguration of bioethical principles', *Journal of Medicine & Philosophy*, vol 2, no 63, pp 365–87.

Engle, K. (2002) 'From skepticism to embrace: human rights and the American Anthropological Association from 1947 to 1999', in R.A. Shweder, M. Minow and H.R. Markus (eds) *Engaging cultural differences: the multicultural challenge of liberal democracies*, New York, NY: Russell Sage Foundation, pp 344–62.

Evens, T.M.S. (2009) *Anthropology as ethics: Nondualism and the conduct of sacrifice*, New York, NY: Berghan

Fung, H., Miller, P.J. and Lin, L.C. (2004) 'Listening is active: lessons from the narrative practices of Taiwanese families', in M.W. Pratt and B.H. Fiese (eds) *Family stories and the life course: across time and generations*, Mahwah, NJ: Lawrence Erlbaum, pp 303–26.

Garland-Thomson, R. (2006) 'Integrating disability, transforming feminist theory', in L.J. Davis (ed) *The disability studies reader*, London: Routledge, pp 257–74.

Giddens, A. (1991) *Modernity and self identity: self and society in the late modern age*, Cambridge: Polity Press.

Goffman, E. (1963) *Behaviour in public places: notes on the social organisation of gatherings,* New York, NY: The Free Press.

Goodale, M. (2009) 'Between facts and norms: towards an anthropology of ethical practice', in M. Heintz (ed) *The anthropology of moralities*, New York, NY: Berghan, pp 182–200.

Gray, M. (2005) 'Dilemmas of international social work: paradoxical processes in indigenisation, universalism and imperialism', *International Journal of Social Welfare*, vol 14, pp 231–8.

Gressgård, R. (2010) *Multicultural dialogue: dilemmas, paradoxes, conflicts*, New York, NY: Berghan.

Haidt, J. and Joseph, C. (2004) 'How innately prepared intuitions generate culturally variable virtues', *Daedalus*, vol 13, no 34, pp 55–66.

Harrison, L. and Harrington, R. (2001) 'Adolescents' bereavement experiences: prevalence, association with depressive symptoms, and use of services', *Journal of Adolescence*, vol 2, no 42, pp 159–69.

Haug, E. (2005) 'Critical reflections on the emerging discourse of international social work', *International Social Work*, vol 4, no 82, pp 126–35.

Hazel, N. (2008) 'Cross-national comparison of youth justice', Youth Justice Board. Available at: http://www.yjb.gov.uk/publications/Resources/Downloads/Cross_national_final.pdf

Headland, T., Pike, K. and Harris, M. (eds) (1990) *Emics and etics: the insider/outsider debate*, Sage eBooks (accessed 1 June 2012).

Heintz, M. (2009) 'Introduction: why there should be an anthropology of moralities', in M. Heintz (ed) *The anthropology of moralities,* New York, NY: Berghan, pp1–19.

Held, V. (2006) *The ethics of care: personal, political and global*, Oxford: Oxford University Press.

Hockey, J. (2001) 'Changing death rituals', in J. Hockey, J. Katz and N. Small (eds) *Grief, mourning and death ritual*, Buckingham: Open University Press, pp 185–211.

Hollway, W. (2006) *The capacity to care*, London: Routledge.

Holzscheiter, A. (2010) *Children's rights in international politics: the transformative power of discourse*, Basingstoke: Palgrave Macmillan.

Hooper, C.-A. (2010) 'Gender, child maltreatment and young people's offending', in B. Featherstone, C.-A. Hooper, J. Scourfield and J. Taylor (eds) *Gender and child welfare in society*, Chichester: Wiley-Blackwell.

Houston, S. (2001) 'Transcending the fissure in risk theory: critical realism and child welfare', *Child and Family Social Work*, vol 6, no 3, pp 219–28.

Jackson, M. (1989) *Paths toward a clearing: radical empiricism and ethnographic inquiry*, Bloomington, IN: Indiana University Press.

Janoff-Bulman, R. (2004) 'Posttraumatic growth: three explanatory models', *Psychological Inquiry*, vol 15, no 1, pp 30–4.

Kellehear, A. (2009) 'On dying and human suffering', *Palliative Medicine*, vol 23, pp 388–97.

Kleinman, A. and Kleinman, J. (1991) 'Suffering and its professional transformation: towards an ethnography of interpersonal experience', *Culture, Medicine and Psychiatry*, vol 15, no 3, pp 275–301.

Lansdown, G. (2005) *The evolving capacities of the child*, Florence: Innocenti Research Centre.

MacKenzie, C. and Stoljar, N. (2000) 'Introduction: autonomy reconfigured', in C. Mackenzie and N. Stoljar (eds) *Relational autonomy: feminist perspectives on autonomy, agency and the social self*, New York, NY: Oxford University Press.

Mattar, S. (2010) 'Cultural considerations in trauma psychology education, research and training', *Traumatology*, vol 16, no 49, pp 48–52.

May, V. (2008) 'On being a "good" mother: the moral presentation of self', *Sociology*, vol 42, pp 470–86.

Montgomery, H. (2009) 'Children and families in an international context', in H. Montgomery and M. Kellet (eds) *Children and young people's worlds: developing frameworks for integrated practice*, Bristol: The Policy Press, pp 77–89.

Montgomery, H. (2010) 'The rights of the child. Rightfully mine!', in D. Kassem, L. Murphy and E. Taylor (eds) *Key issues in childhood and youth studies*, London: Routledge, pp 146–55.

Morgan, D.H.J. (2011) *Rethinking family practices*, Basingstoke: Palgrave Macmillan.

Noddings, N. (2003) *Caring: a feminine approach to ethics and moral education*, California, CA: University of California Press.

Parton, N. (2003) 'Rethinking *professional* practice: the contributions of social constructionism and the feminist "ethics of care"', *British Journal of Social Work*, vol 33, no 1, pp 1–16.

Philip, G. (2010) '"Working at it": an exploration of the perceptions and experiences of managing employment and caring responsibilities of fathers in post-divorce/separation co-parenting situations', unpublished PhD thesis, Department of Social Policy and Criminology, Open University, Milton Keynes.

Philip, G., Rogers, C. and Weller, S. (2012) 'Understanding care and thinking with care', in C. Rogers and S. Weller (eds) *Critical approaches to care: understanding caring relations, identities and cultures*, London: Routledge, pp 1–12.

Raghuram, P., Madge, C. and Noxolo, P. (2009) 'Rethinking responsibility and care for a postcolonial world', *Geoforum*, vol 40, pp 5–13.

Ray, L. (2011) *Violence and society*, London: Sage.

Ribbens, J. (1994) *Mothers and their children: a feminist sociology of childrearing*, London: Sage.

Ribbens McCarthy, J. (2006) *Young people's experiences of loss and bereavement: towards an inter-disciplinary approach*, Buckingham: Open University Press.

Ribbens McCarthy, J. (2011) 'Young people making meaning in response to death and bereavement', in D. Balk and C. Corr (eds) *Adolescent encounters with death, bereavement and coping*, New York, NY: Springer Publishing.

Ribbens McCarthy, J. (2012) 'The powerful relational language of "family": togetherness, belonging, and personhood', *Sociological Review*, vol 60, no 1, pp 68–90.

Ribbens McCarthy, J. and Prokhovnik, R. (under review) 'Embodied relationality and caring after death', Paper under review.

Ribbens McCarthy, J., Edwards, R. and Gillies, V. (2000) 'Moral tales of the child and the adult: narratives of contemporary family lives under changing circumstances', *Sociology*, vol 34, no 4, pp 785–804.

Ribbens McCarthy, J., Edwards, R. and Gillies, V. (2003) *Making families: moral tales of parenting and step-parenting*, London/Durham: Sociologypress/Routledge.

Ribbens McCarthy, J., Doolittle, M. and Day Sclater, S. (2012) *Understanding family meanings: a reflective text*, Bristol: The Policy Press.

Robinson, J. (2010) 'The social construction of deviant identities: the devil wears a hoodie', in D. Kassem, L. Murphy and E. Taylor (eds) *Key issues in childhood and youth studies*, London: Routledge, pp 125–35.

Ruddick, S. (1989) *Maternal thinking: towards a politics of peace*, Boston, MA: Beacon Press.

Rutter, M. (1999) 'Social context: meanings, measures and mechanisms', *European Review*, vol 7, no 1, pp 139–49.

Rutter, M. (2000) 'Psychosocial influences: critiques, findings and research needs', *Development and Psychopathology*, vol 12, no 3, pp 375–405.

Rutter, M. (2006) 'Implications of resilience concepts for scientific understanding', *Annals of the New York Academy of Science*, vol 1094, no 1, pp 1–12.

Sayer, A. (2011) *Why things matter to people*, Cambridge: Polity Press.

Scheper-Hughes, N. (2004 [1995]) 'Who's the killer? Popular justice and human rights in a South African squatter camp', in N. Scheper-Hughes and P. Bourgois (eds) *Violence in war and peace: an anthology*, Malden, MA: Blackwell Publishing, pp 253–66.

Schutz, A. (1954) 'Concept and theory formation in the social sciences', *Journal of Philosophy*, vol 51, pp 257–73.

Sevenhuijsen, S. (1998) *Citizenship and the ethics of care: feminist considerations on justice*, London: Routledge.

Shweder, R.A. (2012) 'Relativism and universalism', in D. Fassion (ed) *A companion to moral anthropology*, Oxford: Blackwell.

Shweder, R.A., Much, N.C., Mahapatra, M. and Park, L. (1997) 'The "big three" of morality (autonomy, community and divinity) and the "big three" explanations of suffering', in A. M. Brandt and P. Rozin (eds) *Morality and health*, London: Routledge, pp 119–69.

Slote, M. (2007) *The ethics of care and empathy*, Abingdon Oxon: Routledge.

Stanley, L. and Wise, S. (2011) 'The domestication of death: the sequestration thesis and domestic figuration', *Sociology*, vol 45, no 6, pp 947–62.

Tronto, J.C. (1993) *Moral boundaries: a political argument for an ethic of care*, New York, NY: Routledge.

Wilkinson, I. (2005) *Suffering: a sociological introduction*, Cambridge: Polity Press.

Wilkinson, I. (2012) February 2nd Keynote Speaker, BSA Presidential Event on Sociology, Suffering and Humanitarianism, British Library, London, UK.

Williams, F. (2004) *Rethinking families*, London: Calouste Gulbenkian Foundation.

Yip, K.-S. (2005) 'A dynamic Asian response to globalization in cross-cultural social work', *International Social Work*, vol 48, no 5, pp 593–607.

Index

Note: the following abbreviations have been used – *f* = figure; *n* = note; *t* = table